HARVESTS OF CHANGE

The Royal Agricultural Society of England
1838–1988

D1493469

HARVESTS OF CHANGE

*The Royal Agricultural Society of England
1838–1988*

Nicholas Goddard

QUILLER PRESS

First published in 1988 by
Quiller Press Limited
46 Lillie Road
London SW6 1 T N

ISBN 0 907621 96 1

Designed and produced by Hugh Tempest-Radford Book Producers
Printed in Great Britain by Purnell Book Production Limited

CONTENTS

Foreword   vii
Author's Preface and Acknowledgements   viii

PART I: THE FOUNDATION OF THE SOCIETY

Introduction   1
Antecedent Institutions   2
The Context of the Society's Formation   8
The Early Development of the Society   25

PART II: THE VICTORIAN SOCIETY

'Storm Centres' of Innovation – the Early Royal Shows   31
'Breaking the Closed-circuit' – the Journal and Agricultural Science   77
Agricultural Consultancy   94
Some Issues and Controversies   104
The Later Nineteenth Century   116

PART III: FROM PARK ROYAL TO STONELEIGH 1903–1963

The Failure of Park Royal   139
From the First World War to the Centenary Show 1914–1939   151
The Society in Wartime   163
Post-war Resumption of Activities   171
Post-war Research and Education   174
The Character of the Post-war Shows 1947–1962   181
The Route to a Permanent Showground   190
'A Great New Concept'   198

CONTENTS

PART IV: THE SOCIETY AT STONELEIGH: THE FIRST
        TWENTY-FIVE YEARS

Establishment at Stoneleigh   205
The Development of the National Agricultural Centre   212
Demonstrations and Technology Transfer at Stoneleigh   242
Royal Shows at Stoneleigh: From Summer Pageant to
    International Agricultural Exposition   262
Education: The Rural Community and Environment;
    the Society's 'Learned Role'   281
The Sesquicentenary of the RASE   293

Notes and References   298
Appendices   323
Bibliography   340
Index   351

FOREWORD

The Earl of Selborne KBE DL

One hundred and fifty years after the founding of the Royal Agricultural Society of England, agriculture is again in a period of change as great as that of the early Victorian era. At a time when the immediate problems of food security appear to be within sight of solution, the mood in the global, European and national policy debate is moving towards a reduction in agricultural protection. At the same time, and on the eve of a single European market of 322 million people becoming a reality, the United Kingdom farm is seeking to position itself in the greater European farm industry.

Once again, as they did a century and a half ago, scientists are pointing exciting new directions to an industry far removed in both social and economic status from that of the early nineteenth century. Against this background few, if any, of the Society's founding members in 1838 could have envisaged either the scale, opportunities or uncertainties of the harvests of change which social, technological and economic evolution would bring.

Nicholas Goddard has charted the course of the Royal Agricultural Society of England across the ebb and flow of the changing fortunes of an industry and its people. The progress of the Society from Hanover Square to the National Agricultural Centre; the development of the Royal Show from country meeting to major international exhibition; the range of technical and rural activities in which the Society is involved; the development of relationships with industry and science from early contact to global network. All these are drawn together as a reflection of the efforts and applications of many thousands of individuals as they shaped the role of a voluntary organisation.

In presenting this record of the Society against a background of agricultural evolution, *Harvests of Change* provides lessons (for those who wish to seek them) which are entirely relevant to the era which lies ahead.

AUTHOR'S PREFACE AND ACKNOWLEDGEMENTS

The research upon which a substantial part of this book is based originated from an interest I developed, while reading geography at Cambridge, in the question of *how* information about agricultural innovation was communicated during the nineteenth century. This directed me to a consideration of the various communication channels available to the farmer in the Victorian age, especially agricultural societies, newspapers and periodicals. In turn, this led to a consideration of the role of the Royal Agricultural Society of England in linking 'science' to agricultural 'practice', an essential part of the mid-nineteenth century intensification of English agriculture known as Victorian 'high farming'.

At St Catharine's College I was grateful for the academic encouragement I received from the then Senior Tutor, Mr A A L 'Gus' Caesar, and at the University of Kent at Canterbury Professor Gordon Mingay was a patient supervisor of my early research. I was most appreciative of the invitation, extended to me by Mr J D F Green (when Chairman of the Society's Education and General Purposes Committee) and George Jackson (the RASE's Agricultural Director) to write the Society's sesquicentennial *History* and I am pleased to acknowledge the help and support that I have received from the RASE during its preparation. It was also John Green who inspired the title of this volume.

I have, in the course of my research, made extensive use of the Society's library at Belgrave Square — a magnificent resource for the agricultural historian — where I valued the advice and interest of the Honorary Librarian, Nigel Harvey, while Mrs Angela Small, receptionist at the RASE's London headquarters, always made me feel most welcome. I met with help and courtesy at the various other libraries and archives I visited in the preparation of this book, particularly at the Museum of English Rural Life at the University of Reading, Cambridge University Library, Wye College Library, and the British Museum Newspaper Library at Colindale.

At the Cambridgeshire College of Arts and Technology I was grateful for support of the project by the former Head of the School of Geography, Peter Speak, while the present Head of School, Peter Taylor, has been most tolerant of the demands made upon my time in seeing this book to press. A number of my colleagues have made helpful suggestions on various aspects of the work and its presentation; an especially valued contribution has been made by Stephanie Plackett — who helped with some of the research — while Peter Hoare provided trenchant criticism of my early writing. A particular debt is owed to Pam and David Soanes, and their daughter Clare, in assisting with the research and final typescript, and enabling me to reach various deadlines. In Cambridge I appreciated the accommodation provided by Mrs Helen Richardson which enabled me to write a considerable proportion of this book in a room overlooking the site of the second Royal Show which was held on Parker's Piece in 1840.

In producing this history it has always been one of my objectives to present more than the record of a great Society — important though that is — in that I feel it is essential to portray the RASE's historical role in its widest social and economic context. This has necessitated not only the consultation of a range of documentary and newspaper sources but also conversations with a number of the Society's trustees, members, and officials in order to gain fuller insight into the Society's affairs and activities over the recent past; I am most grateful to those who have given me their time in this connection. I have also valued the comments and suggestions received on various drafts from Christopher Dadd, Richard Ferens, John Green, Nigel Harvey, John Hearth, George Jackson, Professor C W N Miles, Sir Francis Pemberton, and Christopher York. Dick Jones, of Cambridge, has been immensely helpful in scrutinising the text and in making important stylistic improvements. The errors and ommissions that remain are, of course, entirely my own responsibility.

In the preparation of the manuscript for the press Mandy Whitcombe gave valuable assistance with word-processing and Sarah Skinner, Map Librarian and Cartographer at the CCAT School of Geography, prepared the maps and graphs. I am indebted to a number of institutions and individuals for the provision of illustrative material including the Museum of English Rural Life (University of Reading), the National Portrait Gallery, Gwyn E Jones, Nigel Harvey, and Ray Carter. The editors of the *Journal of Agricultural Economics* and *Journal of the Royal Agricultural Society of England* have kindly given permission to use material first published in those journals for figures 6, 7, and 9. At the RASE Jef Tuyn dealt with my numerous requests for information with unfailing efficiency and, during the final stages of the production of this book, I have enjoyed working with Jeremy Greenwood of Quiller Press, and Hugh Tempest-Radford.

The pages which follow chronicle RASE's varied fortunes since its inception in 1838. 'Change' within the Society and the broader fabric of English agriculture and the countryside is a continuous theme, but there are also certain constancies not the least of which is the Society's role as a *communicator* and *catalyst* of change. The 'harvests' of this have been variable and not always as intended — and uncertainty is still a fundamental facet of agricultural operations. But at a time when farming is dominated by technology, national policy questions, and 'agribusiness', I hope I have been able to convey some of the richness of human endeavour which has underlain the Society's activities. Indeed, the way in which the Royal Agricultural Society of England has harnessed English individualism in voluntary association to promote a collective good may not be the least of the lessons provided by *Harvests of Change.*

Chickenden Farmhouse
Nr Staplehurst
Kent

May 1988

SOURCES FOR THE HISTORY OF THE
ROYAL AGRICULTURAL SOCIETY OF ENGLAND

In 1973 the Society's archives were deposited at the Museum of English Rural
Life, University of Reading. The early minute books have been consulted
during the course of the research for this history: for a full classification see *A
List of the Historical Records of the Royal Agricultural Society of England*,
University of Reading, 1973. The monthly Council meetings of the Society, and
the proceedings of the general meetings, were fully reported in the agricultural
press during the nineteenth century and agricultural newspapers and periodicals have been an essential and indispensible source for this book. For the
Victorian period, the *Mark Lane Express*, *Agricultural Gazette* (published with
Gardener's Chronicle between 1844–1874) and *Farmer's Magazine* have been
extensively utilised. For the twentieth century, *Farmer and Stockbreeder* and
Farmers Weekly have been used. Printed minutes of Council proceedings are
available at 35 Belgrave Square for the period since 1889 (unbound since 1978).

The Society's *Journal* is also a very useful historical source and the less well-
known *Quarterly Review*, which was begun in 1945, also gives valuable insight
into the post-war development of the RASE. This was the forerunner of the
current *RASE/NAC News* which gives detailed information on the Society's
affairs while the annual *Reports of Council* give a continuing overview of
developments.

Unpublished manuscript sources used include the Pleydell-Bouverie MS
(Pusey Papers) at Berkshire Record Office, Goodwood MS (Richmond Papers)
at West Sussex Record Office and the minutes of the War Cabinet (Public
Record Office, Kew).

Newspapers were consulted at the British Museum Newspaper Library,
Colindale, the Museum of English Rural Life, University of Reading, and the
University Library, Cambridge.

For the post-1945 section of the Society's history I have drawn extensively on
conversations with trustees, officers, officials and members of the RASE.
Particularly valuable has been information provided by Canon Peter Buckler,
Ray Carter, Eric Carter, Christopher Dadd, Richard Ferens, John Green, John
Hearth, George Jackson, Sir Francis Pemberton, Jef Tuyn and Christopher
York.

The following unpublished dissertations have been referred to:

Andrews, Martin. 'The Firm of Hare & Co. Commercial Wood-Engravers',
    BA, University of Reading 1976.
Blake, Susan. 'An Historical Geography of the British Agricultural Engineering
    Industry 1780–1914', 1974 (at Museum of English Rural Life).

Cooper, A F. 'The Transformation of British Agricultural Policy 1912–1936'. DPhil, University of Oxford, 1980.

Fisher, J R. 'Public Opinion and Agriculture 1875–1900', PhD, University of Hull, 1972.

Goddard, N P W. 'The Royal Agricultural Society of England and Agricultural Progress 1838–1840', PhD, University of Kent at Canterbury, 1981.

Grobel, Monica C. 'The Society for the Diffusion of Useful Knowledge', MA, University of London, 1933.

Linker, R W. 'Philip Pusey Esq., Country Gentleman 1809–55', PhD, Johns Hopkins University, 1962.

Walton, J. 'The Development of Oxfordshire Agriculture 1750–1850', DPhil, University of Oxford, 1976.

Wilkes, A R. 'Depression and Recovery in English Agriculture after the Napoleonic Wars', PhD, University of Reading, 1975.

PRINCIPAL SOURCES OF ILLUSTRATIONS

Royal Agricultural Society of England collection: William Shaw, William Youatt, Revd W L Rham, Duke of Richmond, Henry Handley, Lord Portman, William Fisher Hobbs, J S Henslow, Charles Daubeny, Smith of Deanston (all by Richard D Ansdell).

Arthur Young (painting by Charles Jagger, 1811), George Webb Hall (painting by James Lonsdale RA).

Pavilion Dinner, Cambridge 1840; views of shows at Oxford 1839, Bristol 1842, Chester 1858, Canterbury 1861, Oxford 1871, and Kilburn 1879 (hand tinted engravings from *Illustrated London News* purchased from Mrs Rachel Pankhurst 26 January 1986).

Edward Holland (painter unknown), acquired by the Society in 1853.

A *Catalogue of Paintings, Engravings and Artefacts* in the Society's possession is available at the library, 35 Belgrave Square.

National Portrait Gallery: John Charles, Third Earl Spencer (painting by Charles Turner, 1832).

Institute of Agricultural History and Museum of English Rural Life collection (University of Reading): Implements of Agriculture, Agricultural Steam Engine, Threshing Machinery, Steam Ploughing, also views of Royal Shows 1928, 1951 and 1960 and the April 1944 conference (originally in *Farmer and Stockbreeder*). I am grateful for Jonathan Brown's assistance in selecting these illustrations.

JRASE: Philip Pusey, Injurious Insects, Sir Ernest Clarke, Sir Harry Verney, Park Royal 1904, C R W Adeane, Sir Walter Gilbey, Prize Winning Tractor 1920.

Illustrated London News: views of nineteenth century shows, and Samuel Sidney (2 June 1883).

Farmer's Magazine: McCormick's Reaper, 'Master Butterfly', Henry Corbet.

Miscellaneous nineteenth century sources include the *Agricultural Gazette* (J C Morton), *Morton's Almanac for Farmers and Growers*, and C W Hoskyns *Talpa* (1852) (the 'Wizard of the Pacific'). The photograph of William Fream was kindly provided by Gwyn E Jones.

The majority of the illustrations in Part IV have come from the Society's photographic collection at Stoneleigh and have often first appeared in the Society's own publications (*JRASE, RASE Quarterly Review, NAC News*).

The photograph on p 166 is attributed to the late Geoffrey Charles.

The photograph on p235 by courtesy of *The Sunday Telegraph*.

PART I:
THE FOUNDATION OF THE SOCIETY

'Farming is in its infancy'

—Third Earl Spencer 1837[1]

INTRODUCTION

THE Royal Agricultural Society of England (RASE) was founded in 1838 (as the English Agricultural Society) with the objectives – embodied in its motto 'Practice with Science' – of encouraging the application of science to agriculture, the stimulation of agricultural progress and development, and the generation and communication of agricultural information. The Society's formation was the outcome of the efforts of a small group of landowners, agricultural writers and farming enthusiasts who attached at least as much importance to the scientific development of agriculture as they did to legislative means for the achievement of rural prosperity. Leading members of this group were the third Earl Spencer, Whig politician and prominent agriculturist, William Shaw, first editor of the *Mark Lane Express and Agricultural Journal* (one of the most influential of the nineteenth century agricultural newspapers), and Henry Handley, Member of Parliament for Lincolnshire. The Royal was not the first national body in England to take an interest in agricultural improvement, but the earlier institutions were either specialised, had agriculture as only part of their programme, or were unsuccessful.

A question which immediately arises is why 1838 was considered a propitious time for the launch of a national agricultural institution. The answer given by Professor J A Scott Watson in his centenary survey of the Society's work was that before this time England was too large a unit to be embraced by a single agricultural association.[2] This is not a very convincing explanation because the difficulty of internal communication, by no means overcome in 1838, was not the reason for the failure of the 'old' Board of Agriculture (the Royal's predecessor) 16 years earlier and the founders of the English Agricultural Society took considerable inspiration from the model of the Central Paris Society and other continental agricultural societies as well as the Highland and Agricultural Society of Scotland. The rapid extension of the railway system in the 1840s certainly made it easier for the Royal to hold an annual national agricultural show in a provincial locality, but the reasons for the foundation of the Society can be best understood with reference to earlier efforts to facilitate information flow among farmers and to the economic and scientific context of the early nineteenth century.

1

John Charles, Third Earl Spencer, who proposed the formation of a national agricultural institution at the Smithfield Club Dinner on 11 December, 1837.

ANTECEDENT INSTITUTIONS

The founders of the English Agricultural Society were aware of earlier attempts to direct agriculture through institutional means and were able to take account both of the successes of previous organisations and of their failings. It is therefore important to consider these antecedent groupings not just for the completeness of the historical record but because the Royal's initial programme and methods owed much to former institutional experience.

The Highland and Agricultural Society which was founded in 1783 and obtained a Royal Charter in 1787, was a source of particular inspiration for the Society's founders.[3] Sir John Sinclair, Scottish landowner and agricultural enthusiast, obtained Government financial assistance for the Society which augmented the funds it could allocate to the award of prizes and grants for agricultural discoveries and inventions. By 1821, the Highland had a membership of over 1,000; the following year it began its own *Transactions*, and established an annual show. At first these were held in Edinburgh, but they became peripatetic after 1829 when the Society visited Perth; the notice that the founders of the Royal Agricultural Society of England took of the activities of the Highland is indicated by the first prize essay topic announced by the English Society which related to the achievements of its Scottish equivalent.[4]

In England there were a number of early national institutions which took an interest in agriculture, or whose activities were of relevance to agriculturists and had a bearing on the Royal's formation. These were, in chronological order, the Royal Society (founded in 1660), the Society of Arts (1754), the Smithfield Club (1799), the Royal Horticultural Society (1804), the Society for the Diffusion of Useful Knowledge (1826), and the British Association for the Advancement of Science (1831). Distinct from these, in that it was almost exclusively concerned with agricultural matters and received some Government money, was the Board of Agriculture which functioned between 1793 and 1822.[5]

The earliest proposal for a national institution to advance the cause of agricultural progress in England appears to have been made by Samuel Hartlib in 1651, although his suggestion was more for a residential agricultural college than an institution of the type the RASE was later to become.[6] The Royal Society founded a 'Georgical Committee' in 1664 which determined to compile 'the history of agriculture and gardening'. With this objective, it drew up a list of *Enquiries* published in its *Philosophical Transactions* which were intended to elicit information on the best practice of agriculture in different parts of the country, a concern which was later taken up by the Board of Agriculture and by the Royal itself. The early agricultural surveys of the Royal Society collected a substantial amount of information which has been described as 'a striking example of that alliance of science and industry which was characteristic of the age'.[7]

After an initial period of activity the Royal Society underwent a decline and towards the end of the seventeenth century suffered from poor administration and uncertain finances. After reorganisation it became much more of an academic body and during the first half of the eighteenth century there was no national institution in England concerned with agricultural improvement. This concern was revived by the Society of Arts, founded by William Shipley in 1754, which although having as its objective more than the promotion of agriculture alone – its full title was, and continues to be, the 'Society for the Encouragement of Arts, Manufactures, and Commerce' – but agriculture was one of six sections for which 'premiums' (awards of money and medals) were offered.[8] The first agricultural premium, announced in 1757, was for the best set of experiments on the nature and operation of manures. Although no successful entries were received it is interesting to note the advanced nature of the topics, for the concern was with understanding how manures worked with stress on experimental method in agriculture. Emphasis was also placed on the practical utility of science rather than on theory as an end in itself, a theme which was to be central to the Royal Agricultural Society nearly a century later. Agricultural trials were instituted by the Society of Arts in 1761 and awards proposed by its Agricultural Committee included the introduction and cultivation of new crops (in which the Society took a particular interest), husbandry methods, implements, manures, soil analysis, and the treatment of animals. Arthur Young, the leading late eighteenth century agricultural writer and commentator, thought that the Society of Arts would be the right vehicle for giving overall direction to English agriculture. He became a member in 1761 and Chairman of its Agricultural Committee in 1764, but his proposal that the agricultural activities of the Society should be expanded was resisted.[9]

The Smithfield Club had the more specialist interest of stock raising. It was founded by John Wilkes of Measham, Derbyshire, and was established at the Woburn Sheep Shearing of 1799 under the patronage of such leading agriculturists as Lord Somerville, Arthur Young, John Ellman, with Francis, Duke of Bedford, as President. More concerned with the fattening than the breeding of stock, the Club's chief objective was to ascertain the breeds of cattle and sheep which could give the best return for auxiliary feeding and the most profitable type of beast. Its early years were somewhat precarious and in 1821 it came near to dissolution when John, Duke of Bedford, withdrew because he thought its objectives had been achieved. The Presidency was then vacant until the Club was revived by Viscount Althorp (later the third Earl Spencer) in 1825 after which it slowly grew in stature. The pre-Christmas show was an important event and was enlarged during the nineteenth century to include crop specimens and agricultural machinery. Nevertheless, the activities of the club led to criticisms which were often justified. The emphasis on feeding and fattening and the fashion that it encouraged for large over-fed beasts gave rise to the gibe that it promoted the production of animals that were 'too dear to buy and too fat to eat'.[10]

The Royal Horticultural Society was much less directly linked to agricultural interests than the Smithfield Club but Sir Joseph Banks, who took the chair at the inaugural meeting, was also a member of the Society of Arts and the Board of Agriculture. The aim of the Society was to encourage all branches of horticulture by means of discussion papers and, most importantly, an annual show.

The Society for the Diffusion of Useful Knowledge was founded by Henry Brougham in 1826 and there was an emphasis on everyday, practical, utilitarian subjects on which the Society published elementary, cheap books. Agriculture was included as a topic and the Society's *Farmer's Series* included volumes on domesticated animals written by the leading veterinarian of the day, William Youatt. Other important agricultural works sponsored by the Society included a

W. SHAW.

William Shaw, editor of the *Mark Lane Express* 1832–52 and leading promoter of the Royal Agricultural Society of England.

three volume *Manual of British Husbandry* in 1834, and articles on farming by the Reverend W L Rham for the Society's *Penny Cyclopaedia*, later collectively published as the *Dictionary of the Farm* in 1844. Spencer was also active in the affairs of this Society, becoming a life member in 1829 and did much to keep it alive in the 1840s; the Society collapsed soon after his death in 1845. Youatt, Rham, and Spencer had a particularly close connection with the RASE in its early years.

The British Association for the Advancement of Science, founded in 1831, had the general aim of giving impulse to scientific enquiry and the removal of barriers to scientific progress. Agriculture was not recognised as a distinct section within the Association until 1912 but topics of agricultural relevance received attention within the early established sections of geology, zoology, and botany. Justus von Liebig's influential *Organic Chemistry in its Application to Agriculture and Physiology*, first published in 1840, was dedicated to the Association.

These various early institutions with an agricultural interest can therefore be seen to have contributed ideas which were to be taken up by the founders of the Royal – the award of premiums, publication of *Transactions* and the holding of annual meetings, sometimes peripatetic, being key examples. Interest in the functioning of the natural world, with its clear bearing on agriculture, is also apparent, while Spencer and others directly drew on the experience of the Society for the Diffusion of Useful Knowledge and the British Association, as well as the specifically agricultural Smithfield Club and Highland Society in promoting the English Agricultural Society. However, the most significant antecedent institution to the Royal was the 'old' Board of Agriculture, founded in 1793.

Sir John Sinclair, the Board's chief architect, believed that a public society with Government finance would have more influence on agriculture than the various private institutions which have been briefly described. This did not prove to be the case, as the activities of the Board, which was perceived as a branch of Government by many agriculturists, gave rise to suspicion in the minds of ordinary farmers even though, paradoxically, Government was at best indifferent to the Board's existence and parsimonious over its finance. A closed corporation, the Board was made up of 30 ordinary members with a President who was elected annually, together with five members drawn from the honorary membership which consisted of gentry, farmers, agricultural writers, and other professional men connected with agriculture. Young, who had early doubts about the Board, was appointed its Secretary in which post he remained almost until the end of his life. In 1820, he was succeeded by George Webb Hall, who was more interested in agricultural protection than agricultural science. Sinclair envisaged that the Board of Agriculture would have the function of providing information on the most advantageous methods of farm management, act as a general collator of agricultural knowledge, and give direction to the numerous

W. YOUATT.

William Youatt, leading veterinarian and prominent early member of the RASE.

local agricultural societies which had been founded in the late eighteenth century on the model of the Society of Arts. The Board's most notable project was a series of agricultural surveys to ascertain the current state of agriculture, together with suggestions for its improvement, and it is the Board's *General Views* of agriculture, county by county, for which it is most remembered. Unfortunately, the surveys were often hastily and incompetently executed and the project was insufficiently financed, so that the early reports soon brought the Board into disrepute.[11]

Other projects included the encouragement of local societies – without much success – and the establishment of prizes for agricultural improvement, some of which were imaginative in conception as, for example, the offer of a premium for irrigation in a district where it had not hitherto been practised. The Board also published its own *Communications* containing agricultural essays of high quality which were issued as separate pamphlets. It attempted to establish an experimental farm, and sponsored Sir Humphrey Davy's lectures on agricultural chemistry at a time when the subject was only a minority interest. It seems doubtful if these endeavours achieved much in the way of tangible results and the Board of Agriculture failed to fulfil the expectations of those agriculturists who had initially given it enthusiastic support. This failure may be attributed to a variety of factors, not least the way in which it antagonised influential elements of Church and State. It was an isolated body, remote from the agricultural community, and oligarchic and aristocratic in nature. Despite these negative attributes, the Board must be viewed in the context of the search for the right medium to give direction to agricultural progress and to diffuse agricultural information. Sir John Sinclair came round to the view that a private institution would be more appropriate for this than a quasi-Government body – in contrast with his initial belief – and the founders of the English Agricultural Society were able to take the Board's experience – and its shortcomings – into account in their design of the new institution. The RASE later met with some of the same criticisms that were made of the Board, such as lack of openness in its constitution. However, its early stress on the principle of annual country meetings can be viewed as reflecting its determination to maintain close links with the agricultural community and avoid the charge of remoteness that came about as a result of the centralisation of the 'old' Board of Agriculture.

THE CONTEXT OF THE SOCIETY'S FORMATION

In the late eighteenth century there was considerable enthusiasm for a variety of agricultural improvements, and information on advances was communicated, albeit inefficiently, through the agency of individuals, a growing number of local agricultural societies, and an increased output of agricultural books, periodicals, and newspapers of variable quality.[12] The 'old' Board of Agriculture

REV? W. L. RHAM.

Revd W L Rham, well known agricultural writer and early member of the Society's Journal Committee.

Arthur Young, prolific agricultural writer and Secretary to the 'old' Board of Agriculture 1793–1820.

unsuccessfully attempted to give direction to this enthusiasm for agricultural improvement. The scientific basis of agriculture developed slowly although there was some interest in agricultural experimentation, and explorations in agricultural chemistry were made by a limited number of individuals such as Earl Dundonald, William Grisenthwaite, and, most notably, Sir Humphrey Davy.[13]

Enthusiasm for agricultural improvement diminished with the sharp fall in agricultural prices which was experienced at the end of the Napoleonic Wars in 1815 and the alleviation of the wartime food shortages; in the 1820s and 1830s interest in agricultural progress was to some degree replaced by calls for legislative support of agriculture such as the maintenance of protection, currency reform, and repeal of the malt tax. Thus the 'old' Board did not survive after 1822 and there was little enthusiasm for a national, non-political institution devoted to the cause of agricultural improvement. The early-nineteenth century was a relatively barren time for the development of agricultural science in England – much more was achieved in Europe by pioneers such as Thaer, Schubler, Berzelius, Sprengel, Boussingault, and

George Webb Hall, successor to Young at the 'old' Board of Agriculture, 1820–22.

de Candolle, and although their writings did not have wide circulation in England it seems that they were read by a small number of agricultural enthusiasts.[14] William Shaw and his close associate Cuthbert Johnston translated Thaer's work as *Principles of Agriculture* in 1844, from which the first two series of the Society's *Journal* carried the following quotation:

> These experiments, it is true, are not easy, still they are in the power of every living husbandman. He who accomplishes but one, of however limited application, and takes care to report it faithfully, advances the science, and, consequently, the practice of agriculture, and acquires thereby a right to the gratitude of his fellows, and of those who come after. To make many such is beyond the power of most individuals, and cannot be expected. The first care of all Societies formed for the improvement of our science should be to prepare the forms of such experiments, and to distribute the execution of these among their members.

This encapsulated the objectives of the Society's founders: the acquisition of agricultural knowledge, the union of science with practice, and the communication of agricultural information.

While agricultural science *per se* made little progress in England during the early part of the nineteenth century, by 1838 there were a number of accumulated agricultural questions of a technical and scientific nature that the more far-seeing members of the agricultural community thought ripe for answer. A prime example was the action of fertilising agents. The use of bones as a fertilizer had increased since the early 1820s, but they had been found to be far from uniform in their efficacy. This led to a consideration of the whole question of the food of plants and indicated a clear convergence of interest between science and agriculture in the understanding of plant nutrition. Such an understanding would, it was hoped, indicate the best means of fertilising the land and hence raising output. The inconclusive Select Committee on Agricultural Distress in 1836 drew attention to the increased divergence of productivity between the heavy claylands of England – which had historically been the best wheat producers – and the lighter soils which had most benefited from the eighteenth century advances in agricultural practice. It also brought publicity to Smith of Deanston's technique of 'thorough draining' as a remedy of these differences. The same year also witnessed experiments in steam ploughing which attracted the attention, among others, of Henry Handley.

Thus when the Society was formed, men such as Shaw and Spencer were convinced that the potential for raising the productivity of English agriculture could only be realised by the methods which had transformed manufacturing industry in the early nineteenth century, in particular the application of 'capital' and 'science', although the precise terms in which this was so and what was understood as 'science' was far from clearly specified. At a presentation of plate to William Shaw in 1843 in recognition of his services to the agricultural community, Sir Francis Pym maintained that agriculture should now be considered as a science and draw upon the knowledge which had raised 'commerce and industry to such a height as almost to throw agriculture into the shade'.[15] Chemistry was seen as having particular relevance to the practice of agriculture and this quest for knowledge was in conformity with the spirit of the times. Spencer talked of agriculture as being in its 'infancy' while Grey of Dilston looked to that 'great desideratum ... of basing the practice of agriculture on scientific principles ...' which had by that time made insufficient progress.[16]

The immediate background of the formation of the English Agricultural Society was the failure of the Central Agricultural Society in December 1835. This institution, though nominally concerned with improvement, had been much more interested in 'political' matters, especially the currency question.[17] The founders of the English Agricultural Society were convinced that an organisation dedicated to the technical and scientific aspects of farming would only prosper if 'politics' were rigorously excluded and this policy was adopted from the outset. This exclusion contributed to the success of the Society in the 1840s especially when the debate over the Corn Laws was at its height, but later led to difficulties – which to some degree have continued to the present – when the range of agricultural questions which were in some sense *political*, but not *party political*, increased.

It cannot be said that the Society's founders had anything like a coherent programme mapped out, nor could one have been reasonably expected, for in 1838 the means by which agriculture could be raised from 'its infancy' were vague. Similarly, the economic basis of the intensification envisaged by the founders was obscure. William Shaw published articles in the *Mark Lane Express* suggesting ways in which agricultural output could be raised, yet he thought that over-supply caused agricultural depression between 1833 and 1835, and encouraged the foundation of the Central Agricultural Society in response. Increasing population, however, was perceived as an important underpinning of the English Agricultural Society's proposed programme of agricultural development: some of the more perceptive agricultural comment-ators, such as Cuthbert Johnston, saw agricultural intensification as essential to counter the dire Malthusian predictions of population outstripping food supply.[18] Chandos Wren Hoskyns – one of the most talented of Victorian agricultural writers, who played a prominent part in the proceedings of the Royal for some 30 years – wrote in the *Agricultural Gazette* of a thousand-a-day increase in population which necessitated 'an indefinitely increasing supply of food to a constantly increased demand'.[19] Interestingly, Hoskyns maintained that it was not the *price* of agricultural commodities which was all-important in determining farming profitability; rather it was the yield from a given space which was crucial. Increased yield could lead to lower prices, but also to an increased demand which could more than compensate the farmer. The ill-fed would then consume more and the wealthy would demand better quality products that would provide the basis of profitable enterprises such as beef and bacon production.

Although opinion leaders such as Hoskyns were in advance of agricultural opinion generally in the late 1830s and 1840s, an inclination to contrast the prosperity of manufacturers with the relative poverty of many agriculturists found a wider response. The success of manufacturing industry was attributed to the application of capital, invention, and lowering the price by 'scale-economies' and it was queried why a 'truth positive to the loom be negative to the plough', while a correspondent to the *Mark Lane Express* maintained that 'in the midst of this activity of the manufacturing and commercial world, the agricultural stands in stupid apathy'.[20]

The extent to which agricultural protection was a necessary concomitant to a programme of agricultural improvement or, alternatively, whether 'high far-ming' was the 'best substitute' for protection was an area where agricultural opinion was anything but unanimous.[21] While *most* of the early Victorian agricultural world was in favour of protection under the continuance of the Corn Laws, and the movement for their repeal was led by manufacturing and commercial interests for whom cheap food for industrial employees was more important than the maintenance of rural prosperity, many of the founders of the Royal Agricultural Society had no great faith in the continuance of agricultural protection and advanced their programme of scientific farming as an alternative. William Shaw's position as editor of an agricultural newspaper placed him in a delicate position with regard to the enunciation of this view but he held that protection could not be justified without a programme of agricultural improvement to produce 'the greatest possible quantity [of food] at the cheapest rate'; Shaw did not maintain the principle of protection in a narrow, blinkered, way and in 1843 he was quite prepared to publish a long article which maintained that protection acted *against* the interests of farmers.[22]

Shaw's views on protection in relation to agricultural improvement are significant given that the Royal was in large part his own creation and that the paper he edited was the most important agricultural publication of the time. Along with writers such as C W Hoskyns and J C Morton, these leaders of agricultural opinion probably saw that protection would eventually be abandoned and there was a clear link here with their interest in more intensive farming. Shaw declared that if the tenant farmer was to be forced into competition, he must have all the advantages that could be afforded him; Hoskyns thought that given improved methods, the English farmer 'would challenge the world to a ploughing match and beat them on their own ground'.[23] The majority of the agricultural community were unconvinced by such sentiments, and this is understandable given that there was little tangible evidence that 'science' could adequately compensate for the lack of protection. In addition, the possibility of higher yields brought with it higher costs for additional inputs, there was little security for tenants' capital, and there was the fear that 'improvement' would bring about higher rentals. In the light of sometimes contradictory economic underpinnings and the fact that the agricultural benefits of 'science' were uncertain, the launch of the new Society was a great act of faith in the idea of 'progress' and the fact that it would attract over 2,000 paid-up members in less than two years was a considerable tribute to the enthusiasm that its leaders were able to generate.

Among these leaders were many who took a wider view of the role of agriculture and its place in the national economy than that which was, in Kitson Clark's words, presented from 'the parlour of their country homes'.[24] As the Royal Agricultural Society was strictly non-political from the outset it took no position with regard to the arguments over the Corn Laws in the early 1840s, but those who suspected that many of its leading figures had no great commitment to the principle of protection were often correct in their view. These suspicions were realised when Spencer made a speech at Northampton in 1843 when he declared his opposition to the Corn Laws and was openly joined by another founder member of the Society whose views were already known, Earl Fitzwilliam, who had written a number of pamphlets attacking the Corn

John Chalmers Morton, editor of the *Agricultural Gazette* 1844–88, and leading commentator on the RASE's affairs.

Laws during the 1830s.[25]

These two leading Whig landowners and politicians were by no means alone in their views. Another early leading member of the Royal who declared himself for free trade was Earl Ducie of Whitfield, Gloucestershire, who created something of a sensation when he appeared on the platform of the Anti-Corn Law League and declared that, under free trade in wheat, not one acre of the Cotswolds would be thrown out of cultivation. Ducie's views were condemned by, among others, H S Thompson (later Sir Harry Meysey-Thompson) who was shortly to play an important role in the affairs of the Society.[26] Ducie is particularly interesting because of his association with the young John Chalmers Morton, editor of the *Agricultural Gazette* between 1844 and 1888. Morton was the outstanding agricultural commentator of the nineteenth century, and figures very prominently in the early history of the RASE. His father John

(1780–1863) was for 40 years Ducie's agent and superintended his 'example farm'. In conjunction with Joshua Trimmer, the agricultural geologist, he wrote in 1844 a pamphlet advocating Repeal from an agricultural viewpoint on the grounds that the farmer himself would come to be one of the largest consumers of grain (for stock feed) and that his business would therefore be helped rather than hindered by a cheapening of that commodity.[27]

There were many other agriculturists connected with the Society in its early years, who were interested in scientific or experimental farming, and in favour of free trade. Edward Holland, a close associate of Morton's, Hewitt Davis, who wrote a number of letters to *The Times* in the 1830s claiming that agriculturists would not suffer under a free trade regime, and Sir Thomas Dyke Acland are prominent figures in this category. This is not to claim that all of the leading founding members of the Society entertained such views: E S Caley MP, Sir William Miles MP, the Duke of Richmond, and Robert Baker (a leading tenant farmer), were also closely associated with the Royal, interested in advanced and experimental farming, but led the opposition to the Anti-Corn Law League in 1844.[28]

It was therefore a gross exaggeration for Earl Stanhope to declare in 1843 that the Royal Agricultural Society of England represented 'the final and fatal triumph of free trade', but nevertheless the founding of the Society was associated with the growth of free trade opinion among agriculturists. In the 1840s this was certainly a minority viewpoint and, while Shaw thought that Spencer's 1843 Northampton speech was ill-advised and 'not stamped with his Lordship's usual discretion', this mild rebuke constrasted with that in the *Farmers' Journal* which roundly condemned what it termed 'the anti-agricultural peer' and his 'cottoncratic allies'.[29] The latter paper may have not been so far off the mark in its claim that not more than a score of the ordinary members of the Royal at that time agreed with Spencer on free trade, but Shaw (in the *Mark Lane Express*) refused to give space to letters attacking Spencer's views – which he described as 'a repetition of opinions which we all knew or ought to have known' – and took satisfaction in the fact that less than one per cent of the Society's membership in 1843 (61 out of some 7,000) felt compelled to resign over the matter.[30] To Shaw and others the Corn Laws were not the semi-mystical symbols of the rural community which united labourers, farmers, and landowners in an acclamation of the ascendancy of land, but a necessary though not very efficacious expedient which could be disposed of given better farming methods and certain concessions to agriculturists, conditions which had not been secured by 1846. Among the leaders of the Royal in its early years, the Corn Laws were probably viewed in more symbolic terms by figures such as Miles and Richmond, but very many more of the ordinary members were simply convinced that they would not survive in the competitive environment which they thought would result from repeal.

Given the intangible prospects of improved agricultural methods in the late

1830s, it was fairly understandable that for many landowners and agriculturists, particularly those on the less favoured heavy clay soils or those who lacked capital, clamours for legislative support for the relief of financial burdens, currency reform, and the maintenance of protection had greater appeal than the unknown benefits of scientific agriculture. Thus there was at least some degree of polarisation between what has been seen as an agricultural 'Party of Memory' who looked back to the remunerative prices of war time which could be revived by government support and the 'Party of Progress' who looked to improved techniques to sustain rural prosperity.[31] These categories were not clearcut, for many agriculturists were, for example, interested in new fertilising agents at the same time as they urged the retention of protection; it was not an unreasonable point of view to argue that protection was necessary to support improved methods in contradiction to the opinion of Hoskyns and others that scientific agriculture would render protection unnecessary. The 'Party of Memory' consisted of those who, at the dinner of the Royal Buckinghamshire Agricultural Association in 1834, applauded the sentiment that

> new fangled nonsense ain't the thing
> to gull the British farmer[32]

while the 'Party of Progress' promoted a non-political national agricultural institution dedicated to advanced farming and communication of best agricultural practice.

Most accounts of the foundation of the Royal Agricultural Society stress the part played by the third Earl Spencer who formally proposed that it be created at the annual dinner of the Smithfield Club held on the 11th December 1837. While Spencer's involvement was crucial, it was William Shaw who may also properly be considered the Society's founder for from 1834 onwards Shaw persistently called for some sort of central agricultural society and produced a plan for a body that was to be styled 'the Royal Agricultural Society'. This was to protect the interests of agriculture but with a significant rider: 'in so far as it may be consistent with the prosperity of other branches of industry'. Shaw placed stress on the models of the Highland Society and the Paris Central Society and looked to the new institution to act as a centre of communications with local and overseas societies, maintain a museum and library, sponsor reports and lectures, and hold an annual meeting in the country.[33]

This proposal was taken up, but not in the way that Shaw had expected. Deputations from various agricultural associations, whose chief interest was in legislative action, met at Aylesbury in November 1835 under the auspices of the Duke of Buckingham and his son the Marquis of Chandos. The outcome of this meeting was the formation of the Central Agricultural Society during the Smithfield show week of 1835. The official title of this body was 'the Central Society for the Protection and Encouragement of Agriculture'. 'Encouragement' was taken to mean the application of science to agriculture but from the start the 'protection' part was very much in the forefront. The Central Society incorporated from its outset an ill-assorted collection of interests: ultra-high Tory landed aristocracy, political economists, country bankers and, additionally, assorted tenant farmers. Their affinity of interest was found in Robert Montgomery Martin's speech at the Society's inaugural dinner when he observed that:

> God forbid that the prayer of the false political economist should ever be realised, and that England should become the manufacturing workshop of the world.[34]

The Central declared that the agriculture of England was the foundation of its national prosperity, sentiments which were representative of the group which sought to uphold the dominance of the old agricultural landed interest, and who feared that scientific farming would lead to changes in the relationship between landlord and tenant and, ultimately, in the traditional basis of rural society.

When it became clear that the main preoccupation of the Central Society was to be 'political' matters, Shaw became more persistent in his calls for a non-political 'scientific' society. In contrasting the increasing economic advantage of manufacturers compared with agriculturists, he claimed that their success and prosperity derived not from the 'liberality of a free trade parliament' but solely from 'their own exertions, capital, and machinery' which allowed them to beat competitors. Shaw then went on to report on the experiments with steam ploughs which had received the attention of Henry Handley, and published a 'Political Companion' to the *Farmer's Magazine* which gave the views of other newspapers on the Central's prosecution of such issues as the currency question, most of which were unfavourable. This also gave prominence to a letter from A G Spiers, MP for Paisley, to Montgomery Martin in which he stated that he could not accept an invitation to join the Central because its objectives were not those of the Highland Society – science and the encouragement of agriculture. The true friend of agriculture, it was maintained, was a more scientific system of tillage not the Marquis of Chandos, 'a nobleman violently Conservative in his politics, hostile to the liberal ministry, advocate of the Corn Laws, and of restrictions and monopolies'.[35]

Support for the Central soon began to fall away as there was some revival of agricultural prices during the year 1837. Shaw continued to allege that the Central, a 'political abortion, the offspring of a confederacy of bankrupt landowners, mercenary speculators, and merciless currency mongers', had given insufficient attention to matters of agricultural improvement. He gave prominence to calls for more agricultural chemistry and focussed attention on the Select Committee on Agricultural Distress of 1836 and its failure to report. C Shaw Lefevre's (later Lord Eversley) *Remarks on the Present State of Agriculture*, which was the only tangible result of the Committee's deliberations, was published in full. This stressed the perceived advantage of lighter lands over the claylands and, in particular, looked to draining, on Smith of Deanston's principles, to help redress the imbalance – Smith's sub-soil plough would be 'as important to the heavy lands as turnip husbandry was to the light lands'. There were calls for the reappointment of a Board of Agriculture and references to 'new discoveries astonishing the world by their results'. Agriculture presented a wide field for improvement and discovery but suffered from 'a want of communication which characterises the manufacturing part of the community'.[36]

This, then, was the economic and scientific context of the formation of the English Agricultural Society. Shaw had done much of the preparatory work through the medium of the publications that he edited, with his calls for a scientific, non-political national agricultural institution on the models of the Highland and the Paris Central Society. Spencer was an appropriate person to propose the new Society formally, given his concern for the efficient communication of information demonstrated by his involvement with the Society for the Diffusion of Useful Knowledge. He was well known to the agricultural community and in 1837 helped to found the Yorkshire Agricultural Society which was for some years to sponsor a premium list which was larger than that of the Royal itself. It was Shaw, however, who induced Spencer to make his proposal at the Smithfield Club Dinner. Spencer met with Shaw at the headquarters of the Club on 8 December 1837 together with Brandreth Gibbs, the Smithfield Club Secretary, and Spencer agreed with Shaw's suggestion that he should initiate the institution on the condition that he would obtain the support of the Duke of Richmond to give political balance. Thus it was no accident that when Spencer made his proposal he had before him 'one of the largest meetings of agriculturists that had assembled at the club'. They were gathered there as a result of much preparatory work, the bulk of which had been carried out by William Shaw.[37]

In his speech to the Smithfield Club Dinner, Spencer suggested that efforts for agricultural improvement should not be devoted to stock alone as was the Club's concern. This, being the metropolis, was 'totally useless for the promotion of the general purposes of agriculture'. Farming, Spencer maintained, was in its infancy and there was as yet little application of science to agricultural practice. But, with successful experiments explained and made practicable, he had no doubt that 'an improvement would soon take place that but few had now any conception of'.[38] The Duke of Richmond extolled the benefits of the Highland Society in diffusing agricultural information and could not see 'why the farmers of England should fail to imitate so excellent an example'. In commenting on these proceedings, Shaw reviewed the failure of the Central and the problems that had faced agriculturists since he had 'commenced the dedication of our labours to the service of British agriculturists'. He urged the importance of cultivating the *science* of agriculture and of enquiring into the

The Duke of Richmond, influential supporter of the proposed English Agricultural Society at the London meeting on 9 May, 1838.

application of *chemistry* to agriculture and emphasised the point insisted upon by Spencer that there would be few important results unless 'politics and all matters which might become subject to legislative enactment' were scrupulously avoided at the meetings of the proposed new institution.[39]

During the early part of 1838, the English Agricultural Society was promoted in a number of ways. Henry Handley made efforts to obtain influential support from other members of Parliament and, in a letter to Richmond, Spencer stressed the need to obtain at least 20 subscribers of £50 each to get the new institution under way. He looked to Handley to achieve this, hoping that he would get the names of some 'outrageous Tories and Corn Law people'.[40] Handley also published an influential 'open letter' to Spencer, in which he alluded to the failure of the Board of Agriculture and maintained that the very time when it failed was when it was most needed, a reference to the agricultural distress of 1822. The answer to lower prices was not Parliamentary interference, but rather the lowering of costs and the utilisation of scientific discoveries which would put farming on the road to prosperity. Agriculture, according to Handley, was far too much dominated by the 'old school' who regarded innovation with suspicion, had no time for 'book learning', confined their lives to their own immediate neighbourhoods, and had minds unwilling to seek or appreciate new information. Thus such improvements as had been discovered were slow to travel. In contrast, Handley claimed that there was a new class of man which would be prepared to strive after knowledge and utilise the new facilities of internal communication. Science – chemistry, botany, entomology, mechanics – was to be the 'pilot' which would steer them into 'hitherto imperfectly explored regions'. Topics in the minds of thinking farmers were such questions as what was the food of plants? How were soils formed? How could manure best be prepared? What was the role of minerals – lime, gypsum, salt? Why had bones acted so well in parts of the Midlands, but failed elsewhere? These were the questions that Handley thought the new Society should consider, and it would additionally help to spread such advances as the improved seeds of Col Le Couteur of Jersey and the machinery which was being developed by Ransomes of Ipswich, but all this could only be achieved if politics were rigorously excluded.[41]

While Handley was eliciting support for the proposed institution, Shaw concentrated on making the provincial press aware of the project. In his first communication to Richmond on the subject he listed some of the most important subscribers who had been recruited and stated that there had been favourable comment in more than 50 local newspapers. He also gave full coverage to this support in the *Mark Lane Express*. The general merits of the proposal were widely debated in correspondence to the *Express* and *Farmer's Magazine* which echoed the points being made by the principals, Shaw, Spencer, and Handley. To Cuthbert Johnston, the new institution would have 'no polar star except the increased prosperity of agriculture'. Another correspondent stressed the difficulty of communicating information about agricultural experiment, the inadequacy of rural education and called for more experimental farms. Others looked to the potential of new and improved communications in spreading techniques from one district to another and quoted the motto of the Society for the Diffusion of Useful Knowledge: 'Knowledge is Power'.[42]

Not all communications were favourable for there were still those who supported the Central Society which, Shaw maintained, existed only in name and had done little for agricultural improvement. Others questioned how much the Highland Society had actually achieved and misgivings were expressed on the potential of science for which so much was claimed. For 'Rusticus', the history of agriculture did not furnish one single instance of any scientific assistance to agriculture for 'our best chemists cannot farm and our best farmers are no chemists'. The shortcomings of agriculture were essentially due to mismanagement. The practitioners of agriculture were not educated in business as they were in other professions: 'I know of a nobleman in England who lately employed disbanded seamen to manage his farm ... When do we hear of a manufacturer employing a seaman or a publican to superintend his manufactory?'.[43]

Late in February 1838 Spencer informed Richmond of his intention to put an advertisement for the proposed society in the *Mark Lane Express* and *Bell's Weekly Messenger* and it was thus with 'no ordinary feelings of satisfaction' that Shaw was able to announce in March 'the first decisive step towards the formation of an English Agricultural Society'. The advertisement alluded to a proposed meeting on 9 May at the Freemasons' Tavern. In April, Shaw was able to publish the addition of the names of Sir Robert Peel, the Marquis of Exeter, and the Duke of Wellington to the growing list of influential supporters.[44]

Immediately preceding the meeting to form the English Agricultural Society, Shaw published a long leader in the *Mark Lane Express* which enunciated far-seeing principles for the new Society:

> The Society about to be formed will not seek to promote or maintain erroneous principles or uphold one class in the state of injury to the rest nor to advocate politically the importance of one branch of national industry to another. The great axiom and object of its exertions will be directed to the advancement of such improvements in every department of agriculture, and to their speedy and general diffusion amongst the whole agricultural community, as may enable them to particularly convert our barren wastes to fertile soil and to render our cultivated lands still more fruitful.[45]

The rationale for this, Shaw claimed, was the increasing population which made such improvements imperative.

At the May meeting Spencer took the chair and reiterated the points which have already been reviewed such as the importance of the exclusion of politics,

22

Henry Handley, Lincolnshire MP who wrote the influential 'open letter' to Earl Spencer in support of the new agricultural institution in 1838.

the example of the Highland, and the need to diffuse agricultural information in a cheap form. He was then followed by Richmond and Handley. At this point there was considerable disruption when a group of dissidents attempted to put a motion to the effect that the proposed Society was 'delusive in principle'. This group had convened a meeting the previous night when it was claimed that the proposed English Agricultural Society disavowed the principle of protection. A representative of the Cambridgeshire Association claimed that the superiority of Scottish farming was due to freedom from tithes and a low poor rate as well as the 'privilege of the circulation of one pound notes'. Handley and Shaw Lefevre had abandoned their commitment to farmers, it was claimed, and it was said that the proposed Society would destroy the agricultural interest and reduce it to 'penury and beggary'.[46] After some disturbance, the dissidents left the meeting. They were representatives of the Central Society but it must be noted that by this time many of the leading supporters of the Central had withdrawn and some, such as E S Caley MP, joined the English Society. The Central went into dissolution at the time of the foundation of the new Society while some of the remaining diehards, who had tried to disrupt the Freemasons' Tavern meeting, went on to form the insignificant Farmer's Central Agricultural Society.

The resumed meeting was then addressed by Sir Robert Peel who made further reference to the importance of agricultural improvement, the application of capital and science to agriculture, and the danger of political discussions.

The following is a summary of the most important resolutions that were made:

> A Society be established for the improvement of agriculture in England and Wales; and that it be called the 'English Agricultural Society'.
>
> It be a fundamental law of this Society, that no question be discussed at any of its meetings of a political tendency or which shall refer to any matter to be brought forward or pending in either of the Houses of Parliament.
>
> That the Society shall consist of two classes of subscribers. The one to be *Governors*, subscribing annually *Five Pounds*, the other *Members*, subscribing annually *One Pound*; either the one or the other to be permitted to become Governors or Members for their lives by the payment of one sum to the amount of ten annual subscriptions.

Additional resolutions included the appointment of a committee to frame rules and appoint officers and to report to a General Meeting to be held on 27 June. It will be seen from these resolutions that the non-political element was at once incorporated as a fundamental rule with important consequences which will be returned to later. There was some opposition to the division between classes of members on the grounds that it might bring a wedge between landlord and tenant. This was denied, the motive for the distinction being essentially financial as it was thought better to raise funds by a higher set class of subscription than to rely on large donations which might give excessive influence to particular individuals; it is worthy of note that the one pound ordinary annual subscription was not increased until 1953. With the election of a large committee to carry on the business of framing rules and to choose officers the following day, the English Agricultural Society had come into being.

THE EARLY DEVELOPMENT OF THE SOCIETY

The Committee of Management appointed at the Freemasons' Tavern met the following day and resolutions were passed with regard to the Society's constitution. It was to consist of a President, twelve Vice Presidents, Governors, and Members. The Society was to be run by a Committee of Management consisting of the President, Vice Presidents, and 50 subscribers elected at the annual meetings, 25 to go out annually by rotation, but eligible for re-election. All Governors were to have the power to attend the meetings of the Committee, but had no voting power unless elected. The President was to be chosen annually and not be eligible for re-election in less than three years. Subscriptions were to be paid in advance, due on the first day of January each year.

The meeting elected Spencer as the first President and William Shaw as Secretary. Spencer's election was, of course, entirely predictable though he had indicated his private concern that the matter should not be decided in advance of the meeting of 9 May. Spencer had given considerable thought to the question of the Secretaryship and he was aware that Shaw wanted the position; although Spencer came to the conclusion that Shaw would 'do better than anyone', he had expressed the view in correspondence to Richmond that Shaw's position as editor of an agricultural newspaper could be considered something of a disqualification – William Youatt and Cuthbert Johnston were among others that Spencer considered in the early part of 1838. Shaw continued as Secretary until 1840 when James Hudson, who was an assistant librarian at the Royal Society, succeeded him. Hudson remained in the post until 1859 when he left under considerable controversy, and Shaw continued to play an active part in the Society's affairs until his sudden departure from England in 1852.[47]

At a further meeting held in May the Committee of Management formulated the following objectives for the Society:

I   To embody such information contained in agricultural publications, and other scientific work as has been proved by practical experience to be useful to the cultivators of the soil.

II   To correspond with agricultural, horticultural, and other scientific societies, both at home and abroad, and to select from such correspondence all information, which according to the opinion of the Society, was likely to lead to practical benefit in the cultivation of the soil.

III To repay to any occupier of land who shall undertake, at the request of the Society, to try an experiment how far such information leads to useful results in practice, any loss that he may incur by so doing.

IV By the distribution of prizes and any other mode of expending a part of the resources of the Society, to encourage men of science to exert themselves in the improvement of agricultural implements, the improved and economic construction of farm buildings and cottages, and the application of chemical knowledge to the food of plants, and in the suggestion of the means of destruction of insects and animals injurious to vegetables, and the eradication of weeds.

V By the same means to promote discovery of new varieties of grain, and other vegetables useful to man, or for the food of domestic animals.

VI To pay attention to any suggestions, which may be made for the proper management of woods, plantations, and of fences; and apply every other mode, which may appear advisable to improve the general resources of the country in its rural concerns.

VII To take such measures as may be deemed advisable to improve the education of those who may intend to make the cultivation of the soil their means of livelihood.

VIII To take such measures for the improvement of the veterinary art as applied to cattle, sheep and pigs.

IX At the meeting of the Society, which shall take place in different parts of the country, by the distribution of prizes and by other means, to encourage the best and the most advantageous mode in which farms may be cultivated in the neighbouring districts, and to give prizes to the owners of livestock, which are best calculated to produce profit in their respective localities.

X At the same meetings, by the same means to encourage labourers in the improved management of their gardens, and in general to promote their comfort and welfare.

Although these objectives stress the practical value of knowledge and experimentation, the Society did not involve itself with farm trials and experiments until the establishment of the experimental farm at Woburn in 1875 although Augustus Voelcker, Consulting Chemist between 1857 and 1883, carried out experiments for the Society at Cirencester Agricultural College and elsewhere. The inclusion of veterinary science may be attributed to the influence of William Youatt who was conducting a campaign for the reform of the Royal Veterinary College and an unsuccessful attempt to link the Society to the College was one of the first actions of the Committee of Management. In 1838 Spencer made arrangements for foreign correspondence to the Society to go through the Foreign Office and by the time of the first General Meeting it was reported that relations had been established with the Paris Society and others at

Lyons, Geneva, and Lille. However, although reports of overseas research and translations of foreign papers sometimes appeared in the *Journal*, links with overseas societies never developed very well. The emphasis on prizes for stimulating the development of knowledge, invention, and excellence followed the pattern established by the Society of Arts and soon generated considerable controversy. It is worth noting that over a century later Sir John Russell, at the time of the foundation of the National Agricultural Advisory Service (NAAS), could comment that these ten objectives of the Society still covered most of the areas of agriculture needing investigation and improvement.[48]

During its early years the Society became involved in a number of projects in connection with its stated objectives, but comparatively few of them had tangible results. Wheat trials to improve the strains available to the farmer were set up in 1839, but the samples exhibited at the Cambridge Show the following year became inadvertently mixed up so that very little was achieved. Another early development was the establishment of a Geological Committee at the instigation of Sir James Graham. This was to conduct soil surveys in conjunction with the Geological Survey, the Director H de la Beche having been made an Honorary Member of the Society, but enthusiasm soon waned and the Geological Committee was dissolved by the end of 1842.[49] Another committee to promote the comfort and welfare of the agricultural labourer in 1844 was similarly ineffectual and when the labourer's question came to the forefront of agricultural discussion in the early 1870s the restrictive interpretation of the Society's Charter precluded the Society's involvement. Thus the activities of the Society came to be rather different from those envisaged at the time of its foundation. The annual country meeting was the event which gave it most publicity and the Society's *Journal* soon became one of the leading original agricultural publications of the day. Agricultural consultancy, particularly the chemical department, was an area of work not clearly anticipated at the Society's beginning. The importance of improvements in veterinary science was recognised at the outset, but the full impact of cattle diseases and the development of measures of a legislative nature to counteract them was something which lay in the future, although the arrival of foot-and-mouth disease in 1839 soon brought this problem into sharp focus.

In outline, the Society's activities during the nineteenth century were as follows. There were three General Meetings of members held in December, May and July (the latter during the week of the Show in a country location); the others at the Society's headquarters in Hanover Square which were acquired in 1841. General business was conducted by the Council at meetings held on the first Wednesday of the month, apart from during a summer recess. At the Council meetings general issues were discussed and reports of numerous committees which dealt with the more detailed aspects of the Society's work – Veterinary, Chemical, Journal, Country Meetings and so forth – were presented. Other Wednesdays at Hanover Square were devoted to open meetings for members to present specimens of plants and crops, ask questions, or send in communications on some agricultural topic; sometimes formal lectures were given by an outside expert or by one of the Society's consultants. These Wednesday afternoon meetings were intended as a sort of open forum, a function in which they succeeded in some degree in the early 1840s but which was not sustained. Agricultural consultancy soon assumed considerable significance and the prevalence of cattle diseases, particularly in the late 1860s and 1870s, gave a continued importance to the veterinary department. The main areas of the Society's work, therefore, during the nineteenth century were the *Journal*, country meetings, consultancy and, later, education. The Society's motto 'Practice with Science' was adopted by the choice of Spencer in 1839 after several others including '*In Manibus Terrae*', '*Arva Bovemque*', '*Ye generous Britons venerate the plough*', and '*Speed the Plough*' had been considered.[50] The Society resolved to seek a Charter of Incorporation during February 1840 and this was granted on 26 March through the good offices of Richmond; it was from this date that the Society took its 'Royal' prefix.

By 1840 the Society had been able to attract some 2,000 members and membership continued to increase until a plateau of around 7,000 was reached a few years later. Thereafter membership slipped back to a figure that hovered around the 5,000 mark until it began to increase again in the 1870s. The higher levels of the 1840s overstate the membership because under the rules of the Society it was necessary to write a formal letter of resignation in order for the name to be taken off the membership list and non-payment of subscription was not in itself deemed sufficient to indicate a resignation. Fluctuations in the early membership of the Society as indicated in Fig. 1 may be interpreted in terms of an initial wave of interest in the early 1840s when the Society was dominated by enthusiasts such as Philip Pusey and Spencer and there was intense interest in the embryonic techniques of 'high farming' such as underdrainage and the application of 'artificial' fertilisers. This was followed by falling membership in the late 1840s which may be related to a more critical view of the potentialities of science for agriculture. The lower levels of membership during the 1850s and 1860s is a trend which is connected with some loss of confidence within the agricultural community about the conduct of the Society's affairs. The increase in membership in the 1870s reflects a heightened appreciation of the work of the Society in such matters as the condemnation of substandard fertilizers and feedstuffs as well as the energetic and popular Secretaryship of H M Jenkins. Additionally, a valued innovation at the Birmingham Show of 1876 was a members' club which provided an additional membership incentive. The rise in membership towards the end of that decade may be related both to this and to the publicity surrounding the preparation for the Kilburn Show of 1879.

It is clear that with the total of ordinary subscribers fluctuating between 5,000 and 7,000 in the most prosperous period of Victorian 'high farming', membership by individual members of the agricultural community was very much the exception rather than the rule. Speakers at the early General Meetings would often complain about the low level of membership, a sentiment which has been reiterated in more recent times, but the Society did very little to 'sell' itself to the agricultural community and it is a criticism of the Royal's early management that it could have done much more for agricultural research if it had been able to generate a higher subscription income. The main privilege of membership was the receipt of the twice-yearly issues of the *Journal* which, with its emphasis on lengthy technical articles and extensive reports, contained little of immediate interest for the ordinary working farmer whose leisure was likely to be given over to less demanding reading such as the local or national agricultural newspaper. Even if he wished to consult the *Journal*, he did not need to pay his annual pound to the Society for it would be available at his local agricultural society or club. There was no member's right of entry to the annual show until 1862, and even then entry on one of the 'shilling days' was a cheaper mode of admission than subscribing to the Society. Members also had the privileges of veterinary consultation and chemical analysis, but there is little evidence that many veterinary consultations were carried out and analysis, although an important part of the Society's work in the 1870s, was also quite widely available

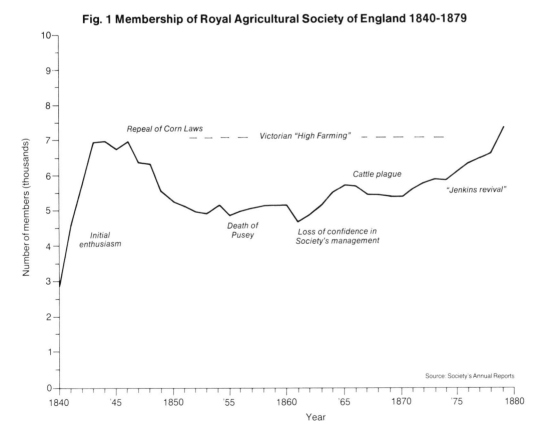

Fig. 1 Membership of Royal Agricultural Society of England 1840-1879

at a local level. Non-members could exhibit stock at the shows and the ordinary tenant farmer had, in any case, little chance in competition against the 'crack' stock breeders of the day such as the Turners, Booths, and Towneleys. As George Turner pointed out in 1874, the small farmer's subscription was most usefully given to his county or local association where he could compete at local shows on more equal terms and where there was a better chance of getting a prize. Many tenant farmers would have welcomed a political element in the Society's proceedings, but this was not possible under the Society's constitution and it was not the Royal's function to lobby on behalf of the agricultural interest. Therefore, although most Victorian tenant farmers of substance belonged to an agricultural organisation of some sort, it was exceptional for the Society to be their first choice. They were more likely to join their local society, or perhaps, in the 1870s, a local Chamber of Agriculture if they farmed on an extensive scale. Numerous local farmers' clubs catered for the 'grassroots' of the agricultural community.[51]

It can thus be queried how far the early influence of the Society reached down to the lower echelons of the agricultural community, while remembering that such influence as there was is not to be measured through direct membership. Even if this comprised solely farmers and landowners – which was clearly not the case – the total number of members made up perhaps two per cent of the total of early Victorian agriculturists. Nevertheless, the Society's influence extended far beyond the relatively restricted ranks of the nominal membership and it is in these terms that its early work should be viewed. Some individual members were the landlords of prominent tenant farmers and took on the role of opinion leaders at the local level, but many progressive farmers did not join the Society. The Society's influence was through the totality of knowledge upon which all members of farming classes could draw if so minded. A small number of the more prominent Victorian tenant farmers took an active interest in the Society's affairs and others followed them through constant reports in the agricultural press. In addition, information generated by the Society was sometimes contained in the local press, while working farmers could attend lectures at local farmers' clubs where research findings were presented. They could also visit country meetings which were given national publicity and thereby exercised some influence on the character of implements and stock available for purchase. Thus although the Society can be demonstrated to have influenced the course of Victorian agricultural change, and the ordinary farmer benefited from its work, there was little incentive for the individual agriculturist to contribute an annual subscription to the Society.

PART II:
THE VICTORIAN SOCIETY

'The agricultural history of the period is as stirring as is the social and political
history in the midst of which we have grown up'

—J C Morton 1881[1]

'STORM CENTRES' OF INNOVATION – THE EARLY ROYAL SHOWS

SELECTION of the location of the 'country meeting' which it decided to hold
in 1839 was one of the first considerations of the Committee of Management; the reason for the choice of Oxford was given as its central situation.
During the Oxford show week, representations were made by a deputation of
Cambridgeshire farmers led by Jonas Webb requesting that the event be held in
Cambridge the following year. There was a determination to visit a manufacturing district in 1841 and Liverpool was selected after some consideration had
been given to Manchester. Location of the first three shows was therefore
chosen on a somewhat *ad hoc* basis, but there was an early resolve to place the
peripatetic scheme – which was a central part of the Society's policy – on a
regular plan. William Shaw established a Committee to consider the formation
of districts to be visited in turn by the Society. The scheme he devised was
accepted together with his suggestion that the districts for the country meetings
for the next four years should be nominated in advance. The rotation of the
districts was applied retrospectively to those towns which had already been
visited (Oxford, Cambridge and Liverpool). Bristol, selected for 1842, was in the
Western District; the North Eastern District was nominated for 1843, 'Middlesex' for 1844, North Wales for 1845, the Northern District for 1846, and South
Wales for 1847.[2]

In 1846 Pusey successfully moved that the district for 1847 be changed from
South Wales on the ground that it was too near Shrewsbury which had already
been visited in 1845; another consideration was lack of a railway connection,
thought to be the *sine qua non* of a successful show after the Shrewsbury
'experience' where inadequate communications had detracted from the success
of the meeting, and thus the Midland District was substituted for South Wales.
This district scheme was kept in operation through the 1850s and 1860s (it was
reaffirmed in 1861) until in December 1867 William Torr brought in new
district boundaries which were thought to accord more with geological provinces than had hitherto been the case. This new arrangement, by thus being
linked with more recognisable farming regions, would give increased importance to the local agricultural context of the country meetings. Some small

amendments to the system of rotation were made in 1870, but it was not long before further reconstitution of the districts was made, a new system starting in 1876. Significantly, the reason for this change was to ensure that each district contained a sufficient number of towns large enough to be able to receive the Society, for by this time the size of the show had grown to such an extent that it was by no means easy to find a place that was able to provide an adequate site for its requirements. The revised scheme was scheduled to begin in alphabetical sequence in 1879 but as other circumstances persuaded the Society to hold a metropolitan show in that year, the rotation did not begin until 1880 when Carlisle was chosen.[3]

In 1841 a list of 'country meeting queries' was drawn up specifying necessary criteria which any town had to fulfil for it to be considered a candidate to receive the Society. The Council had to be satisfied on the following points:

> A statement of the acreage of land on which it proposed to have the showground and to erect the pavilion.

Fig. 2
District schedules for location of RASE country meetings in the nineteenth century

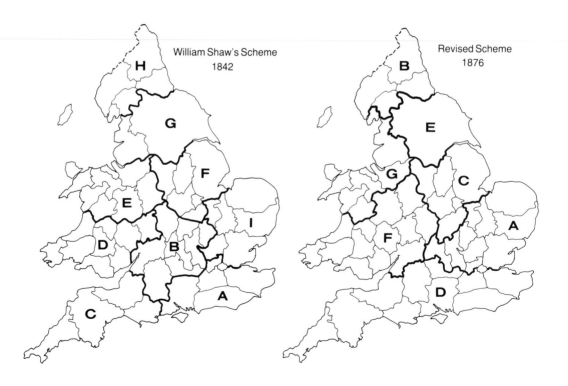

The distance of the showground from the terminus of the railway.

The distance from the centre of the town. Whether a supply of water was available and, if not, an estimate of the price of conveying it.

A statement of the remuneration required for the six weeks that the land was required.

The correctness of the information supplied in answer to the queries was to be certified by the parties providing it who were also required to provide a tracing of the land.

The queries were revised in 1844 when additional information was elicited about the land where it was proposed to conduct the trial of implements – which had rapidly become one of the most important parts of the country meeting proceedings – the distance of the location from the surrounding market towns, and a statement as to whether there was any room in the town capable of containing 500 persons for dinner together with the expense of hiring it.

These queries were subject to further revision and amendment from time to time and reflected the changing character of the show; the Society dinner assumed less significance and implement trials assumed more. Indeed, by the 1870s, the cost of organising trials was one of the most significant items of show expenditure and in 1871 a specific question was added as to the cost of land needed for them.

Given that the district for the country meeting was known in advance it was open for towns within the district to compete for the honour, prestige, and profit of receiving the Society. The normal course of events was for a local meeting to be 'got up' to promote the objective of attracting the Society to a specific location and a subscription fund would be opened in support. These local subscription funds were an important mode of additional show finance and continued to be significant until the end of the 1950s. Deputations from competing towns would then 'wait upon' the Council in the spring of the year preceding the event, though after 1872 full deputations were not required and only two representatives were requested to answer any questions or queries. Competition among rival towns was often intense and considerable bitterness was engendered when a particular town thought that it had been unfairly passed over by the Council. Thus, when the location of the 1872 show was being considered, there was 'little desire on the part of the city or county of Hereford to invite the Royal' as it was 'not forgotten that it was once very undeservedly rejected', a reference to the choice of Worcester nine years earlier. Individuals often set great store on their attempts to attract the Society to their own particular locality and according to H H Dixon ('The Druid'), the choice of Bury St Edmunds over Ipswich in 1867 was a 'staggering blow' to William Fisher Hobbs, after which he only appeared once more at the Council before his death.[4]

W. FISHER. HOBBS.

William Fisher Hobbs, a prominent tenant farmer and Council member who revised the machinery trials during the 1850s.

It was in order to avoid the disappointments and ill-will that was felt when one competing town was chosen over another, particularly when a subscription had been got up and a trials site obtained, that Sir Brandreth Gibbs initiated a change in the selection procedures in 1876. Instead of the queries and competition he proposed that the Country Meeting Committee would draw up a schedule of the requirements of the show, obtain information on the capability of towns within the specified district for the year to fulfil the Society's requirements, and then consider these so that a list in order of preference could be presented to the Council for a decision.

The detail of the adequacy of the facilities of individual towns in meeting the Society's requirements was one vital consideration in the choice of country meeting locations and was very important in deciding the success or otherwise of the event. There were also broader considerations. The greatest difficulty was to balance the desirability of the Society going into more remote districts where it was thought a great deal of good might result in bringing new techniques to the notice of backward regions, and the need to generate adequate income to ensure financial viability. It was not until Chester in 1858 that a profit was made on a show, though it was recognised that in making a financial loss the Society was nevertheless fulfilling its broader educational mission. In the 1870s, however, the expenditure connected with the shows was so considerable that losses were not viewed with equanimity. The following details of the attendances from 1852 (when figures were first kept) until 1879 indicate the importance of the location and particularly the success of urban situations in drawing a large number of visitors.

TABLE 1: Attendance at the Royal Shows, 1853–79

Year	Location	Attendance	Year	Location	Attendance
1853	Gloucester	36,245	1867	Bury St. Edmunds	61,837
1854	Lincoln	37,635	1868	Leicester	97,138
1855	Carlisle	37,533	1869	Manchester	189,102
1856	Chelmsford	32,982	1870	Oxford	75,749
1857	Salisbury	37,342	1871	Wolverhampton	108,213
1858	Chester	62,539	1872	Cardiff	87,047
1859	Warwick	57,577	1873	Hull	163,413
1860	Canterbury	42,304	1874	Bedford	71,989
1861	Leeds	145,738	1875	Taunton	47,768
1862	Battersea	124,328	1876	Birmingham	163,413
1863	Worcester	75,087	1877	Liverpool	138,354
1864	Newcastle	114,483	1878	Bristol	122,042
1865	Plymouth	88,036	1879	Kilburn	187,323
1866 No show – Cattle Plague					

Source: RASE

Between 20,000 and 25,000 people were thought to have visited the first two Oxford and Cambridge shows and attendances in the late 1840s were probably of a similar order to the figures recorded between 1853 and 1857. The attendance at Lewes in 1852, estimated at 18,000, was thought to be half the usual number due to the fact that the show that year was held in the midst of a general election, in an inaccessible location, and particularly suffered from oppressive summer heat.[5] The Royal Shows began to blossom as mass spectacles in the late 1850s. Increased attendance and division of the implement trials contributed to the profitability of Chester and Warwick and steam trials began to become a great attraction at this time. Canterbury was a set-back to the Society partly because the location was inaccessible from many parts of the country and also because the major implement firms boycotted the show as part of their campaign to reform the conduct and objectives of the machinery trials. Leeds, Newcastle, Birmingham, and Liverpool all had large and profitable attendances, in contrast to shows held in the more sparsely populated districts such as Bury and Taunton. This highlighted the dilemma – which was later to become still more acute – that a rural location which might be of great educational benefit would probably be attended with pecuniary loss, whereas at urban locations receipts were swelled by non-agricultural spectators and a sound financial result was more certain. Although it was recognised that a successful meeting could not be judged on financial viability alone, it was a factor which increasingly could not be ignored. The losses in the 1840s were often in the region of £2,000 each year and constituted the greatest single call on the Society's funds. Later, losses exceeded £3,500 at Bedford and Taunton in contrast to profits of £9,153 at Manchester in 1869, and £4,283 at Liverpool in 1877. Although by this time the Society ran a substantial accumulated fund, these deficits took a large proportion of the Society's subscription income which might otherwise have been turned to alternative uses such as the encouragement of agricultural research. The Kilburn exhibition of 1879 lost the Society well over £14,000. This had to be met out of capital, and accounted for about half the Society's reserves which had been gradually built up from life subscriptions over the preceding decades.

Agricultural commentators such as J C Morton and Henry Corbet, (who succeeded William Shaw as the editor of the *Mark Lane Express* and *Farmers Magazine* in 1852), gave a good deal of attention to what they considered a 'proper' location for the country meetings. Morton was not against visits to 'manufacturing' districts where he thought that agricultural machinery would be subject to a searching and worthwhile scrutiny, but he particularly valued expeditions into remote districts where, as at Carlisle in 1855, he thought that the Society had a 'mission' to perform. Morton put forward a three-fold rationale regarding the choice of show locality. The Society could take its members to districts where, as he put it, the area could teach them through its superior general level of farming; Lincoln was cited as an example where it was

Henry Corbet, Shaw's successor at the *Mark Lane Express* and agricultural commentator.

recognised that the implements would be 'more criticized and less stared at' than in backward farming areas such as Shropshire or Devon. Alternatively, the Society could visit more central districts such as Northampton or Warwick where access was comparatively easy for members from different parts of the country and where they could 'teach each other'; or the Society could go to a more backward area, where Morton hoped that the Royal might be instrumental in breaking-up prejudice or stimulating new activity.[6]

As both the attendance and the number of implement exhibits increased, so the number of towns which were in a position to provide the space and facilities required decreased. The first shows at Liverpool (1841) and at Newcastle (1846) occupied seven and ten acres respectively. By the time the Society visited these cities a second time the requirement had risen to 42 acres (Newcastle 1864) and 77 acres (Liverpool 1877). In the 1870s the combined length of the shedding needed to accommodate the exhibits of implements and stock amounted to several miles. At Kilburn in 1879, the most ambitious of the shows yet, there was 22,903 feet of shedding and 11,878 articles exhibited on 704 separate stands. After this there was some contraction in the size of the event, but the 60 acres needed at Carlisle in 1880 was still four times the size of the area occupied when the show first came to the city, 25 years previously.

This increase in the area taken up by the show reflected the expansion of the number of agricultural exhibits – particularly implements – but it was largely accounted for by the extension of the 'miscellaneous' department, where entries often having only a tenuous connection with agriculture occupied an enormous amount of space. This section of the show had a useful function inasmuch as it generated income and attracted the casual visitor – the one shilling entry 'holiday folk' whose attendance helped towards the overall financial viability of the show. Nevertheless, the entries of miscellaneous exhibits got out of control by the 1870s at which time the show had grown beyond a fully manageable size, not least in that it put an immense strain on the judges who had to distribute a handful of the Society's medals for some novelty or useful gadget found within the formidable array of items presented for inspection. At Warwick in 1859 the stewards complained that if they had devoted but one minute to each of the 4000 – 5000 items assembled for their inspection the task would have occupied nine days, and this complaint was often to be repeated. Exception was taken to the necessity of examining such items as:

> apple-parers, alarum-bells, bedsteads, breach machines, beer engines, bells, counting machines, cages, deed boxes, filters, gun-covers, game-bags, hammers, knife-cleaners, machines for aiding digestion, microscopes, odometers, perambulators, roasting jacks, sewing-machines, sign-paintings, trunks, thermometers, urns, varnish, whisks, window-frames . . .[7]

In the 1870s the Society attempted to control the growth of miscellaneous exhibits by increasing the price of showyard space and catalogue entries. After 1872 duplicate entries by individual exhibitors were prohibited but, as Fig 3 – showing the number of items exhibited – indicates this prohibition was not very successful.

These, then, were the financial and logistic constraints that were placed upon the choice of location of the early Royal shows. In the 1860s and 1870s there was a tendency to alternate between the profitable urban site and the unprofitable rural location to achieve financial balance, and an increased reluctance was discernible on the part of many members of the Council to run the risk of financial failure that was likely to attend a show held in a remote area. As Dixon pointed out, by the end of the 1860s it was considered essential to visit some extensive manufacturing district every third year on financial grounds and it was for this reason that in 1869 Manchester was chosen instead of Preston, against the advice of the Country Meeting Committee. The point was further illustrated when the Society returned to the north west in 1877, for when the town had been selected by the Council the previous year the voting was four votes for Carlisle, Preston three and Liverpool thirty-two.[8]

There were three metropolitan shows organised by the Society before 1880. The first two, Windsor in 1851 and Battersea in 1862, were occasioned by the International Exhibitions when it was thought appropriate that the Society should also be in London for the year. Windsor was confined to a stock exhibition, but Philip Pusey was in charge of the agricultural implements at the Great Exhibition in the Crystal Palace. Battersea proved an exception to the

Fig. 3 Number of implements and stock exhibited at the Royal Shows 1840-1879

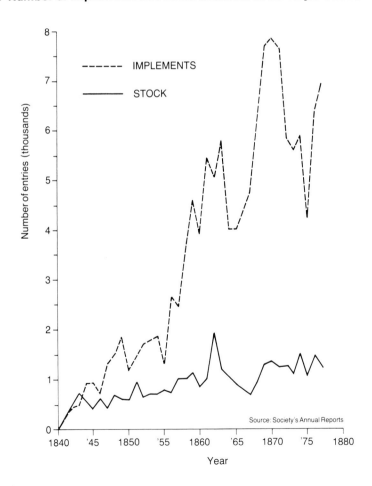

general rule that had been established that an urban location for the show produced a profitable result for the Society: the reasons for the loss were attributed to such factors as the difficulties associated with the supply of green fodder for the stock (which alone cost the Society £900), the relative inaccessibility of the showground, and rival attractions such as the Derby (as the Royal Show was held earlier than usual that year), and the Handel Festival. Dixon maintained that the 'penny-boats' which brought along crowds from the East End did much to mitigate the eventual loss.[9]

The suggestion of a London show was a sensitive issue for the Society with regard to its position in the agricultural community. There were undoubtedly some members of the Council for whom the annual trek to the provinces held little appeal and as early as 1857 Lord Feversham suggested that the time had come for the meeting to be held in London, an interesting proposal considering the later controversy that this idea was to engender. Henry Corbet's report of the Warwick Show in 1859 complained of a tendency to hold the shows relatively close to the Capital instead of in remoter locations; some suggestion was made at this time that a great annual meeting might be held in London in conjunction with the Smithfield Club, with associated local meetings organised by district committees to try out implements first seen at the London show. However, this proposal was not followed up.[10]

The third metropolitan show, Kilburn (1879), was brought about partly by pressure from the implement manufacturers. There was a long-standing antipathy between many of the larger machinery firms and the Society over the operation of the 'prize system' and the conduct of implement trials. In the 1860s and 1870s the manufacturers made repeated complaints about the cost of transporting large tonnages of implements and exhibits to distant parts of the country, especially as the railway companies were increasingly disinclined to give the concessions which they had been anxious to afford during the earlier part of the Society's existence. Alfred Crosskill, a leading implement manufacturer, expressed considerable impatience with the decision to hold the 1867 show at Bury St Edmunds which he held to be inadequately served with railway communications and with general accommodation. There was concerted action against the choice of remote locations in the 1870s, and in 1875 the Agricultural Engineers' Association urged that the trade could best be served by a summer meeting held near to London under the auspices of the Society. In a deputation to the Council the engineers maintained that, although it had been necessary to go to remote districts to bring attention to new techniques and implements during the Society's early years, conditions had so changed that it was now not unreasonable to expect the agricultural public to use the better internal travelling facilities and go instead to the larger centres of population. The manufacturers held that exhibitions and shows in remote parts of the country were no longer an important means of introducing implements to the agricultural community. The overseas trade in implements had also assumed a greater

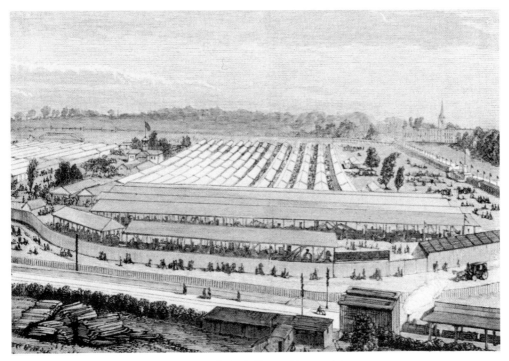

A view of the Kilburn Show, 1879.

importance and foreign agents could not afford to attend the show as it coincided with the harvest in Europe. Although these arguments were considered to be contrary to the fundamental principles of the Society, it was agreed to hold the show in the metropolis as an experiment, Sir Brandreth Gibbs maintaining that the earlier financial loss at Battersea gave no proper indication of the likely success of another London show. The 1879 meeting at Kilburn was enthusiastically promoted by the Society as a great international exhibition of agriculture.[11]

Kilburn had the largest-ever entry of live and deadstock of the early Royal Shows on a site of 103 acres. Its attractions included a working dairy and exhibitions of butter-making on the English, French, Danish and Swedish systems, cheese-making, seed exhibitions, and an assembly of ancient and modern implements to demonstrate the agricultural progress which had taken place over the previous 40 years. This last project did not meet with the approval of manufacturers as it seemed to imply that the shows themselves were responsible for the progress, an idea which they were unwilling to accept. The Kilburn Show has been seen as the first authentic 'Steam Rally' of the sort that has much more recently become a feature of county shows and country fairs.[12] In addition, there was a refreshment department, daily editions of the agricultural newspapers, an improved members' club with reading and writing facilities, and exhibitions of hives and honey with 'bee manipulations'. This show turned out to be little short of disastrous for the Society as it coincided

'Machinery in motion' at the 1879 Kilburn Show. The very wet conditions marred the event.

with one of the wettest years of the century; the incessant rain soon reduced the showground to a quaking morass of mud. Tons of burnt earth were brought in together with thousands of railway sleepers to combat the effects of continuous downpour upon the showground. Because of these difficulties the spirit was 'washed out' and the showyard, instead of being the great festival of agriculture as was intended, presented a 'thoroughly wet and dreary appearance'. Planks, pathways, and wattle hurdles preserved spectators from 'at least falling into more than a certain depth of mire', but the mud spurted up through the interstices and 23 years later Joseph Darby could reminisce that:

> everyone who visited Kilburn retains vivid recollections of its incessant down-pours; of the planks laid down the leading avenues and without which they would have been perfectly impassable . . . one man slipped and falling between two of the planks was so tightly wedged that it was difficult to pull him out.[13]

While the weather was in very large part to blame for the disappointment at Kilburn, it must also be noted that the 'Mansion House Fund' organised by the City of London to support the show had not been very well supported, and in hindsight there were severe criticisms of the ground arrangements, it being alleged that the provision for drainage had been inadequate. The need to sell out a substantial portion of the Society's accumulated fund to make good the deficit led to a resolve to limit the size of the Carlisle Show in 1880. There were higher entry charges for miscellaneous exhibits, and the society's gold and silver medals were restricted to new and 'practically useful' machinery. Some of the innovative features of the Kilburn Show such as the bee manipulations and pisciculture were kept at Carlisle, which also suffered from very wet weather.

By the late 1870s the shows had come a long way in terms of both attendance and range of exhibits, compared to the rather meagre response at Oxford and Cambridge with which there had been some disappointment. Judging of stock was carried out in private until 1862 and the machinery trials were not a major spectator part of the show as the trial grounds were often situated away from the main site; indeed, the trials were sometimes held at a different time of the year. The exhibits of implements and the daily parades of stock were a focal point for most visitors, and as steam power assumed considerable significance in the 1850s and 1860s the 'machinery in motion' section became a great attraction. Parades of horses were always popular although the Society eschewed such 'sensational' elements as 'horse-leaping', made notorious by Samuel Sidney at the Islington Agricultural Hall after 1864, and the Society was at pains to disown the 'leaping' exhibition got up by the Manchester local committee in 1869. It was not until the turn of the century that such features were to be considered an admissable part of the show proceedings.

Most towns which played host to the Society in these early years took considerable trouble to make the visitors welcome. The whole event would turn into a type of agricultural carnival or festival occasion. At Exeter in 1850, for example, the streets of the city were decorated with triumphal arches made of laurel, illuminated with variegated gas lamps, and festooned with banners which proclaimed 'peace and prosperity' and 'success to agriculture'. One thousand two hundred people sat down to the pavilion dinner, there was a balloon ascent, and an outdoor barbecue where the central attraction was a huge joint of beef cooked by gas. At Carlisle in 1855 the houses were decorated with evergreens, flags and wreaths and at Salisbury in 1857 – 'a brilliant success' – there were illuminated fir trees placed around the market square.[14] These shows were all fully reported by the agricultural press and therefore took on much more than local or regional significance; they were attended by many who, like Henry Corbet, looked upon their visit as an 'annual treat'. Not all were equally successful and, apart from Kilburn, to Morton the Canterbury Show of 1860 was 'unquestionably a failure' while to Corbet, who could recall the 'downpour at Gloucester' in 1853, and the 'dullness of Lewes' the previous year, nothing was 'so utterly cheerless' as the Wolverhampton Show in 1871. The town – which was not a 'terrestrial paradise' – was associated with bad weather and 'an unsavoury showground', resulting in the 'most miserable meeting' which the Royal Agricultural Society had ever held up to that time; absent were the 'municipal civilities and hospitalities so common to these occasions'.[15]

The general administrative aspects of the shows were the responsibility of the Secretary and his Hanover Square assistants, but the underlying organisation was between 1843 and 1875 masterminded by Brandreth Gibbs who was also Secretary to the Smithfield Club and partner in the old established seed firm of Humphrey Gibbs & Co. This was an interesting aspect of agricultural continuity for the firm was appointed official seedsman to the Society in 1843, a position which it also held with the 'old' Board of Agriculture. Humphrey Gibbs organised the first few shows, but it was to Brandreth Gibbs that the growth in prosperity of the annual meetings was in large measure attributable. Whatever criticisms there were of the prize system or the conduct of implement trials, and the occasional shortcomings inevitable in any undertaking of such size and complexity, all sources paid tribute to his skill and dedication as Honorary Director. This was recognised by the award of a knighthood on his retirement in 1875, the first time such an honour had been given for purely agricultural services. He was succeeded by Jacob Wilson (later Sir Jacob Wilson) who continued in the position until 1892 and returned from retirement to organise the ill-fated Show of 1905.[16]

As far as the connection of the shows with agricultural progress in early- and mid-Victorian England is concerned, the two great departments were the agricultural machinery and stock divisions. Fig 3, p 39, which shows the number of implement entries at the Royal Shows between 1841 and 1879, conveys the substantial increase of entries which took place during the period and which was frequently the subject of contemporary comment. Although the overall trend is clearly upward, there are marked fluctuations which are worth noting. Distance from the main centres of manufacture may be an important reason for the low implement entries at Exeter in 1850, Carlisle in 1855, Newcastle in 1864, Plymouth in 1865, and Taunton in 1875. The steep rise in the number of implement entries in the late 1850s was checked in 1860 when the leading manufacturers withdrew from the Canterbury Show as part of their protest against the 'prize system'. The lower number of entries apparent in the 1870s was a result of the rule introduced in 1871 to prohibit the exhibit of duplicate implements.

Supporters of the Society were inclined to attribute the increase in the number and range of agricultural implements available to the Society's efforts. The manufacturers not unreasonably rejected this argument though their motive in doing so was linked to their resentment about the way the trials and prizes were conducted and distributed by the Society. H S Thompson, in his review of agricultural progress during the first 25 years of the Society's existence, admitted that it was difficult to prove a causal link between the Royal Shows and the development of machinery, while J Allen Ransome, one of the leading implement manufacturers of the day, made a point of countering Hoskyns's contention, which he advanced at the Society of Arts, that progress

Impressions of stock exhibited at Kilburn, 1879.

45

Views of early Royal Shows: The first Oxford Show, 1839.

in agricultural mechanics up to the late 1850s had come about largely through the Society's influence. Ransome maintained that the limited implement displays at the first few shows could not be taken as representative as the Royal was then a new organisation whose objectives were not generally known. He added that many of the implements in general use by the mid-1850s had been in existence more than a decade earlier and had been improved only in matters of detail during the intervening period. He cited in support of this contention such examples as the drills by Garrett, Hornsby and Smith, the ploughs of Ransome, Howard, and Barrett, the zig-zag harrows by Howard, portable threshing machines by Ransome, Garrett, Barrett, and Exall, clod-crushers by Crosskill, turnip cutters by Gardner, haymaking machines by Wedlake, chaff engines by Cornes, Ransome, Garrett, Richmond and Co as well as a wide variety of rollers – many of these implements having been described by Ransome himself in 1843. He identified the most significant additions to the standard implements available as Garrett's lever horse hoes, Grant's, Smith's and Howard's lever horse rakes, Bestalls's broad share plough, Bushe's, Baxter's and Phillip's root pulpers, Biddell's bean cutter, and a variety of improvements in chaff-cutters and mills.

Bristol, 1842.

He attributed the more general use of standard implements to superior manufacture at no extra cost, the facility of railway transport, the need to cut costs, and (lastly) to the opportunities offered by the Society's annual exhibition for observation, test and comparison.[17]

Whatever the contemporary opinions as to the exact part played by the annual shows in encouraging the development of agricultural implements, the opportunity for viewing, testing and evaluating agricultural machinery was held by Dan Pigeon to constitute a radical 'change of environment' for the implement makers, and the shows provided a focus for what he termed 'storm centres' around which 'successive hurricanes of interest' in types of agricultural machinery 'gyrated'.[18] In the 1840s there was a particular concern for all types of cultivating equipment – improved ploughs, rollers, and clod crushers – as well as seed drills and drainage tile machinery. Steam engines for the farm received a good deal of attention during the late 1840s and 1850s – especially for threshing – and steam tillage was a preoccupation of the late 1850s and 1860s. Reaping and mowing machines were given continuous attention after Pusey's report of the McCormick reaper shown at the Great Exhibition of 1851 and harvest mechanisation constituted the most important department of trials in the 1870s.

The Society's stock exhibition at Windsor, 1851

The first show reports indicated a hint of disappointment at the quality of the implements exhibited. The main prize put up by the Society at Oxford in 1839 was for a gorse crusher and this was not awarded as none of the entries met the specifications laid down with regard to efficiency and price. Numerous drills were shown at Cambridge, but only those by Garrett and Groundsell were deemed adequate, and there was little variety noted in turnip and straw-cutters exhibited. Wood's iron roller was praised along with Crosskill's clod-crusher, but the machine which attracted most attention was a tile and sole maker exhibited by Beart of Godmanchester which was awarded the Society's medal. At Liverpool in 1841 it was noted in the show report that there had been a 'vast stride' in agricultural mechanics since the first show at Oxford and this was attributed to the congregation at a single point of agricultural engineers drawn from a variety of locations: it was also noted that implement manufacture was passing from the hands of the village blacksmith to men of greater skill and capital. Ransome exhibited a portable steam engine for threshing and there were trials of ploughs on Aintree racecourse. At Bristol the following year improvement was particularly noted in drills, including those designed to deposit manure with the seed.[19]

Although the early shows developed in a rather uncoordinated manner, several points emerged as to the usefulness and future potential of the implement department of the annual meetings. The number and variety of exhibits increased rapidly, the standard and finish of the implements was acknowledged to have improved, and it became recognised that trials were necessary to discover merit, although how these could best be carried out was the subject of disagreement. This early experience enabled the Society to be more specific in identifying those developments to which implements were thought to be susceptible; thus the Southampton prize sheet in 1844 stated that the Society wished to call attention to the improvement in apparatus for steaming roots, for smaller portable corn mills, for broad shares for paring stubbles, for horse hoes, and for agricultural harnesses. Prizes were offered for ploughs, drills, scarifiers, and harrows, but the judges had the power to make an award for any invention outside the standard range of agricultural machinery.

A feature of the Derby 1843 awards was a premium of ten sovereigns for the agricultural drain tiles sold at the cheapest rate during the previous year, though account was also taken of durability and local circumstances affecting the cost of production. This prize was not awarded but silver medals were bestowed upon a number of tile manufacturing machines. Josiah Parkes, the Society's first Consulting Engineer, obtained information on production costs and found that the price of tiles ranged from £1 to £2.2s per 1,000 depending on the type of machine and the size of tiles. At Southampton the following year the rate of output of three of the 13 machines on show was tested. The best of these – Etheridge's manufactured by Ransomes – produced 960 tiles per hour, although the trial lasted only six minutes. Parkes claimed that the machine exhibited by Clayton, which did not perform so well because the clay available was in too moist a state, had readily turned out 1,500 pipes per day at a price as low as £12 per 1,000 and had the important added facility of screening the clay of stones which might otherwise impede the manufacturing process.

These trials focused intense interest on the progress of drain tile machines, especially as underdraining was seen in the 1840s as one of the most important agricultural improvements which could be effected, particularly on heavy land. At Shrewsbury in 1845, 14 machines were exhibited of which the judges selected Beart's, Clayton's, and Scraggs's for trial. Beart's – which had earlier been so much praised by Pusey and others – was then found to be inferior and Scraggs's machine, which was constructed on a new principle, drew approval. Subse-

The RASE at Chester, 1858.

quent developments increased the capacity of the machines and there was some criticism of this as not all of the additional output could be utilised and the chief cost of drainage resided in the labour necessary to install the drains rather than in the pipes themselves. By Norwich (1849) there were fewer machines entered and this marked the end of a 'phase of progress' or 'period of special growth' – as Earl Cathcart termed it – in drain tile machines, but they came under periodical scrutiny at later shows in the 1860s and 1870s. At Chelmsford in 1856 the same three makers who had been most successful in the 1840s (Scragg, Clayton, and Whitehead) were dominant, but Whitehead was the only one of these three which remained at the trials at Oxford in 1870; by then the interest which surrounded this department was only a shadow of that aroused during the earlier period.[20]

Given the optimism for the efficacy of drainage in the 1840s, the interest in drainage tile manufacture evident at the early shows is understandable: the parallel enthusiasm for grubbers, scarifiers, clod-crushers, harrows, and various types of improved cultivating equipment indicates a similar concern for improving the growing conditions for plants, as many of these implements had

Country meeting at Canterbury, 1861.

the general purpose of securing a better tilth or seed bed. Alfred Crosskill's clod-crusher received a number of awards at Royal Shows and by 1844 it could be said to be an 'almost universally known and approved machine'; at Northampton three years later its merits were considered to be 'so well known and appreciated'. Awards were also gained by the Uley cultivator invented by John Morton which was found superior to the Biddell extirpator at Southampton on the grounds that it needed less power and travelled further without choking. In 1845 a good deal of attention was excited by a Norwegian harrow which left the land light and loose rather than firm in character, unlike the Crosskill clod-crushing roller. Such an impression was made by the Crosskill implements however that in 1846 the judges recommended the award of the Society's gold medal for the various improvements that had been made to his rollers and clod-crushers over the previous five years or so.[21]

Further interest also surrounded drills and dibbling machines in the 1840s. Drills, which were ousting the broadcast method of sowing seed at that time, underwent marked improvement so that by the early 1860s – as G E Fussell has pointed out – their principles were very similar to those of present day

Manchester, 1869: the agricultural steam-engines are prominent.

machines.[22] Trials of ploughs were also regular features of early shows and these generated considerable animosity between implement makers and the Society as to how proper trials were to be conducted. Ploughs were judged not only for the way in which the furrows were laid, but also for their efficiency in operation. Dynamometers were developed by C E Amos (who succeeded Parkes as Consulting Engineer) for testing ploughs, but it was very difficult to assess from trials whether the plough which gained the prize was necessarily the best fitted for everyday use. Often the trials were only of a few minutes' duration so that nothing could be said about the durability of the instrument, which might have been a very important consideration for the ordinary farmer with limited resources who could not afford to have an implement out of commission.

The general impression of progress in the implement section over a range of farm equipment which became standard in the 1840s is of continuous, small increments of improvement rather than extensive novelty and innovation. The most dramatic advances were looked for in the areas of farm steam engines (which replaced tile machines as the main focus of interest in the late 1840s), steam cultivating equipment, and later harvesting machinery.

A portable threshing machine exhibited by Ransome was the 'great novelty'

The Society's second visit to Oxford, 1870.

of the 1841 Liverpool meeting. The mobility of the machine, which was of simple construction and lightweight in design was particularly noted. No sparks were emitted from the chimney – an important safety feature – and its output of work was far in excess of hand threshing machines tried at the same time. By Bristol the following year the mobility of the Ransome steam engine had been further improved, as it was now shown with four instead of two wheels and with the power of the engine used to give locomotion to the carriage. Four agricultural steam engines were exhibited at Southampton, the prize being awarded to that made by Cambridge of Market Lavington. Efficiency measured by fuel consumption came to be the chief factor considered at successive trials of steam engines, and this led to problems in assessment. Thus the Exeter report of 1850 pointed out that lightness and portability in steam engines were as important to the farmer as sheer economy in work, and it became apparent that there was a danger that engines would be entered for trials which were too expensively constructed and of too large a size to be of practical value but which would carry off a prize by winning the 'race' with low fuel consumption. This led to a call for regulations to limit the capacity of steam-engines to the same nominal power; six horse power was suggested by the Exeter judges, with a

CROSSKILL'S PATENT CLOD-CRUSHER AND ROLLER.

IMPORTANT AGRICULTURAL IMPLEMENT,

DISTINGUISHED FROM OTHERS BY THE NAME OF THE INVENTOR,

AND KNOWN IN THE COUNTY OF SUFFOLK, AS

BIDDELL'S SCARIFIER.

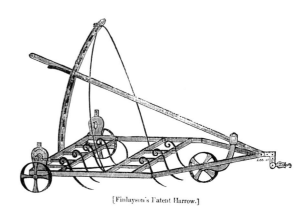

[Finlayson's Patent Harrow.]

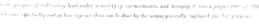

For the purpose of cultivating land under a variety of circumstances, and bringing it into a proper state of tilth
such more effectually and at less expense than can be done by the means generally employed for that purpose.

MADE OF DIFFERENT SIZES, BY

J. R. & A. RANSOME, IPSWICH.

Implements of Agriculture. The 1840s saw intense interest in a variety of cultivating equipment.

54

C E Amos, Consulting Engineer 1848–71.

weight limit of 55 cwt.[23] Despite this caution, however, William Fisher Hobbs made the remark in the 1855 Carlisle report that

> The conditions of competition laid down by the Society for portable steam engines have unfortunately led to the production of engines only intended for winning the Society's prizes and known as racing engines requiring the nicest care ... This result has, I fear, arisen from too strict an attention being paid to conditions relating to the economy of fuel without a corresponding regard having been had to the general character and usefulness of the engine.[24]

He called for new regulations in the trial of steam engines especially with regard to their construction and the length of the period of testing on ordinary farms.

Under a triennial system of trial which had been instituted by Hobbs, steam engines were next seen at Chester in 1858 when no less than 112 were entered in the Show. Some of these were found to be highly dangerous, and led to a regulation whereby competitors had to have the boilers of their machines examined and a certificate of fitness issued before being allowed to get up steam.[25] Tuxford of Boston took the prize for the eight-horse portable steam engine; and Hornsby of Grantham that for the twelve-horse portable – by virtue of the machine's design quality – and Barrett, Exall and Andrews of

55

Agricultural steam engine. Typical of the 1850s–60s, these engines could be put to a variety of uses on the farm.

Reading won the fixed engine class.

There were further trials of steam engines at Worcester in 1863, Bury St Edmunds in 1867, Oxford in 1870 – restricted to fixed classes – and Cardiff in 1872 for portable machines. The Worcester report looked at the economy of fuel question in some detail and, whereas high fuel consumption could indicate that the machine was simpler, and therefore more durable, the high consumption machines could more readily sustain damage to the boiler tubes because of ill-regulated heat. In general there was a tendency to look for durability, refinement of finish, and a good serviceable engine rather than complicated construction designed simply for fuel economy. By the time of the Oxford trial it was said that whereas the main question had formerly been the initial price of an engine, the greater consideration was now the annual repair bill for keeping the machine in use as well as the daily fuel expense. The Bury and Oxford trials were sophisticated in terms of regulations and testing but the merits of the different engines were still assessed by comparing the actual work done in relation to a given weight of fuel. Some of the machines showed 'a general air of bad design and equally bad workmanship' and a winning machine by Clayton and Shuttleworth was found to be seven-and-a-half times more efficient than the worst that was tried at Oxford in 1870.[26]

These fixed and portable steam engines were used to drive farm machinery such as bone mills, guano-breakers, various crushers, cutters, and grinders as well as threshing machines, all of which underwent periodic trial and showed significant improvements in construction and efficiency. The 1858 Chester trial of threshing machines – 'the most important trial of this kind of machinery ever undertaken' – showed some dissatisfaction with the general quality of work performed by steam machines. Only four out of 55 met with approval, and few could complete the work without damage to the grain, or produce cavings or chaff free from corn. Threshing machinery again came into competition at Canterbury and Worcester, and at Bury St Edmunds the judges made approving comment on a new course that had been agreed.[27] This was to offer prizes for both threshing and finishing machines which acknowledged the different values of simpler and more complicated machinery according to circumstances.

Doubts were expressed about the usefulness of much of the finishing equipment, as the crop was often insufficiently uniform to afford an even sample on leaving the machine. Additionally, the motions were too unsteady and irregular for good dressing so the result was often not worth the power that had been consumed. The Bury judges also called for discontinuance of the prizes for horse threshing machines because they were so inefficient and clumsy when compared to the steam machinery available that horse power was no more than 'indicative of the backward condition of agriculture'. Instead, the judges called for a cheap and simple straw elevator or 'any labour saving application', an observation which is indicative of the deteriorating labour position beginning to be experienced on English farms at that time.[28]

The next occasion on which threshing machinery was tried was Cardiff in 1872, where striking advances in finishing machines were noted. Cardiff was the first show at which a prize was offered for a straw elevator, although by that time the apparatus had become, it was said, a 'familiar, as well as valuable' appendage to the threshing machine. In 1872 it was held that the expense of more complicated threshing machines had by their economy superseded the six-penny flail, even though they may have been less efficient in their use of energy compared with hand-labour. This was illustrated with reference to calculations taken from Morton's *Handbook of Farm Labour* which estimated that the labourer could expend 1,400,000 foot-pounds in threshing four quarters of wheat by flail and preparing it for the market. Although this was estimated to be the equivalent of seven days' work, it was still only one-tenth of the power required to do the same work by machine. By their respective costliness however, hand power was 'gold', horse-power 'silver', and steam-power 'copper': 'he who uses hand-power for work that could be done by steam is penny wise and pound foolish' was the judges' conclusion at the Cardiff trials.[29]

The significant advances made in the application of steam power to farm

A	B	C	D	E & F	G & H	I
Spout where the Corn comes out when the Machine is used as a Single Blast Machine.	Spout at which Chobs are delivered.	Second Dressing Apparatus.	Feeder.	Untying Sheaves and handing them to the Feeder D.	Men on Stack pitching Sheaves to E and F.	Engine Driver.

Threshing machinery in operation, manufactured by the leading firm of Ransome and Sims.

operations from the late 1840s onwards naturally led to optimism over the question of steam cultivation. Evelyn Denison (later Lord Ossington) moved that the Society should offer a prize for this at a special Council held in February 1854 and the announcement of a £200 award (later increased to £500) for the steam cultivator that 'shall in the most efficient manner turn the soil and be an economical substitute for the plough or the spade' created intense interest in the agricultural community.

It was thought important that any machine that qualified for a prize should be capable of doing more than merely grubbing or pulverizing the soil and the possible savings in both time and money were taken to be important potential benefits. The Society's prize led to a series of steam ploughing trials at the country meetings in the late 1850s and 1860s and the various types of steam plough tackle which were devised came under intense public scrutiny. At Carlisle the competitors were Usher of Edinburgh whose machine on the moving locomotive principle proved very unsatisfactory under limited trial and Fisken's stationary engine cultivator which, though inadequate under trial, seemed to the judges to offer more promise for the future.

At Chelmsford in 1856 it was considered that there was no reason to doubt that steam, which had brought prosperity to other industries, could and would be used in the daily operations of agriculture. Trials in that year featured apparatus by Smith of Woolston and Fowler of Leeds; Smith's machine was adjudicated to have failed the Society's stipulation that the ground should be fully turned over, while Fowler's, though recommended to the Council for notice, was considered to be insufficiently economical to qualify for the prize. At Salisbury in 1857 there was much less optimism over the potential of steam ploughing, and the ground which the Society provided for the trial proved to be unsuitable for the purpose. Nevertheless, when at Chester the following year the Society's prize was awarded to Fowler, the judges were of the opinion that steam-ploughing would effect real savings over conventional horse ploughs. Among the unsuccessful entries were rotary machines by Ricketts and Burrell and Howard's manufacture of Smith's patent which was awarded the Gold Medal.[30]

Further steam trials during the 1860s have to be viewed in conjunction with the surveys of progress of steam cultivation that were a feature of the Society's *Journal*.[31] The last of these, in 1867, suggested that land tilled by steam perhaps amounted to some 200,000 acres, which (as has been commented upon) was but a negligible proportion of the total arable land of the British Isles. Reports by J A Clarke and others showed that steam cultivation could bring real benefits in terms of work, depth of ploughing, and economy if there were large fields of uniform shape and topography. In his report on the trials of steam cultivating machinery carried out at Wolverhampton in 1871, Clarke looked for a further extension of steam cultivation and noted a contract hire company in Northumberland which employed a capital of £40,000 and which tilled 60,000 acres of land with 20 double sets of steam tackle.

The 'extraordinary economy in costs of steam as compared with horse tillage' was 'taken for granted as already thoroughly proved and well known' by the judges at Wolverhampton and trials resolved themselves then into a public demonstration of well known systems; note was taken of the speed and quality of the work and the technical merits of the different pieces of machinery. The extension of steam tillage hoped for by Clarke did not, however, come about: the conditions for economical steam ploughing were rarely present and there was the further disadvantage of a large amount of capital tied up in the equipment at a time of fast deteriorating economic conditions for the English arable farmer.[32]

Another important focus of interest at this series of shows was the development of reaping machines. Many of the features of the modern reaper are attributed to that developed by the Rev Patrick Bell in 1826. Some of his machines were sent to America and reappeared as McCormick and Hussey reapers at the Great Exhibition of 1851 where they excited a good deal of

Steam ploughing. The operation shows the relatively labour intensive nature of the equipment and the need for flat ground.

interest. Indeed, Pusey hailed them at that time as 'the most important addition to farming machinery' since the threshing machine had first begun to take the place of the flail and pointed to the saving of horse power and the reduction in the employment of casual harvest workers – 'strangers who cannot always be found' – as being the chief advantages that they had to offer the farmer.[33] Thereafter trials of reaping machines became a regular feature of Royal Shows. At Lewes in 1852, where they constituted the 'greatest novelty' and excited 'the most lively interest', Garrett's machine, built on the Hussey principle, was awarded the prize put up by the Society. However, H S Thompson noted that in other trials conducted throughout the country results had been inconclusive as to the best type of machine available, a similar pattern to that of the Society's trials where the decision of one year tended to be reversed at the next meeting. The prizes awarded to Crosskill for Bell's reaper in 1853, Dray for Hussey's at Lincoln the following year, and to Burgess and Key for McCormick's in 1855 indicated to some contemporaries that the contrary decisions were indicative of a weakness of the trial system.[34] In retrospect it is clear that, although the conditions of the trial ground differed markedly – often being unsuitable for the purpose – and the judges' personal preferences sometimes swayed decisions, there was a series of cumulative small improvements which meant that it was unlikely that any one machine would be continuously superior to another, which is itself indicative of the increased pace of agricultural progress.

Substantial advances were made in reaping machinery in the 1860s, and 1870s. Self-rakers were demonstrated by McCormick and Samuelson in 1862 and interest surrounded mechanical, as opposed to manual, delivery at both Plymouth in 1865 and Manchester in 1869. A further development was in one-horse rather than two-horse reapers although at Manchester it was claimed that the one-horse machine would be found to be too heavy.[35]

Between 1875 and 1878 the Society's machinery trials were restricted to mowers and reapers. A prize had first been offered for mowers at Salisbury in 1857, and by Manchester it had been concluded that any of the best machines then constituted a safe purchase for the farmer; at Taunton in 1875 significant improvements were found to have been made in strength, lightness, and cost. At Manchester none of the one-horse mowers had been tried on account of their excessive draught, but at Taunton all 14 entries except the Hornsby's were rejected as being too heavy, although the judges noted distinct advances. Of the two-horse machines, the gap between the best and the worst tried was much narrower than at Manchester and the majority were found to be well-constructed and robust. At Birmingham in 1876 several leading manufacturers abstained from competition; a steam reaper of Aveling and Parkes received notice as did the sheaf-binder exhibited by Walter A Wood. A Gold Medal for sheaf-binders was the only prize put up by the Society at Liverpool the following year but it was not awarded. At Bristol four wire-binders and three string-binders were exhibited: after several had been withdrawn from trial and others tried on unsuitable ground, the Gold Medal was given to the machine exhibited by Burnell, Waite, Huggins & Co (McCormick's) and Walter A Wood's was highly recommended. These wire-binders were disliked by English farmers for fear that lengths of wire passing through the threshing machine could become mixed with straw and injure their stock.[36]

Agricultural commentators in the late 1860s and 1870s were curious as to why the reaping machine came into use much later in the British Isles compared with the United States. H S Thompson accounted for the lack of interest in harvest mechanisation prior to the 1851 Great Exhibition as being due to the continued prevalence of land in high ridges and deep furrows, the costliness of the British machines, the inability of farm labourers to look after the machines properly, and the comparative cheapness of English farm labour up to mid-century. Certainly the reintroduction of the reaping machine at the Crystal Palace coincided with the beginning of a period of increasing labour difficulties in English agriculture – as was recognised in Pusey's report – and this accounts for the interest in reaping trials in the 1850s and 1860s. It has more recently been suggested that 'intermediate technology', in the form of improved hand-tools, was initially preferred to full mechanisation of the harvest, one reason being the need to preserve work for labourers who were still required for other farming operations. Additionally, much of the English terrain was unsuitable for early reaping machines, the surface being much less uniform and flat than

Engraved by J.R.Englehart

Mr Cormick's Reaper.

As Improved & Exhibited by Messrs Burgess & Key of Newgate St London, and to which the First Prize of the R.A.S of England was awarded at the adjourned trial at Leigh Court Bristol, August 1852.

London. Published by Rogerson & Tuxford...

McCormick's reaper, the leading American design of the 1850s.

that of the North American prairies.[37] The luxuriant growth of cereals in the damp climate of the British Isles, encouraged further by the increasing use of additional fertilizers, again acted against the widespread operation of machines which had been primarily developed for North American conditions. Under these circumstances, Thompson's recognition that those who had been among the first to purchase a reaping machine in England had found them something of a hindrance can be readily understood. He detailed a number of difficulties associated with machines constructed on both the Hussey and McCormick principles. These limitations included clogging of the cutting knives leading to frequent stoppages, heavy draught, difficulty of delivery when the crop was heavy, too great a width for standard farm-gates, and their high price – although in the early 1850s he was optimistic that such problems would soon be overcome.[38]

As there was a restricted time each year when improvements could be tried out it may well have been that the Society's trials, carried out in advance of any very *general* demand for harvest machinery, fulfilled a particularly useful function. The amount of labour available to the agricultural sector had declined between 1850 and 1870, and the position then deteriorated still further because of increased migration from the country to the towns, agricultural trade-unionism, and falling prices. It is therefore understandable that there was increased interest in labour-saving machinery on English farms and it was acknowledged in 1875, in a Council discussion on the future of the Society's trials, that its encouragement was all important. It may not be unreasonable to claim that the Society's promotion of reapers and mowers gave the agriculturist, at a time when it was particularly needed, a choice of machinery of greater sophistication and usefulness than would otherwise have been available, although it was also maintained in the *Implement Manufacturer's Review* that the Society did not offer enough prizes for labour-saving machinery when the labour question was uppermost in the minds of 'eighty out of a hundred farmers'.[39]

Stock exhibitions were the other great area of annual shows and, indeed, this sphere of activity was much more important to the Society's founders than the displays of agricultural implements. This is indicated by the relative size of the premiums which were put up at the Society's first two country meetings; 50 sovereigns were offered for a draining plough, 20 for a gorse crushing machine and the same for 'any other' implement at Oxford in 1839. In contrast, stock premiums exceeded 750 sovereigns. The early period of the Society's history saw the implement section of the shows expand far beyond anything that was initially envisaged while the entries of stock underwent a much less dramatic increase; the *range* of animal breeds exhibited, however, showed a marked extension in early and mid-Victorian times.

In the 1840s stock prize sheets had a standard form. Shorthorns, Herefords and Devons were the three divisions of cattle with an extra class for 'any other breed or cross'. The sheep classes were for Leicesters, South Downs, other short-woolled sheep, and for long-wools not qualified to compete as Leicesters. There were divisions for agricultural horses and hunters, and pig classes which were restricted to 'large' and 'small' breeds. There were attempts to bring out the animals specific to the particular localities of the shows and thus there was an extra class for the 'Channel Island breed of cattle' at Southampton in 1844 and for sheep 'most adapted to mountain districts' at both Shrewsbury in 1845, and at Newcastle the following year, while Sussex cattle were prominent at Lewes in 1852. At Windsor the previous year, which was confined to stock, there was an attempt to assemble all the approved breeds known at that time. Thus there were cattle classes for Channel Islands, Sussex, Longhorns, Shorthorns, Scotch Horned, Scotch Polled, and Welsh breeds. Horses during this early period were classified according to type rather than breed.

In general, entries for the various special classes at the early shows were small and Richard Milward, in commenting on what he saw as 'the complete failure' of the Welsh breed class at Gloucester, maintained that the Society should cease to offer prizes for anything but the three recognised breeds of cattle. Milward thought that the five animals shown in response to the Society's prize of £70 for the Welsh breed were not worth that sum in their total value. Twenty shows later Henry Corbet (who had been present at the Gloucester meeting), in reporting the Cardiff exhibition of 1872, remarked that cattle 'peculiar to the district' were those which by that time were known the world over – Shorthorns and Herefords – whereas the Castle Martins, Angleseys and Montgomeryshires were little more than curiosities.[40]

However, the period after Milward's report saw a number of local breeds gain national recognition. The Sussex made significant advances – a *Herd Book* was established for them in 1855 – and they joined the Herefords and Shorthorns as a regular class, although they declined in popularity in the latter part of the nineteenth century. The Norfolk and Suffolk Red Poll cattle advanced in the 1860s, their breeders making a determined effort to monopolise the 'other classes' between 1863 and 1865; thereafter regular classes were provided for them and they gained status when their own *Herd Book* was established in 1873. Longhorns, which had been neglected, underwent a revival at the Birmingham meeting of 1875 and classes were provided for them in the shows which followed. The dairy classes also advanced during the late 1860s and the report of the second Oxford Show in 1870 called for the Channel Islands to be divided into Guernsey and Jersey classes. This was done the following year at Wolverhampton, although some of the exhibitors entered their cattle into the wrong classes.

Extension of variety was particularly a feature of sheep. Although the early shows often had more successful local classes for sheep than they did for cattle – Gloucester was a good example where the Shropshires made a great impression – the first permanent addition was for 'Short-wools other than Southdowns' at Salisbury in 1857. At Chester the following year there were classes for Shropshires, Hampshires, West Country Downs, Oxfords and Cheviots. The Shropshires were given their own class at Canterbury from 1860 onwards and the Oxford and Hampshire Downs, the Cotswolds, and Lincolns had become permanent additions to Royal Shows by the 1870s. There were increasing numbers of pigs at the early shows and horses came to prominence in the 1860s and 1870s with classes for Agricultural (shires), Clydesdales and Suffolks.

These stock exhibitions were attended with a number of problems, not least the question of transporting the valuable and often delicate animals and their housing and feeding over the week of the shows. When Thomas Bates decided to exhibit his famous Shorthorns at the first Oxford Show – where they were one of the leading features of the meeting – he had to convey them by steamship from Middlesborough to London and then by barge up the Aylesbury branch of the Grand Junction Canal, the whole journey taking three weeks.[41] The

MR. RAWLENCE'S HAMPSHIRE DOWN.

MR. G. TURNER'S LEICESTER.

THE BORDER LEICESTER (HAYMOUNT, KELSO).

MR. RIGDEN'S SOUTHDOWN.

MR. MARSHALL'S LINCOLN.

MR. SWANWICK'S COTSWOLD.

Sheep at Oxford Show, 1870. This shows the variety of breeds popular at the time.

extension of the railway system in the 1840s eased these difficulties and enabled the Society to bring together specimens of stock from all parts of the country at their annual events.

As far as there was any recognised objective in the stock exhibition and the award of prizes for superior stock, it was to encourage improved breeding of animals and especially the quality of 'early maturity'. There was, however, continuous controversy over the condition in which the stock should be exhibited and the utility of the stock shows was often questioned.

The over-fed condition of much of the stock shown at the early country meetings of the Society soon generated intense criticism: 'Whoever saw a well-made giant?' queried T C Hincks in 1845, adding that the judges should have instructions not to give awards to animals which were so overgrown that their points were obscured by the accumulated layers of fat that covered over imperfections.[42] With continuous complaints of this kind – the animals exhibited at York (1848) and the decisions of the judges at that meeting were widely condemned – and ineffectual efforts by a few members of the Council (such as Lord Portman) to deal with the problem, the issue was taken up by Earl Ducie in 1852. He was prompted by the experience of the Lewes Exhibition of that year where a number of overfed beasts had died in the extreme heat that was a feature of the show-week.

Ducie formally proposed that as there was widespread agreement that something ought to be done to arrest the evil of high-feeding for exhibition, which was incompatible with the Society's objective of developing the best breeding stock, a committee should be formed to investigate the matter. It was as a result of the Committee's discussions on the best policy to adopt that at Gloucester the following year the Society instituted 'juries' to adjudicate the condition of cattle, sheep, and pigs exhibited, and to indicate that they would be disqualified if found to be in an over-fed state.[43]

Commentators much approved this action, as it was generally considered that over-feeding was a major obstacle to progress in the stock section. At Gloucester, animals which were disqualified under the new system included pigs that 'could not stand', sheep which found some 'difficulty in respiration', and rams which, 'like the Romans of old, preferred taking their meals in a reclining position'. Yet these disqualifications proved to be very controversial. It was claimed that the 'reclining' position of the disqualified rams was only a reflection of their 'docility and aptitude to fatten', and there was determined opposition to the restrictions from Col Towneley and other influential stock-breeders, some of whom boycotted the Gloucester Show on that account.[44]

Thus little progress was made over what was generally considered to be a serious weakness in the Society's proceedings. It was recognised that animals were trained-up specially for the show – the process reminded Corbet of 'the renowned commander who marched his men up the hill for the purpose of marching them down again' – and Pusey said that there was not much

LORD PORTMAN.

Lord Portman, ineffectual campaigner against the exhibition of over-fed stock.

difference between the 'cattle of July' (breeding stock at the Society's show) and the 'cattle of December' (fatstock at the Smithfield Show). Widespread abuses included not only feeding up the show stock with large rations of linseed cake but also, it was alleged, gin, cream, and aniseed. At the Lincoln Show – where the jury-system was abandoned and over-feeding was noted as being very prevalent – additional malpractices were widespread. These included filing the pigs' teeth to give a false impression of youth, and artificial shearing of sheep to accentuate symmetry and to hide defects.[45]

Ducie died in 1853 and much of the initiative for reform was then lost. Thereafter, the over-fed condition of the stock exhibited continued to be perceived as a major problem, but one which seemed incapable of solution in the face of the breeders' general opposition to reform. The show reports contain continual allusions to this unsatisfactory state of affairs; at Carlisle (1855) it was stated that some of the pigs were 'much above the age stated on the certificate and so over-fed that they could not possibly be considered in breeding condition', and at Chester (1858) Samuel Jonas complained of the high condition of the cow and heifer stock which was 'unnatural and opposed to commonsense'. In the 1860s John Dent Dent (a particularly perceptive agricultural commentator) made continual complaints in his capacity as Steward of Stock. At Worcester (1863) many of the pigs were unable to walk from their crates to the pens and some were disqualified, while the sheep had been clipped and trimmed to make 'charming models of symmetry'. At Plymouth (1865) the bulls were 'over-fed and inactive' and difficult to get into the show ring; thus, in 1871, Morton, in answer to the question as to what was meant by 'show condition' was tempted to reply 'a hopeless obesity, a constitution endangered, a system forced to an unnatural extent, a pampered condition of body anything but fitted to withstand the hardship to which cattle are constantly subjected'.[46] Instances were not unknown of animals breaking down under 'severe training', and force-feeding also gave rise to damage in the reproductive system. Many of the leading breeders refused to exhibit – just as some of the implement manufacturers stayed away – and Torr, Bowly, Kingscote, and Booth were among names that were generally absent from the lists.

The problem was a reflection of the extremely subjective nature of animal judging. There was also an inherent contradiction between the desire for the quality of 'early maturity' – which implied a large size at an early stage – and the need for lean stock for breeding purposes rather than fatstock for the butcher. In the 1840s Thomas Bates called for the Society to encourage the all-round qualities of stock and not to merely reward 'the chance obesity of the individual', but his proposals, which included the idea of an award for family groups of stock as an indicator of merit over more than one generation, failed to raise much enthusiasm in the Society: the emphasis continued to be on 'early maturity' with the attendant temptation to produce animals that were unusually large for their age.[47]

The process of judging always posed a number of problems. It was carried out in private during the early years and decisions were kept secret until announced at the Council dinner. The private judging system broke down at Battersea in 1862 under the impatience of the crowd after which public judging became 'the order of the day'.[48] It was often difficult to obtain judges of the right calibre (as many of the acknowledged experts would themselves be exhibitors) and this contributed to a situation where animals which failed to gain an award at provincial shows could be successful at the Royal, or where Society decisions were reversed at, for example, the Highland. In order to preserve anonymity neither the names of animals nor their pedigree were made known during the early years of the shows, but in the 1870s there was intense debate about the way in which the judging could best be carried out and the amount of information that should be given to the judges.

Public debate centred around suggestions made by E A Fawcett, a well-known Shorthorn breeder, on the occasion of the Bedford meeting of 1874. His points included those which had been so widely discussed over the previous 30 years: that prizes were too often awarded to fat rather than breeding animals, that Ducie's proposals had never been seriously acted upon, and that animals were still especially prepared for the shows by feeding with cod liver oil, milk and sugar, rum, brandy, and treacle. In addition, because the same judges acted at more than one show during the year, and because animals were often led into the showring by well-known men, the impartiality of the judges was questioned.[49] The most contentious issue here was whether the names of the owners and the pedigrees of the competing stock should be given to the judges and there was spirited debate over what became known as 'judging by catalogue'. An allied question was whether it should be a condition that, to gain a prize, Shorthorns should have an entry in the *Herd Book*. Here opinion was divided between those who held that an unregistered sire was a 'permanent flaw' and those who considered that too much attention was often given to pedigree alone, which sometimes clouded objective judgement.

For the Birmingham Show of 1876 it was proposed by Dent that the judges should receive the full catalogue.[50] This followed a move by Richard Stratton to relax the pedigree rule – which was rejected – but the argument then was that, if it was desirable for stock to have four crosses of blood, then the judges should know what these were. Full information, it was thought, might counter the exhibition of over-fat animals at a show of breeding stock and that as there was no show where some of the animals were not already known by the judges it was fairer to exhibit them all under the same terms.

This proposal was generally very poorly received in the agricultural community. It was considered that to place the full catalogue in the hands of the judges might serve to shut out the new or rising men from exhibiting; E A Fawcett, whose suggestions had served to make the issue one of central concern, considered the proposal undesirable as the judges could hardly fail to be influenced by the names of eminent breeders. Then there was the suspicion that the pedigree would assume more significance than the actual competing animals, the 'visible merits' being outweighed by 'high lineage'. 'Judging by catalogue' was also seen as likely to lead to the situation whereby the judge would either be charged with favouritism and unfairness or risk refusing a prize to a worthy animal because he happened to be well acquainted with the owner. Against these objections Samuel Sidney maintained that numbers rather than names did not always ensure secrecy and that the best animals were often well known before appearing at the shows. However, it was pointed out that horse shows (for which Sidney was responsible at the Islington Agricultural Hall) were quite different from Shorthorn shows where ownership and pedigree were bound to be taken into account in deciding what was best. In the face of this almost universal opposition from the agricultural community, the Council did not proceed with the 'complete catalogue' proposal, and Dent's motion was defeated.[51]

Another controversial suggestion was the question of using a scale of points to make judging more objective. This was urged upon the Society by Lord Kinnaid, the Scottish agriculturist. Opinion was more evenly divided on this proposal than on the 'judging by catalogue' issue. It was supported in the *Farmer* on the grounds that it had been successfully adopted in Australia and America and that in the hands of competent judges the 'points system' could prove useful in guiding young breeders. It was hoped that a 'points system' would overcome the 'national evil' of over-fed breeding stock. It would make the judging process less 'empirical' and circumvent the predilection of the judges as, for example, whether they were 'Bates' or 'Booth' men. Against these arguments it was maintained that the system could be just as inaccurate as the traditional method, that it would be tedious and take up too much time, and that animals might have qualities that it would be impossible to incorporate objectively into a points scale. The Society's disinclination to take up Kinnaid's suggestion was not generally criticised as it was admitted that when his £10 prize for the best cow or heifer of Shorthorn breed was judged on the points system at the Scottish Midland Counties Show at Kinross, the experiment had not been successful. Later assessments of the points system have shown that it is not particularly useful in picking out small differences between stock.[52]

Thus although there was considerable discussion of the problems of judging the show animals, very little in the way of changes was made and the fundamental problem of acceptable show condition remained largely unresolved. The Kilburn stock report still made reference to 'animals in unprofitable high condition winning prizes year after year' and Thomas Plowman, in his 1885 address to the London Farmer's Club on 'Agricultural Societies and their Uses' referred to the Kilburn report and admitted that prizes were often awarded to over-fed stock. All were agreed that something ought to be done to discourage the exhibition of such animals, yet at the same time it was acknowledged that if all the stock were exhibited in store condition the animal which would not do well under any feeding regime would be placed on the same level as those which possessed the capacity to do justice to the best treatment.[53]

In both the machinery and stock departments the early Royal Shows had a good deal of influence on agricultural improvements and progress, although it is difficult to quantify this with precision. In 1845 Morton wrote in the *Agricultural Gazette* of the importance of the early country meetings and he noted that, as a result of the recently concluded Shrewsbury event, 'it was possible that a valuable implement found its way into a district where it had been hitherto unknown, agricultural engineers had been instructed in the faults of their manufactures, and the pride taken by many exhibitors of stock had been humbled before the evidence of superior skill on the part of others'. The award of premiums had 'to some extent' indicated the qualities in implements and animals deemed to be worthy of praise while the assembled farmers carried home truths and opinions new to them. Morton therefore looked to the shows to encourage the adoption of new implements, to bring about improvements of detail in agricultural machinery, and to facilitate the exchange of ideas among the farming community. He had reservations about the utility of the prize system and the social nature of the occasion, preferring lectures at 'public breakfasts' dominated by 'scientific and practical men' to the lavish pavilion dinners which were a feature of the time.[54] By the late 1870s it was maintained that the Society Show was unquestionably '*the* sight of the year for those of a bucolic turn of mind' and that many thousands of British farmers 'would not like to miss the Royal'.[55] The Society's shows had significant influence in the interchange of ideas and opinion which took place, and in the critical examination of stock and implements in the showground: they also had the general function of stimulating *awareness* of agricultural progress.

As far as implements were concerned, the Royal Shows provided a valuable focal point for the testing of innovations and improvements in machinery. Although many of the leading implement houses, such as Garrett and Ransomes, were already established by 1840, the start of the Society's sequence of shows and trials can reasonably be taken as a major catalyst in the emergence of a fully-fledged British agricultural engineering industry between about 1835 and 1870. Major firms such as Crosskill, Howard, Smythe, Gooch, Bentall, Wedlake, and Hunt came into *national* prominence by exhibiting at the shows, participating in the trials, and winning the Society's prizes.[56]

It is more difficult to find examples of the Society bringing forward a specific innovation by the announcement of a premium; rather manufacturers used the shows to bring innovations and improvements in machinery to the notice of potential buyers, sometimes in advance of a specific demand for the product. J Wrightson, reviewing the progress in agricultural machinery between 1841 and 1877 for the *Agricultural Gazette*, pointed to the chief implement landmarks at the shows as scarifiers, cultivators and dibbling machines in the early 1840s, the

Pavilion dinner held at Cambridge in Downing College, 1840.

development of drain-tile machines and portable steam-engines, steam trials, and the improvement of harvesting machinery, all of which had provided foci of interest at successive shows. Data contained in the Society's annual implement reports have been used to quantify the improvements in agricultural machinery which took place in this important period of agricultural progress, and one conclusion that has been drawn is that the majority of implements and machinery became cheaper without a disproportionate drop in quality, and that where prices rose, there was a compensatory increase in performance.[57]

These impressions are borne out by examination of contemporary comment on the shows and, although agricultural advances can rarely be *directly* attributed to the early Royal Shows, the catalytic nature of the Royal meetings can reasonably be taken as an important factor leading to progress. Nevertheless, it is by no means safe to assume that implements which gained prizes in the showground were necessarily the first choice of the working farmer of the day. Trials and the decisions of the judges were often called into question, and cheapness and durability were often to be preferred to the technical sophistication which won plaudits at the annual meetings. Morton claimed he knew of many classes of machinery that had been awarded prizes, but which had never come into general use and of cases where showground success failed to give any impetus at all to sales. Examples that he cited included Cambridge's roller of which 'thousands were sold' before it was recognised by a prize and Bentall's broadshare which, according to Morton, received 'hundreds of testimonials' before it was appreciated by the Royal. Smyth of Peasenhall was one of the largest drill makers but, it was said, 'always in the background' with regard to prizes, while the Uley cultivator and Biddel's scarifier, which had been so successful during the early days of the Society, appear never to have been generally adopted. Newbury's dibbling machine, which gained several awards in the 1840s was, according to Morton, 'nowhere' in 1864. Of dibbling machines generally, Wrightson commented that he could not recommend the purchase of 'the elaborate machines exhibited at the shows', and W W Good complained that many of the articles seen at the show yards could only be 'worked at a loss'.[58] It was a general criticism that the Society failed to make awards to inventions of the highest importance although giving prizes to useless inventions: judges, it was alleged, would give awards to machines which they would not necessarily buy themselves and Richard Garrett maintained that his customers often specifically ordered *not* to have a prize implement as they knew it would not answer their purpose.[59]

Some of these criticisms were overstated and they can also be turned round to suggest that they derived from the success of the shows in stimulating progress. Dislike of the 'prize system' arose from the fact that many of the implements were so similar in quality that to award the prize to one as opposed to another was to confer too abrupt a distinction on a successful machine, although this uniformity might itself be taken as a reflection of rapid technical progress brought about by bringing together the products of the leading firms at shows for the purpose of comparison and trial. It was perhaps a more just criticism that the Society sometimes encouraged developments in directions which were not particularly useful; emphasis on expensive tile machines with a capacity much above that which could be fully utilised and the promotion of 'racing' steam engines are examples in support of this contention.

A secondary objective of the shows and trials sponsored by the Society was to encourage the adoption of machinery. Generally it seems that the award of a prize for a machine was no guarantee of increased purchases and, if the contemporary statements of some of the leading implement manufacturers are to be believed, showground success could actually depress demand; it is unfortunate that the sales records of nineteenth century agricultural engineers are extremely thin so that they can rarely be used to trace the sales of specific implements or their adoption in a specific locality. In the 1840s commentators give the impression that, despite intense interest in cultivating equipment at the Society's shows, sales were relatively flat, but H S Thompson, who saw the purpose of the country meetings as the encouragement of the general diffusion of the best existing implements and continued progress in their improvement, detailed marked increases in sales of steam engines, threshing machines and drills between 1848 and 1852. He attributed this to the improvements that had been made, particularly in steam engines, under the guidance of the Society's trials.[60] The steep increase in the number of exhibits at the shows in the 1850s may be taken as indicative of increased demand for agricultural implements of all kinds during that period – a view which is confirmed by Morton's statement of 'agricultural experience' in 1861 where he related substantial increases in the output of turnip and chaff cutters, threshing machines, and reapers.[61]

The founders of the Society thought that the Royal would have the function of bringing implements to the notice of farmers in those districts where they were unknown. The show may have had this role in the early years and a communication from the West Cumberland Agricultural Society to Morton maintained that:

> thanks to the Royal Agricultural Society's holding their meeting in Carlisle [1855], I believe that exhibition was instrumental in opening the eyes of many of our Cumberland mechanics. Previous to 1855, our county was wont to boast of her ploughmen, but when it came to the test at Carlisle we were all beaten upon our own soil; not that our ploughmen were deficient in skill, but they had not the implements to work with.[62]

On the other hand, it would seem from the limited evidence available that show success did little to change established local loyalties with respect to implement purchase. It was noted, for example, that Ransomes who took many of the prizes at Southampton in 1844 'never gained a footing there' – while Howard of Bedford who won four of the plough prizes at Chelmsford in 1856 had by 1864 'never sold twenty ploughs within a radius of twenty miles of the place'.[63]

The function of the shows in communicating information about agricultural machinery changed between the 1840s and the 1860s, although the general management philosophy behind the shows did not keep pace with this change. Thus Alfred Crosskill could remark in 1866 that the importance of shows had been diminished because, with the cheap press and the general increase in facilities for communication, there was not the same scope for the shows to extend and exchange agricultural knowledge.[64]

Morton and others attached far more importance to the implement section of the shows than they did to the livestock exhibitions, for it was in agricultural engineering that the greatest advances were looked for in the early Victorian period. In reply to a critic who thought that the *Gazette* paid insufficient attention to the stock (without which the Royal Shows, according to the correspondent, would have 'dwindled away'), Morton maintained that improvements in cultivation exerted an influence over a wide variety of agricultural departments whereas the influence of improvements in breeds of stock was less pervasive.[65] It is clear that for many, the show displays of farm stock were a major attraction and less exception was taken to the notion of giving premiums to prize animals as opposed to implements, even though the condition of show animals was a matter of continuous controversy.

The two main ways in which the early Royal Shows can reasonably be shown to have influenced livestock progress were first, in the encouragement of better breeding stock with the quality of early maturity and hence the more efficient and economic production of meat and other livestock products and second, in the establishment of the new breeds at national level. However, it is difficult to arrive at hard estimates of the improvements in livestock performance which took place in the Victorian period, still less to attribute them to the influence of the show system of which the Royal meetings were the most developed example. There was much criticism of the subjectivity of judging and certainly no thought was given to performance or progeny testing which would have helped to establish the real worth of prize animals – a criticism which, of course, continued to be levelled against stock shows in much more recent times. A number of objections were made in accepting show standard as a specific breeding aim, including the danger that show judgement tended to over-emphasize appearance and points of conformation of individuals which required high standards of feeding and husbandry that could not be sustained in commercial production at the expense of more utilitarian traits.

These criticisms were very evident in the stock awards at the early Royal Shows where the stress was on symmetry and points of conformation in cattle and sheep, an influence which was to continue for very many decades. E A Fawcett was among many who attacked the stress given to the appearance of prize animals: 'straight on this side, straight on that side, and on all sides'.[66] Among the 'utilitarian' traits which were discouraged among Shorthorn cattle – the breed which excited the greatest interest – were the production of lean meat and good milk yields. Thus Robert Smith, in the report of the livestock show at Chester in 1858, asked 'are such animals really in a state for breeding *and* milking, one at least of the uses of the beast? It would be well if more attention were paid to the lean meat of a Shorthorn and less to superfluous fat'. J Dent Dent called attention to the neglect of milking qualities in his 1864 report on the livestock at Newcastle, considering that breeders had too far lost sight of this quality in their desire to produce the utmost symmetry of form and early maturity. At Plymouth the following year he again protested against the breeders of fashionable stock who had entirely ignored the milking qualities of their cattle. The Manchester report stressed the desirability of encouraging milking qualities in all three of the main breeds of cattle at the expense of the desire to secure every additional pound of beef.[67]

The condition of show animals was often unrelated to their practical use on the farm, but Royal meetings did provide a focus at which emerging breeds could gain notice and general standards could be laid down. Breeders in a particular district sometimes monopolised the 'other classes' which in turn would lead to the establishment of a separate category for that specific class. This allowed their points to be demonstrated giving rise to greater uniformity and fixity of type.

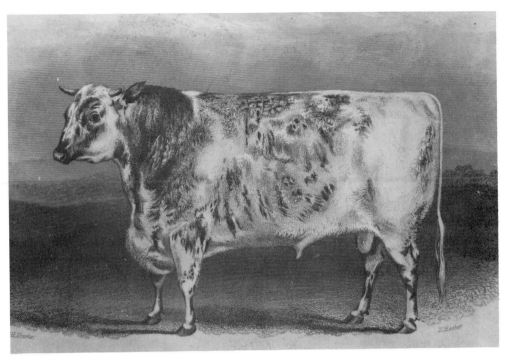

'Master Butterfly', prize Shorthorn at Chelmsford Show, 1856.

Thus in 1863 it was claimed that the Oxford Downs and Shropshire sheep, which had recently made substantial advances, had not yet a sufficient uniformity to make for easy judging. A great variety of appearance was noted among the Oxfordshires, while the Shropshire breeders complained that the judges had mistaken type and gone mainly for size. At Oxford in 1870, which was especially notable for the entries to the different sheep classes, there were still comments on the lack of uniformity in Cotswolds and the Shropshires: by Hull three years later, the latter were noted as making a recognisable advance towards the standard which was laid down by the Oxford judge three years earlier. The early- and mid-Victorian Royal Shows may therefore be taken as instrumental in the general diffusion of the leading breeds of farm animals such as Shorthorns, Herefords, and Devons, and in contributing to the demise of inferior local breeds, although it has been claimed that the location of the meetings did not materially influence the pattern of Shorthorn adoption.[68]

One of the most significant influences of the early Royal Shows was to foster the the trade in pedigree livestock. The award of a prize to a particular animal, especially cattle, conferred upon it a value which was far above that which it would have had for breeding purposes. Col Towneley's 'Master Butterfly', the first-class Shorthorn at the Chelmsford Show of 1856, created a new record when it was sold for 1,200 guineas for export to Australia, but such a price was regularly exceeded by the 1870s. Buyers from the United States, Canada, and Australia were noted as buying many of the best stock at Oxford in 1870, where the price of 2,000 guineas was paid for a seven-year-old Shorthorn cow.[69] The export trade in pedigree livestock which developed in the 1870s put a particular significance upon prize-winning animals. Shorthorns and Herefords were particularly sought after and formed the basis of many overseas herds. It was these herds which were, paradoxically, to provide the meat imports of the British Isles that were a prominent feature of the last two decades of the nineteenth century.

The early Royal Shows can therefore justifiably be seen as 'storm centres' of agricultural innovation and had considerable influence, whatever their short-comings, on English farming. The trials of implements, despite the criticisms of their conduct and of the prize system, brought about cumulative increases in the efficiency and utility of standard implements as new types of agricultural machinery were tried and came to public attention. The annual livestock shows, whatever their limitations, enabled spectators to inspect the products of the leading breeders and to compare their standards with their own stock; in addition, improved standard breeds were brought to public attention at the shows. Contemporaries such as Morton also stressed that the 'gathering' was as beneficial as the show, providing an ideal occasion for the interchange of agricultural opinion. The impact of Royal Shows was increased by the fact that they were national rather than local events and were thus covered by the agricultural press which reported the proceedings and criticised their manage-ment. Fine woodcuts produced by the firm of Hare and Co[70] were used to give the implements prominence in advertisements and reports, and the shows were clearly seen as a focal point for taking stock of agricultural progress. At the turn of the century Joseph Darby could remember the Royal meetings of the 1850s and recalled how he looked to them to demonstrate the best in improved implements and stock.[71] Whatever their criticisms of the show system, and many of these were not without justification, most contemporaries were agreed that they benefited the agricultural community considerably even though with improved management they could arguably have achieved more.

BREAKING THE 'CLOSED-CIRCUIT'— THE JOURNAL AND AGRICULTURAL SCIENCE

Although it was the annual shows which received most attention in the agricultural press and involved the Society's members to the greatest extent, probably the area in which most agricultural advance was made in the early period of the RASE's history was in agricultural chemistry, the science which had given so much inspiration to the founders of the Society. This was promoted by publication of a *Journal* which carried extensive reports of research and good agricultural practice.

In what he has termed the 'Second Agricultural Revolution' between about

1820 and 1880 Professor F M L Thompson identified the increased use of fertilising material from *outside* the farm unit as breaking the 'closed-circuit' of agricultural production, thereby making increased productivity possible.[72] The Society's *Journal* had a key role in this development as its articles and reports increased knowledge about *how* fertilising agents worked, their value for different crops, and the best mode of application. As information generated by the Royal filtered down from its *Journal* to the rural community via more popular media, the English farmer was able to manipulate farming systems with increasing sophistication. This diffusion of knowledge about agricultural science was one of the most crucial nineteenth century agricultural advances and deserves close consideration, after a review of the *Journal's* general publication arrangements and of the range of subjects that it contained.

During the latter part of 1838, the Society considered how best to publish its proceedings. Advice was sought from William Shaw on printing costs and he conveyed an offer from the proprietors of the *Farmer's Magazine* to provide free space in that periodical each month to report the transactions of the new Society.[73] This followed the pattern that was already operated by the Highland Society whose *Prize Essays and Transactions* were published in conjunction with the *Quarterly Journal of Agriculture*. However, after considerable discussion it was agreed that the Society should publish its own *Journal*, to be issued free to members. Given Spencer's enthusiasm for the work of the Society for the Diffusion of Useful Knowledge, it was fitting that he should announce this decision to the first General Meeting held on 18 December. Spencer indicated that the projected *Journal* was to contain prize essays and matter connected with agriculture generally, stressing the importance that was attached to free issue in assisting the spread of information on agricultural topics as widely as possible; to non-subscribers the *Journal* was to be sold at reasonable cost. Initially it was proposed that the Society's *Journal* should be a quarterly publication, but only the first volume, that for 1840, was issued in four parts and publication was formally changed to two parts each year in 1843 in order to contain costs.

How the *Journal's* publication should best be organised to achieve its aim of facilitating the spread of information was, and has continued to be, a topic of debate. Some held that infrequent issues produced bulky volumes that were not to the taste of those modest tenant farmers whom it was especially desired to reach. An open letter to Spencer, published in the *Farmer's Magazine* in 1839, warned that a volume of the *Highland Societies Transactions*, upon which the new publication was in part to be modelled was 'so voluminous, so expensive, and so diffuse in its articles that comparatively few can afford to purchase it and fewer have time to peruse it . . .'.[74] Free issue could circumvent the problem of cost if tenant farmers subscribed to the Society in sufficient numbers, but the question of the best format of the *Journal* was more difficult. It was often maintained that numerous small doses of agricultural information would be preferred to less frequent, more substantial volumes, the sheer size of which was likely to prove intimidating to many readers. It was also held that twice-yearly issue led to the content becoming out-of-date by the time it was received by the reader, a criticism which was particularly pertinent with regard to show reports as these often appeared in the *Journal* as much as six months or more after the country meeting had taken place. However, another line of thought was expressed by H H Dixon who maintained that the Society would be best served by the production of a single annual volume – a sort of agricultural yearbook to be issued during late autumn – which would contain, as well as the show reports and technical articles, features on agricultural personalities, sales, lettings, and general agricultural news to be perused at leisure during the winter evenings.[75] This basic division of opinion, which was difficult to reconcile, was between those who saw the *Journal* as a forum for the exchange of views against a more encyclopaedic permanent record of progress in scientific agriculture. H M Jenkins, who edited the *Journal* during one of its most successful phases, was probably correct when he maintained that it was the interest and relevance of the content rather than the frequency of issue that determined its success and influence in the agricultural community.[76]

Initially the distribution of the *Journal* posed a problem as few of the subscribers were able to collect each part from London. Pusey negotiated the posting on a twopenny stamp but, by the end of 1839, complaints had been received about non-delivery and misdirection of the first issue. In answer to these complaints, Richmond proposed the establishment of a network of booksellers and agents in country towns where the *Journal* could be collected by subscribers. These agents were listed in the appendices of the early volumes, but this mode of distribution later gave way to a postal arrangement.

In 1839 a Journal Committee was established consisting of Henry Handley, C Shaw Lefevre, the Rev W L Rham, J French Burke, J W Childers, Philip Pusey, and William Youatt. With four Members of Parliament – Handley, Lefevre, Childers, and Pusey – and excellent experience of agricultural writing – French Burke edited *British Husbandry*, Rham the *Penny Cyclopaedia*, Youatt the *Veterinarian* – this was a strong committee. In 1839 it was resolved to advertise for an agricultural editor and Pusey, Childers and Lefevre were delegated to draw up a suitable advertisement. They decided upon a combined position of Secretary/Editor and in July James Hudson was appointed to this post at an annual salary of £400. Power of editorial control was however vested in the Journal Committee and the Secretary/Editor was to work under its direction, it being envisaged that he would write reports, translate foreign papers, and edit articles for publication. In fact Hudson wrote very little for the *Journal*: while he supervised the printing and administrative matters connected with its production, Philip Pusey, Chairman of the Journal Committee, was the *de facto* editor. The first 15 volumes of the *Journal*, through his work in editing contributed material, judging the prize essays, and writing articles, bear abundant testimony to his close involvement in its progress. Before 1838 Pusey had written for the *Morning Post* and *Quarterly Review*, but had not been particularly concerned with agricultural matters; it has been suggested that he was prompted by the national question of population increase and the local problem of rural distress in his Berkshire constituency to work so whole-heartedly for the Society.[77]

This editorial arrangement worked very well. Throughout the 1840s Pusey was unchallenged as 'the leading agricultural writer of the day', according to Sir James Caird's retrospective assessment. His 'readable and practical essays' were 'the embodiment of the Society's motto "practice with science"' and he was seen to direct the *Journal* with 'zealous ability'.[78] After Pusey's death in 1855, the editorship and the editorial arrangement became one of the most controversial topics of the Society's proceedings and until 1869, when H M Jenkins was appointed to the editorship, the *Journal* suffered from a period of often uncertain direction.

The development of the Society's *Journal* shows a number of distinct phases. The initial period, when it teemed with short practical articles written by enthusiastic landowners and farmers who had been among the founders of the Society, was followed by a greater reliance upon prize essays. This in turn gave way to specifically commissioned articles and official reports written by recognised specialists. The large number of short articles during the 1840s may well reflect both the enthusiasm that Pusey engendered among farmers for communications on matters of agricultural practice and the care and interest he took in rendering these fit for publication. There is interesting confirmation of this in a letter from Edward Bouverie Pusey to the *Agricultural Gazette Literary Supplement* in 1879. Recalling time spent away from Oxford in his family home in Berkshire, he remembered how his brother would begin his day at 6 in the morning, rewriting letters received for the *Journal* which were badly spelt or ungrammatical in order to pick out that which was valuable while keeping to the facts; E B Pusey was 'all along much interested in his plans because they involved self-denying labour for the good of others'.[79]

The decline in the number of short communications reflected the expansion of the agricultural newspaper press in the 1840s. Although this meant that topical articles could be published more rapidly, this decline was deprecated by many. Charles Lawrence wrote to Pusey in 1854 asking for agricultural experiments to be carried out by farmers and reported in the *Journal*, the pages of which would thereby 'be enriched by a variety of matter highly instructive and useful'. In 1861 Lawrence complained about the policy of relying on the publication of strictly scientific topics and prize essays so 'that the intelligent and observant farmers hesitate to communicate the results as they thought that they might not be valued or worthy of notice', comments which were quoted with approval in the *Agricultural Gazette*.[80]

In the 1840s many learned societies used prize essays as a standard and

Philip Pusey, Chairman of the Journal Committee 1839–54.

uncontroversial mode of eliciting information. The Royal generally announced ten topics each year with premiums typically ranging between £10 and £50 for each essay. The subjects were chosen by the Journal Committee who consulted other members of the Council. Initially the essay topics were seen as falling into distinct groups such as 'experiments', 'manures and soils', 'agricultural operations' and 'implements', but this classification later fell into disuse. All essayists had to abide by rules that were printed in the *Journal* along with the set topics. The most important was that the information in the essays was to be founded on experience and observation rather than compiled from secondary sources. To preserve anonymity, essays sent for competition were to be inscribed with a

81

motto and accompanied by a sealed envelope bearing the motto and containing the name of the essayist. When the essay topics were published quite detailed guidelines were generally laid down as to the information that was wanted and essays which were adjudicated by the Journal Committee had to provide information under specified headings.

From the beginning, the Society had difficulty in obtaining essays of sufficient merit to award premiums, and even unsuccessful essays were sometimes published. Competitors often submitted material which was derived from their own experience and observation as was required, but based on a restricted outlook with little knowledge of the broad compass of the subject which they were covering. These shortcomings were expressed by Professor J S Henslow who read some of the unsuccessful submissions on one of the earliest prize essay topics, 'Diseases of Wheat', in 1840:

> I have . . . seen these essays, and it is evident to me that the authors were ignorant of many of the facts long known to scientific enquiries, respecting the nature of diseases, and the causes producing them. However valuable some of the remarks may have been as a result of the personal and practical experience of their authors, these essays fell far short of what the Society really wanted.[81]

By the 1860s the prize essay system was seen by many to be anachronistic and it was maintained that a more appropriate method of obtaining sound material was to commission acknowledged experts in their respective field to write on defined topics. The subjects announced for prize essays had also been scrutinised and found to be wanting in that they did not always reflect what were perceived to be the relevant and important issues of the day. For example, a review of the prize essays for 1862, which included such items as 'the Agriculture of Staffordshire', 'Haymaking', 'Land Valuing', 'Management of the Home Farm', and 'Any Agricultural Subject', made an unsatisfactory comparison, it was thought, with those articles which had been prepared by Pusey. Morton thought that topicality and relevance had begun to decline and that in 1862 more appropriate topics would have included 'Reaping by Machinery', 'Cultivation by Steam Power', and the 'Relative Merits of Different Breeds of Sheep'. The meagre list presented by the Society was 'a confession of inability and failure' on the part of the Journal Committee.[82]

A review of the list of early *Journal* topics shows that initially there was greater emphasis on subjects that related to practical experience of farming such as modes of root storage, rotations, and results of fertilizer application. Increasingly, topical subjects (such as utilisation of town sewage, theories of plant nutrition, or the nature of cattle diseases), were inappropriate for public competition as they demanded greater technical expertise and specialist knowledge, a development which itself reflected 'agricultural progress'.

Another source of dissatisfaction with the prize essay system was the

PROFESSOR HENSLOW.

J S Henslow, Professor of Rural Economy, Cambridge University, and contributor to the Society's *Journal* in the 1840s.

anonymity of the adjudicators. When the authors of unsuccessful essays had them published on their own initiative, and public opinion did not coincide with the official view of the merits of different essays, the competency of the judges was sometimes questioned. A good example in 1863 concerned the important subject of steam cultivation when the then editor, P H Frere (whose ability was in any case under question), was scathingly referred to as 'walking about with a bundle of essays in his pocket asking for someone to read them'.[83] Such comment, justified or not, undermined confidence in the system. Samuel Sidney, one of the most persistent critics of the Society in the 1850s and 1860s, considered continued adherence to the prize essay system indefensible:

> What did the Council do in this matter of prize essays? They induced a number of men to write on a particular topic; the essays went before a committee existing of nobody knew who; and after a cut-and-dry arrangement an unsatisfactory sketch was placed before the world.[84]

Little good, Sidney maintained, would come of continuing to offer a prize essay for 'he had written a prize essay himself and knew how such things were got up'.[85]

By the 1860s the prize essay system was outmoded and it took a great deal of time to read the essays: time which was wasted when, as Thompson was forced to admit, submissions were often badly written or 'mere twaddle'.[86] Although there was no specific resolution to discontinue the series of prize essays, the Journal Committee minutes show an increasing tendency for known authorities to be approached to write papers for which payment was given. The Committee also considered unsolicited material which was submitted by various authors from time to time. The last premium offered by the Journal Committee in 1869 was £25 for an essay on any agricultural subject. This was awarded, rather curiously, to a paper on the Jersey potato.[87] Although it was held that the Society continued the system after it ought to have been abandoned, the view that it had a deleterious influence on the *Journal* content was by no means unanimous. While there were those who agreed with H H Dixon, himself a prize essayist who maintained in 1869 that 'prize essays and county reports have not done much for the *Journal* so far', in 1873 it was considered that 'many of the best papers in the *Journal* were promoted by the premiums'.[88]

In summary, there were six main types of contribution to the *Journal* in the early years. First, there were the prize essays, the most important sub-group of which were the series of county reports on farming practice. These were inspired by the 'old' Board of Agriculture surveys, and it is worth noting that descriptions of farming have been a concern of the Society in much more recent times. Secondly, there were the commissioned articles which became more important in the 1860s and 1870s, as the prize essay system was phased out. Thirdly, there were unsolicited communications, often in the form of short notes or reports. These were particularly important during the early days of Pusey's editorship. More substantial communications were also received: Lawes and Gilbert, in particular, used the *Journal* to communicate their Rothamsted experiments which were carried out independently of the Society. The three other main categories of *Journal* content were the accounts of lectures given to the Society, either at country meetings or at the London Headquarters; reports of implements and stock at the shows, normally written by show stewards, and investigations and laboratory analyses produced by the RASE Consultants; and, finally, material abstracted from other publications or translations from overseas sources.

Many of the leading contributors to the *Journal* were either directly connected with the Society as consultants or members of the Council, or were practising men of science. Of the remainder, some were well known professional writers such as J C Morton, H Evershed (later agricultural correspondent of the *Field*), J A Clarke, H H Dixon and W L Rham. Others were land agents or connected with land improvement in various ways. The professionalism of the *Journal* content tended to increase so that leisured spectators of the rural scene, who were such prolific contributors to early agricultural newspapers and other periodicals, became much less important as writing on agriculture became, with its increasingly technical sophistication, the province of specialists.

Of the topics represented in the early issues of the *Journal*, surveys and descriptions of farm practice and articles on drainage were important in the 1840s. Articles on pests and diseases such as the potato disease, 'finger-and-toe' in brassicas, and animal diseases, such as pleuro-pneumonia and cattle plague, and various reports of animal health were also well represented. Crops and cultivation, including discussion of various roots, grain crops and their mode of cultivation, and land reclamation were important and there was much description of implements and machinery, including the surveys of progress in steam ploughing, and reports of the implement department of the shows. Livestock articles included methods of animal husbandry, breeds of livestock, and show reports, while food manufacture, markets, and supply became more important in the 1860s and 1870s.[89]

Although Philip Pusey was aware that most of his readers were more concerned with the *practice* than of the *theory* of agriculture, the developments in agricultural science were an extremely important phase of English agriculture during the early Victorian period. At first, papers of a strictly scientific nature were published somewhat apologetically; thus an article on soils had a note appended that 'theory must not pretend how to teach the occupier of land how he is to manage his farm'.[90]

There were calls, however, for scientific directing principles in agriculture: one question of particular interest was how manures and other fertilizing agents were beneficial. In 1841 Charles Daubeny, in a lecture given to the Society, identified three categories of manure: agents such as quicklime used for

PROFESSOR CHAS DAUBENY.

Charles Daubeny, a leading early Victorian scientist with agricultural interests.

improving soil characteristics; animal dung, which had direct influence on plant growth; and 'mineral' substances such as nitrates of soda, bonemeal, and gypsum. It was not known whether these latter substances acted as the 'food' of plants or acted as stimulants to their growth. It was insufficient, he maintained, to find that some substance or other benefitted plant growth on certain soils – precise analysis of the active ingredients was called for, not least so that substitutes could be investigated.[91] Contributors to the *Journal* echoed Grey of Dilston's view that 'the most important branch of our national industry' should no longer be left for its advancement to the 'chance-directed discoveries of the unlettered rustic'.[92]

Early contributors to the *Journal* on agricultural science drew extensively from the work of Liebig whose *Organic Chemistry in its Application to Agriculture and Physiology* had created such a great impression upon the scientific community when published in 1840. The particular interest of Liebig's principles for the agriculturist was the hope that they gave for making manuring a precise science which could raise crop yields by identifying nutrients absent in soils – nutrients which could be supplied externally if their nature was understood. Liebig's work was revolutionary in that he pointed out that carbon, the chief constituent of plants, came from the carbon dioxide of the atmosphere and that traditional manuring agents did not supply additional organic matter to aid plant growth. Liebig's view was that the other constituents of crops such as potassium, sodium, calcium, magnesium, phosphates, and silica were obtained from soluble mineral substances in the soil and that the chemical analysis of the ash of a particular crop would indicate its mineral requirements which, because of the slowness of the weathering process whereby the minerals became available in the soil as rocks are broken down, were not adequate for the purposes of agricultural production.[93] Liebig's view that the mineral constituents of manurial agents were all-important was expressed in the statement that

> the crops on a field diminish or increase in exact proportion to the diminution or increase of the mineral substances conveyed to it in manure.[94]

He therefore thought that, if the land's fertility was not to decrease, it was necessary to restore to the soil those constituents removed from it in cropping. This provided the agriculturist with a logical, easily understood theory which satisfactorily accounted for the action of such substances as farmyard manure and bones – what the farmer removed from the soil in terms of the mineral constituents of his crops had to be returned in natural or artificial manures for fertility to be maintained. The exact balance of the mineral constituents could be determined by analysing plant ash which, it was expected, would lead to the manufacture of artificial fertilizers exactly calculated to provide the different mineral requirements of specific crops.

Liebig's influence in England was at its height between 1843 and 1847 and

Lyon Playfair (later Lord Playfair), who had translated *Organic Chemistry ...* into English was appointed Consultant Chemist to the Society in 1843 and undertook a programme of plant ash analyses in conjunction with the British Association for the Advancement of Science. These were reported in the *Journal* in a series of long articles written up by J T Way who succeeded Playfair as the RASE's Consulting Chemist in 1847.[95]

Liebig held that the nitrogen requirements of plants were supplied by the ammonia in the atmosphere and, in the first edition of *Organic Chemistry ...* , stated that:

> Cultivated plants receive the same quantity of nitrogen from the atmosphere as trees, shrubs, and other wild plants; and this is not sufficient for the purpose of agriculture.[96]

By the third edition (1843) Liebig had moved away from this view stating that:

> Cultivated plants receive the same quantity of nitrogen from the atmosphere as trees, shrubs, and other wild plants; and this is quite sufficient for the purposes of agriculture.[97]

and Liebig's denial that additional nitrogen was necessary for successful agricultural production gave rise to an extended controversy between Liebig and J B Lawes who published many of his Rothamsted research findings in the *Journal*. In the meantime, patent manures for various crops based on Liebig's mineral principles were manufactured and distributed to agriculturists by the firm J Muspratt of Liverpool.[98]

These were given a seal of approval by Liebig who wrote a pamphlet in conjunction with Muspratts explaining the principles and application of the manures. This explained his view that, without phosphates and other mineral elements of the food of plants, ammonia could exercise no influence on vegetable life; it was an error, he held, to regard the nitrogen of manures as the principal source of their efficacy, as nitrogen was always accompanied by other minerals.[99] The Liebig/Muspratt patent manures failed; Lawes tested them at Rothamsted and found that they produced only a slight increase in yield which he attributed to the very small amount of ammoniacal matter that they contained. Nearly 30 years later C S Read recalled his 'disastrous' results when he had used manures based on the Liebig principle.[100] Liebig admitted that the manures sold under his name had failed but refused to accept that this was because his 'mineral theory' was wrong. Instead, he claimed that they had been misapplied and had been manufactured so as to be too insoluble to enter plants. This latter point was particularly important as it was shortly to be realised that soluble salts are not washed out of the soil by rain but are, instead, absorbed by the soil by a complex series of chemical reactions. This was discovered by H S Thompson (who had an important influence on the *Journal* after 1855) and Joseph Spence, a York chemist, and publicised by J T Way in the *Journal*.[101]

In 1847 Lawes published his first substantive scientific paper and chose the *Journal* to introduce to the agricultural and the scientific communities the programme of field experiments which he had embarked upon at Rothamsted. This was a forthright attack on the mineral theory of Liebig where he regretted the 'errors into which Liebig had fallen' and stressed that additional nitrogen was essential for successful plant growth. The mineral theory, he claimed, 'was calculated so seriously to mislead the agriculturist' that 'it was highly important that its failures should be generally known'. The evidence derived from his field experiments gave rise to the view that attempts to increase crops with mineral fertilizers, without additional nitrogen, must 'for ever be abandoned'.[102] Liebig was also attacked by other authorities in the *Journal* such as J F W Johnson who stated that the idea that crops required only mineral matter from the soil had received its 'death blow' from research which had been carried out by Lawes and others; the view that plants obtained all the nitrogen they required from the atmosphere was 'contrary to the oldest and most common experience of practical men'.[103]

Philip Pusey appears to have been soon converted to Lawes's view of the importance of nitrogen and this drew criticism from Liebig who questioned Pusey's qualifications to reject his theories on agricultural chemistry. He claimed that Lawes's experiments were 'entirely devoid of value as the foundation for general conclusions' and in his own mineral theory lay 'the whole future of agriculture'.[104] This brought forth a much more detailed *critique* of Liebig's ideas from Lawes and his co-worker J H Gilbert, and Pusey appended a note to their article to the effect that it established 'the entire failure of the Mineral Theory as a guide to the use of manures in practical farming' and that, having visited Rothamsted, Pusey considered it 'the principal source of trustworthy scientific information on agricultural chemistry'.[105] By the mid-1850s, in what was often an acrimonious debate, Lawes and Gilbert had established certain basic principles on the role of nitrogen which were of tremendous importance for the intensification of English agriculture. In summary, their conclusions were that ash analysis as advocated by Liebig was no key to the manurial requirements of crops, secondly that for the majority of agricultural crops, especially cereals, additional nitrogen inputs were required for high yields, and that, thirdly, fertilizers based on minerals alone would not be successful in producing high yields.[106] The findings of Lawes gained support in the agricultural community when they found that the mineral fertilizers distributed by Muspratts did not achieve the results that had been generally expected. In 1853 Pusey maintained that 'nitrogen is the element mainly required as manure on ordinary soils by our corn crops' and considered that this was 'the only fundamental truth that we possess in agricultural chemistry' comparing its importance to the discovery of the

'The Wizard of the Pacific'. The source of guano off the Peruvian coast.

laws of gravitation in astronomy or the circulation of the blood in medicine.[107]

The early issues of the *Journal* carried numerous reports of experiments by landowners, tenants and others which tested the effects of various fertilizing substances which had attracted a great deal of interest - in particular nitrate of soda, guano (solidified bird droppings obtained from islands off the coast of Peru) and superphosphates. By far the greatest attention was focussed upon the latter two as manurial agents. Guano had first been imported in about 1835 but had not received widespread attention until six years later when Pusey inspected a sample on the occasion of the Liverpool meeting of the Society. The rapid adoption of 'the Wizard of the Pacific' (as Hoskyns termed it) partly depended upon its advocacy in the *Journal* and other agricultural newspapers, but also by word of mouth when its quite dramatic effects on a range of crops were observed by what were initially cautious sceptics. A review of the development of 'Practice with Science' in 1856 maintained that guano had done more than anything else to get rid of the prejudice against science amongst ordinary farmers and commented that those who had first ridiculed its application soon boasted as to how many tons they had applied. As J F W Johnson put it, guano came and, viewing the results, a farmer would resolve 'to try some myself next year'.[108]

Once the efficacy of guano was established, papers published in the *Journal* concentrated on identifying its beneficial constituents and their money value. In the first major statement on guano given to the Society in 1841, Johnson maintained that ammonia and uric acid were its most useful components, although he stressed the wide variation – between 7 and 15% – in the ammonia content of samples that he had analysed.[109] In 1849 Way provided an important

90

paper on the composition and the money value of guano. This was significant because it initiated a phase of work of particular interest both to members of the Society and to agriculturists generally inasmuch as it attempted to ascribe an £ s d value to the beneficial constituents of the substance and thus provide a guide to the purchase of different samples.[110]

Superphosphates posed a particular set of problems: it had long been known that bones could be useful as manuring agents, but their action was uncertain and confined to certain classes of soils. (Indeed, this had been one of the questions proposed by Henry Handley in his 1838 *Letter* promoting the foundation of the Society.) The reason for this is that their fertilizer value depends upon the calcium phosphate contained in bones which is inert until it comes into contact with acid. This was one of the first problems examined by Lawes and it was on the basis of his discoveries that he took out a patent for the manufacture of superphosphates by treating bones and mineral phosphates with sulphuric acid. He began this work in his Deptford factory in 1843, the profits from the enterprise supporting the Rothamsted research.[111]

Early issues of the *Journal* carried a number of reports on experiments with bones treated by sulphuric acid, but the difficulty was to enable them to be used efficiently. Farmers used bones when they could obtain a cheap local source and bone mills became quite widely established, but the problems were essentially solved by proprietary manufacture, for which Lawes held the monopoly, using as raw material either bones, coprolites or overseas mineral phosphates.[112]

In the enthusiasm for artificial fertilizers traditional farmyard manures were not overlooked and there were a number of contributions to the *Journal* which looked at the most efficient modes of management of traditional farmyard manure and sought to identify its beneficial constituents. There was also considerable attention given to the value of town sewage as a manure – a popular topic in early- and mid-Victorian times – because there was great optimism that material otherwise wasted in water courses could be used beneficially on the land. Very extravagant claims were sometimes made for the value of town sewage – indeed one of the most ambitious schemes promoted was the proposed reclamation of the Maplin Sands fertilised by North London sewage conveyed by culverts through South Essex.[113] One protagonist of the value of sewage thought that it would encourage crops to grow rapidly and secrete ozone so that the 'sewage farm' could be combined with a 'health farm' where

> London beauties might come out to recruit their wasted energies at the close of the season and, attired in *costume de circonstance*, with coquettish jack-boots, would perhaps at times listen to a lecture on agriculture from the farmer himself, while drinking his cream and luxuriating in the health-restoring breeze.[114]

Most articles in the *Journal* by agricultural chemists correctly took a pessimistic view of the real worth of town sewage, in contrast to the inflated assessments which were frequently advanced in non-agricultural circles.[115]

The importance of these papers on agricultural science was in their connection with the intensification of English agriculture and, in particular, the increased application of external inputs, such as guano and manufactured superphosphates, to farming systems. This was at the heart of what became known as Victorian 'high-farming' and can be seen as the forerunner of our modern high-input and high-output intensive agriculture. From the point of view of the Society the importance of the publications in its *Journal* was that they spread knowledge of the valuable components of the different fertilizing substances available which allowed their application to be regulated with greater efficiency. In addition, this knowledge was useful in guiding the purchasers of fertilizers. Analysis of the various compounds indicated their real worth for different purposes and farmers could then discriminate between the various types and grades of fertilizing substance offered: it was recognised that any success following the adoption of artificial manures would in part depend upon the attention given by the farmer to the principles which regulated their manufacture. By the 1850s farmers were recognising these principles, especially the identification of nitrogenous matter as an important constituent of manures, particularly for wheat, and the special usefulness of phosphates for root crops. Both these principles can be traced back to the Rothamsted experiments and their communication through the Society's *Journal* under Pusey's editorship.

By the 1870s more popular information on techniques of fertilizing became available to the agriculturist and many of these stressed the pioneering work which had been earlier published in the Society's *Journal*. For example, the Agricultural Cooperative Association's book *Agricultural Economy*, published in 1874, drew extensively upon analyses published in the *Journal* and, in an address on the 'Economy of Artificial Manuring', tribute was paid to the influence of the *Journal* in this respect. In 'Manuring No Mystery', the way in which the somewhat abstract research was utilised was made clear:

> We are not like the Royal Agricultural Society – explorers, pioneers of inquiry, discoverers. We gratefully accept the work done for us in that way by the eminent chemists and agricultural leaders of England and Germany. Our object is to utilise the knowledge thus obtained for the good of many.[116]

In giving advice on the best mixtures of artificial manures, information was in nearly all cases taken from 'results of the experiments at Rothamsted by Mr J B Lawes and of those made by the Royal Agricultural Society under the superintendence of Dr Voelcker'. Recommendations for manure for mangels, cabbage, kohlrabi, potatoes, and sugar beet were taken direct from various items by Voelcker in the *Journal*; Thompson's advice published in the *Journal* in 1872 was adopted for grassland, and for leguminous crops, Lawes's advice on low-nitrogen manures.[117] In this way, at least some of the faith that the Society's founders had in the potential of chemistry became realised.

Another area where there was great enthusiasm for improvement concerned agricultural drainage and in the 1840s the *Journal* contained numerous accounts of drains and drainage experiments. Up to 1843 the views of J Smith of Deanston were generally preferred. The importance of this was that the 'thorough-draining' he advocated involved the placing of drainage tiles at a comparatively shallow depth below the surface of the land. This view came into question after Josiah Parkes was appointed as the Society's first Consulting Engineer in 1843. Parkes's draining experience had been gained near Liverpool in the 1830s on Chat Moss. This consisted of marshy land requiring drainage at considerable depth, and Parkes's view of the efficacy of deep draining was given authority by his position with the Society. He gave the most comprehensive statement of his views in a lecture to the Society at the Newcastle meeting of 1846.[118] Although he recognised that there could be no fixed rules for depth which were equally applicable to all soils, he said that it was his own practice to drain at between four and six feet deep. The evidence was 'irresistible' that any depth less than four feet would not be accompanied by beneficial results and 'a mass of evidence' could be brought forward to show that drainage at greater depth was the most efficient and economical. Parkes's views drew forth a certain amount of support in reports of experiments on drainage communicated to the Society and, as the Society's Consulting Engineer, Parkes's views were accorded a great deal of weight; indeed, it was on the basis of these that money advanced under the provisions of the Public Money Drainage Act of 1846, (which was the first example of public money being given towards the support of agricultural improvement, partly as a *quid pro quo* for Repeal), had to be spent on work carried out under Parkes's principles of deep draining to qualify for the loans at preferential rates.[119]

In 1847 however, a contrary view was put forward and at a Council meeting held in February 1847, William Bullock Webster, a land agent, presented his opinion on draining. He complained that the Society was giving sanction to an unsound system by persistently publishing articles in the *Journal* advocating deep draining. Webster had a paper published on drainage in 1849 where he contested Parkes's four to six foot rule on 'very strong clay soils' where the problem was not from 'under water' (ground water or sub-surface springs). He put forward three main arguments. The first was that on heavy clays it was likely that the rain would not reach the drains, secondly, percolation to the drains was so slow that the ground was not rid of the water sufficiently quickly, and thirdly, deep drains increased the cost of installation which was not compensated by Parkes's advocacy of an increased width between the lines of drains. As Webster stressed:

Error in new systems is quickly propagated. The person who has reduced theory to

93

practice with real or imaginary success is proud of his sagacity and ready to proclaim it. He, on the contrary, who has failed is by no means anxious to call the attention of the world to his mistakes ... Perhaps, therefore, while so many successful experiments in deep drainage are being pressed upon the public with enthusiasm I shall not be doing ill service in ... showing that "profit and loss" on the drainage ledger should have entries as well in the debtor as the creditor side.[120]

In support of this contention Webster cited a number of correspondents who showed that shallower drainage was preferable. The controversy continued, and in 1850 Pusey inserted a note in the *Journal* which stated:

it must now be regarded, not as a wholesome caution but as an established fact, that there are certain clay formations in the south of England on which deep draining is not unlikely to fail.[121]

Modern field drains are generally put much nearer the surface of clay soils than was advocated by Parkes and it may well be that his advocacy of deep draining in the *Journal* caused much of the Government-funded drainage to be put in under erroneous principles and fall short of expectations.[122] It is also possible that the deep drainage principle had currency because good results with deep drains were reported in some communications to the *Journal* in the early 1840s: however, this was probably because they tapped *ground* water, rather than the *surface* water which was the main problem on clay formations. A striking indication of the impression that Parkes's views made is the recollection as late as 1878 that, when there was a public debate between Smith and Parkes at the Society's Newcastle meeting in 1846, the 'advantage was so decisive in favour of Parkes' for whom there was 'enthusiastic cheering'. By the 1870s however, J Bailey Denton, who succeeded Parkes as the leading authority on drainage schemes, held that the required depth of parallel drains in clay soils which was prescribed by the Inclosure Commissioners for the execution of earlier drainage work had not been fully justified and that Parkes's principle that increased depth allowed for increased width was erroneous; Denton admitted that if he had the chance to do some of his drainage work again, he would have done it differently.[123] This episode is indicative of the slow and sometimes uncertain nature of Victorian agricultural progress and in this particular case the Society was responsible for the communication of information which was in some circumstances a hindrance and which arguably led to unwise investment.

AGRICULTURAL CONSULTANCY

The promotion of agricultural science by the Society paved the way for the establishment of agricultural consultants, the first being Lyon Playfair and

JAMES SMITH (DEANSTON)

Smith of Deanston, a pioneer of agricultural drainage.

Josiah Parkes, Consulting Chemist and Engineer respectively. Playfair's increasing scientific commitments made it impossible for him to devote the requisite amount of time to the Society's activities, and he was succeeded in 1847 by J T Way, who was the first Professor of Agricultural Chemistry at Cirencester. Way resigned rather abruptly ten years after his appointment for reasons which are not entirely clear. Although he had devoted considerable effort to the Society and seems to have been popular among the main body of members it was thought that the RASE had not treated him very well and it was deplored that the Society gave 'their old ally but a cold good-bye' in 1857.[124] Way was succeeded by Augustus Voelcker – also from Cirencester – and this began a remarkable episode of agricultural continuity inasmuch that the members of the Voelcker family filled the position of the Society's Consulting Chemist until 1976. Although at first Augustus Voelcker does not seem to have made a very favourable impression, his speaking style being described as 'rambling and illogical', this assessment soon changed and his appointment inaugurated a most fruitful phase in the Society's work. He became extremely popular with the agricultural community, an eloquent testimony to his acceptance being his election as President of the Farmer's Club in 1874. He was

> a model agricultural chemist. He did not dogmatise, he did not theorize, he did not make theory a tyrant in agriculture, but let science and practice go hand in hand.

No man 'ever more happily united "Science with Practice"'.[125]

The Society's Consultant Chemists had two-fold duties. Firstly, they carried out investigations into aspects of the chemistry of agriculture, either on their own initiative or under the direction of the Chemical Committee. Secondly, they performed analyses for members, and it was this analytical work of the Consultant Chemists that was of particular interest for the majority of members.

With the acceptance of artificial fertilizers in the 1840s, which the Society itself had done so much to encourage, came the problem of deliberate adulteration of fertilizers and feeding-stuffs. It soon became evident that there was widespread fraud in the guano trade in particular on top of the notorious variability of that commodity's constituency.[126] The Council of the Society responded to an increasing number of complaints arising from this and Pusey compiled a list of merchants known to be involved in fraudulent dealings. This was the background to the facility of chemical analysis brought in for members at competitive rates in 1849. For a time the Society's efforts led to a diminution of the problem by raising awareness of the extent of adulteration and by 1860 Voelcker was able to state in his annual report that few adulterated guanos had been brought to his notice and that inferior artificial manures did not find as ready a sale as they had done a few years earlier. By now, the re-crushing of oil cake, mixing it with a proportion of waste and then replacing it in the press was of more concern than the sale of inferior guano.

Adulteration again emerged as a problem towards the end of the 1860s as the Peruvian Government's increase in the price of guano encouraged farmers to buy samples at under the 'going-rate'. Many inferior samples of guano were sold as the better quality became worked out, and the commodity was also sometimes damaged by sea water in transit. Shortage of fodder, as in the dry summer of 1868, led to an increasing demand for feeding-cake and with it the temptation of manufacturers and merchants to offer an adulterated or inferior article. Manufactured superphosphate also varied widely and purchase by analysis was often the only way of obtaining value for money.

In 1870 the Chemical Committee drew attention to the very poor samples of bone manure which had been analysed by Voelcker and recommended that they be published in the Council's Minutes. As a result Morton, who had in turn published the report in the *Agricultural Gazette*, was threatened with legal proceedings. In response to this Council determined that they would stand by any report published under its authority and informed Morton accordingly.[127]

This led to a new phase in the work of Voelcker, the Chemical Committee, and indeed the Society generally. It was thought that the publication of names and addresses of merchants engaged in the supply of an inferior article would have a deterrent effect and as a result of this policy of publication it was not long before the Society became involved in litigation. The first case arose from a report of Voelcker's in August 1870 in which he condemned a sample of bonemeal as sub-standard. In the proceedings that followed it came out that the manufacturer named had not claimed that the mixture supplied by him was anything else than that which Voelcker had found it to be – an inferior mixture of bone and bone wastes. It transpired that it had been resold as pure by the manufacturer's agent and, for this reason, a nominal verdict with costs was given against the Society.[128] A second case arose out of the publication of the Chemical Committee's Quarterly Report in the *Mark Lane Express* in March 1872. It was alleged that inferior cake supplied by Ayre and Kidd of Hull to John Wells, a member of the Council, had occasioned the death of cattle. It had been sold as 'best' linseed cake, but Voelcker had found it to be very poor, a 'dirty' linseed cake containing cotton seeds and the sweepings of corn ware-houses. The firm denied this and as their trade was alleged to have fallen off as a result of the Society's publication, damages of £1,000 were claimed. During the case, it transpired that the article supplied was termed 'triangle-best linseed cake' and contained up to 50 per cent sesame seed and bran. It was admitted that some of the cake only had 30 per cent linseed and that this was not put in the advertising circulars; 'we can't put everything in a circular. A baker would not state the number of currants he puts into a cake'. The case went against the Society as it was accepted that the sample had been sold as 'triangle-best' – not 'pure' – and it was recognised that this product would contain a mixture of ingredients. The plaintiffs were awarded ten guineas damages with costs, a

Augustus Voelcker, the Society's Consulting Chemist 1857–84.

derisory fraction of their claim. Although the Society lost this action, a great moral victory was claimed and the second part of the *Journal* for 1872 was delayed in order that the proceedings of the case could be published in full.[129]

After this the Society endeavoured to educate the farmer to buy fertilizers by analysis, and to encourage him not to purchase fertilizers or feeding-stuffs at under the market rate. In this they were strongly supported by the agricultural press. Additionally, the Agricultural Cooperative Association, founded by E O Greening in 1874, worked in close conjunction with the Society in purchasing materials in bulk for the farmer and promoting their distribution and availability. However, buying fertilizers by analysis was by no means the answer for the smaller farmer who might well not consider the outlay on the analysis justified for, as was pointed out in the *Agricultural Economist*, an adequate analysis of his purchase might add up to 10 per cent to the total cost. For such people to buy by analysis was, it was said, akin to the doctor in Punch who 'advertised *gratis* for the poor and then told the washerwoman to give her child unlimited chickens and port wine and take her to Baden-Baden'.[130]

Lord Netherthorpe making a presentation to Eric Voelcker (right), the Society's Consulting Chemist 1938–76, at the time of his retirement.

Around this time, problems of adulteration also surrounded the supply of seeds to the farmer. The Adulteration of Seeds Act 1869, which had been promoted by the Chambers of Agriculture to afford some protection against fraudulent practice in the seed trade, led to the appointment by the Society of a Consultant Botanist in 1871. This was at the suggestion of J Dent Dent, then Chairman of the joint Journal and Chemical Committee. The duties of the post were the analysis of plants and seeds for members, with occasional *Journal* papers. The appointment was given to Charles Carruthers, Keeper of Botany at the British Museum, and in the 1870s he was much involved in investigating fraud and conducting seed trials for the Society. Dishonesty was, in fact, less prevalent in the seed trade than in the fertilizer industry, particularly after the Adulteration of Seeds Act, but malpractices included the killing of cheap seed such as German rape which was mixed with more expensive seed such as turnip or clover. This increased the margin of profit to the merchant while reducing the value of the seed to the farmer. An additional problem was the sale of inferior or old samples of indifferent germination. The botanical service to the members therefore provided for an opinion to be given as to the genuineness and age of the clover and turnip seed samples, examination for fodder infestation, determination of species, and reports on plant diseases. Thus much of the Consulting Botanist's routine work was to prepare reports for members on the purity and germinating power of seed samples and Carruthers soon had occasion to issue warnings on inferior clover and rye-grass seed.[131]

Botanical projects carried out by Carruthers for the Society during the 1870s included the investigation for the £100 prize put up by Earl Cathcart for an essay on 'The Potato Disease and its Prevention'. Ninety-two essays were submitted to the Society, but Carruthers and his co-adjudicators had to report that none of these related anything that was new and most of them to theories and remedies that were already well known. As the essays were unsatisfactory, the funds put up by Earl Cathcart were directed towards the investigation of that part of the life cycle of the potato fungus *Phytophthora Infestans* that was still unknown and to encourage trials of disease-proof potatoes.

Another question that occupied Carruthers's attention was the Colorado Beetle, and it was urged that the Society should investigate the likelihood of this pest being imported into the country. However, this particular project was declined on the grounds of expense. Information was distributed on the Colorado Beetle in all its stages – not just in the final, easily recognisable form – and details were also distributed to members on other injurious insects that could be brought into the country in packaging materials. Too often, any strange insect was reported as a Colorado Beetle and, for this reason, the Society supplied all members with illustrations of the pest in 1877. In 1876 the Society instituted experiments on the longevity of seeds and two years later put up prizes for new varieties of wheat, although nothing came of that particular project.[132]

The area of consultancy which presented the greatest challenge was that of the veterinary department. The veterinary question was one of the first considerations of the Society's Committee of Management and a Veterinary Committee was formed in July 1838. This called for the Governors of the Royal Veterinary College to institute lectures on veterinary education concerning animals other than the horse (which was at that time their chief concern) and the Society offered to defray some of the expenses. The importance of understanding animal diseases was underlined at this time by the appearance of foot-and-mouth disease in England during August 1839: by the end of that year, it had spread throughout England and into some parts of Scotland and continued to affect herds severely in 1840 and 1841. The response of the Society was to issue a circular on the 'epidemic among cattle' to subscribers. The circular, designed by William Sewell, who had succeeded Coleman as Professor at the Royal Veterinary College, described the symptoms of foot-and-mouth disease and advocated sulphur, epsom salts, and bleeding as remedies.[133]

The early efforts of the Society to direct the Royal Veterinary College's

James Beart Simonds, the Society's first consultant veterinarian.

attention to the whole range of farm animals were met with only limited success and Sewell's free lectures, instigated by the Society in 1839, were said to have been a 'miserable fiasco' occupying only a few minutes at the end of an ordinary lecture.[134] It was the outbreak of another severe cattle disease, contagious bovine pleuro-pneumonia during 1842, which forced the Governors of the Veterinary College to create a Chair of Cattle Pathology; this was given to James Beart Simonds, who also acted as Consultant Veterinary Surgeon to the Royal. Born in 1810 of a Suffolk agricultural family, Simonds had entered the Veterinary College at the age of 28. He attended William Youatt's lectures and

101

Youatt seems to have been instrumental in obtaining the post for him. This was the start of a long and not altogether successful association with the Society. Simonds followed William Spooner as Principal of the Veterinary College in 1871 and was forcibly retired 10 years later as a result of illness. However, he soon recovered and he continued his connection with the Society almost to the end of his life in 1904. According to Sir Frederick Smith, his discourses were 'as lifeless and uninspiring as his manner', but he was the dominant influence in veterinary matters within the Society during most of the Victorian era.[135] In the 1840s Simonds lectured frequently to the Council, and at the country meetings of the Society, and a number of his lectures were published in the *Journal*. The Society also made its own attempt to gather information on animal diseases and the Veterinary Committee drew up a list of queries for any members whose stock were affected by pestilence.

By far the most significant veterinary issue was the control of contagious animal diseases, which became of crucial importance with the arrival of rinderpest (or 'cattle plague') in the country in 1865 – one of the most important agricultural events of the nineteenth century. At the joint request of the RASE, the Highland and Agricultural Society of Scotland, and the Royal Agricultural Society of Ireland, in the 1850s Simonds investigated the spread of the disease across Europe. The background to this was persistent reports about a fatal cattle disease extending westwards from Russia and Simonds attributed its diffusion to Russian troop movements. His lengthy report concluded with the observation that 'no fear need be entertained that this destructive pest will reach our shores' so that 'all alarm . . . may cease with reference to its importation into the British Isles'.[136] Simonds reached this conclusion on the basis of the large distances involved and the fact that there was *then* no direct trade with the infected countries. His findings were well received by a number of interests, not least because any restriction on cattle importation – which the theory of the foreign origin of cattle diseases might imply – tended to be interpreted as a 'back-door' reimposition of agricultural protection.

There was an alternative view – that of John Gamgee. In 1857 he had opened his new Edinburgh Veterinary College, in opposition to the established Edinburgh College presided over by Professor Dick, which was as moribund as its London equivalent. Gamgee had an outstanding and original mind and at that time led a crusade against the then prevalent practice of trading in diseased meat. Gamgee's became the most eloquent view in opposition to Simonds's 'establishment' view, also promoted by the Royal, that the country was safe from cattle plague. In 1863 Gamgee convened a congress of leading veterinarians at Hamburg and returned home convinced of the imminent danger of cattle plague being imported because of the improvements in land and sea communications. He warned against this danger in prophetic letters to *The Times* in 1863, but failed to alert either the general public or farming opinion on the matter. The Society was on the sidelines: Gamgee's opinions were much at variance with those of its own veterinary authority and as the measures that Gamgee advocated required legislation and the prohibitions of the Society's Charter were then rigorously adhered to, discussion and consideration of the matter was precluded.[137]

The first outbreak of cattle plague occurred in the metropolis towards the end of June 1865. It is generally accepted that the disease was brought in among a cargo of cattle shipped from Revel to Hull and thence transported to London. A local veterinary surgeon called in Simonds during July who reported to the Privy Council six days later that cattle were dying. It seems probable that Simonds initially failed to recognise the cattle disease and there was some delay in its diagnosis. This, of course, confounded Simonds's earlier prediction that cattle plague would not reach the British Isles. His later explanation was that he had never thought the cattle trade would expand to such an extent as to enable the disease to be directly imported from the Baltic ports, and he had been confident in the measures taken in Germany and Belgium to halt the diffusion of the scourge across country. The disease spread quickly – by 24 July there were 82 centres of infection – and the Privy Council issued several orders under an Act of 1848 which had been originally designed to deal with sheep pox.[138]

The Society formed a Standing Committee to keep in touch with developments and a circular was issued to members on 30 August 1865 which urged cooperation with the various Government orders. The circular deplored the continued trade in diseased stock, advised against the purchase of store animals in markets and fairs, and suggested that newly obtained animals should be subjected to quarantine for up to 14 days. This circular also gave details of the symptoms of the other most important cattle diseases – pleuro-pneumonia and foot-and-mouth as well as cattle plague. The Society did not initiate a concerted response, however, until the December Council Meeting of 1865 when Charles Randell moved that a deputation be arranged to meet the Lord President of the Council. This meeting took place the following day when it urged the cessation of all fairs and markets, and severe restrictions on the live animal trade, slaughter of foreign animals on the point of disembarkation, no movement of animals on public roads from any farm that had suffered from the disease within two months, uniformity of regulations throughout the country, and Government-sponsored experiments on an extensive scale to ascertain the true nature of the disease. The Society was hardly at the head of affairs in these initiatives, however, as numerous local deputations had been got up to press the Government to deal with the matter urgently, and the Society was inhibited in its action because of the restrictive interpretations put upon the Society's Charter. A national conference was held on 8 February 1866, organised by Albert Pell, and it was this which impressed upon Sir Charles Grey the necessity of a slaughter policy. This was incorporated as part of the Cattle Diseases Prevention Act which received Royal Assent within a week, and led to a rapid diminution of the incidence of cattle plague during the remainder of 1866.[139]

In the 1870s the Society was rather less inhibited on the question of animal disease legislation and it thus played a more active and positive role in the development of policy, although at this time its voice was only one among numerous others. Cattle plague was again recorded in 1872 and 1877 and between 1869 and 1872 there was a serious increase in the number of foot-and-mouth disease cases reported. The Society voted funds towards the investigation of these periodic outbreaks and deputations met the Privy Council to urge it to use every power within its means to control the disease. The then Secretary of the Society, H M Jenkins, undertook an extensive survey into the animal trade during the summer and autumn of 1872 and, as a result, the Society's Cattle Plague Committee was able to put detailed resolutions about the appropriate course of action to the December Council of that year. In general the Government was extremely reluctant to take stringent measures against serious, but less extreme, diseases (such as foot-and-mouth) and there was no great uniformity of opinion about what should be done on this matter within the Society's Council. In 1874, when it was decided to send another deputation to the Privy Council on the issue, a policy in favour of slaughter in foot-and-mouth cases was passed by only the narrowest of margins – 15 votes to 14.[140] There were great difficulties in the way of the evolution of a sound and coherent policy on animal diseases: many agriculturists resented the restrictions and interference implied by the necessary regulations, while Government did not view with enthusiasm any restriction in the international trade in animals which could lead to the charge of back door protectionism. The Society's voice was only one among many, but the Privy Council certainly came to regard it as the most influential and important expression of agricultural opinion on what was a very complex matter.

SOME ISSUES AND CONTROVERSIES

The question of the proper role of the Society with regard to the formulation of public policy on animal diseases brought the terms of the Society's Charter into sharp focus, the interpretation of which was one of the most long-running controversies concerning the Society's action and affairs. As we have seen, the restriction on political matters had been instituted at the outset because of the acrimony which then surrounded the debate over the Corn Laws and the issue of protection. Exclusion of a wide range of political issues from the *Journal*, however, soon gave rise to extensive criticisms. Some of the debates of the 1840s such as tenant-right and the game-laws would have caused dissension within the Society if given free expression but in the case of others, such as agricultural statistics, there was a need for discussion to explore various viewpoints. There is no doubt that H S Thompson, who maintained a rigorous control over the *Journal* between 1855 and 1870, interpreted provisions of the Charter extremely conservatively. He made his position clear in his Presidential Address to the Society in 1867:

> As Chairman of the Journal Committee I have been frequently urged to take steps to procure articles on such questions as leases, tenant right, preservation of game etc... not the object for which the Society was founded ...[141]

He maintained that the Society was established for the promotion of the two great branches of agriculture, crops and stock husbandry. Other subjects, however important, were 'forbidden topics' as far as the constitution of the Society was concerned.

This view was openly attacked in the agricultural press and it was complained that Thompson's attitude was obstructive and that it was absurd to maintain that tenure of land was a forbidden topic in a community of agriculturists. The issue of agricultural statistics received a good deal of attention in the early 1850s and Hoskyns, who was an enthusiast for the cause, wrote an eloquent article on the topic which was published in the *Journal* in 1856.[142] This concluded by looking forward to the further development of the subject and was well received, being approvingly referred to as 'the right article in the right place at the right time'.[143] Nevertheless, it met with disapproval in the Council and no further articles on the topic appeared. Yet, as outsiders were not slow to point out, all fundamental questions of improvement were to a degree 'political' and it was maintained that the Highland Society had taken up the question of agricultural statistics with perfect propriety. The restrictive provisions, it was held, were to save time being wasted in fruitless *party* political discussion, not to debar subjects of legitimate agricultural interest.[144] H S Thompson's view prevailed and, as agricultural interest outside of the Society shifted in the late 1850s and 1860s towards the whole range of generally 'political' issues, the standing of the *Journal* and the Society as a whole suffered.

It was the interpretation of the Charter with regard to the Society's position on cattle disease policy that caused the greatest crisis of confidence between the Society and the agricultural community at large during the early part of its existence. In 1863 Edward Holland, a Council member and a close associate of J C Morton, unsuccessfully tried to introduce legislation on animal diseases on his own initiative, being one of the few to take heed of Gamgee's warnings about the likelihood of rinderpest arriving in the British Isles. The following year he argued that it was a proper and urgent matter for the Society to take up the question of how best to prevent possible introduction of the plague into the country. This was resisted, essentially, as we have seen, because the Society's Charter prohibited the consideration of political matters or subjects which might lead to legislative enactment. Many members of the Council took a very narrow view of the terms of the Charter and thus it was for this reason that the Society was slow to take the lead when the cattle plague arrived. Holland

Edward Holland, President 1873–4 and a leading campaigner on cattle disease prevention and agricultural education.

therefore called for changes in the Charter to assist him in 'warding off a national evil' and to prevent the Society from 'being disbarred ... from steadily advancing the interest of agriculture', which he thought would otherwise be the case. It took a local association, the Wakefield Farmers' Club, to organise agricultural opinion on the matter and the Society's initial inactivity on the issue of cattle disease was bitterly resented by the agricultural community. It was thought absurd that the Society would not interfere with anything that was to be brought before Parliament because the Society had been formed in 'the old protectionist times'.

The height of criticism of the Society's attitude came towards the end of 1866, a year when 'the leading agricultural events' included cattle plague and the attendant restrictions on cattle importation and on cattle traffic, the high price of meat, and miserable harvest weather, but the December report of the Society gave more prominence to its relatively insignificant efforts on agricultural education than on these other more pressing topics. Morton, usually temperate in his comments, was exceptionally scathing about the fact that more was said about '£5 prizes won by a lot of schoolboys' than was written about the cattle plague and that the report was more than half taken up with 'important' announcements such as 'F Chubb, E King and W Mortimer, had won four pounds in a recent examination in pure mathematics'.[145]

The frustration felt by many agriculturists over the way in which the Society's Charter inhibited the formulation of a cattle plague policy is well expressed in Corbet's lecture to the London Farmer's Club on 'The Cattle Plague and the Government Measures' in which he referred to discussions at the Royal in the following terms:

> The idea of a number of influential agriculturists gathered together to talk over the cattle plague without, however, venturing to touch upon the means employed to subdue it, is so sorry a joke that I do not believe after-ages will ever credit its occurrence.[146]

The failure of the Society to give a decisive lead in the matter of cattle disease legislation led to the formation of a new organisation, the Central Chamber of Agriculture, which was proposed by Charles Clay, a Wakefield implement manufacturer, in a letter to *Bell's Weekly Messenger* in December 1865. Clay maintained that, since the Royal was precluded by its Charter from dealing with political subjects, a new 'Farmers' League or Association' would not intrude upon its function of encouraging the improvement of stock and machinery. Thus the special objects of the new institution would be to represent the agricultural interest with regard to Government measures and to press for the appointment of a Minister or Board of Agriculture, this latter aim not being realised until 1889.[147]

The Council considered whether the Charter might be changed to allow it to embrace the 'forbidden topics' which it had hitherto eschewed but rejected such a development. By the mid-1870s it was thought that political matters were best left to alternative bodies such as the Chambers and that, on the whole, the clause restricting political discussion had worked well. Commentators on the Society's affairs felt that it failed to give a lead on a number of important issues such as the operation and powers of land improvement companies, river basin drainage and irrigation, and the security of agricultural capital, and there were repeated calls for the Society to become involved in the Game Laws and agricultural labourers' questions during the 1870s.[148]

A rather different sort of controversy concerned the operation of the 'prize system', particularly with regard to the award of premiums for implements at the annual shows: by the 1870s, a 'periodical attack' on the prize system was considered a 'certainty'.[149] It is important to consider the arguments surrounding these prizes as they were the main means by which the Society hoped to promote agricultural progress during its early years.

When a demand arose at the early Royal Shows for implement trials it was soon found that these were difficult to stage and conflict arose between the Society and the manufacturers who frequently considered the trial arrangements inadequate. Some of the ploughing carried out at the early shows was seen by observers to be very inferior and this led to suspicion about the merits of improved implements. For example, a letter from 'a plain Derbyshire farmer' complained in the *Mark Lane Express* that, at Derby in 1843, he had seen furrows ploughed at irregular width and depth and that had such ploughing been seen in his own fields he would have been ashamed for himself, his implements and his workmen. At the Derby Show observations as

'well, we are satisfied in our own ploughs now eh, mates?' was a constant question. 'Why, I think we shall go home contented' was the nearly uniform answer, whilst at every turn some lusty sexagenarian was seen instructing his chubby faced nephews in the danger of novelty.[150]

J Allen Ransome addressed some forcible remarks to the Society on the conduct and purpose of the trials and it is from this time that the almost universal opposition of the major implement firms can be identified. Criticism was aimed at the inadequate trial grounds and the lack of time available for a proper trial together with the fact that conditions at a summer show differed from those which might be experienced on the farm in other seasons, and which would test equipment more severely.[151] After 1855 implements were divided into groups to be tested periodically to give a greater amount of time for particular trials, but criticisms by the agricultural implement manufacturers continued. They said that there should be reports issued on implements rather than the award of money prizes: these conferred too abrupt a distinction upon one implement as opposed to another, when the real differences may have been very small, and may not even have been properly identified by the judges. This did not find much favour in the agricultural community, and, as was pointed out, it was a matter of little substance whether the value of any particular machine was expressed in a favourable report or a £20 note: 'Catalogues would read as well with "took first class report at Warwick" in flaming capitals as "took the first prize of ten pounds at Salisbury"'.[152]

What was perceived as the failure of the Society to take account of the manufacturers' criticisms led to a boycott of the shows at Canterbury in 1860 and Leeds in 1861. The firm of Ransome and Sim gave detailed reasons for the boycott and claimed that, although they had been immensely successful in winning prizes and commendations up to that time, their exertion and outlay were not adequately repaid, and that the public did not put any particular value on prizes as evidence of the character of the manufacturer and the excellence of the productions.[153] Leading critics of the Society claimed that the award of prizes was little more than a 'pleasant occupation for amateurs' which was justified for academic excellence, sport, skill or horse-racing, but was inappropriate for matters of business or invention. Morton was able to cite examples of implements which had won the highest accolades at the Society's shows but had never come into general use, and quoted the experience of one firm who had taken account of the suggestions at the Society's trials and seen his sales fall as a result. When the firm reverted to the old, 'unimproved' pattern, the manufacturer gained sales having been told by his workmen that he had been '"bamboozled" by twenty years' false leading' by the Royal Agricultural Society.[154] While it is probably true that by the 1860s there was little to choose between the established implements of the leading firms and it was impossible at trials 'to fish out the microscopic differences which may exist' in a short trial, it was also the case that the leading implement manufacturers wished to maintain their established positions and deny entry into the field by newcomers who might attain prominence by carrying off the Society's prize. The degree to which the need to compete may have increased the price of products to the farmer is difficult to quantify, but Morton suggested that this contention was not without foundation.[155] By the 1870s the Society began to yield to the manufacturers' criticisms but this was as much on the grounds of the cost of the trials at the annual shows as a belief in the validity of the agricultural engineers' points. The range of equipment that was tested each year was restricted after the mid-1850s and the Society gradually moved to a position whereby the trials were confined to new inventions or to machinery in which rapid developments of particular interest were taking place, rather than the broad range of established equipment. Thus in 1876 the trials were restricted to reaping-machines and sheaf-binders, and the trial grounds were at Leamington rather than the Birmingham showground.

The debate over the restrictions of the Charter and on the conduct of the prize system also reflected the relationship between the Society and the broader agricultural community. In the 1840s there was a great spirit of cooperation in agricultural progress between the wide range of the agricultural interest, but a gulf between the Council and the agricultural community began to become evident in the 1850s. William Shaw fled the country to escape bankruptcy in 1852 and died penniless in Australia while Pusey relinquished the editorship of

Samuel Sidney, first Secretary to the Islington Agricultural Hall Company and the Society's fiercest critic in the 1860s.

the *Journal* in 1854 and died the following year. It was about this time that a feeling began to be expressed that the management of the Society was becoming somewhat distant from the general body of members. Morton remarked in the *Agricultural Gazette* that although the report for 1853 had been received at the General Meeting without criticism, this did not represent the feeling of the membership generally and he criticised the Society for its passiveness and inaction. The General Meeting in 1855 was said to be 'barely more than a meeting *proforma*, held and conducted simply because it was "down in the Charter" that it was to be so held and conducted'.[156]

Underlying this criticism was a feeling that the Society was failing to move with the times, and it was reinforced in 1857 by doubts forcefully expressed over the direction that the Society was taking. These were first articulated by Samuel Sidney, then hunting correspondent of the *Illustrated London News*, at the conclusion of the Salisbury meeting of that year, and was repeated by him at the General Meeting in December. Sidney's criticisms were wide ranging and they included: the small number of members, which then stood at about 5,000; the fact that the Society did little more than hold an annual show; that there was too much encouragement by way of prizes for implements which were standard

110

in design and efficiency; that the Wednesday afternoon meetings were given insufficient publicity and were little more than a farce; that the Society had 'too many gentlemen and too few working men', and that there was too much delay in the publication of important reports and papers given to the Society.[157]

Over the next few years a number of circumstances combined to give momentum to Sidney's campaign, the most important of which was the general dissatisfaction with the editorial arrangements for the *Journal*, which had been run since Pusey's retirement by a triumvirate consisting of Chandos Wren Hoskyns, Thomas Dyke Acland and H S Thompson. Hoskyns was the most gifted writer of the three and was a close associate of J C Morton, contributing much material to the *Agricultural Gazette*. Acland came from one of the largest landowning families in Devon and lost his parlimentary seat after voting for Repeal. He then studied chemistry at King's College, London in order to demonstrate to West of England farmers that scientific farming could prove a better way forward than continued hankering after protection (he had earlier read classics at Oxford and became a Fellow of All Souls). Thompson, who had been one of the chief supporters of the Yorkshire Agricultural Society in 1837, was also interested in scientific agriculture – as we have seen he was one of the first to demonstrate the power of soils to assimilate soluble salts – but after 1849 his attention was increasingly directed towards railway management, becoming Chairman of the North Midland Railway Company in 1854. He entered Parliament as Liberal member for Whitby in 1859.[158]

Whatever their individual merits, the three seem to have been ill-fitted to work together. Hoskyns was talented but sometimes rather whimsical in approach, Acland could be 'dilatory and indecisive' while Earl Cathcart's mostly eulogistic memoir of Thompson nevertheless mentions that contemporaries found him 'distant, aloof and unapproachable'. It was not long before this editorial arrangement was criticised and at the 1857 General Meeting Sidney observed that he had 'never yet known the office of editor conducted as it ought to be, when put into commission like the Chancellor's seal'.[159]

Early in 1858 consideration began to be given to the appointment of a paid editor, one suggestion being that the *Journal* should be jointly edited by Morton and Hoskyns. There was a great deal of resistance in the Society's Council to the concept of a salaried editor as Pusey had not received any remuneration for his efforts, but in May 1858 £300 was granted to the triumvirate for editorial assistance. Later in the year Acland and Hoskyns withdrew from the arrangement - possibly because of a disagreement over editorial policy – leaving Thompson as sole editor but it is clear that he received a great deal of help from Morton at this time. When Thompson entered Parliament the following year the Council accepted a recommendation that a 'literary and scientific editor' be appointed at a salary of £500 a year.[160]

It was confidently expected that Morton, the *de facto* Editor, would be confirmed in the post so that when the almost unknown P H Frere, Bursar of

Chandos Wren Hoskyns, prominent agricultural writer and member of the Journal Committee.

Downing College, Cambridge, was unanimously recommended for appointment out of 25 applicants the announcement was greeted with some considerable outrage. There was immense dissatisfaction in the agricultural community for 'when the committee made its selection it had before it in the list of candidates the name of John Morton ... a feeling of the greatest astonishment was created among the agriculturists of England when such a man was passed by'; there was something 'strange and inexplicable' about the affair and the non-selection of Morton was an 'unwarrantable blow to the cause of scientific agriculture'.[161]

With characteristic vigour Sidney denounced Frere's appointment at the half-yearly meeting in May 1860:

> the gentleman was a highly-educated man and a perfect gentleman he readily admitted; but considering that there are amongst the other candidates several men who had devoted themselves for years to the subject of agriculture and agricultural information, who had learnt by experience both how to write and how to edit an agricultural journal which were two utterly different things—as different indeed as painting and statuary—and who had the confidence ... of the agricultural community, who were on intimate terms with all the best farmers in England, it was with surprise that people saw the Council electing a gentleman totally unknown to the agricultural world – a gentleman of middle age, without experience, without literary reputation, although doubtless connected with influential families—who commenced his editorial apprenticeship for the first time when he entered his duties as editor of the *Journal*.[162]

112

Sidney himself was among the applicants but it seems likely that the Council was not prepared to appoint a professional journalist to the position and that Sidney's observations that he and Morton had been disqualified on the grounds that they 'had both been professional writers connected with newspapers, not amateurs and had not graduated from an English University' had some foundation. A further problem came for the Society in 1859 when James Hudson, who had been Secretary since 1840, was dismissed for the embezzlement of the Society's funds. This led to the resignation of the Finance Committee, and gave added force to general criticisms of the Society's administration. Increased attention was given to Sidney's points of criticism and he was soon no longer seen as the 'accuser-general'; it was impossible to resist 'the rush of general opinion so forceably expressed' about the Society in 1861.[163]

The criticisms related to the full range of the Society's affairs. Detailed examination was given to the composition of the Council and there was support for Sidney's view that over the first 20 years of the Society's existence there had been a change which had impeded progress. Initially, the Council had consisted of nearly one-half 'practical farmers' or 'men of the middle class'. Sidney looked back to the 1840s when those who ran the Society's affairs were 'united by the strongest ties of sympathy to the agricultural and farming class', and included figures such as Spencer, Ellman, Handley, Pusey, and Youatt. By contrast, the Council of the Society had now become

> an agreeable club, the members of which could meet together for a *conversazione* and amuse themselves as a body of amateurs: it had ceased to represent the agricultural community at large. [Cheers]. It reminded him [Sidney] of All Souls College where the qualification was 'to be well-born, well-dressed, and with a little knowledge of music'.[164]

Sidney calculated at this time that there were only 13 members of the Society directly involved with practical agriculture or engaged in cultivation for profit. His case was overstated for it was by no means easy to agree on the definition of a 'practical farmer', but his contention that the administration of the Society was unrepresentative with

> 'twenty one peers, twenty nine sons of peers, baronets, or country members, twelve squires, five lawyers – not yet arrived at the dignity of squires, though they might possibly do so – four engineers and implement makers, one honorary director, twelve breeders and stockholders, and two mayors'[165]

fell on sympathetic ears, especially when popular members of the London Farmer's Club were refused Council seats.

The Wednesday afternoon open meetings were seen to have sunk to a very low level and failed to provide useful purpose:

nine out of ten of these Wednesday meetings closely resemble the Protestant Church in Ireland where Dean Swift began the service with 'Dearly Beloved Roger' and of which Sidney Smith told the story beginning with 'Please your Reverence, she's sick' – members of the Council ... depart in haste and trepidation: for there is a rumour that Mr Edwin Chadwick was waiting ... that he might report for the hundredth time ... the value of sewage. The Journal Committee ... were the first to vanish, Sir Watkin W Wynn mounted his weight-carrier with the grim satisfaction of a man who has 'escaped'.[166]

Calls for much more to be made of these open forums, and for discussions to be modelled after those regularly held by the London Farmer's Club, were generally resisted on the grounds that it would not be desirable for the Royal to become 'a mere debating society'. Apart from continuing complaints about the unrepresentative nature of the Council, the malaise which gripped the Society during the period was mainly a failure to take a lead in agricultural affairs. Dissatisfaction was due to 'shortcomings rather than offences' and a reluctance to take 'bold and popular measures calculated to inspire public enthusiasm and attract an ever-growing body of supporters'.[167]

A further controversy began in 1868 when P H Frere died; this initiated a debate on the future management of the *Journal* and, following long discussion, it was suggested that the office of Secretary and Editor be combined after January 1869. Henry Hall Dare, who had succeeded Hudson as Secretary, applied for the new combined post, but was rejected by the Editorship Committee. A number of alternative options were considered and it was finally decided to dismiss Dare, give him £600 by way of compensation, and advertise the combined post at an annual salary of £400.[168] This was an extremely insensitive way in which to treat Dare, who had supervised the administration of the Society's affairs in an entirely satisfactory manner after the Hudson debacle.

At the time considerable interest was expressed in the appointment and, according to Bailey Denton, the outstanding candidates were Morton, J A Clarke – who became editor of the *Chamber of Agriculture Journal* the following year – and Howard Reed. The last of these had contributed influential papers on the cattle plague and steam ploughing to the Society's *Journal*, later leaving England to edit the *Transactions of New South Wales Agricultural Society* – a publication which was praised by Morton as being a model for what a successful journal of an agricultural society should be, popular in style with an emphasis on practical topics.[169] Forty-six applications were received, though many potential applicants, including Morton and Clarke, were dissuaded from applying by the terms of the appointment. The Selection Committee, which comprised Lord Chesham, J Dent Dent, Chandos Wren Hoskyns, William Torr, and Charles Randell, under the Chairmanship of H S Thompson, unanimously recommended the appointment of H M Jenkins and this was accepted without question by the Council.

The outrage generated by this decision exceeded that caused by Frere's selection when Morton had been omitted from consideration. Aged 29, Jenkins had left school at 14 and, after short periods of work at a seed and corn merchant in Bristol and at a manufacturing chemist, had entered into a minor position as a clerk at the Geological Society of London. There his aptitude and efficiency quickly brought him to the attention of the senior officers of the Society such as Murchison and Huxley, and he eventually succeeded Rupert Jones as Secretary and Editor having acquired sufficient geological knowledge by private study as to be able to contribute scholarly articles to geological periodicals.[170] According to Morton, the members of the Selection Committee had unanimously agreed that the testimonials provided by Murchison and others suggested that Jenkins was the outstanding candidate. It was also considered that his geological knowledge would prove a useful asset in his work for the RASE. This did not impress the agricultural community; Morton led the attack on the appointment and he was less restrained than he had been on the occasion of Frere's appointment as he was not now directly involved. He considered the whole affair as a 'heroic disregard of commonsense'; the best man might have been chosen, but he maintained that this was only a reflection of the misguided nature of the combined post for, however good his career at the Geological Society may have been, Jenkins knew nothing of agriculture. The appointment was so 'ludicrously absurd' as it was a farce to elect an 'entire outsider' as a 'teacher and leader' within a special department of instruction. It was 'altogether indefensible'; a 'wrong thing' had been done and Thompson was criticised for not wanting an editor but a sub-editor – 'the real editorship would be conducted as it had been all along by the Chairman of the Journal Committee'.[171] Thompson put up a vigorous defence of the appointment and Henry Corbet, among others, came to the conclusion that 'a good man had been got in a bad way'.[172] In the event, Thompson's views and judgements were vindicated and within a year there were abundant tributes to the energy and efficiency with which Jenkins carried out his office. In the 1870s he wrote extensively in the *Journal* and lectured widely to agricultural societies and clubs.

It was fortunate that Jenkins exceeded the expectations of the critics of his appointment. The *Journal* in the 1870s, under his editorship, rose markedly in public esteem; by the end of 1870 it was said that not one of the *Journals* of late years had so good a chance of being read as the one just issued by its 'accomplished editor'. By 1873 it was maintained that the *Journal* was now an 'agricultural treasure' and ought to be in the hands of every farmer.[173]

A more active stance by the Society on the question of cattle diseases and their prevention in the 1870s, combined with their action over adulterated fertilizers, did much to enhance the Society's popularity so that it reached a position under H M Jenkins which it had not achieved since the death of Pusey.

H M Jenkins, the Society's very successful Secretary 1869–87.

The Later Nineteenth Century

Writing on the 'Agricultural Lessons of the 80s' Professor J Wrightson recalled that the year 1880 was launched into existence at a period of 'intense agricultural and commercial gloom' and that he would

> not readily forget the feeling of thankfulness with which I regarded twelve o'clock at night on December 31 1879. At any rate, a doleful ruinous year had departed.[174]

The very wet weather of that year, which had in part caused the relative failure of the Society's Kilburn Show, brought home to English agriculturists the depths of the depression in which they now found themselves. The crucial factor was that higher agricultural prices no longer compensated for poor seasons as the historic link between them was swept away on a flood of imports made possible by the opening up of new areas for agricultural production, particularly in the Americas, and scale economies in ocean transport. Thus during the last quarter of the nineteenth century the prices of a range of products were reduced to what were for many agriculturists ruinously low levels. Wheat and wool prices, for example, fell by about half between the early 1870s and the mid-1890s. Other grains also declined in price, but rather less sharply, and cattle and sheep prices fell by between one-quarter and one-third.[175]

Not all areas of the country were equally affected by the depression – the arable south and east was harder hit than the pastoral west and north – and prices stabilised around the lower levels at the end of the century. Dairy prices remained relatively buoyant and there were opportunities for profitable specialisation in such enterprises as fruit and vegetable production or duck and poultry rearing. The Society's *Journal* gave full attention to these and more speculative forms of farm diversification such as tobacco growing.[176]

Although the reality of the agricultural depression was inescapable, the agriculturist's problems were often compounded by a failure to perceive the implications of the changes in world trade that were taking place and the shifts in consumer demand at home. There was sometimes a tendency to take only a short-term view and also to attribute the problems of agriculture to peripheral causes such as the lack of cheap child labour following the 1872 Education Act. Thus some farmers kept to traditional forms of enterprise and failed as a result, whereas the Scottish migrants who bought up land in Essex – one of the hardest-hit counties – claimed to farm profitably even at the prices obtaining during the early 1890s.[177]

The economic topography of agriculture during the later nineteenth century and the farming response has been well-charted; what is perhaps worth stressing – as it had considerable implications for the RASE's affairs - was the growing 'schism' between town and country as agriculture and the problems of agriculturists were pushed into the background as far as public attention was concerned.[178] This was a reflection of the increased preponderance of urban over rural interests; indeed, from the early 1860s there was a tendency for rural affairs to be portrayed in the national press as dull, backward, and something to be ridiculed. The following extract from the *Farmer's Magazine* in 1861 may serve to illustrate the point. It is a complaint about the way in which London daily newspapers reported agricultural shows:

We were much amused, a few years since, with a batch of men from the 'gallery', who, in the dull time, went down specially to the Royal Bucks Agricultural Association at Aylesbury. They began with a good lunch, then they smoked their cigars, and wandered over the town to look at the gaol and the church, or at anything but the cattle show, which they carefully avoided. However, they were ready again in two or three hours for the dinner and Mr Disraeli, with a full report of whose speech they started back again, having a supreme indifference for anybody else or anything else connected with the especial object of the occasion. Then with a proof at his side, the critic of the Sanctum goes to work. If the orator was cheered in the country, he is abused in the town. If he is a popular country gentleman, the most pitiless ridicule and abuse is pretty sure to be his portion; and if the farmer is ever mentioned at all, it is only to be laughed at. Even *Punch* still imbues him with the vernacular of the comic countryman when he 'took up to poarching in the sayzon o' the 'ear'.[179]

Again, consider the patronising air of this introduction to 'Country Newspapers' in 1864:

> The English Farmer is a splendid specimen of the human race. He can generally ride well to hounds and has of late years picked up some queer ideas at Cirencester and other centres of science ... But the sort of writing which is intelligible to ordinary men is to *him* a mystery. He would make nothing of a *Times* leader. He would find the *Saturday Review* as inexplicable as if it were in Sanscrit. His mind has run in other grooves; and he would have much the better of you or me, intelligent reader, if it were a question of judging a Shorthorn or a crop of wheat. Small blame to our agricultural friend if he ignores what you and I think excessively interesting. One cannot do everything.[180]

Thus, when in 1879 W E Bear (who had succeeded Henry Corbet as editor of the *Mark Lane Express* two years earlier) complained of the lack of interest shown in agricultural affairs by the general public, this was a reflection of an already well-established tendency. Bear claimed that the national press devoted more attention to the Boat Race than it did to 'the finest agriculture in the world' during the whole year, and gave several columns to a 'petty suburban [horse] race – a mere bookmakers' meeting' while the problems of agriculturists were virtually ignored.[181]

Despite the declining fortunes of English agriculture in general, much of the last two decades of the nineteenth century were relatively prosperous times for the RASE. Membership, which had begun to increase during the 1870s, continued to climb until the very last years of the century and it is interesting to note that the general membership level was, during these years of agricultural depression, approximately twice that of the prosperous period of 'high-farming' in the 1850s and 1860s. It may be that the work of the Society was relatively more valued in these times of farming stress than in times of prosperity, especially as that work was seen to be relevant to the practical difficulties faced by agriculturists. In addition, the publicity which the Society gained from its fiftieth Anniversary Show held at Windsor in 1889 also gave membership a boost.

In the later nineteenth century the Society continued its established pattern of proceedings and also undertook some important new initiatives, particularly in the field of agricultural education and research. The *Journal*, under the editorship of H M Jenkins, was especially topical during the early 1880s when it reflected the agricultural preoccupations of the day. The onset of agricultural depression hastened the already established trend of converting arable land to permanent pasture and there was an intense controversy as to the best types of grass to employ. This was initiated by C De Laune Faunce in the Society's *Journal* for 1882 in an article which attacked the advice given by leading seed-firms.[182] The Society carried out a number of experiments and trials at Woburn (where the Duke of Bedford had donated land for agricultural experiment in 1875) and elsewhere under the direction of William Carruthers (who continued as the Society's Consulting Botanist until 1909) and in conjunction with J A Voelcker who succeeded his father as Consulting Chemist in 1885. This work investigated the best types of pasture grasses, which were found to be those which were 'nutritious, palatable, and perennial', such as cocksfoot, meadow fescue, and foxtail, while experiments at Woburn demonstrated the superiority of timothy over rye-grass for short leys, although in the arable south and east of the country permanent pastures were by no means easy to establish.[183] The fertilisation of pasture land and root crops was aided by the employment of basic slag (or basic cinder as it was referred to at the time), a by-product of the Gilchrist-Thomas

Fig. 4 Membership of Royal Agricultural Society of England 1880-1902

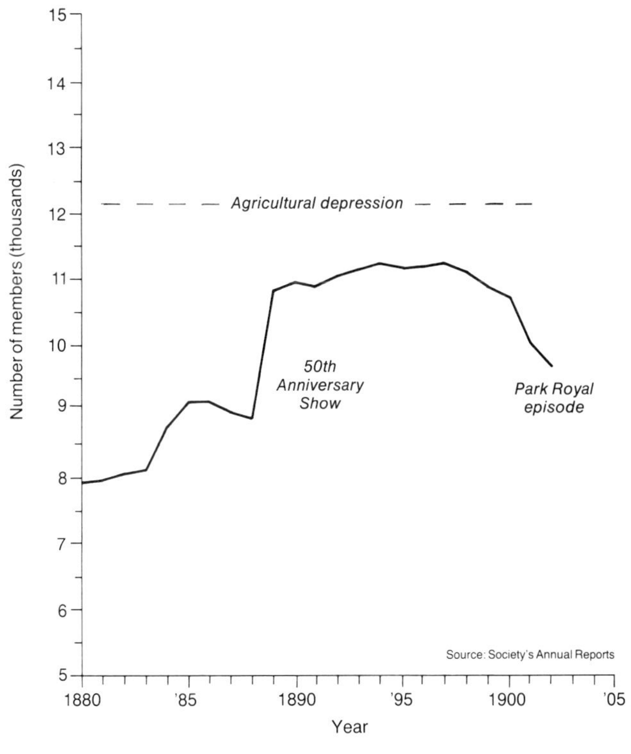

119

William Carruthers, the Society's
Consulting Botanist 1869–1909.

J A Voelcker, Consulting Chemist 1885–1936.

process which used phosphatic iron-ore for steel making. The fertilising properties of the material were the subject of a number of investigations during the 1880s, the results of which were presented in the Society's *Journal* for 1890.[184]

J Wrightson identified ensilage and dairying as two agricultural developments that were particularly associated with the 1880s and both received extensive coverage in the *Journal*. The agricultural press began to give attention to ensilage in 1881 and 1882 and this prompted the Journal Committee, early in 1883, to persuade Jenkins to undertake a full scale survey of the system as practised at home and on the continent. His findings were published in the *Journal* the following year together with Augustus Voelcker's discussion of the chemistry of ensilage, his last major paper.[185]

An International Dairy had been a feature of the Kilburn Show of 1879 – where the Laval cream-separator was first shown – and the realisation that standard British dairy practice had fallen well behind Denmark led to the publication in the *Journal* of Jenkins's report on Danish dairying which he had first prepared for the Royal Commission on Agriculture. By 1890 Wrightson could claim that the best systems of making British butter and cheese were equal to those used abroad, but that superior dairy practice was far from general.[186]

The Society's *direct* engagement in agricultural research dates from 1875, when the Agricultural Holdings Act made statutory provision for compensation to outgoing tenants for unexhausted improvements. This was the first fruit of the campaign for a better system of tenant right started by Shaw, Pusey and others some three decades earlier. Charles Randell suggested experiments to check the accuracy of figures compiled by Lawes on the residual manurial value of different types of animal food. In discussions of his proposals it was said that a 'second Rothamsted' would be beneficial and hope was expressed that 'one day' it would be established. Randell envisaged a number of experiments to be carried out by 'practical farmers' and it is interesting that he thought it a great affront when it was stressed that unless experiments were carried out with as much care as they were at Rothamsted, they would be valueless.[187] After a report on Randell's suggestion was produced by the Chemical Committee, 90 acres of land at Woburn, together with buildings, were offered to the Society by the Duke of Bedford. It was proposed that Lawes and Voelcker should draw up a suitable research programme to be carried out under their supervision and control. This did not please Randell who maintained that 'practical farmers' knew more about animals and feeding than did Lawes and Voelcker. In November 1876 the Chemical Committee made their own suggestions for the study of the manurial value of different feeding stuffs and when these were not accepted the Committee resigned, although the point of dispute was soon resolved.[188]

The first project provided for a study of a series of fertilizer regimes on a three-acre plot. This again did not please Randell, who considered that the proposed experiments were not sufficiently in tune with his original objective. Further controversy was generated when a committee, formed to look into the allegedly foul condition of the land at Woburn, recommended that the farm manager be dismissed. Lawes considered this to be very harsh as the farm had been received in a weedy state and most effort had been expended on getting the experimental plots into reasonable condition. Lawes's reservations went further than this, however, as he claimed that the first experiments had not been properly conducted. He attributed this to the fact that they had been carried out by practical farmers under the direction of scientists residing at a distance and he again stressed the importance of care and training in the conduct of agricultural research if worthwhile scientific results were to be accumulated.[189]

As a result of these disputes Lawes resigned from his connection with the project and thus the start of the Society's association with the experimental farm was not very auspicious. Over the next few decades, however, a range of experimental work was carried out, including investigations into lime loss on light soils, and green manuring, while an annual outing to Woburn for members became an established part of the Society's proceedings. In 1895 E H Hills of Bourne Place, Tonbridge, bequeathed £10,000 to the Society to investigate the 'rarer forms of ash' (trace elements). As a result J A Voelcker went to Germany to learn something of the experimental methods being carried out there and a Pot-Culture Station was opened at Woburn early in 1898, together with a laboratory for analytical work. The experiments on residual manurial values continued and allowed Voelcker to produce a revision of the tables originally drawn up by Lawes and Gilbert for tenant-right valuation.[190]

The Society's involvement in formal agricultural education originated in 1863 when J C Morton posed a direct question at the end-of-year General Meeting as to why nothing had been done up to that time towards the seventh of the Society's stated objects *viz*; 'To take such measures as may be deemed advisable to improve the education of those who may intend to make the cultivation of the soil their means of livelihood'. The question was not altogether unexpected as Morton had complained in the *Agricultural Gazette* about the lack of attention that the Society had given to the matter.[191] The position of the RASE was that the objective was fulfilled by means of the annual shows and publication of the *Journal*, but Morton was looking for the 'professional' education of the sons of farmers in a formal and systematic manner.

The topic had often received attention in the agricultural press and in the early 1840s William Shaw had attached great importance to raising the intellectual level of the general body of agriculturists. His encouragement of lecture and discussion meetings, and of agricultural libraries maintained by local farmers' clubs, was seen as a means of 'self-help' in the absence of formal educational provision. It was this perceived need which led to the establishment of the Cirencester Agricultural College in 1844 and many of the promotors of the venture were prominent in the RASE – Philip Pusey took the Chair at the Southampton Meeting which planned the college. The early years of Cirencester were not very successful – the students were housed in the town where they were subject to certain 'temptations' and the project was under-financed. Further, it was found that the pupils were often so badly grounded in general education that they were ill-prepared to receive the specialised courses given at the College. When, as a result of these problems, the age of entry was increased to 16 and the fees were raised, the College was under-subscribed and limited to the sons of the wealthy who, according to H S Thompson, idled away time or waited until they got commissions in the army.[192] In 1863 most of the distinguished academic staff at Cirencester, including Augustus Voelcker, resigned over an internal policy difference with the Principal and there was further dissension in 1879. This led to the foundation by Wrightson of the Wiltshire and Hampshire Agricultural College at Downton, which was also a new independent centre of agricultural research.

Although Cirencester in its early years seems to have made little overall contribution to agricultural education, the experience gained was used when Morton re-opened the question of agricultural education 20 years after its establishment. His initiative was taken up within the Society by Edward

Holland and T D Acland and a committee was formed to examine how the RASE could best pursue its seventh objective. Holland introduced the subject at a 'Wednesday afternoon' discussion where he covered points previously made by Morton in a lecture at Cirencester. He stressed that to be successful a farmer needed (i) practical skill (ii) business tact and (iii) liberal and scientific education. Holland thought that the difficulty was in persuading farmers to send their sons for additional 'scientific education' after their normal schooling. The role of the Society was, he thought, to offer advice and encouragement for scientific study or practical farm experience.[193]

In the discussion that followed, Augustus Voelcker expressed doubts as to whether the sons of small tenant-farmers could be usefully instructed on a college farm, while Wren Hoskyns stressed the difficulties of educating the poorer sections of the very heterogeneous 'farming class'. The suggestion was made that the Society should offer prizes of scholarships for pupils in agricultural subjects, and Morton called for a system of prize examinations to be conducted by the Society. The Education Committee considered what institutions were available to co-operate with the Society for the education and examination of agriculturists, and negotiations were entered into with the Local Examination Syndicates of Oxford and Cambridge Universities, the University of London, and the College of Preceptors (founded in 1846). In 1865 it was agreed that the Society would provide £300 annually for prizes in special subjects in the Oxford or Cambridge senior or junior examinations, the candidates to be recommended by a member of the Royal Agricultural Society or be in some way dependent on the land for support, or intending to make agriculture a profession. The subjects for prizes were to be related to those needed for work on the farm – mathematics, mechanics, chemistry, zoology, botany, geology. A letter was sent to local authorities, agricultural associations, and similar bodies to inform them of the scheme.[194]

Morton did not approve of these developments or the way in which the education proposal was taken up by the Society and the whole issue became surrounded by controversy. T D Acland, a member of the Education Committee, took the unusual course of circulating his views by way of a pamphlet addressed to the then President of the Society, Sir Edward Kerrison, which argued that the Society should endeavour to improve general, middle-class education as an essential pre-requisite for more specialised agricultural studies; Acland's influence was strongly resented by Morton, Holland, and others. In reply to Acland's question as to what should be the Society's position with regard to the national movement for middle-class education, Morton had no hesitation in replying 'no position at all'. Morton wanted a system of colleges which would provide 'professional' agricultural education *after* general studies: Acland thought that this was useless if there was not first systematic general education. Acland also made a sharp distinction between education in school which was 'vulgarised' by practical experience, and an apprenticeship for business.[195]

In reply to Morton's insistence on 'professional' agricultural education Acland, Thompson and others were able to cite the lack of success of Cirencester as evidence that further institutions of that type would be likely to fail. It was considered in the agricultural press, however, that the 'offering of prizes for a few boys' was 'not what was required on the education question' and that 'little or no good' could come of 'the mere plaything' that the Council had made of the matter'. It was not thought right for the Society to devote funds to general education (which was the effect of the prizes) and the Council, it was alleged, was being 'led astray' in connection with the agricultural education question.[196]

In the face of such criticisms Holland successfully moved for a reconsideration of the scheme and, as a result, the Society instituted its own examinations. These were for candidates aged between 18 and 25 who could prove that they had received a good general education and prizes were offered for competence in the Science and Practice of Agriculture, Agricultural Chemistry, Botany, Geology, Veterinary Science, Field Engineering and Surveying.[197] The first examination was held at Hanover Square in 1868 and examiners were appointed by the Council. Where possible, the examiners were already connected with the Society (such as Voelcker and Simonds) and the examination consisted of written papers and a *viva voce*. Papers in 'Science and Practice' and Book-keeping were compulsory: Land-survey, Mechanics, and Chemistry were necessary for a first-class award which carried with it life-membership of the Society.

In 1874 there were attempts to try and frame an examination to encourage the study of agriculture at middle-class schools, it being felt that the Society should encourage agricultural education at a more elementary level than in the relatively advanced examinations that the Society had instituted. To this end the Society offered 10 annual scholarships of £20 each to be taken up at Cirencester or Glasnevin (Dublin) for candidates from a range of middle-class schools including Ardingly, Bedford, the Devon and Dorset County Schools, Trent College and Whitgift.

The new scheme did not raise very much enthusiasm in the agricultural community and it was commented in the *Farmer's Magazine* that it was 'curious to see how much quasi-importance' was attached by the Society to the examination of 'a dozen or so moderate lads'. Writing in 1878 Jenkins had to admit that the Society's efforts for agricultural education had so far not been very successful. In 1881 the Royal Commission appointed to examine 'technical instruction' made Jenkins a sub-commissioner with the remit of enquiring into 'Agricultural Education' in France, Germany, Denmark and the British Isles. His report showed that agricultural education was much more developed in those continental countries which had direct Government involvement, in contrast to the minimal assistance provided at home. Jenkins's survey had the effect of stimulating further discussion on agricultural education within the Society and there was increasing recognition that the Society's efforts in this direction were inadequate; as J Dent Dent noted in 1890, only 237 candidates had presented themselves for the first 22 of the Society's examinations. Of these, 61 had been awarded first-class, and 30 second-classes.[198]

The increased importance of dairying in English agriculture during the last part of the nineteenth century led to a demand for greater competence in dairy husbandry and a range of dairy operations and in 1895 the Council asked the Board of Agriculture (created in 1889) to convene a conference to consider the appointment of a Central Board of Examiners in Dairying. When there seemed little prospect of a united approach to this project the Society formulated its own plan and in 1896 the Royal Highland and Agricultural Society – which had been involved in aspects of agricultural examination since 1824 and had instituted a Chair of Agriculture and Rural Economy at the University of Edinburgh – approached the RASE with the view of establishing one standard diploma in dairying for Great Britain. A joint committee of the two societies was appointed to arrange and carry out the details of the scheme and thus the National Diploma in Dairying (NDD) was created, the first examinations for which took place in September and October 1897. In 1900 the two Societies combined to administer the National Diploma in Agriculture (NDA) the Scottish diploma having been started by the RHAS as early as 1858.

Linked to this increased concern for agricultural education in the latter part of the nineteenth century was the perception of the need for an adequate agricultural textbook. The most accessible general agricultural work of the time was Morton's *Book of the Farm* series but this covered the different aspects of agriculture in several volumes. It was in response to this need that the Society commissioned William Fream to write *Elements of Agriculture: A Text-Book*, the first edition of which was published in January 1892. Fream was one of the Cirencester lecturers – in natural history – who had followed Wrightson to Downton in 1879 and who had contributed to the Society's Journal quite extensively during the 1880s. The book became an immediate success; the Society kept the price – intially 2s 6d – as low as possible to make the work accessible and by the end of the year 11,250 copies had been printed in three editions.[199] The general level of the textbook was rather more elementary than its modern equivalent – C R W Spedding's sixteenth edition published in 1983 – and its 28 chapters were in three parts: The Soil, The Plant, and The Animal. The following data chart the success of the work from its first appearance to the present:

TABLE 2: Circulation, Price and Editorship of *Fream's* 1892–1988

Edition	Year	Estimated No. printed	Price	Editor
1	1892	1,250	2/6	W Fream
2	1892	5,000	2/6	W Fream
3	1892	5,000	2/6	W Fream
4	1892	10,000	3/6	W Fream
5	1893	11,000	3/6	W Fream
6	1897	5,000	3/6	W Fream
7	1905	9,000	3/6	W Fream
8	1911	9,000	5/-	J R Ainsworth-Davis
9	1914	5,000	5/-	J R Ainsworth-Davis
10	1918	2,000	7/6	J R Ainsworth-Davis
11	1920	33,000	7/6	J R Ainsworth-Davis
12	1932	6,000	10/6	R J Biffen
13	1949	15,604	21/-	D H Robinson
	1951	7,646	21/-	D H Robinson
	1955	4,125	21/-	D H Robinson
	1956	5,000	25/-	D H Robinson
	1959	3,227	25/-	D H Robinson
14	1962	15,470	30/-	D H Robinson
15	1972–82	18,750	£3.50	D H Robinson
16	1983–7	10,000	£19.00	C R W Spedding

Source: H Edmunds, 1974, and RASE

The Society's consultancy services were fully maintained and extended during the last two decades of the nineteenth century. During the early 1880s the number of chemical analyses carried out for members increased substantially (1628 were carried out in 1884) and, indeed, overwork was thought to have hastened Augustus Voelcker's death.[200] In addition to his work at Woburn, William Carruthers carried out important investigations into the quality of farm seeds – the Society was able to obtain guarantees of purity and germination from two leading seed firms in 1883 – and into plant diseases and parasites. On the veterinary side, the Society sponsored research into animal diseases by making a grant to the Brown Institution, a research department of the University of London founded in 1871. The first project made possible by this grant was the investigation of pleuro-pneumonia. The Council evinced considerable impatience with the Royal Veterinary College over its alleged lack of interest in animal diseases but the grant which it withdrew from that institution in 1875 was restored four years later and in 1890 the RASE helped to establish a Chair of Comparative Pathology and Bacteriology.

Following the extreme wetness of the year 1879 there were widespread outbreaks of liver rot in sheep. A grant to an Oxford zoologist, A P Thomas, enabled the life cycle of the parasitical fluke which causes 'rot' (first identified by J B Simonds in 1861) to be pieced together.[201] This research clearly demonstrated the connection between the malady and the wetness of the land, via the snail. Thomas carried out his research in Thames-side meadows north of Oxford – the same meadows which a few years earlier had been the location of Lewis Carroll's first recitation of the *Alice in Wonderland* story.[202]

During the 1880s and 1890s the Society was much less inhibited in pressing for legislative measures to combat outbreaks of animal diseases and, along with other organisations, its repeated deputations to Government were significant in forming public policy on animal diseases. The best known example of this is compulsory slaughter with compensation, which has kept the British Isles *relatively* free of animal disease during the present century. Although there have been serious outbreaks of foot-and-mouth disease (most recently 1967 and 1968) the disease is not endemic.[203]

Understanding how micro-organisms worked (both in animal diseases and in soil processes) was an important area of advance in veterinary and agricultural science during the last quarter of the nineteenth century. Anthrax ('splenic apoplexy' as it was known) was the first of all infectious diseases demonstrated to be caused by a specific organism, and continental research in the 1870s had shown how anthrax spores were very resistant when conditions were unfavourable for their growth. In this way, a piece of ground could remain infected with dormant spores over a long period, especially in the cool conditions of the British Isles. The Society sponsored investigations into anthrax so that its cause and nature became more generally known, and there were experiments using inoculation as a preventative measure. The work of Schloesing and Muntz in France (1877) demonstrated the role of micro-organisms in nitrate formation in the sewage purification process, and Hellriegal and Wilfrath their role in fixing atmospheric nitrogen in symbiotic association with leguminous plants – a vital link which had escaped English research workers such as Lawes and Gilbert.[204] Thus there were cumulative advances in the understanding of the natural systems upon which agricultural production depends, and these were fully represented in the Society's *Journal*.

The Society's established consultancy services were extended in 1882 with the appointment of Miss Eleanor Ormerod as Consultant Entomologist. Earlier contributions to the *Journal* on farm pests had been contributed by John Curtis, who is recognised as a pioneer of farm pest control; these were notable for their detail and fine illustration.[205] Before about 1880 the farmer had few methods available to combat insect pests: hand-picking and ducks were the methods advocated by Curtis to combat the black caterpillar. While these methods have been interpreted as an early example of 'biological control' – which doubtless appeals to the latter-day 'organic' farmer – some of Curtis's remedies such as drawing sticky boards, painted with tar, along turnip rows so that the damaging flea beetles would leap against them and become stuck must have had only limited efficacy![206]

Curtis's work and engravings were important in inspiring Eleanor Ormerod whose independent work on 'injurious insects' attracted favourable notice in the agricultural press, and she did much to establish agricultural entomology as a distinct specialism. This she did by giving public lectures at the South Kensington Institute of Agriculture and publishing such works as her *Guide to Methods of Insect Life* (1884), *A Textbook of Agricultural Entomology* (1882) and *Flies Injurious to Stock* (1901). She also produced regular reports for the RASE which appeared in the *Journal*, and dealt with many hundreds of members' enquiries. Understanding the life-cycles of common insects, together with the methods of chemical control which began to be developed during the latter part of the nineteenth century, enabled the late-Victorian farmer to wage a rather more equal-sided battle against the constant hazard of farm pests than had hitherto been possible. Eleanor Ormerod is particularly remembered for her pioneering work on the warble fly; when she retired from the RASE's service in 1892 because of ill-health, she was succeeded by Cecil Warburton (of the University of Cambridge) who was given the title of Consulting Zoologist.

The Society's Show continued to be its most prominent activity, and in spite of the prevailing agricultural gloom these events continued to be attended with considerable success almost until the end of the century, with the average attendance still above that of the Royal Show's early years; Manchester in 1897, had a gate of 217,980 which set a new record. Costs, however, rose inexorably, and the shows' profitability depended very much on visits to manufacturing districts. The rotation of show districts was reviewed in 1892 at the completion of the second cycle of the scheme established in 1877. This was generally thought to have worked well, but Birmingham and Liverpool (or alternatively, Manchester) were integrated into the schedule on a regular basis as these venues could guarantee a profitable result.

The shows of the later nineteenth century were not attended with quite the same degree of excitement concerning progress in agricultural machinery that had been associated with the earlier years of the Society's 'country meetings'. Sheaf-binders received continued attention in the early 1880s, with an emphasis on binding material other than wire. The Society's Silver Medal for an oil engine was first awarded at Nottingham in 1888; a special prize for these was put up by the Society in 1890 in recognition that the 'petroleum engine had been forcing itself more prominently into notice, thereby proving that it had in effect passed the experimental stage' and the first competitive trial of petrol engines was organised at the Cambridge meeting of 1894.[207]

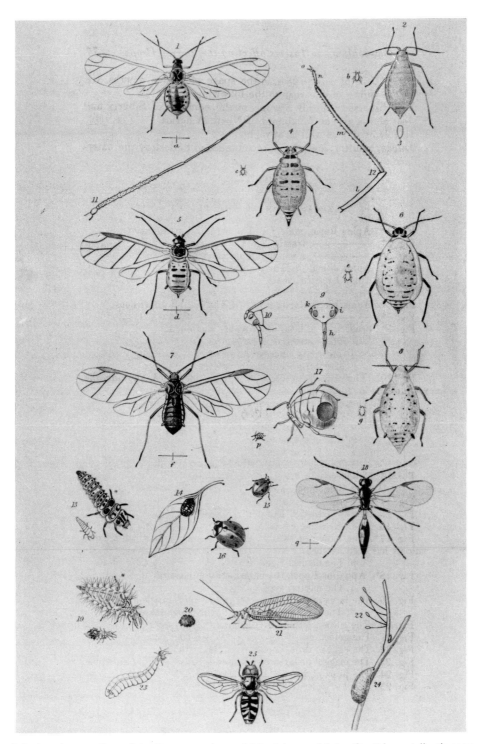

Injurious insects. One of the fine engravings which elaborated John Curtis's contributions to the *Journal* in the 1840s and 1850s.

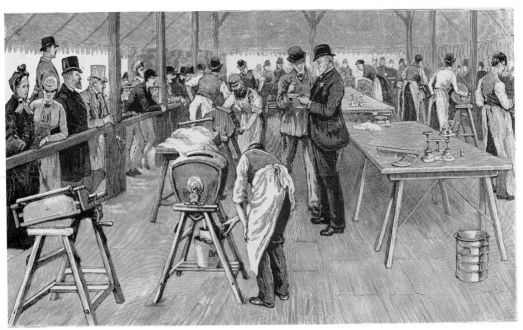

Butter-making competition at the Jubilee Show, Windsor, 1889.

Sir Jacob Wilson gave up the Honorary Directorship of the Show in 1892 because of ill-health. He was succeeded by the Hon Cecil T Parker (Agent to his uncle, the Duke of Westminster, at Eaton) who in turn was followed by Percy Crutchley in 1898.

The success of the Royal Agricultural Society in the later nineteenth century was the inspiration for the foundation of the Deutsche Landwirtschafts–Gesellschaft in Germany in 1885 with which the RASE has ever since maintained a close connection. The common thread between the two societies was the work of Max von Eyth, Head of Sales for the agricultural engineering firm of John Fowler which had participated in many of the RASE's trials. In 1883 von Eyth published *Die Königliche Landwirtschaftliche Gesellschaft von England und ihr Werf* which, by no means ignoring the limitations of the RASE as it was then constituted, revealed his intention to found an equivalent organisation on his return to the Fatherland.

During the 1880s the RASE lost a number of its officers and members who had been amongst its most stalwart servants. Apart from Augustus Voelcker's death in 1884, the Society's *Journal* records the passing of C E Amos, the Society's Consulting Engineer – whose particular contribution was in the development of the dynamometer for testing machinery – and Sir Brandreth Gibbs, the Society's longest serving Honorary Show Director (1843–1875). Thus in the 1880s there were few who could remember the early, pioneering days of the RASE as vividly as could John Chalmers Morton in 1885:

I remember the faces and voices of many of our great leaders present at the Oxford Show – the homely, kindly presence of the late Earl Spencer, our first President; the sonorous voice of the late Duke of Richmond who succeeded him; Mr Pusey's pale and anxious somewhat absent-looking face; Baron Bunsen's staid and placid countenance; the voice, good-nature, and the humour of the Rev Dr Buckland – a distinguished group seated as they were with others at the dais, on the occasion of the Banquet given to the Council at the meeting: Daniel Webster, also evidently a great power both bodily and intellectually; Sir Thomas Acland, bright-eyed, eager-looking, and Sir James Graham – all of them speakers at the Banquet on the following day in one of the College quadrangles.[208]

At the end of 1886 H M Jenkins died, aged only 46. This was a particularly grievous loss to the Society and Morton's obituary notice is especially poignant as he had

opposed his original appointment to the offices which he has held with such signal advantage and ability; and I know that for years he imagined that scant justice was dealt out to him in the weekly journal which I edited ... [but] the family, and friends, and the members of the great Society of which our late friend was Secretary may, however, be assured that no one could bring to the duty which has been confided to me a keener sense of the great loss we have all sustained, a more earnest desire to do justice to the example of his career, or a warmer loyalty to his memory.[209]

The results of Jenkins's labours particularly highlighted by Morton included the vigour of the Society's annual volume, the growth of the annual show, and the great reputation of the Society, both at home and abroad.

In Jenkins's place the Society appointed Ernest Clarke (later Sir Ernest Clarke) as Secretary and Editor from 106 applicants for the combined position. The appointing committee considered that his previous experience 'at the Local Government Board and as Assistant Secretary of the Stock Exchange' appeared to 'fit him eminently for that post'. There was less protest about the appointment of a non-agriculturist to the Society's service than in the case of Jenkins 18 years previously, because Jenkins had confounded the early critics so comprehensively. It was therefore recognised that his precedent could justify the appointment of someone who could demonstrate a 'natural ability, energy, and capacity for affairs'. Nevertheless, there were inevitably those who looked 'a little curiously at the appointment of a young man as editor of an agricultural journal who knew nothing of agricultural affairs' and, as one member protested, Jenkins at least knew something of science, unlike Clarke.[210] Their difference of approach was soon evident in Clarke's approach to the *Journal*, where his chief contributions were a number of historical studies which, however authoritative, had little relevance to the problems which then beset the Society's members.

One of Clarke's first *Journal* contributions was an obituary notice of J C

Sir Ernest Clarke, Secretary 1887–1905.

Morton who died in May, 1888 after 44 years' continuous editorship of the *Agricultural Gazette*.[211] By the time of the Society's fiftieth anniversary show, Sir Harry Verney was the only surviving founding member of those who had gathered at the Freemasons' Tavern on 9 May 1838. There were 42 members who were on the Society's list at the time of the granting of the Society's Charter on 26 March 1840 and these were all made Foundation Life Governors to mark their achievement.

As this account of the Royal Agricultural Society of England in the nineteenth century draws to a close, it is appropriate to ask how far the Society's founders' hopes and expectations for English agricultural progress had been realised. As we have seen, the Society's promoters were conscious of the need for agriculture to respond to the demands that were likely to be put upon it if *national* economic progress was to be maintained. While William Shaw (unlike some of his contemporaries) was 'not inclined to indulge in any visionary expectation of extraordinary discoveries for carrying on agricultural operations at railway speed' the Society's founders were much impressed with the potential for raising agricultural productivity by the adopting of 'scientific' farming hastened by an improved system for diffusing agricultural information.[212] They were particularly inspired by the advances in manufacturing industry made possible by the employment of steam, chemical science, scale economies, and good communications, and hoped that such methods would lead to the

132

'industrialisation' of farming systems. In the 1840s the Royal was an integral part of the movement for more intensive, 'industrial', 'commercial' and 'scientific' farming: the question is, what did the movement achieve in introducing new methods, and what did these contribute to increased agricultural output?

The preceding pages have chronicled many of the main Victorian agricultural advances – the use of off-farm inputs and their manufacture for fertilizer, land drainage by means of cheaply manufactured cylindrical drainage pipes, advances in agricultural machinery, and the development of faster maturing breeds of stock; by 1855 Chandos Wren Hoskyns thought that the RASE had, by its involvement with these advances, 'like an Aladdin's lamp ... summoned up a new race of potent genii, and set them all at work for the farmer'.[213] It is difficult to assess precisely the degree to which these and other aspects of agricultural progress were translated into increased agricultural output, but in outline the position may be summarised as follows.

Between 1829 and 1846 imports accounted for a little over seven per cent of annual wheat consumption in England and Wales, although the population increased by approximately 1,500,000 during this period.[214] When the RASE was founded, it was becoming apparent that the demands put upon agriculture by a population which was growing by 14 – 18 per cent every ten years, were unlikely to be met by methods which already only barely kept pace – expansion of the cultivated area and the adoption of more intensive 'natural' systems. This was because there was little suitable uncultivated land remaining (at home) and 'natural' systems had their own inherent limitations. This explains the intense interest in 'scientific' agriculture among opinion leaders within the agricultural community, and the push for free trade in agricultural produce by the industrial and commercial interests of the day.

Yield statistics for farm crops were not collected on a systematic basis until 1884 and the estimates available before that date have to be interpreted with particular regard for the varying qualities of the land cultivated and deviations associated with short-term climatic variations. Wheat acreage in England and Wales appears to have declined after the mid 1850s (with the increased demand for livestock products) and if the poorest wheat land was the first to be given up, then this process would have the effect of increasing the average yield of that which remained. Climatically, while the weather difficulties of the last quarter of the nineteenth century are well-known, it is worth noting that poor harvests were also recorded in 1850, 1851, 1853, (floods), 1860, 1861, 1864 (drought) 1865, 1866, 1867, 1868 (drought) and these seemingly poor years may well have depressed average yields.[215] With these qualifications in mind we may turn to a sample of estimates of wheat yield which have been available to us since the late eighteenth century.

TABLE 3: Trends in wheat yield 1770–1880

Source	Estimated (England, Wales) yield Bushels per acre
Young, 1770	23
McCulloch, from Board of Agriculture	21
Caird, 1850	26.5
Mark Lane Express, 1861	29
Caird, 1868	28
Lawes and Gilbert, 1868	28.75
Chamber of Agriculture Journal, 1870	30
Agricultural Commission (pre-depression estimate	29.5
Agricultural Commission (pre-depression estimate for 1879)	19.5
Mark Lane Express 1876–82	24.7

These figures indicate a rise in average wheat yield from a little over 20 bushels per acre at the start of the nineteenth century to a little under 30 bushels per acre in the 1860s and 1870s, with a fall after 1875 associated with the adverse weather conditions then experienced and a swing to more extensive farming methods. If this result of all the interest in 'scientific' agriculture that we have reviewed seems less than spectacular (especially when compared with present arable productivity levels) – the figures may be put into context by noting that typical medieval wheat yields appear to have been in the order of 7–10 bushels per acre.[216] Therefore, in the course of 60 years (c1800–c1860) it can be said that there was an *average* productivity increment (7 bushels) which amounted to about 50 per cent of that which it had taken the previous 600 years (c1200–c1800) to achieve. In reality, the Victorian gains in productivity were compressed into a much shorter time span. While it is difficult to distinguish between all the different elements that contributed to increased productivity such as drainage, better preparation of the seed-bed, and drilling of seed, the greatest individual factor was undoubtedly the use of fertilizers such as guano which could produce an instantaneous doubling of yield. This brought with it a profound change in attitudes towards farming operations. This was indicated by Robert Baker of Writtle, who observed in 1855 that many agriculturists would recall that since the RASE was founded if they had been told that a small bag of dried earth, that might easily be carried, would fully manure an acre of ground they would not only have treated the statement as unworthy of credit but fabulous in the extreme.[217]

Although wheat yields provide a convenient yardstick by which to measure agricultural progress, it is well-established that the balance of advantage moved from the arable farmer to the livestock producer during the third quarter of the nineteenth century. Between 1849 and 1868, for example, beef and mutton prices increased by about 50 per cent against a relatively static – but fluctuating – grain price.[218] Per capita meat consumption rose – a reflection of rising real incomes – but at a lower percentage rate than the price increase. This indicated that home production was unable to keep pace with the increased demand, which in turn may be partly a reflection of the failure of the mid-Victorian agriculturist to perceive the long-term demand shift that was taking place. However it also indicates that the more intensive stock-rearing methods that were adopted – feeding with manufactured food, better housing, and improved breeds – did not have a dramatic impact on productivity.

Reliable livestock performance figures are rarely available for Victorian times: in 1878 it was complained in the *Agricultural Economist* that there was no information available on the meat produced from a given quantity of food for different breeds of cattle. James Caird, in his 1890 survey of 'Fifty Years' Progress of British Agriculture' thought that improved systems of livestock husbandry between 1851 and 1874 added about 25 per cent to the weight of home-grown meat.[219]

The achievement of early Victorian 'scientific' farming – and indirectly of the Royal Agricultural Society of England – was to increase food output between 1840 and about 1870. This was a period when Britain's population was increasing at an unprecedented rate and when really large quantities of food were unavailable from overseas sources. Beyond this, the agricultural techniques in use did not – *could not* – sustain a continuously increasing farm output, so additional food requirements were largely met from imports. Thus the continued increase in the per capita consumption of meat (from about 90 lbs per annum between 1861–1870 to 126.9 lbs per annum for the period 1910–1914) took place at a time when the proportion supplied by domestic production fell from 89 per cent to 58 per cent.[220]

Knowledge about agricultural systems increased out of all recognition during the period covered by Part II of this *History* but the great question, as contemporaries pointed out, was whether 'knowledge' would 'pay'.[221] In the face of low-cost imports it did not, for after initial productivity increases, agriculturists had to wait until the twentieth century for additional techniques upon which to draw: it has been observed that British agriculture was only in the early stages of semi-industrialisation in the 1920s.[222]

Sir Harry Verney, longest surviving member of the foundation meeting.

Britain's urban and industrial population of the late nineteenth and early twentieth century was fed by the products of the land which were being brought into cultivation on a world scale. At home 'high-farming' was seen not to be the answer to low prices and, in the 1880s, agriculturists evinced dissatisfaction with what 'Science' had contributed to 'Practice'. For C S Read in 1886 'Science' was a 'two-edged weapon' which had helped the overseas competitor but had done 'nothing' for the British farmer.[223]

The period from the early 1850s to the early 1870s has become indelibly termed the 'Golden Age' of English agriculture although it has been remarked that accounts of prosperity might be made more explicit and Fairlie has observed that only two of the 500 pages of *English Farming Past and Present* are devoted to it.[224] While Joseph Darby, writing in 1903, agreed that the 'golden' appellation was apposite it is noticeable that this, like Ernle's account, was a retrospective assessment.[225] Morton, writing in 1877 when the period of relative prosperity had just come to a close, did not look over the immediately preceding years as part of a 'Golden Age' but rather stressed the agriculturists' 'rough education' since the early 1840s. A history of those times would, Morton thought, include chapters on 'anticipations' and 'expectations' which had never come to full fruition.[226]

Part of this 'rough education' included the various difficulties with which the agriculturist had to contend such as the major animal diseases, the labour

136

question, and higher expenses. Additionally, many of the pioneering techniques were flawed, drainage being a prime example. There are doubts as to whether 'high-feeding' of stock produced the sort of meat that changing consumer preference required: as G T Brown observed in 1886, how to produce lean meat under the system had not been 'discovered' and it may be that the imported meat was more to the taste of the consumer than the home-produced product.[227] The application of nitrogenous fertilizers to grain crops where the cultivars were unchanged could lead to excessively profuse growth and increased susceptibility to lodging, and this was also partly responsible for delaying the mechanisation of harvesting.

It is difficult, therefore, to counter the feeling that Shaw, Spencer and Pusey – who along with others hoped that Britain would not only feed itself but become a net exporter of food – would have shared in the sense of disappointment with the progress of scientific agriculture that was evident in the 1880s. The potential for the 'industrialisation' of farm practice was limited: as P K O'Brien has pointed out, agricultural operations are more separated in time and space than those in industry.[228] There was never the scope in agriculture for the massive scale economies that transformed industrial production and although steam power was successfully harnessed for some farm tasks it had only a marginal impact on cultivation. Further, pest and disease control was, as we have seen, extremely limited.

The founders of the RASE talked of the unity of interest between agriculture, commerce, and industry: implicit in their thought was a sense of the agriculturists' duty to intensify production and so answer the Ricardian fears of a stagnant agricultural sector holding up industrial progress. Industrial society welcomed the productivity increment made possible by the best endeavours of the agricultural community, but when improved transport meant that really substantial quantities of food could be imported at low prices, the agricultural interest was promptly jettisoned until it was belatedly rediscovered at the time of the Second World War. The excessive optimism of the Society's founders was never really fully justified, but it is salutary that in 1882 Pusey, whose memory was still revered among agriculturists, was viewed in *The Times* as being little more than an idle dreamer.[229]

Despite the depression which affected British agriculture during the last part of the nineteenth century the RASE's initiatives in the education and research led C S Read to observe in 1897 that it was a

> great blessing to think that this National Agricultural Society had not participated in the gloom and despondency that had reigned over the agricultural interest generally, but that it went on prospering[230]

There was also, during the last years of the nineteenth century, something of a revival in the appreciation of science among agriculturists for if science had not helped the agricultural community much during the depression, there were ever-increasing advances in agricultural knowledge such as the understanding of the role of micro-organisms in soil processes and in plant and animal diseases.[231]

The last two shows of the nineteenth century – at Birmingham in 1898 and at Maidstone in 1899 – were failures in financial terms and the loss occasioned by Maidstone in particular (£6,382) prompted a thorough review of the Society's conduct of its affairs. It was recognised that the increasing costs of staging an annual peripatetic show could no longer be covered by the Society's ability to attract the non-agricultural public. This was a problem that troubled agricultural shows more generally and was in part a reflection of the changing values of society for as A W Stanton (then editor of the *Mark Lane Express*) observed:

> the man of today expects a great deal more for a shilling than did his father and grandfather before him. He is so accustomed to cheap excursions, both to the seaside and country, that he is apt to laugh at the thought of paying a shilling for the privilege of walking about all day to inspect a lot of stock tied by their heads in sheds.[232]

This was indeed a reflection of the 'contempt' with which the average *fin de siècle* Englishman regarded practical country life.[233]

PART III:
FROM PARK ROYAL TO STONELEIGH 1903–1963

'A great new concept has emerged ... that the permanent base of the RASE must evolve into The Agricultural Centre of England.'
—Report of Fact-Finding Committee, 1961[1]

THE FAILURE OF PARK ROYAL

BETWEEN 1903 and 1905 the Society attempted to establish a permanent showground on a site at Twyford, between Willesden and Ealing in West London, which was designated as 'Park Royal'. The venture was not successful, and its failure had a profound influence on the later history of the Society, not least when the Society again came to consider the question in the 1950s. The circumstances which led to the project and the reasons for its failure therefore demand full consideration.

Concern about the future of the Society's peripatetic show was expressed following the losses at Birmingham and Maidstone. Birmingham was especially disturbing to Council members as visits to large manufacturing districts had hitherto been almost always attended with financial success and while rural locations had seldom shown a profit the loss associated with Maidstone (£6382) was by far the largest (apart from Kilburn) ever recorded in the Society's history. There were, however, particular circumstances to take into account. According to the rotation of districts scheme Maidstone should have been visited in 1898 (having been chosen in preference to Plymouth, its rival for the year) but an outbreak of typhoid fever in the town caused its postponement. Because of the short notice, the site at Birmingham was inconveniently situated and there was less publicity given to the event than usual. When the Society kept its commitment to Maidstone, fears about the quality of the water supply on the showground may have deterred some potential visitors from attending. Nevertheless, the poor financial results which were nearly always associated with visits to predominantly rural locations led to the ironic observation at the end of 1899 that it 'would not do for the Society to repeat very often an experiment which was so thoroughly agricultural in its character'.[2] It was recognised that

> The Society's shows had now reached such a development that a very large expenditure was compulsorily thrust upon it in the building of the show yards, the provision of the necessary staff, and the general administration, which the entry fees paid by exhibitors did not by any means defray[3]

139

and that it was essential to get a large number of paying visitors to ensure financial viability. As the cycle of district rotation was due to be completed in the year 1902 a committee was established to consider what modifications to the show system would be advisable after that date.

The Committee, under the Chairmanship of Cecil T Parker, consisted of Sir Nigel Kingscote (Chairman of Finance), G H Sanday, W Frankish, J Marshall Dugdale, Percy Crutchley, H D Mastal, E W Stanyforth, Sir Jacob Wilson and Sir Walter Gilbey. They undertook a thorough review of the development, aims and objectives of the Society's show since its inception. Among the considerations which were uppermost in the Committee's deliberations was the revolution that the railways had made to the attendance at agricultural shows: with the increased ease of travel that they afforded, the Royal Show did not have the same educational purpose in going into remote areas as during the early years of its existence. The size of the show was now such that a site of at least 100 acres was required, and this was increasingly difficult to obtain at a convenient location. The size was also such that the Society was inevitably committed to an expenditure of £30,000 for each show, which could not be fully recouped if it were held in a remote rural district. Nor could these costs - which had increased with rising labour rates and the price of materials such as timber and canvas – be met from entry fees for stock as the Society had, it was thought, an obligation to provide showing opportunities for its members. In any case, the livestock were recognised as a major part of the Shows' attraction.[4]

The Committee's report, drafted 5 February 1900 and placed before a special meeting of the Council on 7 March, recommended that

> Taking into account all the facts of the case, the Committee have arrived at the conclusion that, if the Society's shows are to fulfil their proper function without an unwarrantable drain upon the Society's general resources, it would be desirable that they should be held upon a permanent location (preferably in the centre of England) which would be convenient for railway access from all parts of the country. In fact, the endeavour of the Society in the future should be to bring the people to the show, and not the show to the people.[5]

In support of this, the Committee held that a permanent showground would 'undoubtedly' be a convenience to the Society's members, the exhibitors, and the regular visitors. A reservation, however, was appended by Sir Jacob Wilson who was not satisfied that every alternative to the proposed permanent showground had been exhausted. He also believed that by various rearrangements the size of the showground could be decreased and economies made in the expenditure on prizes. After a full discussion the Committee's recommendation was accepted by 38 votes to four and the Committee was reappointed to search for a suitable site.

Although the Committee's first thoughts had been in favour of a midland location for the Society's permanent showground, there was an influential body of opinion which favoured London and, in a discussion which has some close parallels with that which was to occupy the Society over half a century later, it was recognised that much of the future development of the RASE depended upon the decision as to whether it was to be based near London or at a provincial site. It was recognised that the midland or northern manufacturing areas had invariably been successful in financial terms when hosts to the Royal Show, but the purpose of holding such an event in these areas had often been questioned. In 1897, for example, it was observed that

> the magnificent array of big burly farmers that were always present at these agricultural shows and the large exhibitions of over-fed grazing stock impressed the inhabitants of those cities with the idea that there could really be no agricultural depression whatever.[6]

On 30 July 1900 the Special Show Committee, which had already been offered a number of alternative sites and needed to know what was wanted, resolved to ask the Council whether the permanent site should be in the metropolis or the provinces. In the discussion on this crucial point the view was advanced that London, described as the 'Hub of the Universe', was best for the Society's purposes and despite the strong opposition of Sir Jacob Wilson and Mr Martin Sutton (of the Reading seed firm) the weight of opinion in Council was for a metropolitan site. The motion 'that it is desirable to obtain a site in the neighbourhood of London for the purpose of the Society's permanent Show-ground' was then passed by 34 votes in favour to 12 against.[7]

Early in 1901 the Special Show Committee entered into negotiations for a site at Twyford, West London. This extended over about 100 acres, with some additional land available if required. The initial intention was to take a lease for 50 years with an option to purchase at a later date, but the Society was able to buy the land in 1902 for £26,146.[8]

To set up the permanent showground needed, however, substantial investment which was beyond the Society's depleted resources at that time. It was therefore decided to launch an appeal for the £30,000 which it was estimated would be required and this was reasonably successful (although only four per cent of the total membership responded) in that it attracted promises of £24,975 by 31 July and £28,000 by the end of 1901. During 1902 work proceeded on draining, levelling, and fencing the land and by the end of the year expenditure on the ground already totalled £42,000 without any provision for permanent buildings. A private company – Park Royal Limited – was formed to raise money and administer the showground. It had a share capital of £15,000 held by the Society augmented by a debenture issue of the same amount. One of the functions of the company was to generate additional funds for the development of the showground by the promotion of its year-round use. One project was an arrangement with the Queen's Park Rangers Football Club; another was the running of a public house 'The Plumes Tavern' adjacent to the showground which drew vehement protests from Martin Sutton who, in 1904, resigned the seat he had held on the Council since 1883.[9]

The three shows held at Park Royal failed to attract anything like the audience expected and produced an extensive cumulative loss for the Society. The 65,013 persons admitted in 1903 (with an associated deficit of £9,671) was disappointing enough but at least in that year the view could be taken that any new venture took time to gain acceptance. In 1904, despite more publicity and improvements to the showground, there were only 52,930 paid admissions and the loss of £6,920 caused considerable alarm. A Special Council Meeting held at the showground resolved 'That the Trustees of the Society be appointed a Committee to consider the present position of the Society, the Committee to be convened by the incoming President [Lord Middleton] and to have power to add to their numbers'.[10]

This Committee embarked upon a full-scale review of the Society's administration and finances, but the immediate pressing question was whether it was advisable to hold a Royal Show in 1905. There was a strong feeling that there should be no show until steps had been taken to put it on a firm financial basis. It was finally decided that the 1905 Show should go ahead if a guarantee fund of £10,000 could be raised to guard against the likely loss which would attend another event at Park Royal. The Show was still in doubt at the end of the year when only £4,471 had been subscribed to the fund but it was eventually agreed to proceed on a lower level of funding than the £10,000 originally envisaged as necessary. Percy Crutchley did not seek re-election as Show Director, so Sir Jacob Wilson was asked to come out of retirement to run the event. Sir Walter Gilbey and his friends put up extra money for show prizes, but despite the efforts and exertions of Sir Jacob Wilson (who died six days after the conclusion of the show) the 'London public, as a whole, sustained their reputation for agricultural apathy' and the total attendance was only 23,978. The actual loss was £7,279 but this was reduced to £241 by the guarantee fund.[11]

Before turning to the wholesale reorganisation of the Society's affairs that the Park Royal episode initiated, it is necessary to consider the reasons for its failure and the inability of the London showground to attract an adequate audience. Professor Scott Watson, at the time of the Society's centenary, stressed that it was still too early to write with assurance about the advisability of the Park Royal venture and the reasons for its failure. He suggested, however, that the deteriorating finances of the Society towards the end of the nineteenth century and the failure to consult with the Society's membership, were important factors. Additionally, he pointed out that it was not likely that farmers would travel long distances to London at what was a busy time of the agricultural year. These are valid points which need amplification and extension.[12]

The deterioration of the Society's finances began in the late 1880s. A substantial reserve fund had made good the loss on the 1879 Kilburn Show and

The Show at Park Royal, 1904. This view gives an impression of the sparse attendance on the showground.

the financial caution exercised for some years after that event enabled the Society to replenish its reserves. Concern about expenditure was expressed in the Society's Report to the General Meeting of 1888 when exceptional items included new entrances for the country meetings at a cost of £1,135, and a loss of £1,004 in connection with the spring show of stallions held at Newcastle in 1887. This was followed by (unusually) a £2000 deficit at the annual show at the same venue, and an ex gratia payment of £1,300 to H M Jenkins's family. An additional £1,800 had been spent on improvements and alterations to the Society's Hanover Square headquarters. These involved an extension to the rooms used as offices and a transfer of the enlarged and improved Chemical Laboratory to the upper rooms of the house which were formerly occupied by the Secretary. Space on the ground floor was given over to 'a general waiting and reading-room for members', a convenience which had been 'an admitted necessity for a considerable length of time' which was indicative of Ernest Clarke's view of the Royal as a great national Society rather far removed from the practicalities of every-day farming concerns.[13]

By the early 1890s 12 Hanover Square was felt to be inadequate for the scale of the Society's activities and part of the site of the adjoining premises known as Harewood House was acquired. The acquisition was facilitated by the Duke of Westminster and Walter Gilbey (as he then was) who purchased the property in order to make it available to the Society. It was estimated that £65,000 was

143

required to buy the freehold and erect a new building and this was financed by the issue of a debenture stock and by a trust which was set up to adminster the scheme.[14] Instead of the new building which had been planned originally, the existing premises were converted to suit the Society's purpose; the cost was again borne by the Duke of Westminster and Walter Gilbey. Although the expense of the new headquarters did not therefore fall directly on the Society's funds, the RASE's occupancy of what was later recalled as a 'pretentious' building had the effect of raising annual expenditure under the heading of rent and maintenance from about £800 to £2,000 per annum.[15] As Scott Watson pointed out, the Society's general administrative expenses rose steeply during the last part of the nineteenth century – from £3,300 in 1884 to £5,700 in 1895. Part of this increase was accounted for by the enhanced salary given to Clarke; further, the post of Secretary and Editor was separated in 1892 (the new position being given to William Fream) and the *Journals* of the 1890s were extensive, costly volumes, which often exceeded 1000 pages annually. A paid assistant for the Honorary Show Director was another item of additional expenditure which the Society had not previously contemplated.

These calls on the Society's resources meant that the reserve fund was halved between 1885 and 1900 – from £38,000 to £19,000. Further, because of the purchase of Harewood House debentures the liquid capital available to the Society fell by two-thirds over the same period – from £31,000 to £10,000. The Society's annual budget was seriously distorted by the large proportion of the membership who were life members. Life composition was obtainable for only £10 before 1890 (£15 thereafter) against the £1 annual subscription. Life compositions were aggregated into the reserve fund upon which there was an annual call of some £3,000 to make up the balance between the annual ordinary expenditure of the Society (c £10,000) and the annual subscription income (c £7,000). This, of course, was before any loss on the Show account was met. It will therefore be appreciated that the operation of the Society's finances was unsound and that it was financially ill-equipped to attempt the Park Royal project, let alone meet the losses that it produced.

The period around the turn of the century was one when the Council took little notice of the general view of the agricultural community, and this is reflected in the decline of membership which was then apparent. Martin Sutton's request that the Council should ascertain the opinion of members on the matter of a permanent showground by means of a questionnaire in the *Journal* was disregarded.[16] There *were*, however, strong reasons for establishing a permanent showground at the end of the nineteenth century and the arguments that surrounded the increased cost of the peripatetic undertaking and the ease of internal rail travel had their validity. Indeed, at one level the Council's decision could be viewed as forward-looking and innovative. Permanent sites for agricultural shows had been successfully established in Canada during the late nineteenth century, prompting the following comment in the

William Fream. A photograph taken at the
Downton Agricultural College in the 1880s.

Ontario *Farmer's Advocate*:

> The conservative old Royal of England has done well to so soon get in line with the
> onward march of procession, and we have not a shadow of doubt that its future,
> under the proposed change of system, will be even more prosperous and glorious
> than the good record which it has made in its own noble work[17]

It seems doubtful, however, if the average English farmer was ready for such a
development and Martin Sutton could claim that he voiced 'the feeling of
thousands of members' who, in 1901, already viewed with dismay the proposed
abandonment of the country show system, and the decision to establish the
permanent showground was attributed to the influence of the 'clique' who then
ran the Society's affairs.[18] Certainly there was resentment against the 'tinsel of
title'[19] that was dominant on the Council while the usefulness of the show itself
was questioned as its appearance did not match the depressed state of farming:

> those who know how matters really stand see no mystery in it as, by looking down
> the list of exhibitors they see that lord this, the honourable somebody else and
> gentleman farmer so-and-so, comprise the bulk of those who exhibit livestock,
> thus clearly showing it is only moneyed men who can afford to enter the lists of the
> Royal.[20]

Holding the Show during late June – the peak of haymaking – also caused
resentment, but there was a reluctance to move the time of the event as it
conveniently followed on from Ascot week.

The Council preference for a London rather than midlands location was the
most controversial aspect of the decision and while there are doubts as to

whether a permanent showground would have succeeded elsewhere at the start of the twentieth century, the Earl of Derby's view of the Show at Park Royal as 'one of the great institutions of the London season' does not indicate much regard for the interest of the ordinary agriculturist.[21]

The promotors of Park Royal thought that its situation would guarantee a large non-farming audience to swell the show receipts, and it is important to consider why this expectation so signally failed to materialise. The previous pattern of show attendance had usually shown a large attendance at locations near populous urban or industrial districts but the exceptions had been when the Show was held near London. Neither Battersea (1862) nor Kilburn (1879, and admittedly wet) nor even the fiftieth anniversary Windsor Show had attracted the audience or the financial results expected. Part of the reason for this is to be found in the observation that the London working-classes were 'not as a whole in the habit of taking as many holidays or of spending as much money in sight-seeing as the artisans of our great manufacturing districts'. This in turn probably reflected the distinctive industrial structure of the metropolis, which was dominated not by large scale industry but, rather, diverse small-scale manufacturing, homework, or casual trades (as in the docks).[22] These were occupations which were inimical to spare-time outings for, if the hours worked by the inhabitants of northern manufacturing towns were long, there was still *relative* security of employment and the tradition of a 'day-off' from the works on holiday or festival occasions. As for the middle-class inhabitants of London's nascent suburbs it may be that, with an increasing range of alternatives, the attractions of an agricultural show did not appear very great and that 'suburban values' caused them to have little regard for country pursuits. The 'industry of agriculture', therefore, was of 'little interest to Londoners'.[23]

When it was apparent that the 1904 Show would be the second failure on the permanent site, a Committee was set up, which had to deal with the greatest crisis in the Society's history. The 1903 losses had been sustained by a bank facility with Harewood House debentures as security; the trustees had to make personal guarantees that £15,000 would be repaid by the June of the following year. There followed a thorough review of the Society's activities, with the *Journal*, and the scientific and consultancy work, all coming under close scrutiny. As an immediate economy measure, staff salaries were reduced (Sir Ernest Clarke's by £300), portions of Harewood House were let, and the Duke of Bedford increased his financial commitment to the Woburn research operation. The main recommendation was that the Society should seek a Supplementary Charter to change the basis of Council representation; this was granted on 11 January 1905.[24] The Supplementary Charter established county divisions for the election of representatives to the Council (a system which, with modifications, has continued to the present). The original scheme provided for two Council members for every 300 members with one extra Council seat for every additional 200 members. The changes also made provision for nominated Council membership.

The Chair of the new Council was taken by F S W Cornwallis (later Lord Cornwallis) on 1 August 1905. The first task identified was to decide upon the future of the Society's shows and the scope of the other operations. Another Special committee was formed to investigate the entire position of the Society and advise on the reforms and economies that could restore the RASE to a sound footing.

This Committee met on 20 and 21 September 1905 and its recommendations, presented to the Council on 1 November 1905, were dramatic: firstly, it asked for the resignation of the Society's entire staff. Second, it was advised that the Park Royal site, and Harewood House (recognised as a 'standing hindrance to economy') be disposed of. In addition the future cost of Secretary and administrative staff should be reduced and the Board of Agriculture requested to help with the Society's scientific work.[25]

These recommendations were very largely adopted. Sir Ernest Clarke was given £1,000 in lieu of salary and Thomas McRow, who had formerly held the position of Chief Clerk to the Society and was latterly Secretary of the Agricultural Hall Company, was appointed Secretary out of 230 applicants. After some delay Harewood House was sold for £45,000 and the Society took the lease of premises at 16, Bedford Square. Some consideration was given to keeping Park Royal as a speculative investment as it was perceived that the Society would be 'parting with land which in future years would be very valuable' (it later became a major industrial estate) but this was rejected because of the expenses of upkeep, which were estimated to be between £1,300 and £1,700 annually. After the original vendors of the site had refused their right of pre-emptive purchase the property was eventually sold for £28,000.[26]

This did not totally discharge the Society's financial liabilities regarding the site. When it became clear at the time of the site's acquisition that major drainage was needed, the Society applied to Willesden Council for this to be done. When the Council refused, the Society applied instead to the neighbouring Acton Council who agreed to do the work, on the condition that an enhanced rate be paid. The Park Royal Estates Company who bought the land from the RASE sold it off to various companies and individuals and collected the rates from them. As some of these purchasers went bankrupt, the chain was broken and in 1928 the Park Royal Estates Company was itself in liquidation. The RASE then found itself responsible for rates on land it no longer owned, and it proved extremely troublesome for the Society to extricate itself from the situation.[27]

It will be appreciated how traumatic the Park Royal venture was in the annals of the RASE. The virtual sacking of Sir Ernest Clarke after 18½ years of service was one of the more unfortunate features of the episode. While it is true that Clarke did little to forge links with the ordinary farmer (as Jenkins had done) his dedication to the prestige of the RASE at the national level was in conformity with the prevailing ethos of the Council at the time. While J A Voelcker's sensitive memoir of him records that he was very much an 'indoor' man who had a certain 'brusqueness of manner' and a tendency to 'cultivate the great at the expense of the small' it is understandable that he should have 'smarted severely under a sense of the ingratitude shown to him' and it is a matter of historical record that no member of the Council represented the RASE at Clarke's funeral in 1922.[28]

Following the election of the new Council in 1905, C R W Adeane, of Babraham, Cambridgeshire, took over from Sir Nigel Kingscote as Chairman of the Finance Committee. As the sale of properties realised more money than expected, the Society's finances were soon satisfactorily reconstituted. The experience of Park Royal, however, led to considerable caution in Adeane's stewardship of the Society's finances, a caution which countinued until 1939. His meticulous attention to the RASE's affairs is revealed by the statistic that he missed only nine of the 272 occasions on which the Finance Committee met over 33 years and, during the same period, only 27 out of 306 Council meetings.[29]

The peripatetic shows were resumed in 1906 when the show visited Derby. The Honorary Show Director was by now Sir Gilbert Greenall (later Lord Daresbury) who continued in the position until 1929. Sir Richard Cooper, a new member of the Council, guaranteed to make good any deficit on the event but a successful show made a small profit – about £2,000. The financial basis of the Society's consultancy work was reorganised and the work at Woburn was continued. Although the consultancy services were seen as one of the main privileges of membership, the number of farmers who were likely to use them, or who were even aware of their existence, may be questioned. This is indicated by an observation by H Rider Haggard in *A Farmer's Year* when, complaining of the cost of the stomach analysis of a dead foal he stated that

> I find ... that the Royal Agricultural Society, to which I belong, will undertake such investigations for its members at very reasonable rates. Charges for various other services such as the treatment of sick animals, inquiry into outbreaks of disease among stock, or the reporting on the purity of samples of seeds etc., seem to be on the same moderate scale. It is a pity so few farmers know where they can find such advantages.[30]

When William Carruthers retired as Consulting Botanist in 1909 he was succeeded by Professor R H Biffen (later Sir Rowland Biffen). The same year S J J Mackenzie was appointed as *Journal* Editor. After Fream had resigned from the editorship in 1900 (possibly because he did not get along well with Clarke) the *Journal* editorship had been delegated to a member of the Society's staff, E H Godfrey. As an economy measure its size was drastically reduced, especially between the years 1904 and 1907, but the content increased after this and this appointment was made possible by additional funds allocated to the

C R W Adeane, President 1917 and Chairman of the Finance Committee 1905–39.

Journal. Mackenzie's editorship, however, was not successful – Scott Watson recalls that his 'oddities of manner, downright habit of speech and impatience of other men's opinions' were 'so combined with natural ability and humour as to have made him a legendary character' and in 1912 he was succeeded by C S Orwin, then Director of the Agricultural Research Institute at Oxford.[31] The *Journal* at this time carried a mixture of 'special articles', a section on 'contemporary affairs', 'official reports', and 'notes, communications, and reviews'. The immediate pre-war issues contained an interesting series of articles on 'minor farm crops' including flax, hemp, tobacco, teasles, peppermint, lavender, poppies, celery, bulbs, chicory, and buckwheat.[32]

Under the new regime the post-Park Royal fortunes of the RASE gradually revived. The shows perpetuated the pre-1902 pattern of showing a profit at urban and industrial locations as at Derby, Newcastle (over £10,000 in 1908), Liverpool (over £5,000 in 1910) and Bristol (£3,115 in 1913). Lincoln, a 'rural' location, where there was a profit of £5,056 in 1907 and the urban site of Doncaster where there was a loss of £1,232 in 1912 were exceptions to this rule. Lincoln saw the revival of the popular local farm prize competition (an earlier series had run from 1870 until 1892 in the district of the annual show) while the loss at Doncaster was a direct result of an outbreak of foot-and-mouth disease almost on the eve of the show. Stock which had already reached the showyard had to be sent back before the show opened, and the animals which were continually arriving were returned immediately.[33]

A leading feature of these early twentieth century shows was the increased attention given to dairy cattle and milking qualities. This was a clear reflection of the increased importance of the dairy sector in a changing agricultural situation where milk production for the urban consumer was one of the most profitable areas of farm enterprise. In 1903 butter classes, and in 1905 milk-yield classes were instituted for each of the recognised milking breeds. Also in 1905, the Society provided classes for Dairy Shorthorns, following the formation of the Dairy Shorthorn Association. In 1911 the British Friesian (then known as the British Holstein) made its first appearance at the Royal Show, the British Holstein Cattle Society having been formed in 1909 after a meeting of the breed's pioneers on the Gloucester Showground.[34]

In 1910 the Society sponsored an important trial of agricultural motors at Bygrave, near Baldock, in Hertfordshire. This followed earlier trials of 'self-moving vehicles' which had been held at Manchester in 1897 and Birmingham in 1898. The 1910 report noted that steam engines had best fulfilled the requirements of the trials but that 'the oil engine will ultimately best suit the farmer's requirements if a general purpose motor tractor is to be adopted for the average farm'.[35] The Society's educational work continued with a complete revision of the Society's textbook (which 'sold as fast as it was printed'). This was undertaken by J R Ainsworth-Davis in 1911; it was from this time that it

Sir Walter Gilbey.

150

became known as 'Fream's'. In 1912 the Society's agricultural examinations were remodelled. Thus the years following the Park Royal debacle were times of cautious reconstruction for the Society with the maintenance of the traditional pattern of its activities.

The year 1914 saw the passing of Sir Walter Gilbey who had been one of the leading members of the Society in late Victorian times and who had opposed the resumption of the peripatetic show system. His own life of successful entrepreneurship combined with a love of the horse and rural afairs symbolised an aspect of an era which was rapidly fading and which was shortly to be finally terminated by the Great War.[36]

FROM THE FIRST WORLD WAR TO THE CENTENARY SHOW 1914–1939

The Great War changed English agriculture considerably: much pasture land was converted back to arable and a wide range of controls and direction were imposed by Government. This was particularly the case after 1916 when disruption of shipping by submarine attacks injected a greater sense of urgency into home food production than had hitherto been apparent. Because of the considerable cost of converting grassland to arable, the Government instituted guaranteed prices for wheat and oats on a sliding scale under the provisions of the Corn Production Act of 1917 (barley was omitted from the terms of the Act in deference to the temperance movement). The guarantees were to last for six years with a review in 1920. The food production policy was overseen by War Agricultural Executive Committees whose members were appointed by the Ministry of Agriculture on a county basis. The task of the 'War Ags' was to arrange for suitable land to be ploughed and for it to be classified according to its level of management, resources and general condition. In cases of very poor farm management, or where individual farmers were unwilling or unable to co-operate, the committees had the power of dispossession, although these powers were used very sparingly.[37]

Thus, although the war brought Government intervention in farming on an unprecedented scale, there was no sense of urgency about home food production until 1917. During the war farm profits generally rose; the main problem that agriculturists initially had to face was a shortage of farm labour. This was brought about not only by the enlistment of farm workers, but also because there were significant losses to higher paid employment in towns.[38]

After the outbreak of war, one of the decisions that had to be made about the operation of the Society's affairs was whether the 1915 Nottingham Show should be held. There was a considerable division of opinion about this; the majority of the Council favoured proceeding with the event but a local meeting in Nottingham came out against, and recommended cancellation. After lengthy deliberations it was decided to press on and the Show attracted an audience of 103,883.[39] A trial of agricultural motors which had been planned for 1915 was cancelled however, as the manufacturers were fully occupied with Government work. A show was also held in 1916 – at Manchester – although the machinery exhibition was considerably curtailed and the 'Machinery in Motion' section prohibited by Government order. On 26 July 1916 there was a deputation on behalf of the Society to the Ministry of Agriculture to ascertain whether permission would be granted for the 1917 show scheduled for Cardiff. Although the Ministry agreed, the representatives of the railway companies made it clear at a local meeting, that they would not be able to meet the transport requirements of the show. At the end of the year the Society received a letter from the Ministry of Munitions rescinding the permission that had earlier been given for the Society to undertake the necessary constructional operations in preparation for the Show; thus the 1917 and 1918 shows were cancelled.[40]

At the end of 1916 the Society became actively engaged in the war effort through the formation of a War Emergency Committee. This was set up by the Selection Committee under the following resolution:

> That the exceptional conditions affecting agriculture and arising out of the war demand that the Royal Agricultural Society of England should in the national interest take action with a view to dealing with questions relating to agriculture, and more especially in regard to the food production of the country during the war; and that a War Emergency Committee be appointed to deal with these matters and advise the Council therein[41]

In supporting the resolution Charles Adeane said that day after day ships were being sunk and tonnage reduced and that 'Although we had not yet begun to tighten our belts, it was high time that we took stock of the situation'. He expressed the view that the Society should come 'out of its shell' to exert all its knowledge and influence to help solve the problem. The main reason for holding back was the Charter exclusion of political matters from the Society's proceedings, but the view was now taken that what were previously 'political' questions had now resolved themselves into a great *national* question to which it was right that the Society should make a contribution. Several areas were identified where the Society had a role. One was in representing the grievances of agriculture in connection with matters arising from aspects of war policy. The Society could also reassure the public that a practical body was devoting its attention to the maintenance of food production. It could monitor the effect of Government orders on food production – some of which were thought liable to defeat their own ends – and counter some of the 'ridiculous' proposals that were being advocated as to what should be done with land. Not least, it was thought that the proposed committee could counter the view (expressed in a provincial paper) that 'the British farmers had no patriotism, and went to market to quaff the toast "May the war last long and still longer so that we may be able to fill our pockets".[42]

During the last two years of the war the Society's War Emergency Committee had regular meetings and advised on methods of increasing food production as well as making numerous representations on behalf of agriculturists, especially on agricultural prices. Early resolutions, for example, included a request to Government to halt the depletion of farm labour and a resistance to the fixing of a *maximum* price for cereals.[43] Representations were also made on such matters as meat and wool prices, the cost of store animals and in 1918 the supply of hay and the future price of milk and cereals. Among various other matters in which the War Emergency Committee took an interest were the need for the provision of rail facilities for the delivery of potatoes, a request for malt to be made available to provide beer for labourers during harvest, an appeal for official assistance in the destruction of rats, and the need for the drafting of orders to be in plain and simple language and given the widest publicity. It was observed that the Ministry of Food had met many of the Society's resolutions and that it recognised the RASE as representing the practical outlook of farmers.[44]

Another aspect of war work carried out by the Society was in its Agricultural Relief of the Allies Committee. This was established in 1915 after the Society had received a request from the Agricultural Society of France for the RASE to assist in the restoration of agriculture in those districts of France and Belgium that had been devastated and to help agriculturists in those areas. The Society immediately decided to organise the collection of money and agricultural materials on a county basis. By 1920, when the fund was closed, its total value in cash and in gifts of agricultural necessities such as livestock and seed amounted to some £253,000. The distribution of the fund – to France, Belgium, Serbia and Rumania – continued until 1923. This was the second occasion that the Society had taken part in relief work for it had organised a 'French Peasants' Seed Fund' to aid reconstruction after the Franco-Prussian War of 1870–1871.[45]

Farming profits, in general, increased during the war but this revival of agricultural fortunes was short-lived. The effect of minimum wages legislation was felt in 1919 and agricultural prices fell after 1920. This caused the Government concern because of its liability to meet the minimum prices embodied in the 1917 Corn Production Act, reaffirmed in the Agriculture Act of 1920. In 1921, therefore, the Government repealed that part of the 1920 legislation which provided for guaranteed prices without the four years' notice that the Act required. Compensation was provided for land already planted at the rate of £3 per acre for wheat and £4 per acre for oats. The Wages Board, and powers to enforce minimum cultivation standards, were also abolished. This dismantling of agricultural policy – in particular the minimum price provision – became known as the 'Great Betrayal' and left a deep impression on the collective agricultural consciousness. As we shall see, it greatly affected attitudes towards food production during the Second World War and then to the formulation of post-1945 agricultural policy.[46]

The fall in agricultural prices was particularly precipitous during the period from the spring of 1921 until the end of 1922. During this time average prices fell by about one-half. The decline was then checked for a while, but further deflation set in during 1924 following the return to the gold standard. The fall in prices during the early 1920s reflected an adjustment to free market conditions: although prices received for agricultural products were some 50–60 per cent higher than they had been before the war, the costs of rental and labour were typically double their pre-1914 levels. Prices for cereals fell further than for livestock and livestock products; thus the area under tillage in England and Wales contracted from a peak of 12.4 million acres in 1918 to under 10 million acres by the end of the 1920s.[47]

Grain prices continued to fall during the 1920s. Mechanisation and more prolific cultivars increased output from the Americas and Australia so that by 1928 world production of wheat was 25 per cent above the pre-war level – considerably in excess of the total demand. At the time of the Great Depression between 1929 and 1933 farm prices fell by about a further one-third. The nadir of the depression was in 1933 when prices were only marginally above pre-war levels: as John Green (pioneer of agricultural broadcasting in the 1930s, former Chairman of the RASE Education Committee and one of the Society's Trustees) has pointed out, the wheat price was only 20s 9d a quarter in 1934.[48] Government policy towards trade agreements during this period was to subordinate agriculture to industry, and the United Kingdom was the largest individual buyer of agricultural produce on the world market. While English agriculture remained largely neglected by Governments, about two-thirds of British food consumption was provided by world and Commonwealth sources. Although the *Farmer and Stockbreeder* perceived 'The Turn of the Tide' at the end of 1934 the revival in prices was very modest and in 1938 the agricultural price index for England and Wales was only one-third above the average for 1911–13.[49]

It is against this general background, therefore, that the inter-war activities of the RASE need to be viewed. It will be seen from the graph (fig 5) that, despite the depressed condition of agriculture there was a rising trend of membership to a peak in 1925; thereafter there was a sharp fall of membership until the early 1930s, followed by a more gradual decline. The post-war rise in membership may be attributed to the relatively high profile that was achieved by the Society during the later years of the war, combined with the short-lived revival of agricultural fortunes and public interest in agricultural affairs. There was also a programme for settling ex-service men on smallholdings, and interest in such activities as poultry keeping and market-gardening. The precipitous decline after 1925 is readily explicable in terms of the worsening economic situation in agriculture, but it was also arguably a reflection of the relative inactivity of the Society and its inability to contribute to the growing debate on how best to improve the agricultural community's lot.

What this community wanted was restriction on food imports and guaranteed prices. There were also calls for programmes of rural reconstruction – or even wholesale land nationalisation – but the terms of the RASE Charter precluded the Society from participating in the debate. Thus to some observers, it was no surprise that, by the end of 1928, the Society had lost some 2,000 members over the previous three years: 'to those who have followed the activities of the Society – or at least, its lack of activities – the surprising thing is that the shrinkage is not more marked'. While it was recognised that the splitting up of large estates, shortage of money, and the increase in the strength of the NFU had all had an adverse effect on the fortunes of the RASE, the failure of the Council to model its organisation on modern lines' or to adopt a 'progressive policy' was thought to account for much of the fall-off of support at this time.[50]

An example of the difficult position of the Society in the inter-war years came in 1932. The issue, which was raised by Sir Archibald Weigall, was whether the RASE should respond to a questionnaire circulated by the Empire Dairy

Fig. 5 Membership of Royal Agricultural Society of England 1903-1938

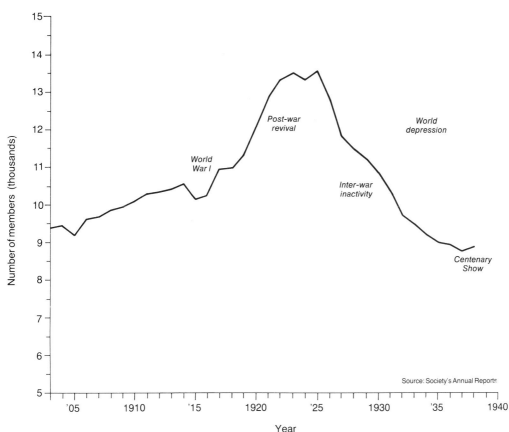

Council. The main aim of the questionnaire was to ascertain how far the Society favoured an import tax on dairy produce, and while it was recognised that if 'a poll were taken of those attending the Council meeting ... probably almost 100 per cent would be in favour of some import duty', the Charter of the Society precluded discussion of these questions. There was, it was pointed out, division in the country over such matters and the National Government was not united in regard to them: under these circumstances Charles Adeane held that it would be very dangerous for the Council of the RASE to give an opinion. Col E W Stanyforth expressed the view that this prohibition made 'the Society an extraordinary useless body' in that when asked for advice on agricultural matters by Government the answer had to be given that, according to the letter of the Charter, the RASE could not give any advice at all. The Society's Selection and General Purposes Committee gave considerable attention as to whether there was any *via media* which would give the RASE a role in considering legislative matters without altering the Charter, but came to the conclusion that this was not possible and that there would be great disadvantages in altering the terms of the Charter. Thus, although it was regretted that the Society, representative as it was of a large and important body of agricultural opinion, was debarred from giving advice to Government on matters of impending legislation, the general inclination among the members of Council was not to press for any alterations in the terms of the Society's operation. The Society did not, therefore, contribute to the widespread consultations that took place before the enactment of the Wheat Act 1932, which re-introduced limited deficiency payments for wheat financed by a levy on wheat flour rather than by general taxation.[51]

With its virtual exclusion from the debate on legislative remedies for agricultural distress (although *individual* Council members clearly had an influence on the evolution of policy) the main areas of activity of the RASE between the wars was in agricultural research and its annual show; in addition, there were the established educational and consultancy activities. Its research activity was inhibited by a lack of funds, while the show, on the whole, became somewhat fossilised into a rather staid pattern which was not associated with significant development or innovation.

After a successful show in 1919, the 1920 event, held at Darlington, produced a deficit of £7,766. This loss was caused by much increased charges by the railway companies and also by the steeply rising costs of labour and materials. The cost of erecting the 1920 show was £35,000 (compared with £18,000 for the previous year) and it was pointed out that 'a few Darlingtons' would soon wipe out the Society's reserve fund and bring the Society back to the position of 1905. A Special Committee was therefore established to review the whole question of the Society's finances. It was requested in particular to report on the cost of the Society's Woburn Farm, and given the power to give notice of the termination of its tenancy if that course of action was considered desirable by the Committee. The annual cost to the Society of the Woburn research was about

£1,200 after taking account of an annual grant of £500 from the Development Commission. It was feared that this subsidy could not be relied upon for the future, and the Committee did indeed recommend that the Society should give up its experimental farm. This provoked intense debate within the Society's Council. Those who were in favour of this course of action – led by the Chairman of Finance, C R W Adeane – pointed to the lack of interest apparently shown in the work by the Society's members. This was indicated by the very small number who attended the annual Woburn visits and a further point was made about the lack of tangible results from the investigations carried out under the terms of the Hills Bequest.[52]

The absence of progress connected with the Woburn pot-culture experiments is interesting in the overall context of the development of agricultural science, for the work carried out by J Augustus Voelcker for the Society has been termed 'a tragic story of a sound idea produced before its time' and 'one of those tragedies from which agricultural science has periodically suffered'. The work failed to uncover the vital role of trace elements in the promotion of plant growth, but only because the quantities that are required of such elements as boron, manganese, zinc, and copper are so minute. The experimental procedures then available were not adequate to ensure the complete absence of these elements in controlled experiments, and it was therefore difficult to arrive at firm conclusions about their impact and importance.[53]

The controversial recommendations of the Special Committee were eventually accepted by the Council and the Society severed its connection with Woburn in 1921. The research work was continued there by Voelcker, being partly funded, until 1926, by the Development Commission with the balance provided from Voelcker's own resources. After 1926 it was supported by the Lawes Agricultural Trust and in 1936, with the agreement of the Duke of Bedford, it was taken over by Rothamsted and provided useful sandy soils to complement the Rothamsted clays in constructing agricultural experiments. The work carried out under the Hills Bequest was transferred to the Cambridge University School of Agriculture; from the 1950s onwards there were repeated applications to the Charity Commissioners to vary the terms of the Trust, but as research work could still be done in conformity with the Trust's original objectives, these were refused.

Those who opposed the Society's withdrawal from Woburn were particularly concerned that the RASE would thereby give the impression that it was relaxing its interest in agricultural science. Sir Henry Rew, in representing the view of the Farmer's Club, thought that the Society should take a lead in agricultural research, and the opinion was expressed that the £13,000 devoted by the Society to livestock prizes each year might be better spent on this activity.[54] In recognition of this concern Lord Bledisloe successfully moved that special representation should be given to agricultural research and education on the Council. This led to the appointment of Professor W Somerville (who had initiated the Cockle Park research programme at Newcastle in the 1890s) and W C Dampier-Whetham (later Sir William Dampier) as nominated Council members. In 1922 it was decided that the Society could afford to devote £2,000 a year to agricultural research and the existing Chemical Committee undertook to examine how the Society's work in this sphere could best be developed. An eight-member Research Committee was formed, which adopted a general policy of identifying promising lines of agricultural research to which it made grants from its annual budget. This policy was followed until 1939, and examples of agricultural research work that the Committee supported during this period included the profitable utilisation of whey, green manuring, trials of malting barley, grassland improvement, the production of 'baby beef', lime loss from light soils, the profitable utilisation of sugar beet tops, mastitis control, experiments in pig-feeding, and grass seed mixture trials. A number of collaborative ventures were entered into, and there were fruitful relationships established with Rothamsted, the Norfolk Agricultural Station (under Frank Rayns) and the Welsh Plant Breeding Station at Aberystwyth under the direction of R G Stapledon (later Sir George Stapledon).[55]

It will be appreciated, however, that £2,000 a year was not a generous sum to spend on research initiatives, expecially as this allocation carried with it the request that the Research Committee would be economical and leave a balance between the amount that it was voted and its actual expenditure. This parsimonious attitude towards the Society's research funding was illustrated in 1938 when there was extensive debate as to whether a £1,000 donation which it was proposed to give to the Rothamsted centenary appeal should be deducted from the £2,000 research allocation. This was at a time when the Society's Reserve Fund, carefully nurtured by C R W Adeane, was approaching £250,000. Adeane's very cautious policy towards expenditure is directly attributable to his reconstruction of the Society's finances following the Park Royal failure and is a prime example of the way in which the Society's experience of its first attempt to establish a permanent site influenced many of its later proceedings.

Two particular areas of inter-war agricultural innovation in which the RASE took an interest were in the application of electricity to farm operations and the development of tractors. The potential of farm electricity first came to the attention of the agricultural community just before the First World War, though at that time its practical usefulness seemed limited. A review of an American work, *Electricity for the Farm* in the *Journal* of 1914, for example, observed that

> the book as a whole bears a strong resemblance to those 'boys' own books' that tell one so glibly and encouragingly how to build a 5 ton yacht and start by sending one to the grocer to beg an old orange box for nothing.[56]

158

but after the war there was a greater appreciation of electricity's agricultural possibilities. One of its pioneers in England was R Borlase Matthews who was elected to the Society's Council in 1928. He equipped his own farm, Greater Felcourt near East Grinstead, Sussex, with a variety of farm-electrical applications and in a lecture to the Gloucester Chamber of Agriculture in 1924 entitled 'Making hay without sunshine and other applications of electricity to agriculture' he identified 200 distinct agriculture uses.[57] Sir Douglas Newton (later Lord Eltisley) encouraged the Research Committee to take an interest in the question but it was recognised in 1927 that the take-up of electricity was very slow. This was attributed to the opposition of vested interests – particularly the gas companies – and the unwillingness (or indeed, the inability) of landlords to pay for the wiring of farmhouses and farm buildings. An Electro-Farming Conference was instituted at the Society's Chester meeting in 1925 and repeated at Reading (1926) and Newport (1927) but the Research Committee reports on the subject did not lead to any significant advance (their findings were considered 20 years behind the times when compared with continental progress) and electricity did not make a substantial contribution to agricultural operations between the wars.[58] By 1939 only 10 per cent of agricultural holdings had an electricity supply and it is salutary to recall that as late as 1954 this proportion had risen to only 50 per cent of farms in the United Kingdom and that only a minority then used electricity for agricultural purposes.[59]

The First World War had led to a consideration of the potentialities of agricultural tractors, given the urgent policy of converting pasture to arable. The work of tractors in the context of the wartime interest was surveyed in the *Journal* for 1918 and the Society sponsored trials of agricultural tractors at Scampton Aerodrome near Lincoln in 1920. In 1930 a much more extensive series of trials was organised by the RASE in conjuction with the Institute of Agricultural Engineering at Oxford. These were held on the Lockinge Estate at Ardington near Oxford and revealed that significant progress had taken place in the performance of tractors during the 1920s.[60] In a talk given to the Tring Agricultural Discussion Society early in 1931 S J Wright, who had been involved with the performance testing of the tractors and was appointed the Society's Consulting Engineer later that year, presented data which showed that in 20 years the cost of ploughing five acres by tractor had fallen from one pound to twelve shillings. Further, the average ratio of weight to horse power had fallen from 355 lbs to 234 lbs over that period.[61] A survey of the progress of the tractor in the United Kingdom has shown that during the 1920s its general performance was unequal to the claims of the manufacturers, with unresolved problems of starting and lubrication.[62] There was more rapid uptake during the 1930s and the production of the Fordson Model 'N' in 1929 (at first manufactured in Ireland but at Dagenham after 1933) set new performance standards. The Society's tractor trials in 1930 might therefore be taken as another example of the RASE's 'catalytic' function in agricultural progress. Nevertheless, although the 1930s witnessed a downward drift in the costs associated with tractor cultivation, take-up of tractors was slow. It has been estimated that in 1937 there were only 1.8 tractors per 1000 acres in use and that prior to 1940 the tractor was not an effective substitute for the horse for the majority of farmers in the United Kingdom.[63]

The work sponsored by the Society's Research Committee was detailed in an annual report which was sent direct to members between 1925 and 1932. In 1933 this was incorporated into the *Journal* as 'The Farmer's Guide to Agricultural Research' and this remains an established feature of the *JRASE* format.

During the inter-war years the *Journal* editorship continued as an individual appointment. C S Orwin resigned in 1925 to be succeeded by C J B Macdonald, the youngest of the renowned Scottish family of agricultural journalists and, like William Fream, also agricultural correspondent to *The Times*.[64] Macdonald died after three years in the post, however, to be succeeded by Professor J A Scott Watson. The Society's Secretary, Thomas McRow, resigned in 1920 because of ill-health and was followed by T B Turner who came to the Society from the Peterborough Show. McRow had had a connection with the Society over a period of 43 years: other examples of extremely long service worthy of note during this period of the RASE's history include F S Courtney, the Society's Consulting Engineer who retired in 1928 and who had first assisted at the Wolverhampton Show in 1871, and Thomas Brown who had been a foreman in the show fodder yard and later become Clerk of Works. He retired in 1936, also after 57 years' service with the Society.

Notable topics in the *Journal* during the inter-war years included the reports on various marketing schemes that were set up to bring some order to the home market in, for example, hops, pigs, and milk.[65] There were also surveys of successful farming enterprises, examples being Chivers' fruit farms at Histon near Cambridge, S F and J E Alley's mechanised farming, and Leckford in the Test valley where the fishing department was recognised as an important ancillary enterprise.[66] The *Journal* was revised and improved in 1938; Volume 100 was in three parts, made up of the *Farmer's Guide*, show reports, and special articles together with shorter reviews and notes.

The greatest part of the Society's efforts during the inter-war years went into the Show. This was a point of criticism for, as Lord Bledisloe pointed out when making his plea for the Society not to disengage from agricultural research, the RASE could not really rest content with an exhibition of livestock; nevertheless the impression that the organisation of the annual show was the only thing that the Society did was not altogether unjustified given the Society's rather modest involvement in other areas of agricultural activity at this time.[67]

The shows of the early 1920s were relatively successful affairs despite the generally depressed agricultural conditions, although there were often substantial financial losses associated with the event. Every effort was made to

Tractor trials. Winning entry in the RASE's 1920 competition.

overcome various difficulties: the Reading Show of 1926, for example, proceeded in an unruffled manner despite foot-and-mouth disease, the general strike, and difficulties associated with railway transport. The entries of livestock were particularly high during these inter-war years and the parade of cattle at the Royal Show was a scene that 'had no parallel in show yards of this or any other country'. The growing involvement of breed societies in the Royal Show was considered a notable feature of the event in the early 1920s and the information bureaux that these societies set up were also welcomed.[68] The Society was involved in a constructive initiative in the pedigree livestock trade by its promotion of a quarantine station. Lord Bledisloe considered that finding better markets for home livestock should be foremost among the Society's priorities and, in terms that have a familiar ring in the late 1980s, he observed in 1927 that 'in every department of agriculture it was one thing to produce the best possible products, and it was quite another to market them with satisfaction and profit to the producers'.[69]

Lord Daresbury retired from the Show Directorship in 1930. During his quarter-century in the position he had established himself as a very distinctive Show Director. A review of his Show experiences included the extreme difficulties associated with the 1912 Doncaster Show and the ways in which provincial showgrounds were obtained – not least the case of the autocratic owner of the site at a northern venue who only agreed to provide the facilities that the Society required on being provided with a lunch which finished with

A day out at the Royal Show, Nottingham, 1928.

his favourite 1885 port.[70] Lord Daresbury was succeeded by U Roland Burke (later Sir Roland Burke) the Duke of Devonshire's agent who had first been elected to the Council as a member for Sussex in 1919.

The shows of the early 1930s were attended with increased difficulties and that held at Southampton in 1932 was particularly unsuccessful as it suffered from a site which was difficult of access, and there had also been a pre-show rumour that the event was to be abandoned. By this time the show was identified as having a threefold purpose: providing guidance and incentive for traders, education for the agricultural and general publics, and business opportunities for the exhibitors of live and dead stock.[71] But although the Royal Show provided a fine spectacle, contemporaries questioned whether these broad objectives were being achieved; suggestions for its development in the early 1930s included a call for a drive to attract more townspeople, the promotion of home produced food, and more educational exhibits. Sir Douglas Newton rather controversially suggested that the Society should feature dog-racing at the show, although this proposal was not taken up.[72] A greater degree of attention was given to publicity for the show and the considerable success of the 1934 event at Ipswich – the first time the Society had visited the town – was attributed to increased efforts in this direction. The potential of broadcasting for bringing the show to public attention was given consideration at this time. Lord Daresbury had given a wireless talk about the Royal Show as early as 1924, and the Ipswich Show was featured on the programme 'In Town Tonight'.

In 1935 Walter Elliot, the Minister of Agriculture, wrote of 'The New

Outlook' in farming which included the raising of the acreage of wheat under the Wheat Act, the regulation of marketing, and a growing awareness of rural neglect.[73] Strategic considerations also led to a reappraisal of the condition of agriculture: as was observed in the Society's Council at the end of 1934 the food situation had been critical in the 1914–1918 war and 'that there was no reason to suppose that if we do have another war (with all respect to our "peace at any price" people) we shall get our food over as well as we did in the last war'.[74]

Despite the worsening European situation the Society planned for its Centenary Show in 1939 with enthusiasm and confidence. The event was held in Windsor Great Park (the scene of the Jubilee meeting) after some consideration had been given to Oxford (the site of the first Show) and a midlands location. The Centenary Show brought together the largest exhibition of livestock – there were 4,548 combined entries for horses, cattle, goats, sheep and pigs – ever assembled at a Royal Show. The classes demonstrated the extension of the range of breeds that had taken place since the nineteenth century with prizes provided for no less than 12 breeds of pigs. Whether such a number served any useful purpose, however, was an unanswered question which Sir Douglas Newton had earlier raised in Council.[75] Dairy cattle were also very strongly represented, the Dairy Shorthorn being the most numerous breed. The Society's Council was entertained at a banquet in the Waterloo Room at Windsor by the President, King George VI, and the Show programme was extremely varied with a large forestry exhibition, an extensive schools section, and an outstanding flower show.[76]

Although the Centenary Show was viewed as the 'greatest exhibition in the annals of the Society' the attendance, at 118,036, was not particularly high and once again confirmed the comparative indifference of Londoners to the event. Post-show comment in the *Farmer and Stockbreeder* questioned whether, in all the circumstances, the event had been as big a success as it might have been. Pre-show publicity was again thought to have been deficient and there was a call for the Society to 'move with the times and adopt modern business methods'.[77] It was to be another two decades before such calls were fully heeded.

THE SOCIETY IN WARTIME

The outbreak of war meant that the range of the Society's activities had to be curtailed, and it was decided that the normal meetings of Council and the Standing Committees would be suspended. The Selection and General Purposes Committee therefore recommended the appointment (under the provisions of the Society's byelaws) of an Executive Committee to oversee the Society's affairs. This initially consisted of Lord Mildmay of Flete (Chairman), Sir Roland Burke (Deputy Chairman), Sir Arthur Hazelrigg, Sir Merrik Burrell and Sir Archibald Weigall, with the power to co-opt as appropriate. It was decided that it would not be possible to hold a show during the period of the war but when hostilities were over, Lincoln would be the first place to be visited. The Society leased a house in Guildford in case the London headquarters had to be evacuated, and the Royal's pictures were dispersed, the majority being lodged at Knepp Castle, Sir Merrik Burrell's West Sussex estate.[78]

The success of the Windsor Centenary Show was recorded at the December meeting of Members and Governors but, less encouragingly, it was reported that the ordinary membership stood at only 9,483 despite expectations that the anniversary show would have boosted the number considerably. The main feature of the December meeting was the presentation of the Society's Gold Medal to Sir George Stapledon in recognition of his work on plant breeding and grassland improvement, part of which had been sponsored by the Society over the preceding years. During his acceptance speech, Sir George said that for one who had, since the First World War, devoted his research activities and energy to preparing for such an emergency as had now befallen the Country, it was difficult to avoid a feeling of failure with respect to the continued and undiminished amount of land in second- and third-rate permanent pasture. He observed that 'as long as we, as a nation, are content to allow such a huge acreage of this fertile little country to remain in such a condition which, to all intents and purposes, is not farmed at all, we cannot say that agriculturally we are very much good' . Sir George's 'terse appreciation' of the Society's honour was reported with approval in the agricultural press.[79]

Apart from the Show, the Executive Committee was able to maintain many of the peacetime concerns of the Society during the early years of the war, and towards the end of 1942, at the first Council meeting held since December 1939, the President reported that such matters as animal diseases, the testing of tractors, shortage of farm labour, long service awards, examinations, research grants, and the publication of the *Journal* and *Fream's* had been carried out along pre-war lines.[80] Despite this, there was a view that the Society could have played a more important role in the war effort. In the *Farmer and Stock-breeder* the Council meetings were said to be 'purely ornamental, not to say superfluous' and that:

> With its great experience, its brilliant membership, not to mention its high accumulated idle balance of £260,000 the RASE ought to be playing a part in today's great drama very different from that of the slumbering Rip van Winkle which it appears to have chosen.[81]

This criticism was discussed by the Executive Council and considered quite unwarranted. Rather than write to the *Farmer and Stockbreeder* and generate controversy, a reply was sent directly to its Managing Director, R W Haddon (later Sir Richard Haddon), in refutation.[82] Later, Haddon returned, in conjunction with Anthony Hurd (later Lord Hurd), with proposals as to how the RASE's usefulness could be enhanced.

A new issue with which the RASE became involved at this time was that of artificial insemination (AI), a technique which received considerable attention in the agricultural press, and it was thought by some that the Society should take a lead with regard to the regulation of the practice. The Agricultural Improvement Council[83] had investigated the process, and it now appeared that AI could have some practical application and value for British stockbreeders. While the potential worth of the method was appreciated, there were also considerable reservations among the breed societies as to how far development of the practice was desirable. Within the Society there was some internal disagreement about the extent to which it should become involved with the new issues that the technique raised. One view, put forward in Council by Col Wheatley, was that the Royal Agricultural Society should take the initiative and lay down sound principles and practice. This was rejected by Sir Merrik Burrell and others, because Government legislation was being prepared. The objectors recognised that the Society had a legitimate liaison function between the agricultural world and the Ministry (which had already taken cognisance of the Society's advice in the matter), but beyond that it was thought far better for individual breed societies to lay down rules for their own members. Nevertheless, members of the Society's Council had informal meetings with officials from the Ministry of Agriculture concerning impending regulations, and minutes of a meeting between the Society and the Ministry on 8 October 1942, were circulated *confidentially* to the breed societies. This was a good example of the influence that the Society was able to bring 'behind the scenes'; the link that it provided between the breed societies and the Ministry continued when there were further meetings early in 1943.[84]

One particular wartime food production initiative with which the Society was associated was the Victory Churn Contest, for which it provided a challenge trophy for inter-county milk production at the request of the Minister, R S Hudson (later Lord Hudson). Although this was later recognised as a useful incentive in encouraging increased milk output, it also provided ammunition for critics who considered that it was at best a peripheral activity and that the Society should have assumed a more central role in agriculture's contribution to the war effort.[85]

In retrospect the Society's greatest influence during the war period can be seen to be the development of the post-war agricultural policy and, in particular, the framing of the 1947 legislation which, with various modifications, was the foundation of British agricultural policy until the accession to the EEC in 1973. As post-war agricultural policy stemmed from wartime food production efforts, it is therefore necessary briefly to consider these and, in particular, the reaction of the agricultural community to the demands which were put upon it during the war years.

Wartime ploughing campaign. Ploughing bracken in Montgomeryshire, 1942; the driver is Nigel Harvey, now the Society's Honorary Librarian.

The growing awareness of the strategic importance of a thriving home agriculture, which was apparent in the mid-1930s, was reflected in the Agriculture Act of 1937 which provided some modest measures to promote agricultural intensification including subsidies on inputs such as lime and basic slag and deficiency payments for oats and barley. In his 'Kettering Speech' of July 1938, however, Neville Chamberlain denied the need for increased home agricultural production and declared that Britain would not starve in the event of war, but after the invasion of Czechoslovakia plans for increasing home food production were announced. The Agricultural Development Act of 1939 provided grants for grassland improvement or conversion to arable, a deficiency payments scheme for sheep (which did not rely on imported feeds) and a national reserve of tractors and of fertilizers placed at the disposal of new agricultural executive committees.[86]

The essential elements of wartime agricultural production policy were announced by the then Minister, Sir Reginald Dorman-Smith, in October 1939. The main policy was (as in the latter part of the First World War) to plough up much land which would not normally have been considered remunerative under peacetime conditions, in order to economise on vital shipping space otherwise taken up by imported food. Agricultural executive committees ('War Ags') were again set up for each county in England and Wales to supervise farming practice, the chairmen for these having been selected even before Munich. As between 1914–1918, these committees had very extensive powers: they could determine cropping systems and agricultural practice, and, again, in extreme cases occupiers of land who were unable to come up to the required standard of husbandry or who did not obey directions were dispossessed. All of this took place within a comprehensive framework of guarantees and price control, grants for ploughing up, and, on the demand side, a stringent system of price control and food rationing. The official inter-war neglect of agricultural research and development (despite a few palliatives such as the establishment of the Agricultural Research Council in 1931) can be put into perspective by the observation in the War Cabinet that the 'plough-up' campaign – the central part of the drive for home food output during the early part of the war – would, by the conversion of 1,000,000 acres of grass to tillage, be only equivalent to raising the average overall arable yield per acre then obtained by five per cent.[87]

The agricultural community was ready to accept the challenge, but there was at the same time a great deal of suspicion that at the end of the war there would be a repeat of the 'great betrayal' of 1921. The NFU took the view that 'the will to help' was 'endangered by a lack of confidence' and, looking forward to the return of peace, it was hoped that no food would be imported that could be produced at home.[88] This view had widespread support among agriculturists and the sentiments expressed by Lt Col J Creagh-Scott in *Farmer and Stockbreeder*:

> Restrict him here, restrict him there, the agitating brute,
> But its 'work like blazes farmer' when the guns begin to shoot.
>
> When U-boats sink imported foods he's made the Nation's pet,
> Let's hope the farmer isn't fooled! Let's hope he don't forget! [this time]
> [*With apologies to Kipling*][89]

readily found echoes in the agricultural community at large; there was a great deal of concern that wartime policies, including the various measures of agricultural support, would be abandoned at the end of hostilities, and that there would not be continuity of agricultural policy between wartime and peacetime. The NFU formed a committee to investigate the question of future agricultural policy in 1940, and a Government Committee was formed to consider the matter early the following year. In the light of these developments, the Royal decided that it should formulate its views and appoint a witness to give evidence to the Government review; Sir Merrik Burrell had also been invited to present his opinion and he circulated a memorandum on the subject to members of the Society's Executive Committee. The RASE then established

Wartime tractor. The driver is J D F Green, now a Trustee of the Society and Chairman of the Education and General Purposes Committee 1974–83.

an *ad hoc* committee on post-war agricultural policy which sent a further memorandum to the Minister; at his request this initially remained confidential, although permission was later given for the memorandum to be circulated to other Council members.[90]

Thus the Society gave attention to the matter of post-war policy at an early stage although their views did not at first have very wide circulation. However, many other bodies became interested in the question of post-war agricultural and rural policy and similar undertakings were obtained to restrict circulation of various ideas. This restrictive policy became difficult to sustain when Government Committees issued reports which had some bearing on post-war agricultural conditions. One of these was the Uthwatt Committee which published a report in 1942; this made little impression on the Society's senior members – Sir Arthur Hazelrigg went so far as to say that he fell asleep while reading the first two pages. More importantly, the Scott Report on post-war rural conditions, although meeting with a great deal of general approval, had a minority report appended to it 'written by some nineteenth century economist' which appeared to envisage no post-war development or improvement in agriculture: this occasioned considerable disquiet within the Society and the agricultural community.[91] By 1943 the ministerial embargo had been lifted, and eventually memoranda from the Society and other bodies could be more generally circulated – that issued by the Royal was the first statement to come to public attention. The basis of the Society's thinking was that a statutory body, similar in organisation to the Forestry Commission, should be responsible for food production. Prices would be stabilised, and these guaranteed prices would be linked to guaranteed wages. The general policy was that the fertility of the land would be maintained or increased in contrast to the inter-war neglect.[92]

It became apparent from subsequent memoranda published by other bodies that there was a good deal of unanimity in the views put forward, and the Executive Committee adopted the following resolution at its meeting of October 1943:

> That the Minister of Agriculture be informed that the Royal Agricultural Society of England, whilst adhering to its views on post-war agriculture as set forth in its memorandum, have observed that reports and recommendations of the National Farmers' Union, the Highland and Agricultural Society of Scotland, the Group of Peers, the Council of Agriculture for England, the Central Landowners' Association and other bodies have also been submitted to the Ministry and that there are in these memoranda and reports many points of agreement which might well be taken as a basis for an agreed common policy.[93]

A second resolution authorised the Executive Committee to approach the various bodies named to confer on common action to urge the Government to produce its post-war agricultural policy as soon as possible.

As a result of these initiatives, the Society was able to call together a conference which took place on 12 April 1944, and attracted representatives from all the leading agricultural organisations. This was very successful in drawing together the main strands of opinion and so closely did these agree that the main task of the conference was to appoint a Drafting Committee to decide on a suitable form of words for general circulation.[94]

The main plank of the policy which was eventually agreed was an emphasis on the prime importance of a healthy agriculture, which yielded an adequate return to those engaged in it, consistent with rendering the best possible service to the community. Mixed farming was to be encouraged to maintain soil fertility and regular employment. There was to be an orderly regulation of production and marketing and the functions of the Ministry of Food in regard to the importing and marketing of competitive foodstuffs were to be combined in a statutory body, supported by an Imports Board. The most contentious issue was the degree of direction that owners and occupiers of land should accept in return for guaranteed prices. Other points included the need for the expansion and development of agricultural research, revision of the impact of taxation, maintenance of reasonable credit facilities, improved rural housing, extensions of water supply, gas and electrical facilities, and an increased attention to land drainage.

According to Sir George Courthope (later Lord Courthope) 'the success of the Conference more than justified the initiative which the Council showed in summoning it'. This success had been achieved through the unanimity of views

The RASE conference on post-war agricultural policy, 12 April, 1944.

that it had been possible to reach, combined with supportive press coverage. However, it was also held that 'the impression of unanimity was partly illusory having been obtained by a measure of window dressing' and to some critics the emphasis on mixed farming already looked old-fashioned.[95] While the follow-up to the Conference was impeded by the very difficult conditions which obtained in London during the latter part of 1944, there was also increasing dissatisfaction among agriculturists concerning the failure of either the Minister or the Government to make a pronouncement about post-war agricultural policy. This dissatisfaction had been apparent at least a year earlier when a House of Commons debate had failed to extract any clear statement on the subject and in the course of which Christopher York (then sitting as Conservative Member for Ripon), had declared 'Mr Hudson's speech a smoke screen and Mr Williams's a gas mask' and the agricultural community had further been astounded to learn that the Minister was 'under instruction not to talk about post-war policy'.[96]

While assurances had been given that there was to be no immediate stop to wartime policies, this absence of a longer term commitment gave rise to increasing concern. It can no doubt be linked to W S Morrison's observation in Cabinet that, left to themselves, farmers would formulate elaborate and expensive demands, and certainly the financial basis of the policy which the agricultural community demanded was not spelt out.[97] With the approach of the election in 1945, the leading political parties showed a reluctance to declare their policies, although when their manifestos were published there was considerable uniformity between them on agricultural matters, the bogey of land nationalisation having been disposed of as far as Labour policy was concerned. Thus, the 1947 Agriculture Act contained very many of the elements which had been put forward by the farming community during wartime and the leading role of the Royal in bringing together the various interests involved deserves due recognition. A further example of this ability of the Society to represent a wide range of interests by virtue of its impartial status was shown during the food crisis of 1947 when another conference was convened by the RASE and detailed recommendations sent to the Ministry. The conference called by the Society in 1944 can thus be seen to have had a very direct influence on the 1947 Act and, by extension, the nature of post-war governmental support for the industry. This was remarkably consistent among all parties, despite criticisms, up to the transition to the CAP in the early 1970s.[98]

POST-WAR RESUMPTION OF ACTIVITIES

Only two members were present at the first meeting of the Executive Committee after the termination of the war in Europe. Sir Roland Burke congratulated the President, Sir George Courthope, on his elevation to the peerage. In return the President reported the message of victory congratulations that had been sent to the King on 12 May. Apart from the members of the Society who had been killed on active service, a number of long standing members who had served the Society had died during the war. These included Percy Crutchley (the father of the Council, having been first elected in 1887), Charles Adeane, Sir Walter Gilbey, R H Evans, Col Wheatley, and Borlase Matthews (tragically killed in a swimming accident off the North Wales coast). Thomas McRow, the Society's former Secretary, died in 1942.

There were a number of changes in the Society's administrative affairs immediately after the war. The Secretary, T B Turner, had been due to retire in February, 1945, but had been persuaded to stay on by Sir Roland Burke until the Lincoln Show, planned for the following year. Later in 1945 Alec Hobson was appointed Secretary. Hobson was very well known to the agricultural community as a partner in the leading firm of livestock auctioneers Thornton, Hobson and Co which, with his brother Harry, he had founded in 1928. Earlier, Alec Hobson had been the first Assistant Secretary to the British Friesian Society, (his brother being Secretary),[99] and from there had gone to the National Pig Breeders' Association. He had also been very active during the War in connection with the Small Pig Keepers' Council, services for which he was awarded an OBE. An Assistant Secretary, Carol Fellowes, was appointed in 1952 and continued in that position until his retirement in 1959. Towards the end of the 1940s the Council considered whether the premises which it occupied in Bedford Square were adequate for its purposes, although it did not move to its present London headquarters at 35 Belgrave Square until 1956. In 1948, a Policy Committee was set up to look at the future activities of the Society and its services for Members. Its recommendations included an increase in subscription, the first which had taken place since the Society was founded, and modifications to the Charter which were eventually enacted in 1953.

The Society looked forward to the resumption of its full range of activities with considerable enthusiasm and also towards achieving a higher level of prominence in the agricultural community than it had enjoyed in the 1930s. There was a feeling that whatever recognition the Society had received regarding its efforts on agricultural policy, it had lost something of its standing during wartime when, under the Executive Committee, its administration and operations had appeared particularly 'closed'. Early in 1944, following some of the press criticism already noted, Anthony Hurd, who had recently been elected to the Council as Member for Wiltshire and was liaison officer at the Ministry of Agriculture, approached the Executive Committee (together with R W Haddon) with suggestions for increasing the Society's usefulness. This resulted in the establishment of an Advisory Committee on Propaganda and Publicity to assist the Society in its future work, and the appointment of L F Easterbrook to lecture on the Society's activities and edit a new *Quarterly Review* which was launched in 1945. This was the forerunner of the present *NAC News* and served as an additional link between the Society and its membership. Early in 1946 the Society's President, Lord Bledisloe, wrote to *The Times* urging all three sections of the agricultural industry – landowners, tenants and farmers, and agricultural labour – to work together. Meanwhile Alec Hobson was active in stressing the benefits of membership of the RASE.[100]

The most immediate concern of the Society at this time was the question of when the first post-war show could be held. A preliminary meeting to consider the question had been convened in March 1944 when there was a widespread hope that a show would be possible very soon after the end of the War. However, it was also recognised that the problems, particularly with regard to labour and materials, would be immense. Causes for optimism included the fact that the Society had carefully looked after many of the necessary items which were at the moment in short supply such as timber and canvas, some of which had been newly acquired for the Windsor Show, and that the Lincoln Show site, with a generous local fund of £2,000 had had some preliminary work completed on it. Nevertheless, it soon became clear that it would be impossible to hold a show in 1946.

The question of a 1946 show was partly out of the Society's control as a Government licence was necessary; Sir Roland Burke and Sir Archibald Weigall put the Society's case to the new Minister, Tom Williams (later Lord Williams), on 23 August 1945 stressing the importance of agriculture in the

Lord Bledisloe speaking at the presentation of the RASE Gold Medal, 30 July, 1947; with Rt Hon Tom Williams, Minister of Agriculture, and Lt Col Sir Archibald Weigall Bt.

national interest and the undesirability of a delay to 1947. The Government decision was that with the extensive calls on labour, materials, and transport which large agricultural shows demanded, it would not be appropriate for the Royal to be held in 1946 and that Government support would not therefore be forthcoming. This decision was not at all well received by members of Council and Sir Archibald Weigall reported that 'he had turned almost purple with rage' when he met the Minister to discuss the matter.[101] A particular source of contention was that the Minister's reply had indicated some lack of sympathy with the way in which the pre-war shows had been run and, as Anthony Hurd observed, the Society had not been able to demonstrate to the Minister the Royal Show's utility and worth in the difficult situation which still prevailed.[102] Although many felt that the Royal Agricultural Society without a Royal Show was without its essential *raison d'être*, there was some agreement in the agricultural community that the show's early resumption could not be justified. In the absence of the national event the Society made funds available for awards at county agricultural shows held in 1946.

Official clearance for the 1947 Show had still not been granted by June 1946, and considerable concern was expressed about the uncertainty which obtained. Permission for the Show was finally confirmed for 1947 after informal contacts between Alec Hobson, Anthony Hurd, and the Minister and the support of Mr Williams in persuading the Ministry of Works to overcome the remaining difficulties was something to which Sir Roland Burke was pleased to pay tribute.[103] Thereafter strenuous preparations for the Lincoln event went ahead despite the considerable problems which the Society faced. Materials were still in very short supply and tubular steel had to be obtained to supplement the lack of timber in constructing the showground. At the Annual General Meeting of 1946 – the first for seven years – the President was able to express the hope that, in spite of the austere conditions, there was every prospect of a highly successful show for 1947. The newly established Publicity Sub-Committee recommended that £3,000 should be available for advertising – more than twice the amount that had been allowed for the immediate pre-war shows – and new advertising agents were employed. Considerable attention was given to the question of bill posting, the design of the show brochure, and a short publicity film of the Windsor centenary event was released to advertise the show in Lincoln cinemas. In the expectation of a large attendance Sir Archibald Weigall was delegated to approach 'Butlin's Hotel at Skegness' in order to secure additional accommodation for Lincoln Show visitors.[104]

Preparation of the Lincoln Showground was made particularly difficult by the exceptionally severe weather in the winter and spring of 1947, but the number of entries indicated the widespread interest caused by the show's resumption. There were 71 entries for the Silver Medal new implement award and the response of implement exhibitors generally was considered embarrassingly large.

In the event, the occasion surpassed the most optimistic expectations and the 240,323 paid admissions constituted a new attendance record. So great was the press of people wishing to gain entrance to the showground that the turnstiles could not cope and stewards collected admission money in their bowler hats.[105] The Lincoln Show was judged 'a marvellous accomplishment', although it was also recognised that many people went merely for the spectacle, and its very success brought with it unforeseen problems. Not the least of these were the difficulties concerned with traffic flow and car parking at the showground where visitors were subject to interminable delays and which gave rise to questions about the character of the show which became increasingly pressing in succeeding years.[106]

POST-WAR RESEARCH AND EDUCATION

At the 1946 Annual General Meeting Lord Bledisloe identified six tasks which he hoped that the Society would make its own in addition to the Royal Show. These can be summarised as follows:

1 Close and friendly contact and collaboration with all the leading national agricultural organisations and especially the National Farmers' Union

2 Special encouragement of the Young Farmers'
Clubs Movement

3 Outspoken and active sympathy with agricultural
education and research

4 Raising the average standard of British
livestock to that of the best and the steady
elimination of animal diseases

5 Friendly co-operation with agriculturists in
every part of the British Commonwealth

6 The determination that the Royal by its
progressive activities, shall remain the
premier agricultural society of this country
and the British Empire.

In the following years several initiatives were taken along the lines that Lord
Bledisloe had indicated. Special Royal Show tickets were made available for
Young Farmers' Clubs at the end of 1946 and facilities for overseas visitors were
improved at the Lincoln and succeeding shows, although these were not fully
developed until the Society became established at a permanent base and a
permanent International Pavilion was built. The foundation of the Royal
Agricultural Society of the Commonwealth, on the initiative of the Duke of
Edinburgh during his 1957 Presidency of the Society, was another step in the
direction that Lord Bledisloe envisaged. The Society resolved to limit cattle
shown at the Royal Shows to those from accredited herds from 1948 onwards
and, as soon as possible, to those also free from contagious abortion. Sir Merrik
Burrell provided liaison with the breed societies and this was again an initiative
which received a general welcome. Lord Bledisloe himself instituted an inter-
county dairy herds trophy administered by the RASE to encourage the
promotion of accredited herds. This award was given, in conjunction with the
Milk Marketing Board, to the county which could show the most rapid progress
each year in the number of accredited herds within its area.

The Society's wider role in agricultural research was an area of some difficulty
immediately after the war because of the greater state involvement in agricultural advisory services and research following the foundation of the National
Agricultural Advisory Service (NAAS) in 1946.[107] This diminished the significance of the Society's involvement in the agricultural consultancy sphere as it
had resources far beyond the capacity of a private voluntary institution. The
formation of the NAAS, coupled with the retirement of two of the Society's
consultants, Sir Rowland Biffen and Cecil Warburton, prompted a reconsideration of the scope and nature of the Society's advisory services. One suggestion
canvassed was that botanical inquiries by members could in future be referred
to the National Institute of Agricultural Botany (NIAB), but such an arrange-

ment did not prove to be possible. Instead, Frank Rayns, Director of the Norfolk Field Station, was appointed to deal with botanical questions as part of his role as the Society's crop husbandry officer and F R Petheridge of Cambridge was recruited as the RASE's entomologist. The reorganisation of the Society's advisory services at this time led to a proposal that the existing 'Botanical and Zoological (Forestry and Orchards) Committee' be renamed the 'Agricultural, Horticultural and Forestry Advisory Services Committee'. This was, however, a very cumbersome title: the President's suggestion that it be shortened to 'Biological and Forestry Committee' was rejected by Sir Archibald Weigall because of his horror that if this abbreviation was adopted he could see 'the cultured committee going down to history as "the B F Committee"'. The title finally decided upon was the 'Forestry and Biological Committee'.[108]

For some time before the war it had been apparent that the number of inquiries made by members to the Society's advisors had been declining, but the RASE's consultancy services were some of the longest standing privileges of membership and it was felt that personal, as opposed to official services, continued to be preferred by many members. Nevertheless, the number of inquiries received by the Society declined still further in the 1950s with the greater availability of both state and commercial agricultural advisory agencies. Therefore, when F R Petheridge retired in 1958 it was resolved that his position would not be replaced and by the early 1960s all the remaining consultants acted only in an honorary advisory capacity. One of the last of these, Eric Voelcker, retired in 1976 after a continuous family service of 120 years.

On the agricultural research side, the Society had continued to support the grassland trials under Sir George Stapledon's direction during the war years. There were also experiments on the disposal of beet tops and straw trials at the Norfolk Field Station under the supervision of Frank Rayns, experiments of cake feeding on grassland at Rothamsted, and Dr D H Robinson had been commissioned to produce a revised edition of *Fream's*. It was, however, becoming increasingly obvious that with the general expansion of post-war agricultural research activity, the Society's continued involvement in this area lacked focus and rationale.

At the heart of the problem, as Sir John Russell and others recognised, was the fact that the Agricultural Improvement Council had the same role as that traditionally carried out by the Society – to make the bridge between the experimental station and the farmer – but with much greater resources than anything that the Society could reasonably hope to command. If the Society continued its traditional policy, there was a danger that it would be left with only the problems that the Agricultural Improvement Council did not consider worth taking up or as some appendix to a more promising investigation the main credit for which would go to the AIC and not the Society. This was a position which was considered to be 'undignified and unsatisfactory', and a suggestion was made by Sir John Russell to resolve the dilemma and identify a valid role for the Society in agricultural scientific activity. His idea was that the Society should embark on 'operational research' whereby information would be obtained from some of the most outstanding farms of the day, collated by the Society, and relayed to members.[109] This, he suggested, could be done by publishing details of first class farming enterprises, reporting on the farming of different counties or on agricultural specialisms such as beef or fat lamb production, an initiative which might, he thought, need the appointment of an agricultural officer to oversee the reports. Contact was also made with Dr W K Slater of the Agricultural Improvement Council for information about the sort of work with which the NAAS was engaged and asked for suggestions as to how the Society could co-operate. The response included the suggestion that the Society could join with the University Grants Committee in order to initiate research, that the Society help with the entertainment of visiting overseas scientists, and also that the Society could collaborate with agricultural surveys which had been started by NAAS.

The first two of these suggestions did not meet with very much enthusiasm on the part of the Society, but the idea of agricultural surveys appeared a more fruitful line to pursue. The advice of Professor J A Scott Watson was taken, who was in broad agreement that the preparation of County Surveys would be a valuable and appropriate activity for the RASE to embark upon. The Society therefore began a new series of agricultural surveys, the general aim of which was to give an overview of the present day agriculture of particular counties, broadly on the lines of the old nineteenth-century surveys, with a level of exposition set to appeal to farmers, advisory officers, students, and members of the Young Farmers' Clubs. It was expected that each county survey would have sections on the physical background, the historic setting, farming systems, possibilities of agricultural extension, intensification and specialisation, layout and mechanisation, problems of social economy, together with examples of successful enterprises. Each survey would be about 80,000 words long. This project continued through the 1950s and 1960s; indeed, the last survey to be published, P J O Trist on *Suffolk*, did not appear until 1971.[110] As production costs increased, financial support for individual surveys was obtained from some county councils. The series did not have as wide a circulation as was originally expected and neither was there anything like the total coverage envisaged. Technical change in agriculture and the associated geographical change in farming systems and specialisms went ahead faster than the project could be executed and, increasingly, book form was not a suitable medium for the presentation of information about superior farming methods. These recent surveys remain, however, as a valuable source for the agricultural historian at a time of exceptionally rapid technical change in agriculture as do the more extensive series of prize reports sponsored by the Society in the mid-nineteenth century.

In 1948 the Research Committee recommended support of the straw disposal experiments at the Norfolk Agricultural Station to the extent of £250 and also gave funds for similar work at Rothamsted. Reports of animal production trials at this time produced useful information but had the limitation of giving insufficient information about cost. Restoration of land to agriculture after opencast mining operations was another concern of the Society at the time.

Perhaps the most significant research sponsored by the Society during the early 1950s concerned field beans. The background to this was the Society's connection with the Cambridge School of Agriculture which had continued to investigate lithium salts under the terms of the Hills Bequest. The Research Committee had reservations about the usefulness of this work and considered whether it was able to widen the scope of the trust arrangements. After some consideration and consultations with Sir Frank Engledow (Head of the Cambridge School of Agriculture) the work continued with particular orientation towards beans. These were a potentially important crop at that time as the most useful source of home produced protein for animal feeding, but where very little improvement in average yield had taken place since the 1890s. The Research Committee therefore resolved to widen the research supported by the Society and, after some discussion with the Finance Committee, was able to sponsor bean research in conjunction with NIAB to the extent of £500 per year for three years. These funds were welcomed by research centres as they allowed greater freedom in the planning of work than was possible with Government funding alone, and the grant was later extended so that by 1957 the Society had contributed over £4,000 to this project. This bean research sponsorship was a good example of the Society identifying an area where work needed to be done, where practical benefits could be expected to accrue, and where the work would act as a catalyst in encouraging a particular research line to be followed by others who could then bring more resources to bear upon it. Interestingly, the performance of field beans since the 1950s has not matched other crops such as cereals in terms of yield increase, and diseases such as chocolate spot can seriously reduce yields in particular years.[111] This indicates that work still needs to be done in this area, over 30 years after the Society's initiative.

Another sphere in which the Society encouraged progress at this time was in the development of agricultural machinery. At the suggestion of Lord Bledisloe a forage harvester competition took place in 1950, with substantial awards offered by the Society and a public demonstration near Oxford during the September of that year. In 1951 there was an open competition for potato harvesting machinery, and the Society also organised a number of original 'crop-drying for conservation' competitions at this time. Similar competitions and demonstrations were held throughout the decade.

When Professor J A Scott Watson was appointed to head the new advisory service in 1946, Dr E M Crowther, retiring Principal of Harper Adams College, was appointed Editor of the Society's *Journal*, a post he continued to occupy until his retirement at the age of 84 in 1960. He was succeeded by Dr D H

Robinson, who already had an association with the Society as Editor of the 13th revised edition of *Fream's* published in 1949. During this period the *Journal* did not undergo any marked change in form, with the established mixture of special articles, the *Farmer's Guide to Agricultural Research*, and the report of the annual show constituting its main elements.

The Society, in conjunction with the other national agricultural societies, continued to administer the NDA and NDD examinations, although these had been severely criticised by the Luxmore Committee on Agricultural Education to which the Society gave evidence in 1944. In 1955 Frank Russell, Secretary of the Small Pigkeepers' Council and wartime associate of Alec Hobson, was invited to become the Society's Education Officer to oversee the running of the examinations. He also played an important part in the production of the Society's *Journal* during his appointment. The Queen's Prize for the best candidate in the National Diploma in Agriculture Examination was instituted in 1954 to mark the occasion of Her Majesty the Queen's Presidency of the Society. Another educational award established by the Society was a medal

Fig. 6 National average yields of field beans 1885-1987 compared with wheat

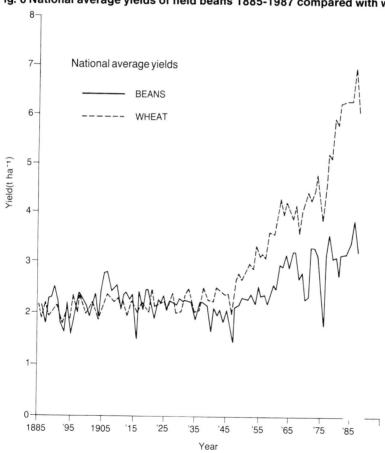

179

The Royal Show at Cambridge, 1951.

presented to the candidate securing the highest number of marks in the practical examination in agriculture then conducted by the Chartered Land Agents' Society. This was a supplement to the Talbot-Ponsonby prize for agriculture instituted in 1943 by Mr Arthur Talbot-Ponsonby, a past President of the Chartered Land Agents' Society and Chairman of the Society's Finance Committee.

A number of significant awards and distinctions were founded by the Society for various aspects of agriculture and land management during the post-war period. Under the revised Charter of 1953 provision was made for the election of not more than 50 Honorary Fellows who were to be people of eminence and distinction in the agricultural field. In 1954 the Society instituted a research medal for work of benefit to agriculture, which carried with it a monetary prize of 100 guineas to be offered annually, but not necessarily awarded. To mark his 90th birthday on 21 September 1957, Lord Bledisloe made a Deed of Gift of £3,000 for the award from time to time of a Gold Medal to a landowner 'having done outstanding service in encouraging (not necessarily on his own property), the application of science or technology to some branch of British Husbandry', the first recipient being the Earl of Iveagh the following year. The achievement

Fig. 7   The diffusion of T.T. milk production in England and Wales 1939-1962

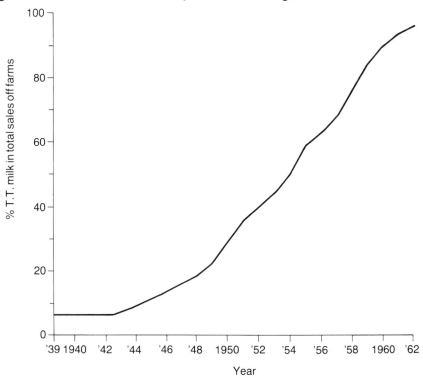

of full country-wide accreditation of dairy herds by the end of the 1950s was marked by the establishment of the Bledisloe Veterinary Award for persons who had made outstanding contributions to animal health. This was in place of the Inter-county Dairy Herd Trophy which the Society had awarded between 1946 and 1957. The first recipient of the revised award was, appropriately, Sir John Ritchie, Chief Veterinary Officer of the Ministry of Agriculture, for his work on the eradication of bovine tuberculosis.

THE CHARACTER OF THE POST-WAR SHOWS, 1947–1962

The buoyant character of the Lincoln Show in 1947 was repeated the following year at York which had 237,827 paid admissions. There was a further advance in implement entries – which, significantly, now equalled the livestock section in numbers – and a growing emphasis on agricultural science and rural economy was apparent in the showground. Visitors could see a much increased range of educational exhibits sponsored by such bodies as the Ministry of Agriculture, the Young Farmers' Clubs, Women's Institutes, Foresters, Rural Craftsmen, and the many organisations and occupations which made up English rural life. Despite severe traffic problems, the event was 'crowned with success', although an unwelcome sign of change was the number of beer bottles strewn about the showground. This led Sir Merrik Burrell to complain that it was hardly possible to walk around the showground for broken glass. At Shrewsbury the following year there was a diminished attendance – 186,678 – but a record number – 660 – of trade stands. Well-received new features included a tractor parade in the main ring on each day of the Show (apart from the first) and sheep carcase demonstrations jointly organised by the National Sheep Breeders' Association and the Ministries of Food and Agriculture. A further development was a dried grass competition initiated by the Society's Research Committee and carried out in conjunction with the NFU and the NAAS. The number of overseas visitors approached 1,000 with representatives from 31 separate countries, an indication of the increasing international character of both the Society and the Show which had been foreseen by Lord Bledisloe and which was later to expand still further.

The Oxford Show of 1950 was marred by heavy rain, but the view was taken that 'if we were horrified at the sight of a little mud on our boots, we would have no right to call ourselves an agricultural society'.[112] This is a significant observation, since the depth of mud in the avenues at Oxford was remembered throughout the following decade, and the possible recurrence of such adverse conditions led more and more people to favour a permanent showground. The Oxford Show was Sir Roland Burke's last as Honorary Director, and the occasion was marked by the award of the Society's Gold Medal to him at the showground. In addition, at the end-of-year Annual General Meeting he was presented with his portrait to commemorate the 20 years that he had completed in the position, a subscription having raised £1,364 to enable the Society to commission Sir Oswald Birley to execute the work. His successor, Michael Mason, who had acted as Assistant Show Director at Shrewsbury and Oxford, was thought to have 'got off to a flying start' at Cambridge the following year. Innovative prizes at the Cambridge Show included the Burke Trophy for the best new implement and awards for the best pair of dairy, dual purpose and beef cattle. The Trumpington site, which had been used by the Cambridgeshire Agricultural Society at the invitation of Francis W W Pemberton (later Sir Francis Pemberton) when he was President of that Society in 1949, was particularly notable for the good signposting of stands, and avenues laid out with grid references requiring, altogether, 28,000 separate letters. Another landmark of the Cambridge Show was that this was the first to be televised.[113]

At Newton Abbot the following year there were severe limitations on the showing of stock because of an outbreak of foot-and-mouth disease, and this was thought, in some quarters, to have robbed the show of its chief attraction. The Society was determined to provide alternative exhibits, and the University of Reading assisted in this by moving the entire Museum of English Rural Life to the showground at short notice. In the end, the event was described as a 'gallant recovery from adversity'. The show emphasised the reduction of

Sir Roland Burke. Portrait by Sir Oswald Birley presented to the sitter to commemorate his Honorary Show Directorship 1931–50.

agricultural production costs together with increased efficiency of operation. Particularly noted were the crowds around the Ministry's agricultural exhibits which were thought never to have been equalled in simplicity and utility.[114]

Shortly after Newton Abbot, Mason resigned as Honorary Show Director. Part of the reason for this was his belief that the Ministry of Agriculture should pay for its showground space, but, more particularly, it was related to his dissatisfaction with the division of authority between the Honorary Show Director and the Society's Secretary. The Council appointed a committee to investigate the dispute which, of course, it did not wish to receive too much publicity. The Selection and General Purposes Committee accepted Mason's resignation and recorded their full confidence in the Secretary while requesting that he delegate more authority to his recently appointed assistant, Carol Fellowes. At the Annual General Meeting of 1953 Mason complained about the lack of attention given to the reasons for his resignation in that it had, he claimed, given rise to speculation that he had committed some outrage or offence. He therefore explained that in the spring he had told the late Chairman of the Selection Committee (Sir Archibald Weigall) that 'a certain paid servant of the Society would have to go'. He acceded to the request that the matter

183

should be left until after the Newton Abbot event and, when he did not get the support of the Society's Committee, he resigned. After this, the Society brought in a rule that tenure of the Honorary Show Directorship should normally be limited to five years.

Mason was succeeded as Honorary Show Director by Lt Col Guy Blewitt (between 1953 and 1955) and then by W A 'Billy' Benson who continued in this capacity until 1962. Gales at the Blackpool Show in 1953 caused considerable damage to the show structures and one of the chief memories of Blackpool was 'of wind interspersed with sharp, squally showers'. The show was sited on a former rubbish tip which had been grassed over. Some impression of the enormous effort needed to get the expanded shows of the early 1950s into operation can be gauged by the following statistics: at Blackpool, 30,000 railway sleepers had to be laid down, 8 miles of electric cable put into position together with 9 miles of mains and services, 20,000 post-holes dug or mechanically bored, and 1,100 tons of timber assembled for pavilions and shedding to be covered by 120,000 square yards of canvas.[115]

The return to Windsor in 1954 took place in the week that food rationing ended. The Show itself was considered to be one of the best planned ever, although the level of attendance was thought surprisingly low. Despite this, traffic was still a problem, and there was also considerable concern about managing the all-time record entry of livestock. Protests were voiced at the poor accommodation provided for the attendant stockmen. After a heavy thunderstorm flooded the livestock marquee the stockhands had to sleep in very damp conditions. This led to criticisms that the Society was oblivious to such problems which had been subject to continuous complaints since the Show's resumption in 1947.

In 1954, the Society entered into an agreement with the Dale Electric Company to hire its own generating equipment to reduce the costs of the electricity required for the shows.[116] The site at Nottingham the following year was the largest so far – 166 acres – and the show was generally well received despite the difficulty of walking on uneven ground. The show achieved a new post-war record for the first day's gate and the Nottingham Show 'occupied an especially pleasant niche in the memories of the regular Royal fans'. The Newcastle Show in 1956 presented particular difficulties of arrangement on the Town Moor site, and the leading pavilions had to be positioned at the end of the main ring instead of facing the grandstand. Gales before the show caused damage amounting to some £10,000 but its all-time attendance record of 242,548 paid admissions was thought by some to 'display the advantages of taking the Royal to the people'. There was some showground gossip of the possible withdrawal of tractor and implement manufacturers and of other leading exhibitors from the 1957 and 1958 shows. There were also complaints from exhibitors about the way pitches had been allocated and the fact that

Her Majesty The Queen inspecting the Burke Dairy Trophy winners at Windsor, 1954.

business was not commensurate with the effort and expenditure incurred. The record Newcastle attendance was partly accounted for by the Society being able to draw upon support from north of the Border to the considerable detriment of the Royal Highland Society whose show in that year had a deficit of over £25,000.

The 1957 Show was held at Norwich, on the newly established permanent Royal Norfolk Costessey Showground. Attendance slumped to 135,621, fulfilling earlier warnings that the Society could no longer count on good attendance at peripheral locations badly served by road communications. Although the livestock entries at Norwich of 3,834 were an advance on those of the previous year, the downward trend in attendance was repeated both at Bristol in 1958 when only 87,727 admissions were recorded and at Oxford in 1959, where the Show was held at Kidlington Aerodrome and sun and extreme heat replaced the rain of the earlier visit.

The declining gates at Norwich and Bristol, financial losses on all of the post-war shows after York, and the growing disaffection of many exhibitors, led to a rising chorus of criticism of the Royal Shows towards the end of the 1950s and at the conclusion of his Presidency in 1957, the Duke of Edinburgh sent a

185

memorandum to Council urging a rethink on the show and the Society's policy and future direction. On the evidence of the Bristol experience the President of the Agricultural Engineers' Association observed that the character of the Royal Show would have to change although to many observers the argument was not so clearcut: as Robert Trow-Smith later recalled, much of the press criticism of the time was destructive without any very positive alternatives being advanced by the show's detractors.[117] A persistent demand, partly prompted by the attention that the Ministry's educational exhibits received, was that the show should be more instructive, and reports of the Newton Abbot event called for machinery demonstrations which had established a recognised place at continental shows. The Newton Abbot site, one of the most scenic of the post-war sequence of peripatetic shows, presented considerable difficulties with regard to size and layout, and it was gradually realised that the choice for the Royal Shows lay increasingly between 'utilitarian airfields' on the one hand and picturesque (but otherwise unsuitable) grounds on the other.[118]

The decision of the Yorkshire Agricultural Society to 'go permanent' – their showground at Harrogate opened in 1951 – was received with considerable interest for it represented a trend seen as likely to influence the whole organisation of agricultural shows. Indeed, in 1957 the opening day's attendance at the Great Yorkshire was double that achieved by the Royal at Norwich and, whereas the Royal events were making increasing deficits, profits at Harrogate in the order of £50,000 were realised. As was observed in the *Farmer and Stockbreeder*, Alec Hobson, who was present at the Harrogate event in 1957, 'must have gone back to London with copious notes for his Council to digest'.[119]

Further, it was observed that permanent sites gave scope for demonstrations that could not be mounted under the peripatetic system. The reason advanced by the Society for the poor attendance at Bristol was that the weather had kept people away, but this was not found to be very plausible when scrutinised: it was by no means as bad as on several previous occasions, and in addition it was felt that the publicity had been more than adequate. Although the Society was always at pains not to put much stress on 'the gate', reports of low turnout tended to have a cumulative effect in reducing attendance. It was also pointed out that the cost of visiting the show for the urban population (which the Society hoped at least in part to attract) was far too high in relation to what was provided for the non-agricultural visitor. There was intense criticism of the fact that at Bristol there were no reduced admission charges for those who could only go late in the day after work and, in any event, very little in the way of ring attractions or general interest for the afternoon and early evening visitor. Certainly the 'post-show inquest' in the farming press revealed the feeling that the Society was complacent and that 'the humdrum outlook of the show authorities was peaceful and undisturbed'.[120]

Partly as a response to these criticisms the last three shows of the pre-Stoneleigh sequence developed some new features, particularly associated with

The return to Cambridge, 1960.

the demonstration area first established at Cambridge in 1960. This concept developed out of conversations at the 1959 show between Alec Hobson, Francis Pemberton, John Perrin (the Eastern Regional Controller of the Ministry of Agriculture), and Peter Buckler (then Chief Agricultural Advisor to the firm of R Silcock and Sons). These led to the establishment of the demonstration area of about six acres in 1960. This featured slatted floors for stock and 'haleage' for storing winter fodder as an alternative to hay and silage. Its organisation owed much to ideas seen at the Norwegian Show at Olso which had been visited by Peter Buckler.[121] There was also a display of irrigation equipment which was demonstrated periodically throughout the show period so that visitors could inspect and see various systems and compare alternatives rather than have to search out manufacturers' stands scattered over the showground.

Press comment on this development was extremely supportive and the concept was well received although the paid 'gate' at the 1960 Cambridge Show was 91,892, very similar to the disappointing figures realised at Bristol (87,729) and Oxford (94,341) and 39,441 less than the total recorded at the previous Cambridge event in 1951. Nevertheless commentators recorded that there was 'a distinct, if modest, departure from tradition' and that the 'wind of change' was, 'rustling the time honoured canvas'. Of the 'skilfully contrived demonstrations' it was said that:

It would be hard to think that the Royal's introduction of this practical farming into its show would have got off to a more auspicious start than in the imaginative

187

Fig. 8 Membership of Royal Agricultural Society of England 1939-1962

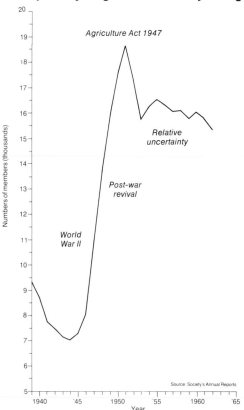

and eminently helpful display here at Trumpington.[122]

The Royal Show was again held at Trumpington in 1961 in order to reduce expenditure, and the demonstration area was expanded to 16 acres. This again featured slatted floors with the emphasis on cows on slats, displays of mechanised bale-handling equipment, and an exhibit by the Milk Marketing Board which illustrated concepts of animal breeding by means of 'Ferdy', an electronic simulation of genetics, together with the display of two bulls that had been progeny-tested. Other demonstrations included liquid manure disposal by gun spraying (to the discomfort of some of the passengers on the adjacent railway line), commercial rabbit production, beef and sheep recording, potato silage making and the laying of farm roads and yards with ready-mix concrete.

Attendance at Cambridge in 1961 – 93,764 – showed a modest increase over the previous year. This was encouraging to those who supported a permanent site, as there was a view that two years on the same ground would cause attendance to diminish. Of the extended demonstration zone, Robert Trow-Smith, noting that at 'no time on the first three days, when the serious man does his serious looking, were the demonstration site rails not lined two or three deep', commented that:

188

Never, one supposes, had more questions, and more penetrating questions, been asked at any agricultural gathering than were posed at the demonstration area of the Cambridge Royal Show. The virtues of these 16 acres were two-fold: the newest techniques were shown without frills or puffery; no one tried to sell anyone anything. One just stood and talked and how stimulating and productive of ideas that was![123]

At the Newcastle Show of 1962, which had a radial layout as an experiment, a 10 acre demonstration area featured aspects of livestock improvement, including intensive fat lamb and intensive cereal-fed beef production developed from work carried out by the Rowett Institute. Two examples of sheep improvement were Mr Oscar Colburn's 'Colbred' combinations of Clun Forest, Border Leicester, Dorset Horned, and Friesland Sheep and Cockle Park's more conventional Clun Forest flock which had been used in a long-term breeding experiment to improve commercial performance in sheep. Cockle Park, King's College, Newcastle, experimental station, also demonstrated cross-bred poultry, BOCM Ltd showed beef performance testing, the Pig Industry Development Authority demonstrated performance and progeny testing of pigs and its commercial application with an emphasis on carcase and meat quality, while the intensive fat lamb production feature showed forward creep grazing based on a system developed by King's College, Newcastle, School of Agriculture.[124]

The Newcastle Show of 1962 is, however, most remembered as 'the nine days' wonder' of reconstruction after 80 mph gales razed most of the trade stands to the ground and ripped nearly all the canvas to shreds. This followed earlier damage from gales in February, the total cost of the devastation amounting to some £120,000. It was abundant testimony to the 'superhuman effort' of the Honorary Show Director, Billy Benson, his Deputy Francis Pemberton, the 1,500–2,000 men who worked under their direction to repair the damage, and the many offers of help which poured in, that the show was able to take place at all. The four day attendance was 187,124, confirming the large measure of support that the Society had always enjoyed at the Town Moor location despite the difficulty of preparation and further dismal weather during the show week.

The three Royal Shows held between 1960 and 1962 therefore represented a transition away from the social nature of the event as it had been when largely dominated by the stock-judging and static machinery displays to a more purposeful and commercial agricultural exposition. The way in which these pioneering demonstration areas caught the imagination of the show visitors owed much to the enthusiasm and energy of the Director of Demonstrations, Peter Buckler; his firm's Chairman, Richard Silcock, also gave assistance and financial help to the demonstration concept and, indeed, over 50 other firms helped in staging the first Cambridge demonstrations. This was the beginning of the sponsorship and commercial involvement which has more recently contributed so much to the success of the National Agricultural Centre concept

Devastation of the Newcastle showground, 1962.

and it is interesting to note that before 1960 the RASE had eschewed any commercial sponsorship of its activities.

THE ROUTE TO A PERMANENT SHOWGROUND

The demonstrations initiated at Cambridge were a belated response to a feeling that had been evident in the mid-1940s that the post-war shows ought to be more practical and useful in their character than the majority of those of the inter-war years, and that the non-farming public should also be encouraged to participate. The 'War Ags' had pioneered agricultural demonstrations which came to be seen as a necessary part of the shows of the future, and the war itself encouraged a much increased pace of agricultural change. In the introduction to D H Robinson's *The New Farming* (1938) the author commented on the 'considerable lag' – up to ten years – between the discovery of a new principle and its employment on the farm but by 1951, in the third edition of the work, the lag was 'much shorter'.[125] The experience of wartime farming, it was thought, would leave the taste for 'something stronger, something more instructive' than the amusement and 'social nature' of the pre-war shows. There were also suggestions that a permanent site for the Royal Showground should be seriously considered, and some adverse comment was made about the decision to go to Lincoln for the first post-war show rather than near a centre of urban population.

The very large attendances at the first two post-war shows reflected partly the increased national interest in agriculture brought about by recognition of the wartime contribution of the rural community and also the desire for a little 'jollification' (as Sir Roland Burke put it), but the problems of traffic, parking, and catering raised the question as to whether the peripatetic system could continue without drastic revision. While there was widespread feeling that permanent buildings would alter the particular character and atmosphere that surrounded the Royal Show, there was also the possibility that increased ease of transport might outweigh the disadvantage of losing local contacts.

Despite rising costs the York Show of 1948 made a profit for the Society of approaching £50,000. This deflected some of the criticisms and there was optimism at this time that profits from the shows could be used to sponsor and support agricultural research. However, a serious difficulty that soon became apparent was the sheer problem of obtaining sites that were sufficiently large and well-appointed to house the show adequately. Two suggestions were put forward late in 1948. One, from Col Harry Cator, was that the Royal Show should be held on a permanent site. This found almost no support and Cator's motive was probably to stop speculation rather than to endorse the idea of permanency. The second suggestion, from Lord Hazelrigg, was that the Society should consider the advisability of purchasing grounds, possibly in three different parts of the country such as the north, midlands, and south, to be used in addition to those places where the Society knew it could get suitable sites. Caution was urged by Lord Bledisloe who stressed the experience of the Park Royal 'fiasco'.[126] The question was floated in the Society's *Quarterly Review* for February 1949 and was given added impetus by the decision of the Yorkshire Agricultural Society to establish their permanent site at Harrogate. Sir John Dunnington-Jefferson (the Honorary Director of the Great Yorkshire) contacted Sir Roland Burke to consider whether the Harrogate site could be one of three permanent grounds suggested by Lord Hazelrigg. There was however at the time a view in Council that the various press criticisms which had been levelled against the Royal showgrounds, such as inadequate accommodation for stockmen, lack of lavatories, and insufficient and confusing signposts were part of a campaign in support of a permanent showground rather than substantive items needing attention, and a strong commitment to the peripatetic system remained among many Council members.

In July 1950 Christopher York and Anthony Hurd contacted Alec Hobson to inform him of their wish to raise the following item at the next meeting of Council:

That a special committee be set up to consider the provision of permanent sites for the Royal Show and to report on all the factors including the cost of moving the show if it remained peripatetic; such report to form the basis for a full discussion by the Council of this subject.[127]

This suggestion did not gain support, but it was noted that the Policy Committee, which had been instituted in 1948 to consider the future of the Society's activities, would make recommendations about the show which would be taken account of in due course. In 1950 the Finance Committee proposed that the Secretary should prepare a report on the possible effects if the migratory system for the Royal Show were dropped in favour of either one or several permanent sites. The following year two reports were circulated on the future of the Royal Show, one written by Alec Hobson and the second produced independently by Sir Roland Burke.

Hobson's report reviewed the reasons which had been urged upon the Society for a permanent site, and considered in detail the relative costs of a fixed site compared with moving the show each year. In conclusion, he said that while he was now as convinced that the peripatetic system should be continued as he had been in favour of a permanent site before he 'saw things from the inside', he also appreciated that the costs of dismantling, transporting, and re-erecting the modern Royal Show had become so considerable that some modification of the existing system might be forced upon the Society in the future. The holding of the show on the same site for possibly two successive years could make biannual savings of up to £50,000. The dilemma was that while the peripatetic system in its present form caused great difficulties because of the sheer size of the operation it continued to be considered essential to the future of the Society and maintenance of its character. Another possibility, that of holding the show less frequently than annually, was not considered to be attractive to either the Society or its exhibitors. Sir Roland Burke's report also rejected a permanent site.

This thinking was reflected in 1952 when the Secretary was asked about the desirability of a permanent site at the University of Reading Farming Club and he maintained that the advantages were not at all clear. Farm workers and urban dwellers, it was thought, would never go to the Royal Show if held in a central place: a compromise might be a fixed pattern where perhaps ten sites could be visited in turn. This would reflect the national character of the Society's work and also maintain local enthusiasm.

A possible way of operating such a system was suggested by F Neville Gascoigne in 1954.[128] He envisaged that the Royal could go round the country visiting the showgrounds of permanently sited regional societies, although it was recognised that this carried with it the danger of a loss of identity. While such a plan had a number of adherents, the impractical nature of the idea became more apparent with closer scrutiny. The permanent showgrounds which were then becoming established by regional societies would only be able to take a much reduced Royal event and they would not want to make special adaptations to their grounds for a Royal Show which would not recur on much less than a ten year cycle.

Blackpool in 1953 illustrated the arguments on both sides of the debate for while it 'did wonders in cementing town and country relations', gales wrecked some of the marquees, and livestock exhibitors complained of the high transport costs associated with a peripheral location. The lack of enthusiasm for a permanent site shown by the reception of the reports prepared by Alec Hobson and Sir Roland Burke did not close the internal discussion – a minority of Council members continued to voice alarm about the problems of a peripatetic show, not least from the financial viewpoint. Sir John Dunnington-Jefferson, then Chairman of the Finance Committee, pointed out that the average loss of the four shows held 1949–52 inclusive was £6,500 per show.[129] This was a marked turn-around from the favourable financial results of the first two shows after the war, especially as these losses took into account support by local funds. These averaged £8,500, making the real losses in the order of £15,000 a year. Show losses were met by drawing on the Society's ordinary account and this inhibited the Society's other potential activities.

At this time Christopher York drew attention to the proposal to visit Norwich in 1957 and expressed grave doubts as to the advisability of taking the show to a location so close to the coast. The attendant problem of access, he claimed, would almost certainly give rise to a substantial financial liability. This generated considerable debate, particularly as the Policy Committee had recently reaffirmed the peripatetic system. Harry Cator, the Chairman of that Committee, thought that, in the longer term, the Society would make a grave mistake if the system of migratory shows was abandoned, as the 'glamour factor' would be lost and show finances would consequently deteriorate still further.[130] The alternative view was that the holding of shows at outlying districts cut it off from the great majority of the Society's members and that to support Norwich as a suitable show location was, according to Christopher York, to 'bury one's head in the sand'. A greater service would be provided if the show were kept within a reasonable circuit in 'the central oblong of England'. When Blackpool continued the trend of show losses there was a suggestion that income from the membership account could be used to defray the deficits, given that the show, rather than the Society's other activities, was the chief attraction for most of the members. Lord Bledisloe suggested that the show be held only near large centres of industrial population; Lord Hudson maintained that the profits from the York and Lincoln shows could be used to produce income to subsidise these later shows. It was too early at that time, he held, to determine whether the trend of loss-making post-war shows would be continued.

Early in 1955 a motion was moved by Mr Douglas J Bird that a committee be appointed to produce a report on the advisability or otherwise of Council acquiring a site which, over a period of years, could be developed for use as a

Royal Showground every four to five years and a memorandum was circulated among Council members by the supporters of this idea to facilitate discussion. This looked to the development of central showgrounds because of the increasing costs associated with the transport of materials and their erection at different sites each year. Instead, a site could be developed with permanent roads and services. It would be used to store materials and equipment during intervening years. Another consideration was that machinery trials and new implement tests could be better carried out at a 'field headquarters worthy of our great Society'. This led to another full discussion where it was recognised that the majority of the Council was still committed to the peripatetic system even though it was increasingly difficult to visit the more out of the way places. It was thought that permanent sites which were not continually in use would pose problems because of the possible deterioration of the roads and other facilities, while the savings on storage of show materials would be far outweighed by the cost of transporting these materials to different show sites. Although some urged the investigation of the possibility of using the county showgrounds, the conclusion was that this would not work. What the discussion did advance, however, was the notion of a 'field headquarters' for the Society which, as Christopher York pointed out, several people were beginning to have in mind.[131]

The Policy Committee considered these suggestions further in 1955 and early the following year the Selection and General Purposes Committee formed a sub-committee to consider the possibility of acquiring some 300 acres for a showground and car park near to London and to look at the various requirements which would result from such a development. The report of this sub-committee was considered late in the year when it was resolved:

> That, in the near future, the time may come when the Society will have to change its migratory show policy to one based on a permanent showground and that appropriate steps be taken to consider the implication of such a change with special reference to finance and possible venues for a site[132]

At this juncture Col Cator asked to be relieved of the Chairmanship of the sub-committee, Lt Col Walter Burrell taking over at the Selection Committee's invitation. The Council considered an amendment moved by Sir John Dunnington-Jefferson that 'in the near future' be deleted and 'has' substituted for 'may' and that the word 'immediately' be inserted after the work 'taken'. This was particularly prompted by the deteriorating financial situation of the show because, despite the record attendance at Newcastle that year, there had still been a considerable financial loss and the potential deficit at Norwich looked to be in the order of anything from £11,000 to £20,000. Had the amendment been accepted it would have committed the Society to a permanent show site there and then. The Council was not yet ready for this, but the financial implications of the peripatetic system were never more baldly stated. The fear of many Council members was – with the Park Royal experience still being cited – that a permanent site could lead to an even more acute financial difficulty for the Society.

One suggestion put forward at this point was that there should be a referendum of members to resolve the impasse. The sub-committee approached the problem by examining closely the structure of show costs over the past ten years to establish a yard-stick of expenditure on which to base consideration of future policy. It would also enable them to evaluate the various suggestions that had been made such as holding the show on the same site for two consecutive years or, alternatively, to obtain a permanent showground.

Events began to gather pace in 1957, especially after the final result of the Newcastle meeting revealed a loss of £12,931. This was more than had been forecast and, as Lord Cornwallis observed, the deficit 'was really rather frightening' given the record attendance at that particular venue.[133] A sense of urgency was apparent to both Sir John Dunnington-Jefferson and Christopher York, who said that the Council as a whole did not see this and was proceeding in a far too leisurely manner. Christopher York therefore put a further motion at the Council meeting held during the Norwich Show week asking that the Policy Sub-Committee be requested to present its report, or an interim statement, at the October meeting of the Council. The first recommendation of the Show Working Party was that certain economies could be made to achieve savings at Bristol and Oxford, to which the Society was already committed for 1958 and 1959. There was also the suggestion that if two shows could be held on the same site for 1960 and 1961, with possibly another two shows on another site in 1962/3, the Royal Show could continue in its present form until 1964, that period giving the Society the necessary time to assess whether the change to a permanent site was desirable and feasible. The same Cambridge site that had been used in 1951 was available for 1960 and 1961, if required. Immediate savings could be achieved thereby as the cost of transporting materials from Nottingham to Newcastle had been £6,000 and from Newcastle to Norwich £8,000.

The final account of the Norwich Show revealed a loss of over £20,000. This led Harry Cator, who had previously been in favour of maintaining the peripatetic system, to suggest that immediate steps be taken to establish a show on a permanent site and his views were communicated to the Working Party. This presented its report to Council at a special meeting held on 23 October 1958. The decision was made to search for a place, preferably in the centre of England, and well served by road communications, which would act as a permanent site. However, such a site would still not preclude visits to other parts of the country which could be supported by funds built up from profitable shows at the central location. Part of the discussion surrounded the nature of the show itself and the old consideration of the importance of 'gate'. Was the show mainly interested in the professional agriculturist, it was asked, or was it a wider public entertainment? Non-professional agriculturists had always been important in attracting an adequate 'gate', yet this could conflict with the fundamental rationale of the show venture. There was still the possibility, as Christopher York pointed out, that a smaller, more compact, professional show could continue to rotate and serve the agricultural community while maintaining a sound financial footing, and a smaller show of this type would facilitate site selection. Other possibilities included the suggestion, particularly advocated by Willy Freund, of a permanent showground with some adjacent national trials ground.

The discussion of this report demonstrates a great variety of thinking within the Society at this time, some of it, it has to be said, far from clearcut. A full commitment to the concept of a permanent site was still lacking. Sir John Dunnington-Jefferson pointed out that the objective of permanence, which he favoured, was to give a much better service to members than was possible on temporary showgrounds in addition to meeting the very real need to reduce costs. If this was the case the recommendations which had so far been made, he said, would not meet either of those objectives. Despite the range of opinion within the Society at the time the feeling gradually swung towards a permanent site and it was resolved to enter into discussion with the Agricultural Engineers' Association, MAFF and NFU and issue a press statement. The report was circulated to members asking for observations and comments to be given to elected members of the Council, with a further special meeting to be convened to inform members of the decisions. By May 1959 Sir Walter Burrell reported that 61 letters had been received by members of the Council of which 37 favoured a permanent showground. Four were against departure from the existing show system, while the remainder offered various suggestions which the Council were reviewing. Discussion between the stockbreeders, exhibitors, machinery manufacturers and with the Ministry indicated a consensus opinion that there should be a permanent showground in the Midlands.

On 27 July 1959 a special meeting of Council was convened to consider future show policy and in particular two specific recommendations:

1 That the Society should acquire a permanent base on which to stage the Royal Show.
2 That the site for a permanent base for the Royal Show should be acquired in an area thirty miles north of London.

The second recommendation was not in accordance with that of the Show Policy Committee, which had preferred a Midlands location. Points in favour of London included the greater likelihood of achieving a large 'gate', ease of access for overseas as well as home visitors, and the possibility of attracting other agricultural organisations and events to a site near London. An additional argument was that a showground in this location would not infringe the territories of other regional or county societies. Sir Walter Burrell urged the adoption of a Midland rather than a London location. John Bourne, looking to the future, envisaged a much wider range of show attractions, permanent buildings on the ground, and a high standard of accommodation. In support of Sir Walter's amendment, Lord Hazelrigg pointed out that London had never been a very satisfactory site for the Royal and that, whereas agriculturists might visit London in the winter, as they did for the Smithfield Show, they were much less likely to do so in July. Against this, Christopher York voiced the opinion that a Midlands location would mean the Royal Show tending to degenerate into just another large regional show: the prestige of the Royal decreed that it should be in easy reach of the capital. It was certainly wrong, he maintained, to attach any importance to the experience of Park Royal over 50 years previously. On a vote the Burrell amendment in favour of a Midlands location was carried by 48 votes to 18.

Having adopted the principle of the permanent showground, the search was then on to find a permanent site. The location favoured by some of the 'pro-London' group had been for a situation on the A1 at Bignells Corner in Hertfordshire, but with the decision to have a Midland-based Royal, other options had to be considered. Nottingham was considered: it met the criteria of a suitable physical site, a central location with good road communications and the benefit of particularly supportive local and county authorities. Lincoln and Oxford had also been advocated at various times during the 1950s as providing the requirements for a suitable base for the Royal. An ex-factory site in Staffordshire also had its advocates. Most attention was initially given to Wroxall Abbey in Warwickshire, but negotiations broke down at the time of the Cambridge Show in 1960. Shortly after that, Lord Leigh suggested that his Home Farm at Stoneleigh, between Coventry and Leamington, could meet the Society's need and this site was inspected at the end of August. Sir Walter Burrell, commending the site and location to the Council, stressed its good road communications, adequate rail service, and the reasonable hotel accommodation in the vicinity. The showground could be located on flat land in a ring contour which would facilitate drainage.[134]

At a meeting on 11 October 1960 between Sir Walter Burrell and Lord Leigh and his agent, basic terms were agreed in outline. These were for the Society to lease about 460 acres and four cottages for a period of seven years at a rental of £4,000 per annum – a figure which represented fair agricultural rent plus loss of amenity to the owner and any special value which there might be in the show site. The terms of the agreement proposed were that after two shows – 1963 and 1964 – the Society and Lord Leigh could decide whether they wanted to negotiate a further lease at a rental which would then have to be agreed. If either party did not want to do this, then the lease would end in December 1967 which gave the Society three years in which to look for an alternative. If both

" PSST—LOVELY PERMANENT SITES TO LET—BY TENDER ! "

The search for a permanent site, as depicted by 'Chrys' in 1960.

parties wanted to continue, then a long lease could be negotiated and the Society could embark on expenditure on its permanent base. This arrangement had the clear advantage of giving the Midland site a fair trial without irrevocable commitment and although there was unease expressed in Council about the leasehold terms the decision to proceed along the lines suggested was agreed. Thus after years of indecision the Society had a permanent site by the end of 1960, at least for an experimental seven-year period.

'A GREAT NEW CONCEPT'

To some senior members of the Society, the debate on the permanent site was part of a larger question of the role of the RASE and at a meeting of the General Purposes Committee 27 January' 1960, Christopher York moved that a sub-committee be established to examine the issues and to discover the extent to which the Society was fulfilling its purpose. In support of this motion Christopher York had circulated a memorandum which suggested that each section of the industry should be examined in turn to discover what services were required and what organisation – RASE , MAFF, NFU etc – was best fitted to meet the needs identified. The sub-committee should consider what type of machinery was necessary to fulfil those functions seen to be particularly within the province of the RASE. Two other memoranda were also circulated at this time. Sir Walter Burrell urged that other interested bodies such as the NFU, CLA, and NUAW as well as trade exhibitors' organisations should be represented on the Society's Council. This would lead to a change in the Society's constitution with the number of nominated members of the Council being increased from the then permitted maximum of ten. It was also suggested that an advisory committee might be established to seek out ideas and advertise the fact that the Royal wished to provide what the agricultural industry as a whole required. A memorandum from the Secretary pointed to a number of issues concerning the future of the show, particularly the audience to which it was expected to appeal and the degree to which the Society should have demonstrations on or close to the show site, some of which might well be held at other times of the year than during the show week itself. Hobson also asked whether it was desirable to erect exhibition halls where selected exhibits could be shown at any time of the year, and which might well be used by other representative bodies. The show itself, he thought, should be more than just a 'super' county show and be established in a category by itself. This would require the collaboration of other powerful and representative bodies capable of using the show to pursue their own objectives. The acquisition of a permanent site and an extension of the scope of the RASE's activities would necessitate a widening of the composition of the Council, as also envisaged by Sir Walter Burrell, and in particular that part of it especially concerned with the functioning of the show.

After some discussion of Christopher York's proposal and the memoranda which had been circulated, a 'Fact-Finding Committee' was appointed under the terms suggested consisting of Christopher York (Convener), John Bourne, Sir Walter Burrell, Willy Freund, Clyde Higgs, Francis Pemberton, Frank Sykes and Alec Hobson, with power to co-opt.

The Fact-Finding Committee proceeded by distributing a questionnaire to members of the Society with the July 1960 issue of the *RASE Review*. The Committee held a number of meetings throughout the country and the Graham Cherry Organisation provided assistance as the full burden of the work could not be placed on the Society's own staff. In the course of its investigations, the Committee interviewed 60 expert witnesses and analysed over 2,000 sets of replies which had been received from questionnaires – a very good response which indicated the degree of interest in the future development of the Society among many of its members.

The 64 page report, with extensive appendices, was available for members of the Council before the Cambridge Show of 1961 and was considered by the General Purposes Committee that September. Its chief recommendations were not made known to the general body of members, however, until as late as 1965 when they were outlined in the *RASE Review*. Even at that time, as commentators on the Society's affairs have pointed out, the concept of the permanent agricultural centre was only just finding acceptance, and the proposals were prefaced with the statement in bold type that 'it should also be emphasised that the recommendations in the report have not necessarily been accepted as Society's policy. Indeed, some are controversial'.[135]

Because the Fact-Finding Committee's Report is so influential regarding the later development of the RASE it is essential to consider its methodology and findings in some detail. The evidence that the Committee had accumulated revealed that the main strength of the Society was perceived as its being above sectional interests and that its particular roles were to provide leadership and education in the practical, economic and scientific problems of the industry and to lead opinion through its educational work, demonstrations, publications, and the co-ordination of interests. The main criticism which emerged was that the Royal had failed to provide the leadership expected and had not appreciated quickly enough the rapid strides in agriculture since 1945. The Committee considered that at a permanent base, the Society could provide a range of services for the agricultural industry, greatly extending its usefulness, and in particular could meet needs not provided by other organisations, especially in the field of demonstrations, exhibitions and experiments.

As far as the annual show was concerned, the greatest problem identified from the assembled evidence concerned the area of livestock, but the central thrust of the report was that the permanent base, to which at that stage the Society was committed, should exist as more than just a place to hold a show. 'A Great New Concept' emerged from the Committee's enquiry: that the permanent base of the RASE should evolve into 'The Agricultural Centre of England'. This would require resources beyond its existing capability but the Committee was confident that these would be forthcoming. It was no longer feasible, it was maintained, for the Society to cater primarily for the farmer or breeder who followed tradition and outdated methods; rather it had to assist agriculture to grapple with the problem of economic production in an increasingly competitive world, recognising that science dominated agriculture as it did most other industries. The Committee concluded that the Society must immediately take up the challenge 'or die of atrophy'.

Following logically from this view was the idea that from the outset the permanent site should be designated an agricultural centre which would demonstrate all that is best in agricultural practice, rather than an annual showground. The agricultural centre would continuously reflect new ideas and be visited by all progressive landowners, farmers, manufacturers and traders so that they could keep up-to-date. There would be close and continuous liaison with research and development institutions, marketing boards, and any representative body capable of contributing ideas and techniques. There would be demonstrations within the showground during the period of the annual show, and also on the periphery of the site on a year-round basis. A farm buildings centre was suggested, together with long term forestry and woodland areas, management centres, and performance- and progeny-testing stations.

Alec Hobson, Secretary 1946–61.

Further recommendations dealt with the machinery and equipment aspects of the annual show, proposing the separation of professional equipment and every-day household wants; the updating of the amenities and services including the need for good support roads, convenient car parks – incorporating a caravan park – and club facilities for members. Events would continue within the show ring, with the entertainment factor not ruled out by the envisaged new developments.

The General Purposes Committee approved the report in principle in 1961. This meant that a framework was then adopted to which Council could work, but that individual recommendations would have to go before the appropriate committees. This was accepted by the Council, although considerable doubts were expressed, particularly as to whether the concept was within the Society's financial resources and whether it could be realised on a leasehold site.

At the end of 1961 Alec Hobson retired as the Society's Secretary because of ill-health, after 15 years of meticulous and dedicated service. He had first attended the Royal Show at Cardiff in 1919 and had only missed two shows, because of illness, ever since. As he explained at the Annual General Meeting when he was presented with a desk and chair together with a cheque in recognition of his service to the Society:

> The job of a Secretary was really quite an easy one ... in the case of the Royal, for example, the Chairmen of the Committees were always so clear and so concise in their summing up of situations, that the preparation of minutes was child's play.

201

At the Royal Show, exhibitors were always delighted with their allocations of stand space; they didn't mind a bit not being in the middle of the grand ring, and of course they enjoyed themselves immensely working in co-operation with the trade unions; they never asked for too many tickets! As for members and Governors, they were in a class by themselves; they never complained – well hardly ever; they didn't mind walking from the back row of the car park about a mile from the showground; they were always delighted with the catering regarding it as one of the outstanding features of the show – the sumptuous meals, hot soup, the quiet efficiency of the waitresses and so on! Members of the Council and Stewards, were also most considerate. They never asked for permission to bring their cars onto the showground. They were most considerate about that. And of course the appreciation of the stockmen was most noteworthy. They liked their shower baths and their accommodation – they might sometimes complain because of water being rather too hot! Generally therefore, a Show Secretary's job is quite simple. Instead of being a task, as some people might think it, it was an enjoyable experience ...

As his son John Hobson recalls, the Royal was Alec Hobson's life.[136]

In Alec Hobson's place as Secretary, the Society appointed Mr R R Meyric Hughes, who was Deputy Secretary of the County Councils' Association. Tragically, however, Meyric Hughes died suddenly at the Society's London Headquarters in February 1962, only one month after taking up the appointment. All who came in contact with him during that brief time formed a very high appreciation of his ability and enthusiasm. For the rest of 1962, Paul

Fig. 9
The growth in numbers of five agricultural innovations in England and Wales 1937-1962

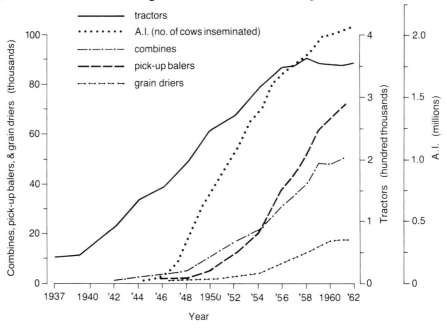

Osborn, the Deputy Secretary (who had succeeded Carol Fellowes in 1959) was the Society's chief administrator.

The 1950s were a time of unprecedented progress in English agriculture when there was rapid adoption of a range of innovations in farming systems. The data in figure 9 presented at a conference on the diffusion of agricultural innovation in 1963, illustrates this with respect to five specific areas.[137] In many respects the Society had been left behind in this process of change and had not been at the forefront of agricultural affairs during what can now rightly be viewed as the beginning of a new – or perhaps the only – 'agricultural revolution', as was recognised in the evidence gathered by the Fact-Finding Committee. The National Agricultural Centre concept was the way in which a number of senior members of the Society thought that the RASE could again place itself at the head of agricultural progress, particularly in the technical and communications domain, and it is how that concept became translated into reality to which we now must turn.

The first news conference at Stoneleigh. Francis Pemberton addressing the press in a farm building on the Stoneleigh estate.

PART IV:
THE SOCIETY AT STONELEIGH:
THE FIRST TWENTY-FIVE YEARS

'Those who had the early vision would have been, or are, immensely proud to see this ongoing institution so well established and so full of promising prospect.'
—Lord Netherthorpe 1977[1]

ESTABLISHMENT AT STONELEIGH

STONELEIGH was first launched on the public on 26 April 1962 when about 150 invited guests were received by Francis Pemberton and Mr J E Benion, Chairmen of the Society's Publicity Committee. Representatives of the press and local civic authorities were brought together to tour the site with a question-and-answer session inside a cattle shed where queries were dealt with by a panel which included Sir Walter Burrell, Billy Benson, Frank Sykes and Mr S J Wright (the Society's Consulting Engineer).[2]

The initial layout at Stoneleigh was largely planned by Alec Hobson and Francis Pemberton during 1961, when there were many meetings at Trumpington on its development. The central spine road in the present showground was originally a farm track, while deep ditches traversed the site with hedges and fences in the bottom of the trenches. These had to be piped and filled before further work could proceed, and the whole site was poorly farmed and wet – indeed, at an early inspection of the site Francis Pemberton had remarked to Sir Walter Burrell that they would have 'to make a silk purse out of a sow's ear' as Stoneleigh was 'the best West Midlands location that they had seen'. Grass-seeding of the area was undertaken by the Home Farm, Stoneleigh, and the Trumpington Farms Company Manager, Charles Reed, who travelled across weekly to oversee the operation and supervise the farm foreman, Fred Healey.[3]

It was significant that, following the loss of Meyric Hughes, the Society advertised for a 'Technical Director and Secretary' and it was to this post that Christopher Dadd was appointed with effect from 1 January 1963. Dadd came to the position from the NAAS where he had been on the East Anglian Regional Staff as a Crop Husbandry Officer. A contemporary[4] of his on the Cambridge post-graduate diploma in agriculture course (which Christopher Dadd read after taking a First in the Natural Sciences Tripos) recalls that he worked twice as hard as anyone else and this capacity for extreme industry was to prove a vital asset to the Society during the next 15 years. Paul Osborn, Acting Secretary during 1962, was appointed Deputy Secretary and Adminis-

205

Sir Francis Pemberton, Honorary Show Director 1963–7; President 1975–6.

trative Officer.

In the transition of Stoneleigh as a site for the Royal Show to a year-round agricultural centre, a crucial role was played by the Honorary Show Director, Francis Pemberton, who was appointed to that position in 1961 as successor to Billy Benson. Sir Francis recalls being told by the then Chairman of the Council, Sir Robert Gooch, that the appointment was seen as 'a calculated risk' because it was feared he would proceed with too much hurry and it was thought he 'might upset quite a number of people' on the way. It was hoped, however, that his business skills would be utilised to further the objectives of the Society and build up the showground at Stoneleigh. Since first joining the Council in 1951 (in succession to Owen Webb, a member of the well-known Cambridgeshire farming family who had served on the Council for many years) Francis Pemberton had accumulated much first-hand knowledge on the practical operation of Royal Shows and had acted as a Steward dealing with traffic, car parking, and catering. To those, therefore, who suspected that the Royal in 1963 was insufficiently 'non-feudal' to run Stoneleigh in a modern idiom, it could be shown that the administrative structure was organised very much on company lines with an Executive Committee (consisting of the Secretary and Technical Director, the Honorary Show Director, and Willy Freund as Finance Director) meeting regularly and reporting back to the Council. Tragically however, Freund was lost to the Society in September 1963, victim of the Swiss *Caravelle* air disaster.[5]

The immediate task after Christopher Dadd took up his appointment was the

206

preparation for the July Show. The idea of the National Agricultural Centre was an uncertain concept for many members of the Society and still less understood in the wider agricultural community. Christopher Dadd's appointment emphasised that Stoneleigh's future function was to be more than the holding of an annual agricultural show and that it could 'become a unique platform for the discussion of important topics which could be brought together under an impartial organisation of farmers, industry, and politicians if necessary'. The work of building the 1963 Show commenced in the August of the previous year when the Clerk-of-Works, Mr Cadwallader, moved from Newcastle to Stoneleigh and the Royal Pavilion was erected on sleeper foundations on which it stood (just!) until rebuilt in 1985 for the 1986 Show.[6]

By the time of the Society's Annual General Meeting in 1962 Francis Pemberton was able to report that the grass was well-established and that the initial roads had been put in. There was a perimeter road around the showground with demonstration areas planned beyond this boundary. Utilities were in the process of being connected, the Grandstand had been erected, and livestock shedding was in the process of construction. Early in 1963 work slowed down on account of the exceptionally severe winter but apart from some killing of the grass there were few long-term effects and time lost was soon made up. In planning the layout of the showground the experimental radial plan tried at Newcastle was abandoned; apart from facilitating signposting and directions, the grid plan was also suited to the configuration of the site. The showground layout has not undergone major alteration during its first quarter-century. The 140 acres of showground area utilised for show stands were bisected by a 20 foot wide road running east to west from the main entrance, with the Grand Ring, Royal Pavilion, and offices almost in the centre. Close by were the Farm Buildings Centre – the first of the permanent demonstration units – and a forestry area established to the north of the ground. Five public entrances were planned with car parks covering 120 acres and a separate 27 acre caravan park.

The plans for the show announced by the Society were well received by the agricultural press which looked forward to the 1963 event with 'restrained optimism'. In his show preview Robert Trow-Smith wrote in the *Farmer and Stockbreeder* of the easy access of the site and its green, peaceful environment 'redolent of rural Britain at its most typical'. Doubts about accessibility were dispelled when, at a press view in April, journalists from London, the Welsh Borders, East Anglia and the north Midlands were assembled together and it was noted that it had taken none of them much more than two hours to drive to the site. Greater doubts surrounded the more immediate access to the ground as 'the medieval winding lanes, now tarmacadamed and classified, are still as tortuous as they were when they served the needs of the monks of the Order of Citeaux when they moved to their new home, Stoneleigh, in April 1156'.[7]

Although the Honorary Show Director was at pains to stress that the success or otherwise of the first Stoneleigh Show was not to be judged by the size of 'the gate' and that he would like 'to tear down the comparative attendance boards', the recorded number of visitors was only slightly below the average of the previous three years (which was augmented by the large attendance at Newcastle in 1962):

	Stoneleigh 'Gate' 1963	
Day	*Stoneleigh*	*Three-year average*
Tuesday	13,939	12,294
Wednesday	30,297	33,721
Thursday	48,705	46,285
Friday	18,975	32,035
Totals	111,916	124,335

More significant was the recognisable tendency for a new type of visitor to be seen. This was in keeping with the 'commercial look' associated with the venue, and a move away from the 'middle-aged, fashionable, and rather equestrian bias of the past'.[8]

Visitors to the Show expected the benefits of 'permanence' to be more evident than they actually were, especially as the event suffered from particularly wet weather with four inches of rain the month before and some thunderstorms during the Show week. Most of the initial investment had been put into the perimeter road and many of the main avenues and intersecting lanes lacked sleepers or other surfacing material apart from hastily laid straw and gravel to alleviate the worst of the underfoot conditions. As Francis Pemberton pointed out, to do everything necessary with regard to the Showground development would have entailed an investment of about £1,000,000 and the final decision to 'go permanent' at Stoneleigh still had to be made; the guiding principle during these early years was that not more would be spent annually than the cost which would have been incurred by continuing with the peripatetic system.

The 1963 Show featured a demonstration area of 57 acres under the direction of Peter Buckler, divided into two main sections: the Farm Buildings Centre was devoted to a comprehensive display of pig buildings including housing for in-pig sows, farrowing and rearing, and a number of fattening houses. In addition, new intensive beef fattening units, sheep housing, and cow cubicles could be inspected. The field demonstration area featured the growing of early potatoes and especially the use of herbicides to eliminate cultivations after plant emergence. The disposal of slurry and liquid effluent was also demonstrated – linked to the exhibits at the Farm Buildings Centre – with additional space devoted to water preservation for irrigation, and land drainage, thereby illustrating a number of aspects of water management on the farm.[9]

An early Press inspection of the Stoneleigh showground.

Reflecting on the demonstrations in the Society's November *Review*, Peter Buckler noted some of the resulting questions of organisation and layout.[10] There had been some problem in finding the way from the Farm Buildings Centre near the middle of the ground to the Demonstration Area on the periphery, while the field demonstrations had been difficult to label adequately. This meant that the visitor could have been not fully aware of what was actually available to be seen. The Demonstration Area in 1964 continued to be divided into two parts. On the buildings side, there was an emphasis on pig management with the greatest innovation being a demonstration involving a full herd of dairy cows to illustrate aspects of mastitis control. The field displays featured plots organised by chemical manufacturers, the National Institute of Agricultural Botany, and the National Institute of Agricultural Engineering. The Show had a greater emphasis on the 'ring' in 1964 and more 'popular' events. The *Daily Express* sponsored a pastoral pageant, staged five times during the four days of the Show, entitled 'This Earth, This Realm' which included special scenes using farm tractors and machines in presentation of a 'ballet'. A 'gala evening' was staged on the Thursday of the Show which featured a singing group, 'Billy J Kramer and the Dakotas'.[11]

The first two shows at Stoneleigh were generally well received, despite the problems with mud on the showground, and traffic bottlenecks around the car park exits. Organisations participating in the Demonstration Area were thought to 'have risen splendidly to the occasion', and the show and demonstrations combined were judged to be a qualified success: 'The grand strategy, was right, even inspired, but it fell down in detail'. For skilful adaptation to various needs the layout was 'masterly' but the roads which had been built were considered too narrow and the members' accommodation fell short of what was considered adequate. However, these were recognised as small faults which could be rectified and the new receptiveness of the show management to points of criticism was appreciated.[12]

Improvements to the showground put in hand before the 1964 Show included some road widening, sleeper roads in the livestock areas, and reorganisation of the implement yard. A limited number of the new roads were of concrete – with the Cement and Concrete Association making a contribution to the materials – while others were soil stabilised with 1,200 tons of fly ash, waste provided by the CEGB from solid fuel power stations.

The 1964 Show was crucially important: it was after this that the Society had to decide whether to take up the option of a long lease at Stoneleigh and the event's success or otherwise would strongly influence the decision. At the Show preview Francis Pemberton was able to point to the improvements that had been made since the previous year. These included not only the physical aspects, but also a greater range of exhibits for women, improved facilities for overseas visitors, and easier car parking.

The judgement after this second show was that Stoneleigh stood 'clearly revealed as the most convenient site the Society is likely to find: idyllically situated, centrally placed, capable of being made easy of access, and adaptable to any purpose'. 'Blythe' 'came away from Stoneleigh feeling that the Royal really is going to be of increasing practical use to ordinary farmers like myself', and the Show had everything – 'gate, glamour and gusto'. The 'gala evening' was well received by a rural-urban audience of some 50,000 while the overall show attendance – 138,000 – comfortably exceeded the 1963 level. Even John Cherrington, arch-crusader against the 'Bowler-hat Brigade' and by his own admission the most 'jaundiced' of the Royal's observers, found a few complimentary words to write about the site and the demonstration areas.[13]

Apart from the success of the 1964 Show the 'admirably staged' National Grassland Demonstration at Stoneleigh the same year attracted an attendance of 33,000 and further indicated the utility and promise of the permanent site. This was the first major event to be held there apart from the Royal Show and even those who had been sceptical about Stoneleigh – and it must be emphasised that some of the site's promotors continued to entertain doubts about its suitability – found no good reason to go elsewhere especially as considerable investment had already been made and no viable alternatives had been presented.

The decision to take up the option of a 99 year lease at Stoneleigh was taken at a meeting of the Council held on 14 October 1964; the lease was signed in May the following year. The main point of discussion within the Society surrounded detail of the lease rather than the basic principle. Christopher York, now converted to Stoneleigh after his earlier preference for a near-London base, pressed for the lease terms to be so drawn that no restrictions could be placed on the site's development at a later date. It was stressed in Council that the Society was taking the land on the basis of its use as an agricultural centre, and the rent was to be linked to that use.

The decision to stay at Stoneleigh, the most momentous in the Society's history, gave rise to two important related issues regarding Council representation and subscription levels. In anticipation of the Society remaining at Stoneleigh and the change in the Society's character that this would mean, the Finance and General Purposes Committee put a recommendation for consideration by the Council that members' county representation should be modified. This was because legal opinion was that the Society's Charter obliged it to maintain its *national* identity. The point at issue here was the strong possibility that counties adjacent to the Society's new West Midlands base would gain members at the expense of more distant areas by virtue of location and while it was right that counties with a high level of membership should have full representation on the Council this could conflict with the RASE's national standing – it was not to become a large regional agricultural society. Frank Sykes therefore drafted an amendment to the existing Byelaw of the Society which would reduce the Council representation of the larger membership divisions. His proposal provided for each 500 Governors and members in divisions in excess of 700 to be able to elect one additional ordinary member of the Council to a maximum of seven, whereas the existing regulation allowed for one additional Council member for each 200 over 700 to a maximum of twelve. The effect of this amendment was to reduce the likelihood of a small group of counties around Stoneleigh having a preponderance of Council representation. This change was attended with a certain amount of ill-feeling, particularly from Warwickshire which had achieved a large membership increase after the Society had indicated Stoneleigh as its probable permanent location.[14]

The permanent site and its location also had implications for the Members' and Governors' subscription rates. The initial development of Stoneleigh called for very considerable investment quite apart from the demand for better facilities in general. The early 1960s were difficult financial times and in 1963 the Society had a non-show loss of £5,567 brought about by rising costs of administration, salaries and rates, while its income from investments was falling, and some of the Society's assets had to be realised to release capital for the build-up of Stoneleigh. In December 1964 the Finance and General Purposes Committee decided to recommend that the basic member's subscription be kept at the then existing rate of £2 – unchanged since 1953 – but with an optional additional fee to cover Showground privileges. The idea of a differential membership fee was again in recognition of the Society's national standing as it was considered that those members who lived well away from Stoneleigh would be less likely to attend the Show, or to use the other facilities at the site, and had therefore lost most on the cessation of the peripatetic system. The new proposed category of 'Show Club' members at £5 would include additional show facilities and entry to the agricultural centre throughout the year; the £2 members would have a more restricted range of membership benefits but would not be asked to pay for privileges of which they could not take full advantage. A particular concern was that this suggestion would create a 'two-tier' membership with 'first-' and 'second-class' connotations and there was also the view that the jump from £2 to £5 was too large. After lengthy discussion and consideration of various amendments to the proposal, the new membership structure was accepted but the scheme was not at all well received; 'ordinary' members appeared to get little for their subscription while for the 'Show Club' members, admission to the Showground was perceived to be a somewhat involved business as the £5 fee only gave access to the Members' Pavilion, Flower Show, and Grandstand whereas previously membership had been enough to gain admission to the Showground.[15] The two-tier membership never gained full acceptance and, after some further modification, the £2 subscription was phased out in 1973.

The National Agricultural Centre was not officially opened until 29 September 1967. The opening ceremony was performed by Mr G T Williams, President of the National Farmers' Union, who described it as 'a venture which will give a new lease of life to the pioneering spirit of British agriculture'. An address of welcome was given to 250 guests by the Society's President for the year, the Marquess of Abergavenny, who described the NAC as 'the most interesting and exciting project the Society had ever sponsored'.[16]

The majority of the Society's staff were transferred to Stoneleigh in 1969. Some consideration has since been given as to whether the Society should maintain its London headquarters at 35 Belgrave Square, most notably in 1976 when there were plans to dispose of the lease, but the need for a national society to maintain a London base has been considered essential. The lease of the Mews at Belgrave Square was sold in 1983 and space not utilised within the building has been let to a number of tenants with agricultural or rural interests, most notably the British Agricultural Exports Council in 1976, itself the subject of strong support from the Society's Chief Executive in the face of general apathy from the agricultural industry as a whole.[17]

THE DEVELOPMENT OF THE NATIONAL AGRICULTURAL CENTRE

The development of Stoneleigh since the Society decided to remain at the site can be considered under three broad headings: the search for the right

Conference to form the National Agricultural Centre Advisory Board.

administrative structure and framework; finance and investment; and changes in the Showground's physical character together with its extension in size.

On 2 December 1965 the Society's President, Lord Netherthorpe, called a conference at Agriculture House (Headquarters of the NFU) which was attended by delegates from no less than 56 separate organisations with an interest, or potential interest, in the Society's venture:

Organisations Represented at the RASE National Conference
2 December 1965

Agricultural Central Co-operative Association
Agricultural Education Association
Agricultural Engineers' Association
Agricultural Land Service
Agricultural Machinery & Tractor Dealers' Association
Agricultural Research Council
Agricultural Show Exhibitors' Association
Animal Health Trust
Association of Agriculture
Association of British Manufacturers of Agricultural Chemicals
Beef Recording Association (UK)
British Beekeepers' Association
British Egg Marketing Board
British Electrical Development Association

British Horse Society
British Show Jumping Association
British Veterinary Association
British Wool Marketing Board
Cement & Concrete Association
Compound Animal Feeding Stuffs Manufacturers' National Association
Country Landowners' Association
Farm Buildings Association
Farm Buildings Centre
Farmers' Club
Fatstock Marketing Corporation
Fertilizer Manufacturers' Association
Forestry Commission
Guild of Agricultural Journalists
Incorporated Society of Auctioneers and Landed Property Agents
Land Agents Society
Livestock Export Council of Great Britain
Milk Marketing Board
Ministry of Agriculture, Fisheries & Food
National Agricultural Advisory Service
National Association of Agricultural Contractors
National Association of Corn and Agricultural Merchants
National Cattle Breeders' Association
National Farmers' Union
National Federation of Young Farmers' Clubs
National Grassland Demonstration Committee
National Institute of Agricultural Botany
National Institute of Agricultural Engineering
National Pig Breeders' Association
National Sheep Breeders' Association
National Union of Agricultural Workers
Pig Industry Development Authority
Potato Marketing Board
Poultry Stock Association
Produce Packers' Association
Royal Association of British Dairy Farmers
Royal Forestry Society of England, Scotland, Wales & N Ireland
Royal Institution of Chartered Surveyors
Royal Smithfield Club
Rural Industries Bureau
Seed Trade Association of the United Kingdom
Timber Growers' Organisation

The purpose of the conference was to discuss the role of the National Agricultural Centre and, in particular, Lord Netherthorpe's view of Stoneleigh which was – following closely the Fact-Finding Committee's recommendations –

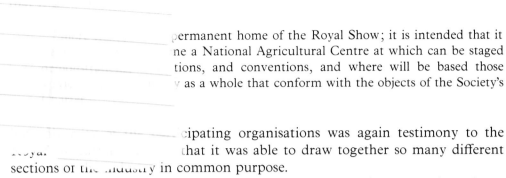

ermanent home of the Royal Show; it is intended that it
ne a National Agricultural Centre at which can be staged
tions, and conventions, and where will be based those
as a whole that conform with the objects of the Society's

cipating organisations was again testimony to the
that it was able to draw together so many different
sections of the industry in common purpose.

The organisations invited had first been asked to complete a questionnaire as
to how the development of the centre should be handled and a selected number
were specifically invited to speak. Leading the conference on overall policy were
Sir Harold Woolley (National Farmers' Union), Brig A F L Clive (Country
Landowners' Association), and Lord Collison (National Union of Agricultural
Workers). Among a variety of recommendations on ways in which the Centre's
activities could be developed, the most significant was the unanimous opinion
that Stoneleigh should be developed as a National Agricultural Centre and that
a representative organisation should be set up to administer it. This led to the
proposal to create the National Agricultural Centre Advisory Board (NACAB)
to advise the body administering the Centre. Final executive authority would
rest with the Council of the RASE. Delegates to the NACAB would be drawn
from the 56 participating organisations, represented in proportion to their
interest in the development of the NAC and including the requisite industries,
professional bodies, marketing organisations, exhibitors' associations, and export promotion groups; some members of NACAB would be afforded nominated status on the Society's Council thus welding into the executive body the
representation of those who had a stake in the development of the NAC. This
was an important broadening of the Society's Council beyond the traditional
County representation in the way that had been envisaged by Sir Walter
Burrell, Alec Hobson and others at the time of the Fact-Finding Committee's
deliberations.

On 19 January 1966 the Finance and General Purposes Committee set up a
Sub-committee consisting of Sir Robert Gooch (Chairman), Sir Walter Burrell,
Lord 'Eddie' Digby, John Everall, Sir Peter Greenwell, Francis Pemberton,
Captain Henry Tupper and Christopher Dadd to recommend the formal
procedure for setting up the NACAB. The Sub-committee met on 23 February,
and considered how the various sectors of the Board's separate interests could
best be administered.
It set out three alternatives:

    (i) A main board of the NACAB to make recommendations through its nominated and co-opted members which would be considered by the RASE Standing Committees affected for submission to the Council

or

(ii) A policy-making Board with advisory committees or groups to deal with specific subjects and make recommendations through appropriate channels to the RASE Council

or

(iii) A main board and a steering committee, with or without special committees or groups

The Sub-committee identified some subjects which needed to be dealt with by specialist committees or groups of the NACAB. These included the Royal Show, Demonstrations, Livestock Improvement, Conferences and Exhibitions, Exports and Publicity. The timetable for setting up the NACAB was reviewed when the Sub-committee's proposals were considered at the March meeting of the Finance and General Purposes Committee. This Committee's recommendation would be put to the May meeting of the Council, followed by invitations to interested organisations to be represented on NACAB, the announcement of the plan at the pre-show press conference, with the inaugural meeting of the NACAB being called by the Society for late July with the first full meeting in the autumn. Liaison between the NACAB and Committees, and between the Council and the NACAB was carefully planned with cross-representation of both bodies on all committees.

These proposals were accepted by the Finance and General Purposes Committee on 23 March and by the Council on 4 May. The meeting to convene the NACAB was held on 28 July and the first full meeting on 19 October under the interim Chairmanship of Lord Netherthorpe. This meeting nominated seven members of the Board to serve, together with seven RASE representatives, on a Central Executive Committee. The NACAB nominees were Mr C H M Wilcox, representing the Ministry of Agriculture, Mr Gilbert Hunt, ex-President of the Agricultural Engineers' Association, representing machinery interests, Mr A Steele-Bodger, past President of the British Veterinary Association, representing livestock interest, Mr T D Dampney (National Farmers' Union), Dr Joseph Edwards (MMB), representing statutory marketing boards, Mr J B C Carr, Director of the Fertilizer Manufacturers' Association Ltd, representing fertilizer, chemical and ancillary industries, and Mr J V Thatcher representing the Agricultural Show Exhibitors' Association. These NACAB members were also made nominated members of the Society's Council. The Central Executive Committee met on 25 November when Francis Pemberton was elected Chairman.

Representation of organisations on NACAB was in three groups. Group 'A' comprised organisations with individual representation:

Agricultural Engineers' Association

Agricultural Engineers' Association
Agricultural Show Exhibitors' Association
Beef Recording Association (UK)
British Agricultural Export Council
British Veterinary Association
Cement & Concrete Association
Country Landowners' Association
Electricity Council
Farm Management Association
Ministry of Agriculture, Fisheries & Food
National Association of Agricultural Contractors
National Cattle Breeders' Association
National Farmers' Union of England & Wales
National Federation of Young Farmers Clubs
National Grassland Demonstration Committee
National Institute of Agricultural Botany
National Pig Breeders' Association
National Sheep Breeders' Association
National Union of Agricultural Workers
Pig Industry Development Authority
Poultry Stock Association
Royal Association of British Dairy Farmers
Royal Smithfield Club

Group 'B' consisted of organisations represented jointly according to interests held in common, each sub-group having one representative. All these organisations received Board papers and had the right to be represented individually when there were matters of specific concern to them:

Corn & Seeds
Institute of Corn and Agricultural Merchants
National Association of Corn and Agricultural Merchants
Seed Trade Association of the United Kingdom

Equestrian
British Horse Society
British Show Jumping Association

Farm Buildings
Farm Buildings Centre
Farm Buildings Association

Fertilisers and Chemicals
Fertiliser Manufacturers' Association
Association of British Manufacturers of Agricultural Chemicals

Land and Property
Chartered Auctioneers & Estate Agents Institute

Chartered Land Agents' Society
Royal Institution of Chartered Surveyors
Incorporated Society of Auctioneers & Landed Property Agents

Statutory Marketing Boards
Egg, Milk, Potato and Wool Marketing Boards

Group 'C' was made up of organisations which received all meeting papers and had the right to apply to be represented at Board meetings when there were items which concerned them:

Agricultural Central Co-operative Association
Agricultural Education Association
Agricultural Machinery & Tractor Dealers' Association
Agricultural Research Council
Animal Health Trust
Association of Agriculture
British Beekeepers' Association
Compound Animal Feeding Stuffs Manufacturers' National Association
Council of Industrial Design
Farmers' Club
Fatstock Marketing Corporation
Forestry Commission
National Institute of Agricultural Engineering
Produce Packers' Association
Royal Forestry Society of England, Scotland, Wales & N Ireland
Rural Industries Bureau
Timber Growers' Organisation

Mr J V Thatcher was elected Chairman of NACAB and Francis Pemberton, on completion of his term of office as Honorary Show Director in 1967, became Honorary Director of the NAC; members of the Board visited the NAC on 3 January 1968 when he was requested to draw up a five-year plan for its development.

These administrative arrangements were not without their problems. There were some in the Society who felt that the National Agricultural Centre, 'a geographical location and not an organisation' was, by the end of 1967, beginning to assume an independent identity, while the NACAB was equally anxious *not* to draw away from the Society, but move closer to its activities, administration and traditions. The Honorary Show Director had warned in 1965 that 'as in the case of almost every great enterprise, there will be many difficulties to be overcome before complete success is achieved' and two years later it was said that the 'growing pains' of the NAC had been 'excruciating'. As the Chairman of the NACAB observed, they were all feeling their way 'along routes entirely uncharted'. The representation of the NACAB on the RASE Council through a small number of nominated members led to some confusion as also overlapping of commit-

view of the administration of
put forward to increase the
RASE Council included the
the right to attend and speak at
Executive Board be formed,
and the Advisory Board, which
would carry out the Council's instructions quickly and would have the right to
report directly to the Council. It was additionally suggested that when action
was required on individual projects, working parties composed of Council and
Advisory Board members should be empowered to deal with them. This would
mean that the number of the Society's standing committees could be reduced.

The Council agreed to the formation of the Executive Board on 6 March
1968. This initially consisted of Sir Walter Burrell (Chairman of Council),
Christopher York (Vice-Chairman of the Finance and General Purposes
Committee), Lord Netherthorpe, W D Akester, J B C Carr, Lord Digby, E
Maxwell Howard, A A C 'Archie' MacArthur (Show Director from 1968),
Francis Pemberton, Alastair Steele-Bodger, Frank Sykes and J V Thatcher.
The Executive Board replaced the existing RASE and NACAB executive
committees and met monthly. It had three principal functions: drafting broad
outline plans for future policy, dealing with matters delegated to it by Council
or committees, and acting on urgent matters.

By the late 1960s the administration of the Society had become far more
varied and complex than when its prime responsibility had been the Royal
Show. The technical and demonstrations side of Stoneleigh was expanding
rapidly and it was recognised that the direction of the NAC was itself a full time
job. In March 1968 it was agreed, in principle, to appoint a paid Director of the
Centre, and Christopher Dadd undertook this role in 1969, his post changing
from 'Secretary and Technical Director' to 'Director of the National Agricultural Centre' with the particular responsibility of developing the technical aspects
of the Centre's work as well as strengthening the links with other organisations
in the research, development, and practical fields. In this task he continued to
be assisted by W Ray B Carter, 'loaned' to the Society by MAFF from 1 October
1966 as Deputy Secretary (National Agricultural Centre). To deal with the
rapidly expanding general administration of the Society a new post of Director
of Administration was created, W D Draffan (formerly General Manager of
Kenya Co-operative Creameries Ltd) being appointed to that position with
effect from 21 July 1969. As the Society's constitution required it to have a
Secretary, Howard V Fox, who succeeded Paul Osborn in 1968, assumed this
position which was revised so that it was combined with the new post of Deputy
Director (Administration).

The review of the Society's committee structure, called for in 1968, was

219

Christopher Dadd and Ray Carter at an instructional exhibit in animal health at Stoneleigh.

undertaken by the Executive Board and the Finance and General Purposes Committee and completed two years later. The main recommendations were that the Society's committee structure be streamlined. This would mean merging the Executive Board and the Finance and General Purposes Committee – where there had been particular duplication of responsibility – and the establishment of four standing committees – Technical Development, General Purposes, Royal Show, and Works. Working parties and sub-committees would be set up as needed. These changes came into effect at the start of 1971.

Following this reorganisation the Executive Committee established a working party to examine the staff structure to ensure that it was able to meet the demands put upon it. The years 1970 and 1971 were difficult for the Society, a particular area of concern being the need for more revenue at a time when some leading exhibitors were withdrawing from the Royal Show. The development of a marketing strategy was seen as a key priority. The Working Party examined staffing, job specifications, and organisational structure in detail and recommended that there should be one Chief Executive, or Managing Director, responsible for effecting all the aims and objectives of the Society. A specialist firm of Management Consultants was engaged to advise on this appointment and a Selection Panel to discuss the scope and remit of the post was set up consisting of Sir Walter Burrell, Francis Pemberton, Capt Steve Player, Christopher York, John Cumber and 'Archie' MacArthur. As the financial position of the Society was not strong in 1971 it was made known 'that some very good friends of the Society' would underwrite the salary involved for five years. These 'very good friends' – Lord Rank, Sir Joseph Nickerson, and Francis Pemberton – thus enabled the appointment to be made early in 1972 and Mr J D M Hearth took up the appointment of Chief Executive of the RASE with effect from 5 April.[20]

John Hearth came to the Society from the Cunard Shipping Company where he had been a Director, with earlier experience in the Colonial Service and journalism. His appointment was received with scepticism in some quarters because of his lack of an agricultural background. However, it was explained that the Society had access to all the agricultural skills and knowledge required particularly as for five years Christopher Dadd would be remaining as Agricultural Director.[21] It was felt that the NAC required business and management skills to complement the existing agricultural expertise. Another significant development was the appointment of Mr P R Taylor, the Society's Head of Public Relations, as Head of Marketing with responsibility for all that the Society sold.

In his first report the Chief Executive identified a number of areas of the Society's affairs which needed reappraising. Apart from concern at the apparently high overhead costs of running the RASE and the need to develop more income-generating activities, it was considered that lines of authority and responsibility within the Society were not clear and that administrative procedures needed reappraisal. Further, the Society's image within the agricultural industry was not right and needed attention.

Although the changes in the Society's committee arrangements instituted in 1971 were considered an improvement, certain difficulties of procedure soon became apparent and in September 1972 John Cumber (who had succeeded Francis Pemberton as Chairman of the Executive Board) proposed a Working Group to reassess the RASE Council and Committee structure. This working party was chaired by Capt Steve Player and, after very extensive deliberations, reported to the Council in March 1974.

The report was addressed to two main areas of the Society's affairs: representation on the Council, and the nature of the RASE Committees. On Council representation, it was considered essential to develop links with the counties in order to maintain the Society's national character and guard against the tendency of counties near the NAC to have a disproportionate voice. This, as we have seen, manifested itself as a problem as soon as Stoneleigh was selected as a permanent site. Reorganisation of local government, with the establishment of six metropolitan counties with effect from 1 April 1974 was another factor which made reconsideration of the county basis of Council representation timely. The recommendation was that the new county structure should be based on 38 counties including Greater London, plus Scotland, Wales and Northern Ireland. Three metropolitan areas with more than 1,500 farm units were to be considered as counties with separate representatives (West

Lord Netherthorpe, President 1965, Chairman of Council 1974–75.   C M T Smith-Ryland, Chairman of Council since 1976.

Yorkshire, South Yorkshire, and Greater Manchester), metropolitan areas with less than 1,500 units (West Midlands, Merseyside and Tyne and Wear on 1973 figures), and counties below that level would be attached to adjacent counties. The working party presented two alternatives regarding the proportion of Council members to county membership and that which gave relatively more representation to counties with small membership totals was preferred. This also provided for a maximum of five Council members per area as opposed to seven under the existing scheme.[22]

In the light of two years' experience the working party maintained that it was necessary to review the position of the Standing Committees in order to delineate more clearly responsibilities of committees and their relationship to Council, and to improve efficiency where possible. Consideration also had to be given to getting the right balance of knowledge and experience of Council members on the appropriate committee. It was recommended that the Executive Board and Selection Committee should be replaced by a Chairman's Committee which would have the function of an executive cabinet. The Technical Development Committee would have enhanced status so that it would be fully recognised, with its supporting sub-committees, as a high-level technical policy-making group. The General Purposes Committee's responsibilities would be enlarged to deal with education, the *Journal* and other

222

The RASE's management team 1988: from left G H Jackson, C A M Sparrey, C H Richardson, J D M Hearth, J Perrott, A D Callaghan.

publications, leisure and rural pursuits, and senior staff appointments. The Finance Sub-committee of the Executive Board would revert to its former status as a main Standing Committee. These changes, which came into effect in 1975, have largely remained in force. The present Chairman of the Council, Charles Smith-Ryland (the Lord Lieutenant of Warwickshire) succeeded Lord Netherthorpe in 1976.[23]

Associated with this is the permanent staff structure of the RASE. Under the overall executive direction of J D M Hearth there are five distinct areas of operation: the agricultural and technical work of the Society under the Agricultural Director (G H Jackson, who succeeded Christopher Dadd in 1977), Accountancy under C A M Sparrey, Marketing under C H Richardson, and Secretarial (under A D Callaghan who succeeded H V Fox in 1982) and the Showground Director (J Perrott appointed in 1976, formerly Manager of the Farm Buildings Information Centre). The Society's staff currently totals about 140. Two of the longest serving staff members are Rosemary Bartlett (Livestock and Sponsorship Executive) – who retired in September 1987 but remains with the Society part-time – and the Society's Surveyor, Ron Treves, with 27 and 28 years' service respectively.

223

It was not easy to achieve the right administrative structure for the Society and the NAC, especially as the range and complexity of its operations had expanded greatly since the late 1960s. Different administrative and committee structures were appropriate at different periods of the Society's development; the NACAB for example (which ceased to exist as a recognisable entity following the Player Committee recommendations) contributed a great deal by many ideas which have been used in later developments at the NAC.

The key to these developments has been the generation of adequate finance which has again been by no means easy. Early development of Stoneleigh was financed by the Society's own resources and input from commercial interests which contributed much to the establishment of the demonstration units. When Lord Netherthorpe brought together the wide range of agricultural interests into the NACAB it was stressed that this was *not* with the intention of calling for financial support, but it soon became clear that the full potential of the NAC would be difficult to realise from the resources of the Society and commercial sponsors alone. Thus in 1968 consideration began to be given to the establishment of the Development Fund. The preliminary work on this was kept confidential on the advice of the Society's fund-raising consultants (the Wells Organisation) but Christopher York was able to announce to the July Council that a feasibility study had revealed that a sound target for the campaign could soon be determined and expenditure of £5,000 was authorised to enable the scheme to be started, although full details were not revealed at that time.

The Development Funding Operation proceeded during 1969 by the establishment of contact with individuals and organisations to elicit initial gifts, to be promised prior to the public launch of the campaign. By September 1969 it was reported that the Initial Gifts Committee (chaired by Lord Abergavenny with Lord Netherthorpe as Vice-Chairman) had almost finished its work. Their conclusion was that £1,500,000 was an achievable target for the Development Fund.

The Development Fund was publicly launched at the Cafe Royal on 15 January 1970 and was supported by the Minister of Agriculture, Mr Cledwyn Hughes (now Lord Cledwyn), who reviewed those areas of agriculture needing attention and investigation, and commended the NAC concept. The Marquess of Abergavenny, the Society's President, stressed the Society's intention to make the NAC a focal point for presenting British Agriculture nationally and internationally, as a base for the demonstration of potential exports, and for more effective marketing of home-produced products. The NAC was to serve as a hub of communications and bridge the gap between developing agricultural technology and general farming practice. The identification of impediments to productivity would be of particular importance.[24]

At the time of the Development Fund launch some £550,000 had already been pledged to the campaign with leading gifts from Lord Rank, the Massey-Ferguson Group, and Fisons Ltd. It was considered that the target sum should be allocated between demonstration units (£75,000), development of the centre (£290,000), provision of services (£250,0000), sales promotion (£75,000), communications (£110,000), and general amenities (£25,000).

The Development Fund launch was backed up by regional campaign committees pioneered by Christopher York in Yorkshire, who also spent a considerable amount of time in helping to set up others around the country; indeed, a great deal of effort was put in by Council members and the leaders of these local campaigns in listing individual and business contacts and identifying trusts which might be able to help. The Society also had a professional fund raiser to assist the appeal (Mr P S Luckin, succeeded by Mrs Peggy Pardoe). By the end of 1970 the Development Fund had reached £841,000; it passed the £1 million mark in 1972 as a result of a donation of £45,000 from the Frank Parkinson Trust (arranged by Christopher Dadd) but by the time the first cycle of the Development Fund was closed at the Royal Show of 1974 it was some way short of the planned target. By far the greater amount of the money raised came from a small number of large donors – individuals, firms, and trusts – and since 1974 the greatest amount of attention has been given to the renewal of existing covenants and contacting new donors. In this way the Development Fund has continued, but not as a *public* appeal of the sort that was appropriate at the time of the initial campaign.

One of John Hearth's first conclusions after his appointment as Chief Executive was that the Society's revenue-earning activities needed to be increased in respect of all its operations but particularly in relation to the considerable proportion of the NAC facilities which lay dormant for much of the year. Thus there has been since this time considerable effort to extend the range of events at the NAC beyond those directly connected with technical events and demonstrations, to those which can help to raise revenue to support these activities and spread the fixed costs of the Centre.

A major event instituted in 1972 was the Town and Country Festival held on the August Bank Holiday. This was very much on the initiative of Peter Buckler. It was seen as a way of making use of the showground outside the Royal Show time, as an opportunity to create stronger links between the Society and the local community, and as a way in which agriculture could be interpreted to the urban population. It was not originally seen primarily as a source of revenue, but over the years it has contributed significantly both to the Society and also to charitable purposes. Its unique pattern, blending the resources of the Society and the skills of its professional staff with the voluntary input of enthusiasts in numerous different fields of activity and hobbies, has made it the largest event of its kind in the country and with an attendance of over 140,000 in 1987, it is the second largest event held at the NAC each year.

The right sort of additional events have not been easy to find: restrictions in the Society's lease, local planning regulations, and the nature of the RASE all limit the options that can be considered for Stoneleigh. Experiments were made

View of Town and Country Festival, the second largest annual event held at Stoneleigh.

with equestrian and country sport events in the mid- and late-1970s but failed to become established while a major leisure event, the Barclaycard Leisure Festival 'Recro' 1980, upon which the Society had high hopes, failed. Although this occasioned a considerable financial loss, it was noted at the time that it was the first of 31 major events since the inception of the permanent site to have brought about a significant pecuniary liability. Large scale events in the spring pose problems because of the preparations for the Royal Show and the need to have the Grand Ring in peak condition for early July. A May 'Model, Craft and Country Show' which ran between 1982 and 1984 never really achieved success

226

Presentation of charity cheque from the proceeds of Town and Country Festival 1981.

while the National Pet Show which took its place in 1985 was not successful, prompting the observation in the Society's *Report of Council* for the year that 'Competition in the leisure business is as keen as in agriculture itself'. A recent initiative to achieve a more all-the-year-round revenue raising utilisation of the Stoneleigh facilities has been to encourage more exhibitions and conventions, and some of the stock accommodation lines have been modified for this purpose.

Between 1972 and 1980 some £3,200,000 was spent on capital works at Stoneleigh; about half of this was from donations and it is worthy of note, therefore, that the RASE spent during this time as much from its own resources as it did from those who helped the Society. In recent years the Society has *budgeted* for a surplus of £100,000 to £150,000 – amounting to about 2.5–3.5% of revenues of around £4–5 million. As the Society's annual financial statement noted in 1986 'no commercial concern would contemplate comparable, sometimes high-risk, activities on so fine a margin' and much of what has been achieved at Stoneleigh has been built on a policy of calculated risk-taking.

The development of the National Agricultural Centre and the growth in the Society's activities that has followed can be well illustrated by reference to the

Arthur Rank Centre.

annual accounts. For the twelve months ended 31st December 1961 the RASE's income was £219,879, with a surplus of £26,009. Ten years later, in the twelve months ended 31st December 1971, in a difficult year, the Society's income was £395,738 and there was a deficit of £67,208. After a further ten years, for the twelve months ended 30th September 1981 the Society's income was £3,095,000 and there was a surplus of £171,400. By 1988 the Society's income was in excess of £5m per annum.[25]

From this outline of the administrative and financial background to the development of Stoneleigh we may turn to the build-up and extension of the site. Initially, many of the buildings were inherited from the peripatetic days; the black-and-white Secretary's office, for example, remained in use until new office accommodation was opened in 1969 to coincide with the transfer of staff from London. Much of the development during the 1960s was of basic infrastructure, while the demonstration units depended on commercial sponsors.

Major additions came during the 1970s. The Arthur Rank Centre was opened during the Royal Show in 1972, originally with a threefold purpose: providing a

The Rank Village, a major addition to the Stoneleigh facilities opened in 1979.

reception point for the NAC as a whole; social facilities for the NAC staff; and a permanent Church Pavilion for the Royal Show which could also act as a base for chaplaincy work during the remainder of the year. The project originated when Lord Rank, President of the Society for 1970–71, and a lifelong Methodist, visited the existing Church Pavilion during his tour of the showground and was not impressed with the quality of the building – it had formerly been the Basic Slag Stand. Following meetings with Peter Buckler and Lord Rank, in January 1972 Christopher Dadd took plans for a replacement to Lord Rank who promised funds for the project to the extent of £20,000. Lord Rank died in March of that year but the building was completed, in conjunction with Messrs Colt, in time for the show.[26] Although it did not become the planned general reception centre, it has developed into a unit with extensive interests in the well-being of the countryside and the rural community and as a base for the rural ministry. Its first Director was Peter Buckler, who had done so much to pioneer the technical demonstrations at Stoneleigh and who had himself been ordained into the Anglican Church in 1966. The original Colt buildings were extended in 1980, and in 1983 Peter Buckler was succeeded by Canon A J

229

Princess Alice, Duchess of Gloucester opening the Royal Pavilion in 1986. The new Royal Pavilion preserves the distinctive style of the traditional building.

Russell. Tony Russell continued the development of the Arthur Rank Centre's activities in a different style from Peter Buckler, but with equal brilliance, until he was elevated to the Bishopric of Dorchester, in Oxfordshire, in 1988.

A major addition to the NAC facilities, the Conference Hall, opened in 1973 and provided accommodation for 320 people. This was made possible by a substantial donation from the Wolfson Foundation and the Frank Parkinson Agricultural Trust. The provision of a Hall of Residence (for which Lord Rank had made available £110,000) was also considered at this time but was postponed because of the implications that it had for additional support services such as storm water drainage, road improvements, and electrics, as well as catering – all of which were beyond the Society's resources at the time. Residential accommodation had to wait until 1978 when work began on what was described as 'the most significant project of the RASE since it moved permanently to Stoneleigh'. This was the provision of a 'village' – now known as the Rank Village – to provide much improved accommodation for herdsmen and women during the Royal Show. At other times of the year, it also made residence available for visitors – delegates to conferences and so forth – thus enabling the potential of the NAC to be greatly enhanced. The project was made possible by a donation of in excess of £320,000 by the Trustees of the J Arthur Rank Group Charity.

In 1979 ambitious plans were announced to develop the south side of the Central Concourse of the Showground. Some of the existing buildings were in poor condition, having been erected shortly after the move to Stoneleigh and known to have a limited lifespan, while the Council and Stewards' Pavilion was destroyed by fire in 1978. The Royal Pavilion, dating from 1906, needed extensive refurbishment every year while the existing Members' Pavilion was, by the late 1970s, incapable of meeting the demands put upon it. The plans announced took into account the need for good design, the increasing demand for space, and the requirement for year-round use. The work was planned to be carried out in several stages, with the replacement of the Council, Stewards', and Governors' Pavilion as a priority. The initial plans were later modified, and substantial savings made on the original estimates; also, the traditional style of the Royal Pavilion, which did not feature in the original specification, has been retained and the new Royal Pavilion, opened in 1986, saw the completion of the project.

Apart from specific RASE developments, various commercial and Government interests have established permanent buildings at Stoneleigh and the planning of what, in total, is part-town, part-exhibitions centre, and in part almost akin to a university campus, has presented complex problems. As early as 1969 Mr J D F Green expressed concern about achieving unity in the design of the centre, pointing out that a permanent establishment posed special problems connected with the aesthetics of buildings, traffic, landscaping and amenities: he warned that attention needed to be directed towards this before it was too late.[27]

General view of the Central Concourse area.

Early in 1973 a small working group was established to look in detail at the planning of the NAC and reported to the Planning and Works Committee the following year. The committee identified 17 zones on the site as a whole. There were decreasing demands on some of these, while there was pressure for growth in others as, for example, in the International and Leisure Areas. As the Society's Consulting Architect (A R Laing) pointed out, the sort of temporary buildings which were satisfactory for a peripatetic four-day annual show were not always visually acceptable throughout the year and, although commercial concerns naturally wished to maintain a distinctive identity, harmony needed to be maintained outside the show period for the benefit of visitors to the NAC and for those who work there throughout the year. The Chief Executive recognised that there was no straightforward solution to the problem of maintaining architectural harmony where it was the very essence of the exhibition business that each exhibitor wished to be different.[28] Thus, while the Society has given considerable latitude to individual concerns wishing to establish permanent buildings, the care given to the overall planning and design problems posed by the NAC has allowed the Society to avoid much of the 'shanty town' image outside the Show period.

It was always hoped that the National Agricultural Centre would become a base for a range of agricultural organisations apart from the RASE. An important early development was the establishment of the Farm Buildings Centre at the start of 1964. The Society accepted an invitation to undertake the administration of the Farm Buildings Association, and the Association's *Journal* was edited by Derek Stannard, Editor of the RASE *Review* and the Society's Public Relations Officer. An Electro-Agricultural Centre was developed in 1965 and operated on a trial basis prior to its permanent opening at the 1967 Royal Show. It was promoted by the Electricity Council to provide information on all applications of electricity in agriculture, to serve as a liaison centre on behalf of the electricity services with the various demonstration units which were being established at the NAC, and to provide utilisation training courses, lectures, demonstrations, and conference facilities for all concerned with electricity in agriculture. The facilities and services of the centre were made available on a national, regional and local basis.[29]

One of the earliest national associations connected with agriculture to transfer to Stoneleigh was the British Beekeepers' Association which, in 1965, took advantage of a one-acre site that the Society made available to create a National Beekeeping Centre. This aimed to facilitate meetings for beekeepers, to hold field days, instructional courses and conferences, with a permanent apiary to demonstrate the purposeful utilisation of honeybees in the fertilisation of farm crops. The bee garden which has since been established – with nectar-bearing flowers, shrubs and trees together with a demonstration apiary and hives – greatly enhances the exhibition at the Bee Pavilion which attracts great interest at the Royal Show.[30]

A very significant development came in 1966 with the decision of the British Horse Society to move its headquarters to Stoneleigh and create there a National Equestrian Centre; the following year the British Show Jumping Association also moved from London to the NAC to combine in the venture. An indoor riding school was opened at the Royal Show in 1968 and began to put on courses for riding instructors in the Autumn of that year. The School, under the Directorship of Mr Dorian Williams, opened with what many considered to be the finest instructional facilities in the world. Three hundred founder members, each subscribing 100 gns, provided over £30,000 towards the £75,000 necessary to establish the School, with additional funds from the BSJA, money raised from the BHS former offices in Bedford Square (which were sub-let), and a Government grant. Since the late 1960s, a model stable yard and hostel have been built and the forge reconstructed to extend the popular demonstrations of shoeing and iron work that had been long-established at the Royal Show and provide routine shoeing at the NEC, as well as a venue for farriery courses.[31]

Thus by the time of the official opening of the NAC in 1967 a number of outside organisations had been attracted to Stoneleigh including – apart from those mentioned in the preceding paragraphs – the Farm Management Association, the Beef Recording Association (later incorporated in the Meat and

Livestock Commission), the Milk Marketing Board, the Agricultural, Horticultural and Forestry Industry Training Board, and the National Federation of Young Farmers' Clubs. Although some other organisations have been inhibited from moving to Stoneleigh by the leasehold nature of the site the list of organisations represented has grown significantly over the years. In 1987 the following (apart from demonstration units run directly under the auspices of the Society and sponsors) were established at the NAC

Agricultural & Food Research Council
Agricultural Development & Advisory Service
Agricultural Training Board
Association of Independent Crop Consultants
British Equestrian Federation
British Limousin Cattle Society
British Simmental Cattle Society
British Texel Sheep Society
Farm Holiday Bureau
Farm Buildings Information Centre
Farm Electric Centre
Farmers' Publishing Group (*Farmers' Weekly*)
Grand National Archery Society
Health & Safety Executive
Institute of Agricultural Secretaries
National Beekeeping Centre
National Farmers' Union – Warwickshire
National Federation of Young Farmers' Clubs
National Master Farriers', Blacksmiths' & Agricultural Engineers' Association
National Proficiency Tests Council
Rare Breeds Survival Trust
Shorthorn Cattle Society
Warwickshire College of Agriculture
Warwickshire Young Farmers

It will be seen from this list that there is a mix between official or Government organisations and those which are independent, with a wide range of agricultural and rural interests represented.

Of all these various activities, the Rare Breeds Survival Trust deserves particular notice. An interest in Rare Breeds at the NAC dates from 1967 when Sir Solly Zuckerman, now Lord Zuckerman (the chief Government Scientific Adviser) was looking for a home for a 'gene bank' – a collection of rare breeds that he had established ten years earlier and kept at Whipsnade Zoo. Space was needed to house white rhinos from Kenya and without a new home the rare breeds could, as Christopher Dadd recalls, have become 'lion fodder'.[32] A joint working party of the RASE and the Zoological Society was formed, chaired by Sir Dudley

Michael Rosenberg, Honorary Director of the Rare Breeds Survival Trust 1973–85.

Forwood, to investigate means of ensuring the survival of rare breeds and this led to the formation in 1973 of the Rare Breeds Survival Trust. This project created extensive media interest and through the efforts of Mr Michael Rosenberg, an American financier, who was until 1985 the Trust's Honorary Director and Editor of its monthly Newsletter *Ark*, Joe Henson, Mrs E R Wheatley-Hubbard and others, and grants from Volvo UK and Shell Chemicals to assist the Trust's work, a great deal of success has been achieved in keeping blood lines going which were very near to extinction. A good example is the Norfolk Horn breed of sheep; this was down to six ewes, six rams and eight cross-bred Suffolks when the remaining stock were transferred to Stoneleigh at the suggestion of Sir Peter Greenwell in 1968. The Trust now has its permanant office at the National Agricultural Centre and there has been a permanent Rare Breeds Pavilion on the Showground since 1983, while the thriving Autumn Rare Breeds Show and Sale – the largest pedigree stocksale in Europe – is an

1 Rare Breeds Survival Trust	10 Farmers' Club	19 Forge	28 New Zealand 'Agrodome'
2 Conservation Advice	11 Stoneleigh Park Pavilion	20 Rank Village	29 Livestock Export Centre
3 Children's Farmyard	12 Members	21 Sheep Shearing	30 Rural Enterprise Centre
4 Vegetable Garden	13 Royal Pavilion	22 NSA	31 Exhibitors Club
5 Farm Electric Centre	14 Governors, Council & Stewards	23 Cattle Breed — Promotion Area	
6 Science into Practice	15 Press Centre	24 RASE Machinery Awards	
7 Post Office	16 ATB	25 Goats	
8 MAFF	17 FBIC	26 Carcase Hall	
9 International Pavilion	18 Arthur Rank Centre	27 Tropical Agriculture Centre	

T Toilets   ♨ Catering   ☎ Telephone

✚ First Aid   ♿ Disabled   🍺 Bars   ? Information

Showground plan.

established part of the Stoneleigh calendar.[33] The work of the RASE in assisting the whole project was recognised in the form of a generous donation to the Society by Michael Rosenberg in 1981 which enabled it to rebuild the showground sheep and, later, the pig accommodation lines. The association between the Trust and the Society continued with the appointment in 1985 of Alastair Dymond, formerly Deputy Agricultural Director at the NAC, as the Trust's Chief Executive.

Michael Rosenberg's farsighted work for the Trust was recognised in 1986 by his appointment as an Honorary CBE for, in the words of the Minister of Agriculture Mr Michael Jopling, his 'unique contribution to genetic conservation through the survival of rare breeds'. The Minister added that his 'unfailing energy and enthusiasm as Honorary Director of the Rare Breeds Survival Trust Ltd', had made it 'an important preservation organisation'.[34]

From this outline of developments at Stoneleigh, the present position of the NAC can be understood in its chronological context. The visitor to the Centre proceeds through the main entrance – built in 1982 when landscaping of the Showground approaches was undertaken - where the main Avenue M leads to the administrative offices situated south-west of the Grand Ring. To the north of these offices and to the west of 8th Street are the Governors', Council and Stewards' Pavilion, linked to the Royal Pavilion and Members' Pavilion, on the

236

John Cumber.

south side of the central concourse. To the north of the open area, with its Clock Tower and Grandstand, are the International Pavilion and Farmers' Club Building. At showtime, the majority of the machinery stands are to the east of the Grand Ring with the stock lines to the south-east of Avenue M. The Rank Village is also to the south, adjacent to Entrance 5, and the National Equestrian Centre further to the west. The John Cumber Park, to the west of 'Ring A', commemorates John Cumber, a former Vice-President of the Society and whose wise counsels did much for the progress of the Society over a lengthy period. John Cumber bequeathed £25,000 to the Society and this was used to redevelop the area in time for the Royal Show in 1981; the area had for some time been used for the heavy horse lines but had quickly become soft in wet weather and very dusty under dry conditions, so the area was tarmacadamed and landscaped. It now provides an attractive car park for the Conference Hall year-round, and is used for heavy horse stabling and parking for horseboxes during the show period.

The south-west corner of the showground contains the area used for the magnificent flower show which is a feature of 'The Royal', the Town and Country Centre, and the lake (a legacy of the 'Water '76' event) which provides a natural focus for country sports. The year-round demonstration units are in an arc on the north-west periphery of the main showground area; to the north-

View of the flower show at the Royal.

east adjacent to the arable unit, are plots used for demonstrations by NIAB and ICI Plant Protection Ltd, together with land devoted to forestry and farm woodlands.

As the range of activities and demonstration units, and particularly technical events, expanded at Stoneleigh during the late 1970s, so there was a pressing need for the Society to increase its landholding. The original lease gave the Society some 600 acres next to Stoneleigh Abbey and its provisions included a rent review every 14 years, the rent to be negotiated four years in advance. As the two sides could not reach agreement by Christmas Day 1974 (when the first review was to be completed) recourse was had to arbitration and, after the arbitrator's award, both sides decided on a major Deed of Variation. This incorporated changes which were felt to be necessary in view of the way that the NAC had developed over its first decade. The 'mammoth task' of the renegotiation took three years and the Society's file on the subject fills seven volumes; principal responsibility for the negotiation on the RASE side was undertaken by Sir Francis Pemberton and John Hearth with Mr Jim Eve of Savills acting in a professional advisory capacity. The new arrangements included provision of a rent review every ten years; provision for the Society to have its own road access from No. 4 Entrance to the B4115, thus in the fullness of time enabling it to operate without using the Grecian Lodge Drive; and, perhaps most important of all, implicit recognition for the first time of the Society's right to hold non-agricultural events. Most significantly, in terms of the NAC's development, was that an additional 150 acres of land on the west side of the showground between the B4115 and the A45 Kenilworth by-pass were made available to the Society under a 21-year partnership agreement with Lord Leigh.[35]

The Society's landholding was greatly extended in 1980 when 296 acres to the south-east of the showground, between the A444 and A445 roads, was purchased from the Stoneleigh Estate, the sale being prompted by the need to finance death duties following the death of Lord Leigh. The purchase was made possible by the generosity of Sir John Eastwood (who revolutionised the poultry industry in the late 1950s) in arranging to give the Society £1 million over ten years through the Sir John Eastwood Foundation. In what was described as 'an imaginative form of sponsorship' Barclay's Bank made a fixed-interest loan available at an advantageous rate to facilitate the acquisition. In commenting on his gift Sir John said:

> The creation of the NAC has been a considerable achievement by the RASE. I have spent my working life in the agricultural industry, and it gives me great personal satisfaction to be able to assist in the further development of the centre.[36]

This land was designated the 'John Eastwood Farm' in recognition of the benefaction, while the 45 acres of the No. 1 car park opposite the main entrance to the NAC, which was also acquired (formerly being held by the Society on lease) was named the 'No. 1 Barclay Park'. This brought the land in the Society's long term possession to 911 acres: 570 on 99-year lease plus the 341 acres purchased, with medium and short term agreements on a further 125 acres. Further recent acquisitions include the Manor Fields Farm of 112 acres adjacent to the NAC which was purchased in 1982, with an additional 46 acres adjoining Manor Fields purchased in 1983. This was followed by another nearby 81 acres in 1984. In 1979 a revised Supplementary Charter was granted to remove the original limitation that the Society was not to hold more than

Sir John Eastwood. This portrait by Bernard Hailstone RA, was unveiled by HRH Duke of Edinburgh on the first day of the Royal Show 1980, to commemorate Sir John's gift to the Society.

£50,000 in land. These acquisitions had a two-fold purpose: to provide an additional 'lung' to meet the needs of the permanent demonstration units and, secondly, to ensure that there was sufficient land on a secure basis to allow an adequate rotation of the series of increasingly complex and demanding specialist events and demonstrations.

The Society also has two farms away from the NAC, both arising from initiatives and personal relationships of Christopher Dadd. It was the wish of William Scott Abbot, owner of the 575 'acre Sacrewell Farm at Thornhaugh, near Peterborough, that his life's work on that holding should be perpetuated through the form of a charitable trust. He died in 1959 but his wishes were realised by his wife Mary who conveyed the farm freehold to the William Scott Abbot Trust to be operated under the auspices of the RASE. The Society is the

240

Corporate Trustee and operates the farm through a management committee, nominating Trustees to act on its behalf. The objects of the Trust are very much in conformity with those of the Society's own Charter:

(i) To encourage agricultural education and training with particular emphasis on pre-college experience for pupils

(ii) To stimulate and assist Agricultural Research, stressing the value of Economics to the farm business

(iii) To foster the well-being of the Land, the Agricultural Industry and all engaged in it[37]

In contrast to Sacrewell – a lowland farm on the eastern side of the country – in 1968 Mrs Louise Ryan gave the Society her 100 acre Stowford farm near Ivybridge in Devon.[38] Both of these farms have proved extremely useful in aiding the Society's work, enabling a range of projects to be undertaken and providing venues for demonstrations of practical farming, regional events, and educational and farm interpretation exercises. Stowford has meant that the Society has been able to focus attention at first-hand on the problems of profitable farming in a marginal upland environment. Policy at Stowford is at the time of writing under review: the aim is to establish a farming system which reflects not only the problems of upland farming, but the ways in which an integrated land use policy can be developed – reflecting current and future pressures on the land use aspects of the agricultural industry.

The National Agricultural Centre has developed into a sophisticated hub of agricultural communications as a result of the vision of those who compiled the 'Fact-Finding Report', the dedication of the Society's officers and staff, and the generosity of individual and institutional benefactors and sponsors. At his retirement in 1977, Christopher Dadd was able to show that of 36 recommendations in the 'Fact-Finding Report' action had been taken on half, while a few had been tried and failed and others were no longer relevant.[39] This progress has not been achieved easily and has, to a degree, followed the cyclical fortunes of the agricultural industry as a whole. There have been some exceptionally good years for the Society and others when, sometimes because of chance events, things have gone less well; 1970 and 1971 were, for example, very difficult years for the Society as the critical funding operation was not yet underway and some leading firms withdrew from the Royal Show. In 1976, with rampant inflation, limited progress on the lease negotiations, problems with rating and VAT, the Society was 'embattled on a good many fronts' while 1980, with a very wet show and the failure of the major leisure event, was the 'most difficult year since the Society went to Stoneleigh'. This was in complete contrast to the previous year which was 'one of the best the Society had ever had'.[40] More recently, by the end of 1985 it was noted that the Society was not immune from the hard times that were facing the agricultural industry generally; the Society's response was to promote its image and corporate identity by means of a redesigned logo, a restyled *NAC News*, and a member-ship drive under the direction of a Membership Development Officer.

There is some uncertainty about the developments adjacent to the Stoneleigh site following the decision of the present Lord Leigh to leave the Abbey, while few present participants or observers of the agricultural scene would feel able to be confident about the short- or medium-term prospects for English agriculture. However, it is arguable that it is in times of uncertainty, change, and adaptation that the Society's work is at its most important, even if this makes its funding more problematical. At the heart of the NAC are the demonstration units and a year-round programme of events which have the crucial role of linking research and development to farm practice and it is to these technical areas that we must now proceed.

DEMONSTRATIONS AND TECHNOLOGY TRANSFER AT STONELEIGH[41]

At the time of the acquisition of Stoneleigh the demonstrations were an established part of the Royal Show following the success of the pioneering efforts at Cambridge and Newcastle but the concept of year-round units was still uncertain. The first permanent demonstration was the Bull Performance Testing Unit for which a timber building was constructed during the early part of 1963 and opened on 15 August. The Devon, Hereford, Lincoln Red, and Sussex Breed Societies sent bulls although the response was disappointing in that only 33 out of a possible 64 places were taken up.

The unit which established the pattern to be followed at Stoneleigh was that which was established for pigs. This developed out of the 1963 Farm Buildings Demonstration Area which included several specialist pig houses; there were no live pig classes that year because of countrywide outbreaks of swine fever, but regulations allowed pigs to be brought in from Warwickshire to demonstrate 'controlled environment' housing for the fattening pig. Later in 1963 Peter Buckler encouraged his firm of R Silcock and Sons Ltd to become involved in the running of the demonstration unit on an all-the-year-round basis and a 40-sow unit was established with advice taken from the Pig Industry Development Authority on sources of stock of the right quality.

As the pig unit expanded, and plans were made for other units, it became clear that the original site – on what is now the Town and Country Centre – would not be adequate for the purpose and the move was made to the northern perimeter zone of the Stoneleigh site where the various demonstration units are now grouped. The Bull Performance Testing Unit was used for temporary housing during the transition period. The pig unit was redeveloped in 1968 when the PIDA (later taken over by the Meat and Livestock Commission) made a grant of £25,000 and in March 1969 a meeting between the MLC,

Silcock and Lever Foods Ltd, and the RASE at Stoneleigh determined future policy and financial responsibilities, with a Management Committee answering to the RASE Demonstrations Committee (as it then was). A four-year plan of demonstrating the natural cycle of pig production was decided upon – the Pregnant Sow (1969), the Sow and Litter (1970), Rearing and Weaning (1971), and Fattening (1972) with each stage demonstrated under five main headings: Housing, Management, Recording, Breeding and Health. The Manager of the pig unit for the first eight years was Keith Thornton whose first connection with the RASE had been in helping to reconstruct the Showground in 1962 while reading agriculture at Newcastle University. At a presentation at the 1972 AGM Christopher Dadd recognised that 'the success of the pig unit had been due very largely to the hard work, imagination and, above all, the technical efficiency of Mr Thornton'.

In the 1960s the pig industry underwent a rapid transition to much more intensive systems and the pig demonstration units provided a particularly useful function in bringing innovative techniques to the attention of the farmer in a working environment. Especially important was the initial sponsorship of Silcocks who provided finance and staff because, as D H Robinson pointed out in his 1968 survey of the formation of the National Agricultural Centre, many official and trade bodies were initially cautious and the success of the Pig Demonstration Centre showed more than anything else the potential of the whole NAC concept and encouraged interest by other commercial firms.[42] A Poultry Demonstration Unit was opened in 1966 under the sponsorship of Spillers followed by a Beef Unit. This was firstly concerned with the maximum use of grazing and conserved grass throughout the life of an animal: later a calf-rearing unit was opened in March 1967 and divided into four sections showing a controlled environment house, converted Dutch-barn, straw-bale shack, and a hardening-off area. The outbreak of foot-and-mouth disease late in 1967 delayed plans for a Sheep Demonstration Unit. This eventually opened in 1968 with the prime objective of indicating ways in which sheep profitability could be increased. Thus forward-creep grazing was shown, and there was a demonstration of intensive indoor fattening of early-weaned lambs. In 1971 attention was directed towards ewe productivity based on Dorset Horns, which can be mated more than once a year so that a flock can lamb three times within a two-year period. A Dairy Unit opened in 1970 with the main aim of demonstrating modern techniques in dairy husbandry, including buildings and equipment.

As the number of demonstration units built up attention began to be focussed on how best to make the facilities of the NAC available to the farmer on a year-round basis. Initially, most of the work of the NAC was seen at the Royal Show while some of the commercial sponsors arranged for their clients to view the work of the units, but it was far from straightforward in the early days to bring what the NAC was doing to the attention of the ordinary farmer. A first 'open day' at the Centre in October 1967 (shortly after the official opening) attracted

Pig demonstration unit at Stoneleigh.

only 70 visitors and gave rise to a certain amount of press criticism. This was considered not altogether justified as the Centre was then finding its way in how best to open the facilities and receive visitors.

Nevertheless, the enforced closure by foot-and-mouth restrictions of the Centre late in 1967 did provide an opportunity for a 'rethink' on viewing and demonstration policy; when the NAC reopened there was a system of 'viewing-days' on the first Tuesday and third Thursday of each month, 'theme days', and 'sponsors' days' with separate 'student days' to allow the Centre to make its special contribution to agricultural education. General open days were found to be not particularly useful because the specialist nature of the demonstration units meant that it was unlikely that many visitors would need to see all that was available. The best use of time at Stoneleigh was therefore achieved by identifying the particular interests of visitors and ensuring they obtained the maximum amount of information pertinent to them. The day-to-day arrangements for visitors and their reception was overseen by Jef Aartse Tuyn, then Assistant Demonstrations Officer, while the staff at the individual units had to run the farming operations at a high level of sophistication and also to give talks to the viewers of their units. Ray Carter, who found himself not only in overall charge of the demonstration units but also responsible for such things as the domestic and catering arrangements at the staff hostel, recalls the energy and enthusiasm of those working at the NAC during the late 1960s.[43] This enabled the Centre to overcome the considerable difficulties associated with its early phase, which was, in the words of the NACAB Chairman John Thatcher, 'a long hard sweat'.[44]

Apart from the disruption caused to the developing programme at Stoneleigh, it will be appreciated that the foot-and-mouth outbreak caused enormous problems at the NAC given the number of intensive livestock units and the difficulty of isolation because of the various people working at, or using, the Centre. The MMB 'lay-off' Bull Centre had some very valuable animals and there was the particular problem of manure and slurry disposal. When this very necessary operation was carried out in the spring of 1968 by means of spreading on fields adjacent to Stoneleigh the smell caused considerable outrage and protest among the village residents.

In the late 1960s and early 1970s a good deal of attention was given by NACAB as to how the Centre could best be developed – in retrospect, it was its formulation of ideas and forward planning that was the Board's largest contribution. In 1969 papers were circulated by Christopher Dadd and W Emrys Jones (later Sir Emrys Jones) outlining views on the development of the NAC over the next decade. Projects considered suitable for the RASE included field drainage, grassland productivity, animal health, and agriculture and natnature conservation, with activities orientated towards those problems which were likely to have the greatest economic significance in farming practice.[45]

It was suggested that the NAC might consider a development programme in these activities both at Stoneleigh and through a system of 'link farms', backed up by a comprehensive information centre. In discussion there was general agreement that 'communications' in the broadest sense were all important and that it was not the Society's role to undertake fundamental research. There was a good deal of support for the 'link farm' concept which could involve farmer-members of the RASE – and possibly also regional and county agricultural societies – in dealing with problems or trying out new techniques.

Further papers were prepared by Mr O G Williams (Agricultural Director of Fisons Ltd) and Mr A J Davies (Deputy Director, NAAS) on their view of the development of agriculture during the 1970s and its implications for the NAC. These papers, which were presented to the Society's Demonstrations Committee in March 1970, again emphasised the potential of the 'link farm' idea and the importance of the NAC as a complete communication system, and O G Williams emphasized the importance of 'minimising losses' as well as increasing production. Another facet was pollution, with the suggestion that Stoneleigh should be a focus of how agriculture could cope with environmental problems. There was also a stress on countryside amenities, with interested parties coming together under the NAC umbrella to devise schemes for farming to cope with the increased demand for countryside access. A J Davies stressed that the NAC should not be 'all things to all men' but should concentrate on specific aspects of agriculture at a given time and vary the theme according to circumstances.

With these and other papers (including presentations from Christopher York and George Jackson, then Principal of Warwickshire Agricultural College), together with discussions at NACAB and elsewhere, there were plenty of ideas formulated for the development of NAC. However there was still much to be done in terms of basic provision at Stoneleigh and financial resources were very limited. Indeed, when members of the Works Committee toured the ground early in 1971 they were disturbed at the magnitude of the task which lay ahead and were concerned at the dilapidated state of many of the buildings. This led them to the conclusion that the immediate priority had to be one of consolidation rather than expansion, with no new units until the condition of the existing roads and buildings had been considerably improved.[46] The Development Fund Appeal improved the financial position considerably and by the end of 1973 £240,000 of the money raised from that source had been put into capital works and some £300,000 into an endowment fund for the future support of the technical enterprises.

A major boost for the NAC came in 1971 with the decision of the Minister of Agriculture Mr James Prior (now Lord Prior) to base a unit of the newly formed Agricultural Development and Advisory Service (ADAS) at Stoneleigh. This followed contacts made by Sir Walter Burrell and Francis Pemberton when it was indicated that following the reorganisation of the Government agricultural advisory services it would be possible for the Ministry and the Centre to work in conjunction. The Minister was quoted as being 'impressed by the imaginative concept of the National Agricultural Centre – those concerned with farming helping themselves to raise the industry's productivity' and the unit, led by Mr Guy Haines, arrived early in the Spring of 1972.[47] There were specialists in pig and dairy husbandry, crops and grassland, farm mechanisation, land drainage, veterinary medicine, farm buildings, and land use aspects of conservation, recreation and amenity. The unit's dual aim was seen as assisting the NAC to achieve a high standard in its demonstration and communications work, and to develop the opportunities of the Centre for advisory work and in the communication of technical information to the agricultural industry. Members of the ADAS team were particularly involved in the development of 'link farm' projects and in assisting with the Society's expanding conference programme.

Thus with the Development Fund, the establishment of the ADAS unit, together with the appointment of a Chief Executive and the opening of the

Conference Hall in 1973, the early 1970s were a significant period in the overall development of the NAC's technical side. As Ray Carter observed at a presentation in 1971 in recognition of his work at Stoneleigh 'the ship launched five years ago had finished its first round, had come back to port, been repainted and refitted, and was ready to sail again'.[48] In this connection a major conference was convened on 1 November 1973 to plan the work of the NAC over the next five years, and leading figures from the agricultural industry put forward their views of the Centre's priorities. The Chief Executive identified six main points of consensus arising from the varied contributions:

(i) The NAC had a useful role to play in extending field-scale machinery demonstrations nationwide.

(ii) The Society's role in agricultural education was 'post-graduate', eg in farm management.

(iii) The role of the NAC as a centre for the collation and distribution of information should be expanded.

(iv) The NAC should lead the study of the economic implications of changes in farming systems.

(v) The Centre had a 'shop-window' function for British agriculture and should provide a permanent display of machinery, livestock and food to both British and overseas visitors.

(vi) That the RASE had an important role in the interpretation of agriculture to the general public and that it should pay particular attention to urban-rural relationships and care of the countryside.

One of the themes that runs through all of the various contributions to the forward planning of Stoneleigh is that of the NAC's role as a centre of communications. As Christopher Dadd pointed out, the RASE was neither wholly educational nor a wholly advisory body although involved in both forms of communication as it provided 'an opportunity for all engaged in agriculture to learn about and to understand new ideas, techniques, machines and systems of "improving agriculture", and by so doing improving the livelihood of those earning their living through the practice of farming'.[49] Since the early 1970s this 'technology transfer' has been achieved with ever-increasing sophistication by the demonstration units, technical events at Stoneleigh and at other locations around the country, and by conferences and symposia; developments in each of these activities will be reviewed in turn.

The Pig Unit, recognised as 'Stoneleigh's pride and joy' by 1971 formulated a second five-year plan in the autumn of 1972. This forecast that the average size of herds was likely to increase and that economic pressures on producers meant that a change to weaning earlier than five weeks was likely to occur. Thus the herd size at Stoneleigh was substantially increased and weaning began at three weeks in a heated temperature-controlled flat-deck weaner house which generated very considerable interest. In January 1975 a new farrowing house was erected with innovative design in the farrowing crates, followed by a finishing house to fatten the progeny of an increased herd.

Thus in the first ten years of its existence the Pig Unit had kept in the forefront of the industry's rapidly changing demands. In 1976 attention was focused on service management as the three-week weaning system, though successful in terms of the young pig, had not been found to attain the improved farrowing index that had been expected; the NAC unit was also much involved in pregnancy testing using hand-held ultrasonic testers. Later in the 1970s further attention was given to pig housing, including the development of combined rearing and finishing houses, investigations into problems of ventilation, and the trial use of new types of early weaning kennel which were devised on the unit. Other important areas of interest included the investigation of alternative feeding systems, development of new weighing systems, and the marketing of entire boars (which have advantages for the producer because of superior liveweight gain but suffer a financial penalty from the meat trade).

A further five-year plan was formulated in 1979 with prime considerations being animal welfare, effluent disposal, and the containment of energy costs. In order to keep up to date with rapidly changing pig housing systems, manufacturers were invited to sponsor buildings and equipment. In 1984 the managing sponsor, BOCM Silcock, announced a £250,000 expansion enabling the unit to be extended by 120 sows. Much of the development was planned to respond to new welfare codes and, as the first large-scale commercial application of the use of electronics in sow feeding, it allowed the return to bedding systems, the earlier problems of which had led producers to adopt intensive stall systems. This was yet another aspect of change in a dynamic – if notoriously cyclical – branch of the agricultural industry which under the successive management of Keith Thornton, Gerry Brent (1973–1979) and Bernard Peet has been so successfully demonstrated at Stoneleigh.[50]

The Dairy Unit, which opened in time for the Royal Show of 1970, pursued a number of objectives through the 1970s.[51] Special attention was given to feeding regimes and a mastitis control programme was started in 1971. Another early development was metabolic profile testing, started in 1972, which was designed to assess the nutritional and metabolic status of the herd by testing the blood for abnormalities. By 1973 a Dairy Unit plan had been formulated which allowed for expansion to 75 cows on the 40 acres then available and this was achieved by 1975. With advancing herd sizes in the late 1970s and rapidly changing technology, a major expansion took place in 1978 with the number of cows increased to 180, but with the original herd managed as a separate entity as a 'family farm herd'. Apart from the facility of comparing alternative management and feeding policies, the Unit has been able to monitor a number of specific aspects of milk production, the weighing and condition scoring of cows, assessment of cubicle bedding, feeding for high yields and butter fat production,

Beef-crosses at Stoneleigh.

behavioural studies of cows not grazing on grass through the summer, general questions relating to economic milk production, and the publication of records. Following reorganisation of the Unit associated with a change of sponsor in 1983 the indoor herd was disbanded and a herd of 160 cows established, based on a grass silage winter feeding regime. The imposition of milk quotas in 1984 gave the Unit the opportunity to evaluate response options and more recently the Unit has undergone a major planning exercise in order to anticipate trends and technologies of dairy production into the 1990s. A particularly notable feature of the Dairy Unit's work has been studies of milk and dairy hygiene in demonstrating ways of improving cow and milk cleanliness on farms.

The Beef Demonstration Unit was much expanded early in 1971 – opening at the Royal Show of that year – and, although both Units had their own management committees, it was run with the existing calf-rearing operation as one unit. Major investment in 1973 was put into permanent housing and finishing systems for cattle. An important contribution of the Unit has been in providing information on health practices designed to minimise disease and reduce calf losses, together with the refinement and communication of grass and cereal finishing systems linked with work on practical hygiene to contain disease problems such as ringworm.

It has been found more appropriate for the Unit to stress indoor finishing in the management of beef production than grass finishing, as the latter is difficult to demonstrate effectively to short duration visitors. The Unit has shown a range of systems available to the industry, with particular success in both cereal fed beef and silage/cereal finishing. A particular recent role for the Unit has been to demonstrate that lean beef, consistently demanded by the public, can be of good quality. The detailed records kept on the performance of different breeds and crosses, and the economics of production for specific markets under different feeding regimes, has meant that the Unit *Newsletters* have been able to provide the kind of detailed cost information which farmers need in a sector of production where margins are notoriously variable and fine. The additional land which became available at the NAC since the late 1970s has been of particular benefit in extending the range of systems that the Unit is able to demonstrate.[52]

By 1973 three different demonstration flocks had been established at the Sheep Unit and the overall theme of the work demonstrated was 'systems of finished lamb – throughout the year'. The systems used were early spring lamb from winter-born Dorset Horns, traditional summer and autumn lambs produced from intensive grassland flocks, and heavy winter hoggets finished on fodder crops. Promising results from the Dorset Horn Flock suggested expansion of this demonstration and 120 ewes and 40 ewe lambs were bought in April 1974; however but two years later it was considered that the attempt to establish an eight-monthly breeding cycle had met with only partial success. The decision was therefore made to revert to annual early lambing, with the introduction of Finn/Dorset Horn rams to increase prolificacy. There was particular interest in the 1970s in the Follow 'N' Flock which was formed in 1972. This intensive system involved rotational fertilizer applications on a grazing sector with a proportion of land retained for the production of conserved fodder. The system depended on a high stocking rate – fifteen ewes per hectare in 1978 – allowing for a productive grass break in a cereal rotation which was financially viable in its own right as well as having the benefit of incorporating organic matter into the soil.

In 1983 the Sheep Unit was reconstituted, with additional joint sponsorship and major investment by the RASE in new facilities, in 1985/6. The closure of the Bull Performance Testing Unit (consequent on the changing pattern of breed performance work) made some additional building resources available and allowed room for an extension of its site; the additional land at the NAC was also very helpful in this respect. Other work at the Sheep Unit which is worthy of note has included the use of low-cost plastic structures – originally designed for horticultural use – for ewe housing, the development of the circular sheep-dip, and the employment of ultrasonics in pregnancy and litter size determination (which is valuable in deciding winter feeding needs). Recent trials and demonstrations include monitoring of toxoplasma immunity in bought-in replacements (a joint venture with Liverpool University), the performance of

Low-cost plastic sheep housing developed at the Stoneleigh Sheep Unit.

lambs from rare breed ewes (in conjunction with the Rare Breeds Survival Trust), forage systems for winter housed ewes, winter shearing, indoor finishing of early weaned lambs on cereal diets, and the use of progestagen sponges to induce early and synchronised breeding.[53]

Poultry have been difficult to demonstrate on a scale which relates to the requirements of the modern industry but important work has been done on particular facets of egg and poultry meat production. The Unit was closed during 1968 when the original sponsors withdrew but it reopened in 1969 (under the sponsorship of the firm of J E Hemmings & Son Ltd). The first project was to compare the performance of twelve strains of brown-egg laying hens, subsequently extended into a study of the economics of white and brown egg production. Although the birds had all been vaccinated, an outbreak of Fowl Pest was confirmed on 24 November 1970; mortality in the laying flock was low and this occurrence was used to monitor the effect of the disease on egg quality. In 1980 a Poultry Review Group at the NAC assessed the entire structure, work, and future objectives of the Unit and a development plan was initiated.

An interesting aspect of the Unit's work in the 1980s has been the investigation of alternative systems of egg production. Intensive battery cage production systems have always had their critics and there is a limited – but increasing – demand for non-battery produced eggs. Thus both a free-range unit and a deep litter system have been established to allow detailed comparisons with the battery cages in terms of performance and, particularly, economics. The study has shown that free-range flocks can generate an additional margin over battery systems on account of the premium price realised by the eggs. This indicates that such an alternative system is viable so long as the consumer is prepared to pay an extra price for the non-battery egg. Whether the *majority* of consumers would ever be prepared to do this is, of course, highly doubtful.[54]

The most significant addition to the established Demonstration Units during the 1970s was the Cereal Unit, opened in 1977 and redesignated as the Arable Unit in 1983. The early NAC Units concentrated on livestock, which was relatively more easy to demonstrate in a restricted area, but with the appointment of Mr N A Barron as Technical Assistant to the Agricultural Director in 1973 additional attention was given to the services which the Society could provide through the NAC for the arable farmer, and an Arable Policy Working Group was set up to make recommendations to the Technical Development Committee. Although the opportunities for arable demonstrations at the NAC were limited, considerable scope was recognised for the Society to organise events elsewhere, particularly in co-operation with other organisations such as the Potato Marketing Board, British Sugar Corporation and so forth. In 1974 an Arable Fair was held at Sacrewell, the Society coordinated the information services at BP LANDWORK held at Bawtry on 25 and 26 September, and there was a major arable demonstration at the Royal Show.

The Cereal Unit was established as the result of initiatives taken by Christopher Dadd, Sir Francis Pemberton and Dr P Wellington (then Director of NIAB, Cambridge). It aimed:

> to indicate to farmers and others how developments in soil management, crop establishment, plant breeding, variety testing and seed quality, fertilizer practice, mechanisation and crop protection can be integrated into commercial systems of farm production and marketing (market requirement) and to collect such relevant data as may be necessary in order to:
> a) establish the relevance and viability of these developments
> b) provide new information of value to the Industry in general.

A particular feature of this Unit has been its establishment of a *national* programme based on four regional groups:

Wheat '84 at Cambridge.

Region	Group based at
Eastern	Cambridge
Northern	Askham Bryan College, Yorkshire
Midland	Royal Agricultural College, Cirencester
Southern	Hampshire College of Agriculture

Regional activity has been coordinated through the Society's national programme of events – particularly the National Cereals Demonstration, beginning with Wheat '77 at the invitation of the Trumpington Farming Company at Cantelupe Farm near Cambridge. When in 1983 the Unit was reconstituted and designated the Arable Unit, the scope of its work was widened to include potatoes, sugar beet, oilseeds, pulses, etc with a particular emphasis on combinable crops.[55]

The participation of farmer groups has been especially important to the development of the Unit's work. In 1977, for example the Cereal Unit, in conjunction with Mr H V Hughes, Principal of the Royal Agricultural College, Cirencester, brought together a group of Cotswold farmers to investigate optimum management systems for winter barley production. Particularly interesting was the way in which this initiative integrated local experience with available experimental findings to maximise yield and profitability in environmental conditions which presented a specific challenge; Barley '79, organised by the Society at the Royal Agricultural College, Cirencester, presented this group work amongst the exhibits and was the most comprehensive event of the decade for barley growers.[56]

The Arable Research Centres – a farmer-funded experimental industry activity based at the RAC, initially servicing the Cotswolds – were a direct consequence of the event and the contacts made there. This has proved such a successful approach that under the vigorous leadership of its Director and guidance of its Council the Arable Research Centres have now established a chain across the country.

Another early initiative of the Cereal Unit was the encouragement of crop recording to provide the farmer with data for future planning. More recently, the importance of both formal and informal farmer groups coming together to share knowledge and experience has been recognised as an important means of technology transfer: in 1985 the Unit published a directory of farmer discussions, farm walks, and trialling groups as a means of fostering regional self-help developments and in conjunction with *Farmer's Weekly* produced a *Guide to On-Farm Trialling* which can help growers to 'fine-tune' systems for local environmental conditions.

The Demonstration Units work closely in conjunction with bodies not specifically concerned with production *per se* – the ADAS unit, the Farm-Electric Centre (formerly the Electro-Agricultural Centre and renamed in 1971) and the Farm Buildings Information Centre (reconstituted in 1975 after a period of difficulty) – which also monitor developments in their particular areas, collect information, and contribute to exhibitions and demonstrations, conference and seminar programmes. The Agricultural and Food Research Council, which established a permanent base at Stoneleigh in 1982 with a full-time liaison officer (Mr J Hardcastle) also has links with the various activities while the *communication* of information generated by the demonstration activities was much enhanced by the establishment of an Audio Visual Unit at the end of 1979.[57]

The range of the demonstration units at Stoneleigh and their sophisticated nature has been made possible by commercial sponsors who have enabled the best of up-to-date systems information to be made available to the farmer and grower. The collaborating sponsors who have contributed so much to the success of the Stoneleigh enterprise are listed as an Appendix. It may be noted that there is no Horticultural Unit at Stoneleigh (although this was discussed in the late 1960s) and that the emphasis is very much on *production*; at a time when many would see the key to the maintenance of farm profitability in 'added value' and sophisticated marketing, it is perhaps surprising that there is no specific 'marketing' unit to explore such areas as contract farming, packaging and processing on-farm (or in co-operatives), manufacture, direct sales etc. The programme at Stoneleigh has, however, recognised individual value-added

Deer Farming Exhibit at Stoneleigh.

initiatives which have taken place and has featured these through conferences and other meetings. These initiatives have been promoted, jointly with the National Farmers' Union and others, through a Directory of Country Foods and the encouragement next of the effective promotion of farmhouse holidays as alternative farm enterprises through the Farmhouse Holiday Bureau. In mainline agricultural enterprises, the view has been that because the highly structured processing and retailing sectors of the food industry dominate the food distribution chain and are the farmers' prime customers, the value-added emphasis in production should be on showing how farmers can meet the increasingly demanding requirements of these sectors.[58]

Not all the units have been 'permanent' and the Deer Unit, which operated between 1979 and 1983 under the management of Alastair Dymond, obtained useful information on a nascent enterprise which attracted a good deal of attention from those exploring alternative operations in both upland and lowland situations. This is indicative of the way Stoneleigh has perpetuated the RASE's traditional 'catalytic' role in farming progress. All the demonstration units are reviewed by the joint sponsors on roughly a five-year cycle, when special attention is given to the continuing role of particular units.

255

During the 1970s the range of technical events sponsored by the RASE both at, and away from, the NAC showed a dramatic increase. As already indicated, the National Grassland Demonstration was one of the first externally sponsored national demonstrations to be attracted to Stoneleigh, and by 1972 this covered a demonstration area of 150 acres with some 75 separate demonstrations. A major breakthrough occurred in April of that year with the move of the International Dairy Show to the NAC. Although compared with the 'glossy Olympia spectacular' the new venue was then perceived as 'rough and barely ready' the show was thought to have been highly successful in that it was

> a working show for thoughtful working milk producers eager to examine their own techniques in the context of a changing market and yet outwardly looking with the opportunities and difficulties of Europe in mind.[59]

The following year the Royal Association of British Dairy Farmers (RABDF) took the International Dairy Farming Event, as it is now called, to Harrogate as an experiment. This was not successful and the event returned to Stoneleigh where it has been ever since.

The National Sheep Fair held at Stoneleigh in September 1973 brought together the largest and most varied turn-out of rams, ewes and lambs seen on a single site.[60] The 1,570 attendance was, however, a disappointment and the event was not repeated in 1974, being replaced by sheep demonstrations based at the Sheep Unit, but was then re-launched in a somewhat different form and has since grown on a biennial cycle to be an immensely successful national event – since 1983 being based at Malvern.

The Arable Fair held at the William Scott Abbot Trust, Sacrewell Farm, in 1974, though judged a success in terms of technical content, still only attracted 1500 visitors which was disappointing to the Society and the difficulties associated with the early development of the Society's technical events illustrate the problems involved in the establishment of the Society's year-round programme for

> New events take time to become established. People who attend are usually the professionals; they are not there for a day out; they go to learn; they want to move in, have a thorough look round and be out again smartly, particularly when the combine is poised and ready to go as many were in the area last week[61]

However, since these early days, the Stoneleigh specialist events have developed to the extent of attracting audiences from the whole of the United Kingdom and, increasingly, from other European countries.

An important new development for the Society was Muck '75 which was a technical presentation of working and static exhibits with a range of farm waste management methods and demonstrations of different manure-handling systems such as tankers, slurry guns, tractors and loaders, and spreaders. One of the newest techniques shown was slurry injection and there was also sprinkler irrigation for liquid separation from the solid content of slurry. This event occurred at

> A critical time in farming history. Tough anti-pollution legislation has forced farmers and researchers to look hard at the possibilities of recycling farm waste. Unrestricted spreading of manure on the land is no longer permitted. Meanwhile each year farmers are spending about £260 million a year on fertilisers and at the same time wasting or using inefficiently some 13,000 million gallons of effluent weighing 60 million tons and containing plant nutrients worth as much as £100 million.[62]

The event was repeated in 1977 – 'the biggest slurry show ever' – when it featured the 'widest range of equipment assembled in Europe for handling and treating farm waste'. One of the problems of Muck '75 had been a lack of slurry (as one of the storage tanks had collapsed shortly before the event) so that coloured water had to be utilised instead but this was not a difficulty in 1977 and 'visitors who carried the perfume of the day home with them could appreciate the efforts being made to reduce drift and smell to manageable proportions'. The 'Muck' events have since become a regular part of the Stoneleigh programme.[63]

The first arable event at Stoneleigh was a two-day 'From Seed to Harvest' potato demonstration, in association with the Potato Marketing Board, in March 1976 which attracted 5000 growers from as far as the North of Scotland and Cornwall. This was a 'split' event featuring trade stands on the Showground and 40 acres of demonstration plots a mile away with a coach service between the two. The repeat in 1978, again with the PMB, was the largest demonstration of its kind in Europe, while Wheat '77, at Cantelupe Farm, Haslingfield, was 'an idea on a grand scale' although some of the high yield systems demonstrated did not reveal their full potential because of the soil type.[64]

By the late 1970s therefore, the specialist demonstrations were settling down into a successful pattern and were seen to be a very efficient mode of effecting 'technology transfer'. They took the place of the 'link farm' programme which, although achieving a certain degree of success with projects on oil-seed rape, maize silage, and rotary parlours in the early 1970s was found to be less cost-effective in conveying information: by contrast, as many as half of all growers by *acreage* have been represented at the large arable events which have been held at Stoneleigh and at other locations during the 1980s

For 1985/6 the RASE technical events programme was as follows:

October	National Small Farming Event and Goat '87
April	National Pig Fair
	(Sponsored by MLC and *Pig Farming*)
May	European Poultry Fair

The Goat and Small Farming Event 1987.

June	Landscape Industries '88
June	Cereals '88
July	Sheep '88 (Three Counties Showground, Malvern)

and other events, such as Beef '82 and '86, and UKF Grassland Demonstration '87 are featured in the programme on a periodic basis. The National Small Farming Event and Goat '87 is an interesting development in that it began as a goat show to mark the anniversary of the Goat Society in 1982 which attracted an unexpectedly large response. Since that time goats, far from being a 'cinderella' animal, have attracted serious interest as an 'alternative enterprise'. The event was broadened in 1987 to include a range of farm 'diversification' areas including 'organic' crops, small woodland management, farm tourism, deer farming, duck and goose production and mushroom growing with an emphasis on 'adding value' with displays of processing, packaging and marketing.[65] The development of the goat event and its extension is another example of the 'catalytic' function of Stoneleigh which has always been part of the

258

RASE's prime purpose. It is also indicative of the way in which the Society is of assistance to a range of agricultural and rural interests in addition to the large specialist grower or stock-rearer.

The third main sphere of year-round activities at Stoneleigh is the conference programme. The first RASE conference was held in November 1963 (at the Chesford Grange Hotel, Kenilworth) on the subject of 'Profitable Farming in a Competitive World' followed, in 1964, by 'Breeding for Beef – A Discussion'. The conference programme developed, albeit slowly, during the late 1960s but it was not until the arrival of the ADAS unit and the completion of the 320-seat Conference Hall in 1973 that major expansion was possible – some of the early conferences at the NAC were held in quite primitive conditions. Since the early 1970s the conference programme has been arranged jointly by the Society and ADAS and the proceedings are published.

The annual lists of conference topics provide an interesting insight into agricultural progress and changing concerns. The following, for example, was the programme for 1973/4:

Farm Waste Disposal	Progress in Grassland
Housing of Young Calves	Milk Research
Pig Health and Productivity	Calf Health and
Oil Seed Rape	Productivity
Damage to Ware Potatoes	The Development of the
Dairy Herd Health &	Farm Business
Productivity	Livestock Environment
Beef Production from the	Escalating Machinery Costs
Suckler Herd	Tree Planting on Farms
Straw Utilisations &	Heavy Lamb Production
Disposal	Non-ploughing on Arable Farms
Pig Research – What's in	Dairying in the EEC
the Pipeline?	Annual Pig Conference
Livestock Disease Control	Annual Poultry Conference
in Europe	Sheep Health and
Tourism and Recreation in	Productivity
Farming	

and there were also experimental three-day 'in-depth' conferences and seminars on such topics as fish-farming and farmgate sales.

More recently, the following topics (selected from the full programme) are indicative of changing farming preoccupations:

1981   Pitfalls and Opportunities for the Next
        Generation of Farmers
      Growth Promoters: Safety with Profit
      On-Farm milling and mixing

1982 Energy on the Farm
The Alternative Farming Ladder
Recreation and Access to the Countryside

1983 Quality Lamb – Efficiently
Growing Oilseed Rape and Peas Better
Growing Wood for Fuel
Joint Ventures in Farming

1984 Slurry and the Environment
Straw Incorporation – the Methods & Machines

1985 Cultivating the Bank Manager
More Lambs per Ewe – Can science really help?
Planning a Future with Milk Quotas
Soils Workshop (including guidelines for
Straw Incorporations)
Agreeing on Access

1986 Lower Input Farming – Myth or Reality?
Compensation for conservation – a Review of
Experience
Organic Farming – the Natural Alternative?

The full programme for 1987/8 was:

November   Mohair or Cashmere Production – A New Farm
Enterprise
Water Pollution – The Farming Perspective
Recent Advances in Improving the Health of
British Farm Livestock
The National Agricultural Outlook Conference – The Outlook for
Eastern England
(St Ives, Cambs)
January   Alternative Combinable Crops – Harvesting and
Storage
Stockmanship in Pig Production
February   Setaside – What Will it Mean for you?
The Rational Use of Pesticides
Milk Product Manufacturing on Farms –
An Opportunity
March   Fresh Income – The Change in Planning
Controls
Animal Health: Human Health in Agriculture
April   Harnessing Working Horses for the Future
May   Progress in Poultry Production

International Symposia at Stoneleigh. Delegates to the Animal Health Symposium 1985.

The 'Outlook' conference has been a regular feature of the programme in the 1980s focusing on a different part of the country in turn. The list above clearly mirrors the current shift of emphasis in farming concerns away from production *per se* (although this is still important) to alternative income sources and wider environmental issues.

An important continuation of the conferences since 1983 has been the establishment, largely on the initiative of the Agricultural Director, of a programme of International Symposia, one of which is always conveniently held at Stoneleigh during the week prior to the Royal Show, enabling delegates to attend both functions. The 1983 Symposium dealt with Advances in Cereal Technology, and other Royal Show symposium topics have dealt with Education and Training for International Agricultural Devolopment (1984), Animal Health (1985) and Bioscience in Crop Improvement (1986). The 5th Royal Show International Symposium in 1987 was held on the theme of Communications in Agriculture at the conclusion of which delegates asked the Society and

261

the Agricultural Director to consider the establishment of an International Association to promote interest in this important topic in a world which was shrinking and in which the pathways of information and technology-transfer globally are beginning to change. The selection of themes is always forward-looking and is based on areas of activity in which UK excellence provides a fundamental strength.

The 1988 Royal Show Symposium was based on the theme 'Towards an Agro-Industrial Future'. Other themes have included topics like Farm Electronics and in May 1987 there was an important contribution in the form of an international seminar exploring the Role of Women in Agricultural Extension. This was held jointly with the British Council and sponsored by the Technical Centre for Agricultural and Rural Co-operation. As George Jackson pointed out in his preface to the 1987 Symposium the RASE's Charter provides in its second objective for the Society to confer and correspond with those 'from both home and abroad' and to communicate this information, and the international programme is therefore part of a 'global web' of agricultural communications of which Stoneleigh has become an integral part.

The year-round range of activities at the NAC has enabled the RASE to be a potent force in agricultural development . Not only do the demonstration units attract many thousands of visitors each year but the publication of unit newsletters further facilitates the exchange of experience. In addition increasing farmer involvement, as in the Cotswold cereal group and the farmer – plot "competitions" at the Royal Show, enables research to be incorporated into practical farming systems. It is in this way that many of the hopes of the original 'Fact-Finding Committee' have been translated into reality.

ROYAL SHOWS AT STONELEIGH: FROM SUMMER PAGEANT TO INTERNATIONAL AGRICULTURAL EXPOSITION[66]

'The real test of a permanent Royal, everyone has said, will come with the third show on a permanent site.' So began the report of the 1965 Royal Show in the *Farmer and Stockbreeder* and its judgement was that even if there were 'threads of nostalgia for the old, mobile days running through some conversations' to most visitors 'a return to an itinerant show was unthinkable'.[67] The general reaction to the event was favourable although there was some criticism of the paucity of working demonstrations in comparison with static displays. This was coupled with a warning that with the permanent site now accepted as a reality, the Society needed to look for innovation and development. The show period was again wet, but underfoot conditions remained reasonably firm, there were few problems with the car parks and traffic moved smoothly.

Any tendency towards repetitiveness was avoided in 1966 because of new trade representation, a significant extension of the range and scope of the demonstration area, and through 'subtle changes in the entertainment pro-gramme', but the event was marred by torrential rain on the first day. This meant that, for the rest of the week, the stock lines, in particular, were often ankle-deep in mud: 'permanence', however, was beginning 'really to show its value in the part of the demonstration area devoted to crops'.[68]

The 1967 event was 'one of the best Royal Shows within living memory' and, in almost ideal weather, a good deal of business was transacted; on the first day, there was 'scarcely a fashionable woman or a bowler hat – only thousands of people scuttling along with much too much of importance to see in too little time'. Under these conditions 'the top brass was rather less keen than in the past to dismiss the gate as irrelevant'. Thus Stoneleigh was attended with a 'sweet smell of success' and, on completion of Francis Pemberton's term as Honorary Show Director the 1967 Royal was seen as his 'crowning triumph'.[69]

By the late 1960s the Royal had reached new heights of purposeful agricultur-al exposition and although retaining its position as the Society's most important single event, it was as part of the programme of year-round activity that has already been reviewed. This 'new concept' was seen to be 'working out as its authors – notably Lord Netherthorpe, Mr Francis Pemberton, and Mr Christopher Dadd – planned that it should'. Under 'Archie' MacArthur's Directorship the 1968 Show had 'enough new lines to be significantly different from the previous year' and the demonstrations were crowded with spectators. The following year it was said that the Royal had transformed itself 'painfully and with some rancour into a show better than which it would be difficult to find anywhere in the world'. The £1 entrance fee was doubled in 1970 with little detectable effect on the attendance and the admission charge was seen to represent good value.[70]

The early 1970s were, however, difficult years for the Royal Show. The agricultural industry was suffering under an increasingly severe price-cost 'squeeze' and home sales of agricultural machinery, in particular, suffered as a result. In 1970 and 1971, therefore, many of the large machinery firms were missing from the show – although it was noted that their products were to be seen in the showground on the stands of various distributors – and this had a serious effect on the show receipts, trade stand fees being down by some £18,000 in 1971. The Society's response was to re-organise the machinery lines for the 1972 show by grouping like products together for ease of viewing and to provide space in which machines could at least simulate their intended activity. This was coupled with a much more intensive marketing drive to sell stand space, particularly to potential overseas exhibitors; as a result of these efforts the losses were soon made up and significant improvements were made to the crop demonstration areas.

In the early 1970s decisions also had to be made about the future development of the general character and emphasis of the show. The 'commercial look' had been emphasised since the first demonstrations at Cambridge in 1960 although

263

'Alcoholic Sociability'. To Robert Trow-Smith in 1972, part of the charm of the Royal Show.

it was always recognised that events for the non-agricultural visitor had their place. One view, however, was that the Royal offered neither a comprehensive demonstration (other than the permanent units which were better visited on specialist days) nor unanimous trade support because of the cost of exhibiting. On the other hand, it could provide an interesting and carefree day while to Robert Trow-Smith its 'alcoholic sociability' was part of its charm, 'a demonstration centre dressed in fine trappings for four days in July and in sensible denims for the rest of the year, when the men who really matter come'.[71]

In 1972 the decision was made to limit the main ring attractions to show jumping and massed piped bands as, in the words of the Society's then Head of Marketing, P R Taylor, it was considered that the show could 'stand up as a major agricultural event without the trimmings'.[72] Under the successive Honorary Directorships of Sir Dudley Forwood (1973–7), Joe Harris (1978–82) and Richard Ferens (1983–7) the technical and professional content of the show became increasingly sophisticated and it is in this context that the show attendance and Society membership since the move to Stoneleigh needs to be viewed:

TABLE 4: Royal Show Attendance since 1963

Year	Show Attendance	Year	Show Attendance
1963	111,916	1967	151,521
1964	138,803	1968	134,418
1965	132,349	1969	127,116
1966	144,182	1970	125,372

Year	Show Attendance	Year	Show Attendance
1971	124,134	1980	225,804
1972	165,383	1981	226,561
1973	178,262	1982	228,311
1974	186,220	1983	224,675
1975	226,330	1984	224,123
1976	191,684	1985	214,318
1977	196,843	1986	203,102
1978	194,418	1987	214,375
1979	211,988		Source: RASE

The figures for show attendance before 1972 underestimate the total number of people present on the showground as they relate only to those who paid and exclude exhibitors, members, guests, officials and so forth – the equivalent lower figure in 1986 would have been 163,000.

The show statistics illustrate the very buoyant nature of the event through the mid and late 1970s with a peak of 226,330 visitors in 1975 and attendance around the 200,000 figure was quite usual. The fall-back of attendance in the early 1980s was of concern to the Society and was in part attributed to a reduction in the number of children attending. This in turn was put down to educational cutbacks, the teachers' strikes, and the lack of agricultural content in the school curriculum.[73] The success of the August Town and Country Festival was also thought to have reduced the local audience on the Thursday. It will be noticed (from fig 10) that the membership of the Society fell during the late 1960s and the greatest loss was in districts remote from Stoneleigh where potential members were less likely to avail themselves of Show or other NAC facilities; this led, indeed, to the charge that the Society was 'becoming the Royal Agricultural Society of Warwickshire'. Emphasis on demonstrations and events away from Stoneleigh then led to an increase in membership especially during the late 1970s since when it slipped back as farming entered a more difficult economic climate. There has been debate as to whether the institution of a joining fee in 1982 has depressed membership, while further consideration has been given to a two-tier membership pricing structure to take account of the difficulties of those living considerable distances away from the showground. A number of country meetings have been held in recent years at locations distant from the West Midlands in order to maintain links with the membership. Recent examples of these are Boyton, in Wiltshire, in 1985 at the invitation of Mrs E R Wheatley-Hubbard (the Society's Deputy President for the year and formerly Chairwoman of the Technical Development Committee), Werrington Park, Cornwall in 1986, hosted by Mr Robert Williams, and at

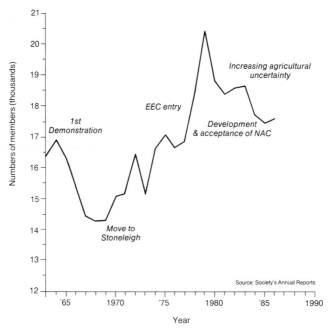

Fig. 10 Membership of Royal Agricultural Society of England 1963-1987

Numbers of members (thousands)

1st Demonstration

Move to Stoneleigh

EEC entry

Increasing agricultural uncertainty

Development & acceptance of NAC

Source: Society's Annual Reports

Year

David Carr-Taylor's Westfield, Sussex, Vineyard in October 1987. It is hoped that the National Celebration of British Food and Farming planned for 1989 – the year of the sesquicentennial show – will help to bring the membership back to the 20,000 level. In the case of both the show and membership, the RASE has been recruiting from a significantly declining number of those engaged in practical farming during the time that is has been based at Stoneleigh while, as John Hearth stressed in 1973, many of the benefits of membership are also available to non-members.[74]

The opening of the Show changed to Monday from Tuesday in 1972 with the emphasis on the professional viewer on the first two days; a suggestion for Sunday opening in 1978 created a considerable furore among trade exhibitors and breed societies alike.[75] The Agricultural Engineers' Association opposed an extra day which, it was thought, would not generate sufficient extra business to defray costs; the claim that the Sunday would prove attractive to the non-farming public was treated with suspicion and the proposal was later dropped. Linked to the matter of Sunday opening was the question as to whether the four-day Show period needed extension, for by the late 1970s the Chief Executive's view was that the limit of four-day attendance had been reached, and there were acute problems in accommodating as many as 100,000 people on the Showground on one day.[76] It is a matter of some surprise to overseas journalists that the Royal is limited to four days as no other comparable event in Europe is so short, but the exhibitors take the view that this comparison is unfair: there are fewer shows in Europe in relation to area and the Royal has to fit into a programme of other events which also make calls on the exhibitors' resources. The Sunday is now used as a 'rehearsal' day when overseas visitors, VIP guests, etc, can be given a preview while a change in 1987 was to equalise the admission charges over all four days with discounts for those attending after lunch. The effect of this was to reduce the distinction between the former early 'professional' stress and the later more 'popular' emphasis and to even out business over the whole of the show period.

Many of the Royal Shows during the 1970s benefitted from fine weather – slurry spreaders were used to lay the dust (with water!) at times. The vulnerability of the event to adverse weather conditions was brought sharply into focus in 1980 when the NAC received near record rainfall totals during the preceding June, combined with a very wet Show-week. As a result 'disaster threatened daily' in the grassed car parks, and some were closed or restricted in their use.[77] Thousands of bales of straw, and coarse gravel, were used to form access tracks. This was the first time that really adverse conditions had been experienced at the Showground since 1974 and substantial sums were diverted into car parks, road, and drainage improvements before 1981. However, full scale concreting of all the car parks (estimated at £2,600,000 in 1980) or the provision of access roads, was, and remains, far too expensive for the Society to contemplate, quite apart from environmental considerations. One consequencee of the 1980 experience was the abolition of car-parking charges at the Royal in order to speed access and traffic flow.

As the attendance figures show, there was a drop of some 20,000 in the number of visitors to the 1980 Royal, but the deficiency was thought to consist mainly of the non-farmers. This is a vital qualification of any consideration of the trend of Royal Show attendances, for the Society has always stressed that it is the *quality* of its audience which is more important than its size. Regular surveys of the profile of Royal Show attenders confirm its 'professional' character. The survey of the 1972 visitors for example, estimated that over 26,000 farmers and farm managers farming a total of 11 million acres visited the Show and that 60% of all men attending were connected with agriculture; in 1975 36% of all male visitors were farmers, farm managers, or farm workers – a figure which had increased to 43% by 1983.

Significantly, the 1983 *Audience Profile Report* found that as many as 83% of the farming visitors had a 'buying influence' – either as a purchaser or recommender of a purchase – in an identifiable area of agriculture. Apart from 'general interest', nearly one half of visitors in the 'farming' category visit the Royal to see new products and developments; and the opportunity to obtain technical or product information is also a major incentive to attend. Of those farmers, farm managers and workers attending the 1986 Royal Show, audience research revealed that 93% expressed an interest in exhibits, 54% planned to buy, 66% made a purchase on the basis of what they had seen within seven months, and 26% changed purchasing or working policies as a direct result of their visit.[78]

If 'people doing business' is the modern idiom of the Royal Show, there is still much to hold the interest of the non-professional viewer with the extensive Town and Country Area, Flower Show, 'Best of Country Living Feature' country sport area, conservation and rare breeds exhibits. All of these make a visit to 'The Royal' high on the agenda of those with an interest in rural life and the countryside. Livestock and machinery remain the chief foci of interest for many professional visitors with the arable area, featuring a range of 'alternative' crops and 'farmer trialling' plots an aspect which has recently assumed increased significance. Established technical exhibits include the 'Science into Practice' exhibition, while all the Demonstration Units mount special displays for the Show period.

The Farm Woodland Area always attracts extensive attention at the Royal Show and almost since its inception the Society has taken a keen interest in the management of timber and estates awarding highly prized Silver Medal Awards through competition to various categories of plantation. The regional Woodlands and Plantations Competition now runs on an 11-year cycle covering the various counties in sequence over the period of each cycle, and is organised jointly with the Royal Forestry Society of England, Wales and Northern Ireland. The awards are presented in the Farm Woodland Area during the Royal Show – an area which reflects not only companies servicing the forestry and farm woodland industry but provides also a strong educational element typified by the establishment of the Tree Collection in 1978. The work of the Farm Woodlands Sub-committee, which includes Forestry Commission representation, under the Chairmanship of Lord Clinton, has broadened the scope of the area to include the permanent demonstration of biomass production, and jointly with the Sheep Unit, a large scale demonstration exploring the new techniques of agroforestry using part of the John Eastwood farm for the purpose. This sphere of activity is likely to grow in future years.

Livestock exhibiting at the Royal underwent a major change in the early 1970s following the recommendations of the *Crathorne Report* (which runs to over 200 pages) in September, 1970. The Report had been commissioned two years previously to advise on the 'potential value of competitive livestock classes at the Royal Show'. For many years the organisation of livestock exhibiting had been left largely to the Breed Societies with RASE essentially the provider of space, and there had been a certain amount of questioning of the commercial rationale of show objectives. Among the wide range of the Report's findings – including the need to explore all avenues (such as sponsorship) to raise the level of prize money – were the recommendations that performance data should be displayed in the stocklines and that there was an overwhelming need to improve the promotion of livestock exports.[79]

One of the essential purposes of the Royal Stock Shows was seen as the provision of facilities for the best representative sample of the breed to be viewed enabling a 'contemporary comparison' to be made in a competitive

Livestock at the Royal Show.

context. The Report's key finding, however, was that the pedigree lines had failed to satisfy the requirements of commercial producers. While not rejecting the traditional emphasis on conformation and pedigree concepts, *Crathorne* stressed that there were other factors related to those qualities required in commercial stock and these needed to be discussed in relation to 'The Royal'. It was therefore recommended that the Breed Societies should take a critical look at all their competitive classes and advise the Society accordingly.

The most important concept to come out of the Report was that of Breed Promotion and Sales Centres, to which a whole chapter was devoted. The competitive stock lines had two chief functions: maintaining improvement in the conformation and soundness of stock, and acting as a 'shop window'. It was felt, however, that in the latter respect the system did not provide an adequate approach to sales as the potential buyer was given insufficient information on which to make a judgement. The system was also considered unsatisfactory for export sales, as it was geared more to selling a few animals at exceptional prices rather than large numbers at moderate prices. Prizes in the Royal Show Ring, by the early 1970s, were no longer seen as a guarantee of substantial sales for winning stock; rather, more information on the various scientific assessments was required. Thus 'Promotion and Sales Centres' managed by Breed Societies with comprehensive displays of information, orientated to specific require-ments, and indicating specific qualities, were strongly advocated.

Four major British cattle societies pioneered the Breed Promotion and Sales Centre concept at the 1970 Show, but at Stoneleigh 1971 'West Germany and France polished their already shining image as efficient supermarket operators in the livestock export fields. The contrast with Britain's small shopkeeper approach was stark'.

The Breed Societies pointed out that the West German and French exhibits were backed by national export agencies whilst the 'missing' British breeds stressed that they had no sponsors to back their promotions. In 1972 continental breeds of cattle were very much in the forefront – Charolais, Limousins, Simmentals, Maine Anjou, Meuse-Rhine-Issel, Red and White Canadian Friesians, Canadian Holstein Friesians, Canadian Herefords and Blonde d'Aquitaines (which were making their Royal Show debut). Against the overseas challenge were South Devons, Sussex, Dairy Shorthorns and with some Friesian AI organisations also represented, but the main British beef breeds were absent from the promotion area. It was claimed that there was no money for promotional work on an individual breed society basis, whilst a spokesman for the Hereford Herd Book Society said 'we take the view that if anyone wants to see our breed, they can do so in the judging ring, which shows the real competitive role of the breed'. Breed export business increased in 1973, although a particular point of contention was that the relatively easy access to the UK for European cattle did not meet with the same degree of reciprocity.[80]

The 1970s saw developments in livestock showing at the Royal Show very

Officials and Staff at the 1965 Royal Show as seen by 'Mac'.

271

much along the lines envisaged in the *Crathorne Report* with much more emphasis on the provision of performance records as a basis for commercial assessment. In 1978 breeds competing for the Dairy Burke Trophy were represented by two females, rather than a female and male as had hitherto been the rule. This change reflected the feeling that it was correct to place emphasis on the female line, while still recognising the influence of the sire through the quality of the daughters. New sheep classes that year reflected the increasing emphasis on export markets and carcase quality; more recently, carcase displays have been extended at the Royal Show although the NAC lacks a purpose-built carcase hall.

Livestock exhibiting had a major boost at the end of the 1970s with much increased sponsorship – most notably from the National Westminster Bank – and the Wellcome Foundation, Dalgety-Spillers and Calor Ltd have since provided additional generous sponsorship. Awards for the best promotion of livestock in the lines were instituted in 1982 and classes have been constantly modified in consultation with Breed Societies to reflect changing trends and requirements. There have been particular developments in sheep during the 1980s with the National Sheep Association being especially active in breed promotion and in 1982 a 1240 square metre sheep area was opened. The value of competitive showing of pure-bred pigs has been questioned, as most replacement breeding stock is produced with the emphasis on hybrids, but the continued support by the exhibitors of pure-bred stock with an interest in exporting are a counter to the charge that pig showing is no more than 'a fanciers' hobby'.[81]

Showing facilities have been much improved following Michael Rosenberg's sponsorship of the redeveloped sheep and pig accommodation lines, and the involvement of the RABDF in the cattle area, while improved accommodation has been provided in the Rank Village for those involved with stock showing. Show classes for the smaller breeds are important for their survival to which the Society has a clear commitment while competitive classes also provide opportunities for developing livestock interests – continental cattle breeds and, most recently, goats, being prime examples. After the somewhat hesitant start, British breeds are much better represented in the breed promotion areas and, for the 1987 show, the RASE and MLC joined forces to mount the Livestock Export Information Centre. This acted as a meeting place for overseas buyers, breeders and export agents, as well as advising buyers on appropriate stands to visit and providing information on such matters as export certification.

The Royal Show has traditionally been a focus for exhibits of agricultural machinery and an opportunity for innovations in agricultural engineering to be seen at first hand, and this area of activity has been developed since the Society has been at Stoneleigh. Significant refinements to the judging process for the Society's Silver Medals for new machinery were made under W H Cashmore, who succeeded S J Wright as the Society's Consulting Engineer in 1964. The

Machinery at the Royal Show.

emphasis for this award was on innovations which had been tried and tested in working conditions, and in 1972 the judging panel was strengthened by the addition of pre-judges (Claude Culpin, then President of the Institution of Agricultural Engineers and Chief Mechanisation Adviser to ADAS, Peter Jones, Machinery Editor of *Farmers' Weekly*, and T B Muckle of the Mechanisation Department of the National College of Agricultural Engineering, Silsoe) to the panel of 'farmer' judges and as a supplement to on-farm experience. In 1970 a Gold Medal award was instituted for manufacturers of machines or equipment which had made an impact on farming generally, or in a specific branch of agricultural horticulture, the first award in this category going to Wright Rain Ltd for irrigation equipment; other winners are listed as an Appendix. In 1982 this award was modified so that the Gold Medal was given to the outstanding entry in the Silver Medal award scheme, and the Burke Perpetual Challenge Trophy given to a company selected for its outstanding contribution to mechanical development. This award is based on consultations with a panel of about 20 referees who are invited to submit names of three companies in order of merit who have made, and are making, an outstanding contribution to mechanisation development.

Claude Culpin, who succeeded W H Cashmore as the Society's Consulting Engineer in 1974, outlined the essential elements of the Society's highly regarded Silver Medal scheme in the RASE *Journal* in 1983.[82] The award has the primary aim of assisting potential users of new machinery in the identification of sound qualities as soon as this can be safely done on the basis of practical information gathered from commercial use. Entry guides are sent to potential exhibitors at the Royal Show and a list of at least six users is provided who are able to receive visits from judges. To gain an award the RASE insists that spare parts and service are available, that an instruction book is provided, and that the equipment will continue in manufacture for the foreseeable future. The full judging panel, convened by the Consulting Engineer, meets in November and May and consists of the Senior Steward of Implements, four former members of the Panel selected by Senior Officers of the Society, the Senior Mechanisation Officer of ADAS, a Scientific/Technical Officer from NCAE, representatives of the publicity media, and a Senior Officer of the Health and Safety Executive Agricultural Division. The entrants discuss the machines with the panel either at the NAC or in London and for the award of the Silver Medal some important new feature is essential. An award is a recommendation that a potential user should include the winning machine on any 'short list' that he intends to study in detail. It also signifies that the equipment can do what is claimed for it, that users find it satisfactory and would buy again, and that the judges are not aware of serious faults or inadequacies. Claude Culpin was succeeded as Consulting Engineer by W E Klinner in 1985 and a recent change to the operation of the scheme is to publish machinery trial reports under one of two options at the choice of the entrants.

The machinery award winners are paraded and demonstrated at the Royal Show and there is a wide range of displays of equipment and tackle; over the years there have been persistent calls for more moving, rather than static, machinery exhibits. The 'trade' has generally resisted competitive trials; suspicion of this mode of assessment is very reminiscent of the controversy that surrounded the 'prize system' in the nineteenth century and which has been reviewed in an early part of this *History*. Particular facets of machinery demonstration during the Society's time at Stoneleigh which are worth highlighting include demonstrations of tractor safety cabs in 1972 when the Dutch stunt man Simon Van Schaik gave a twice daily demonstration of rolling a tractor into a pit and emerging unscathed from a safety cab. This was done against a background of an uncabbed tractor and crushed dummy, with a commentary that stressed that 28 tractor overturnings in 1970 had resulted in the death of the driver.[83] Also at this time the 'Eurotechnik' display attempted to show – not altogether successfully – 'the latest developments of agricultural machinery from any part of Europe and the United Kingdom, to bring together European agriculturists and manufacturers'. More recently the Tropical Agricultural Machinery Centre was an innovation at the 1984 Show, encouraged by the address of Sir Shridath Ramphal who opened the Show the preceding year. This is devoted exclusively to machinery and equipment suitable for tropical,

View of the Demonstration Plots at Stoneleigh.

arid and Mediterranean climates. Among products on show in the centre, which was staffed by personnel from the RASE and BAEC and sponsored by *Middle East Agribusiness*, were 'water weed cutting boats, ox-drawn carts, coffee machinery, hand held sprayers, irrigation and slurry handling equipment, disc ploughs, harrows and ridgers – and electric fencing suitable for fending off anything from the smallest wild animals to elephants'.[84]

In the difficult economic climate for agriculture in the mid and late 1980s the Royal Show provides a good opportunity for the agriculturist to consider at first-hand various 'alternative enterprises'. In 1984 the Arable Area for the first time embraced all the crop production interests on the Showground, drawing together the Soil Centre, Soils Marquee, Field Vegetable Centre, New Crop Opportunities Demonstration plots, Arable Marquee, farmer wheat system

Alternative Livestock Enterprises. Royal Show exhibit 1987.

plots, NIAB's and ICI Crop Protection Ltd's plots (the latter tended since 1964 by Harry Fox), together with related trade stands. Among new crop opportunities shown have been rye, lupins, peas, linseed, triticale and durum. It is appropriate to note the particular problems which are associated with getting

276

the crop demonstration plots ready for the show visitor. Small areas are very vulnerable to damage from wildlife and the Stoneleigh oaks are home to a number of squirrels, while bird damage is high because of the agreeable environment provided by the adjacent Livestock Demonstration Units.[85] In 1987 a new display, sponsored by Savills, featured alternative livestock enterprises including llamas, ornamental and table fish (koi, carp and trout), quail, sheep milking, goats, and a major display of deer farming.

Although the emphasis for the professional visitor to the Royal Show is clearly on the production side of agriculture – productivity, efficiency and cost reduction, and diversification – the Society has attached considerable importance to the involvement of the food trade with the event, but this has been far from easy to achieve. In 1970, for example, when National Pavilions of various overseas countries were under consideration for establishment at Stoneleigh, concern was expressed about the apparent lack of interest by the various organisations and companies in putting on an exhibit which would amply demonstrate English food. The Show Director ('Archie' MacArthur) observed that:

> Some two years ago he had been anxious that they should demonstrate at the Royal Show an exhibit of British food stuffs. They had called a meeting in Belgrave Square of all the major organisations dealing with British foodstuffs. They had all thought it a splendid idea and that the RASE should get it going. The Society had offered to provide the facilities but not the finance, and this had been the stumbling block. The food organisations had not been prepared to meet the cost.[86]

A specific Food Hall was first a feature of the Royal Show in 1973, with home and overseas products about equally represented. The Society contacted 4000 firms concerned with the processing, packaging and handling of food: 38 responded and helped with the launch.[87] In 1975 when the food exhibition moved to the Tate and Lyle purpose-built building, there were only 17 British stands out of a total of more than 50, while one estimate was that 42.3 per cent of the space was occupied by firms selling drink; as the editor of *Farmers' Weekly* commented, 'perhaps we are missing the opportunity of forging a closer link in the housewife's mind between the hoof and the hook or the silo and the loaf before the idea gets engulfed by drink and delicacies'.[88] The first co-ordinated promotion of British foodstuff was presented at the 1977 Royal Show under the 'Taste of Britain' banner when the RASE took the opportunity to state its collective belief that British food is second to none in quality and that 'this should be shouted from the rooftops, that the farmers who produced the food should know that it is being properly promoted, and that given the chance the consumer would prove the quality of British food by buying it'.[93] Since the late 1970s the food exhibition has grown in stature; a major development came in 1981 with the participation of the firm of Marks and Spencer who have a large

The Food Exhibition at the Royal Show.

stake in quality food retailing. Their stringent market requirements and high quality specifications have had significant implications for production systems. The food exhibition was re-launched in 1983 with support from the Food from Britain Organisation and currently about 30 companies, large and small, are represented in the Food Hall exhibition. This is now an established and popular part of the Show although still dwarfed when compared with, for example, that at the Paris Agricultural Show.

If one theme is to be picked out of all the various changes in the Royal Show since it has been permanently located at Stoneleigh, then the ever-developing international dimension of the event stands pre-eminent. The potential of Stoneleigh as an international business centre for agriculture was revealed at the very early shows; in 1965 for example 'overseas visitors were everywhere' and export orders, including $1 million worth of tractors for the United States, exceeded expectations. In 1969 it was observed that 'it would do a lot of industrialists a lot of good to be grasped firmly by the coat collar, taken to Stoneleigh, and made to realise how much export potential this little 'three per cent of our gross national product' occupation of ours contains'.[90]

A major development came in the early 1970s with the establishment of various national pavilions at the Royal Show. The first was that of France in

Frank Sykes.

1971 which exhibited representative samples of several French breeds of cattle and sheep, and had sections devoted to machinery, with details of French agricultural and horticultural production. In 1972 pavilions were established by Germany, Canada, New Zealand and Abu Dhabi and it was the first at which the ordinary farming visitor and the average trade exhibitor were thought to have noticed a real overseas emphasis. Thus, 'according to one's viewpoint' the 1972 Royal Show went down in history 'either as the event at which the Royal's struggle for an international image genuinely began to succeed or as the birthplace of consciousness of continental competition'.[91] By 1973 the increased number of national displays had been grouped together in one area and the French pavilion – one of the largest on the Showground – embraced subjects from native cattle to wine production and tourism. This was described as the most European show yet, and the Society's President Sir Christopher Soames (then an EEC Commissioner) stressed that British Farmers should view the CAP as Europeans; it is worth noting that one of the busiest areas was the Intervention Board section of the Ministry exhibit.[92]

In the late 1960s and early 1970s the official overseas attendance was in the order of 3000 at each Royal Show, and overseas awareness of the event during the early years at Stoneleigh was promoted by the Society's International Relations Officer, John Keyser. The international reputation of the Royal Show is, however, based very much on the foundation of the work done by Frank Sykes, farmer, author, and between 1950 and 1971 agricultural adviser to Her Majesty the Queen. With his wide range of contacts, and the help of his

279

assistant, Miss Cynthia James, the International Pavilion – rebuilt for the 1976 show – was very much his creation. In 1978 the French Government created him a Chevalier of the Legion d'Honneur – an honour rarely bestowed on British subjects and never before to an agriculturist – in recognition of his 'long standing work for the improvement of French/British relations in the agricultural field'.[93] Largely as a result of the efforts of Frank Sykes, by the late 1970s there were some 7,500 overseas visitors attending the show and such has been the advancing reputation of the Royal as an international event that this figure has since doubled. Surveys conducted for the Society have shown that agricultural machinery and livestock feature very prominently as attractions for overseas visitors of whom as many as half are active farmers; the Royal Show is now 'one of the world's agricultural meeting points, like Paris'.[94]

The Royal Shows at Stoneleigh have sometimes been organised around specific themes, but the size and complexity of the event now means that there is too much to be encapsulated in this way. Preparation for the event is a year-round effort and catering for the needs of over 200,000 visitors, exhibitors, journalists and officials over a four-day period is an immensely complicated operation. While the responsibility for putting the show together falls on the Executive, the Honorary Show Director has a very important role. If the nature of the Honorary Directorship has changed since the rather autocratic days of Lord Daresbury or Sir Roland Burke, the modern equivalent continues to be responsible for the honorary stewards and judges, their selection, appointment etc, and for all the very important committee and sub-committee work involved as well as such matters as the ring programme, consultations arranged between the RASE and Breed Societies and Exhibitors' organisations, and arrangements for official and Royal visits. While 'the Royal' is highly professional in its execution, it continues to depend very much on voluntary effort from the stewards who see to the efficient running of each of its sections. The 'bowler-hat brigade' retain their traditional symbol of office but those who act as stewards today essentially do it for the appreciation of involvement and as a welcome change from their normal occupation; as Peter Adams pointed out in 1980 'spending the week in a car park or in charge of manure disposal tends to sort the enthusiasts from the glory hunters'.[95]

So many different people have contributed to the success of the Royal Show at Stoneleigh since 1963 that it is invidious to pick out individuals, but in 1970 Mr Ernest Dillamore retired as Show Administration Officer after 24 years with the Society and a total of 42 years' service to agricultural shows; in 1975 W C Robinson retired after 27 years with the Royal, acting as the Society's Surveyor until 1964, then as Show Ground and Exhibitions Manager and Head of Works. Robinson's retirement severed one of the last links with the peripatetic show days – his first show had been at Shrewsbury in 1949. He recalled working with seven different Directors including Francis Pemberton with whom he had first come in contact at Cambridge in 1951. Looking back to the first years at Stoneleigh he remarked that:

> Mr Pemberton was always on the Show Ground before six o'clock in the morning on show days, and on several occasions I had thought 'I will beat him tomorrow', but when he arrived at 5.30, he always found him sitting on his horse, with a cheerful 'Good morning Robinson, don't worry, everything is under control'. You could not really win.[96]

EDUCATION: THE RURAL COMMUNITY AND ENVIRONMENT THE SOCIETY'S 'LEARNED ROLE'

The end of the Society's *formal* involvement in agricultural education followed the recommendations in 1966 of the Advisory Committee on Agricultural Education (the Pilkington Committee) of which Christopher Dadd was a member. This had been set up two years previously by the National Advisory Council on Education for Industry and Commerce which advised the Secretary of State on technical education. One of the main points at issue was the possibility that the Industrial Training Board would insist on uniform standards of training – with implications for the education services throughout the various industries for which it was responsible. Therefore, if agriculture did not make some move in this direction it might find a pattern imposed upon it. The Journal Committee, which oversaw the Society's interest in agricultural education, agreed that there was a need for a central body of some kind to co-ordinate the activities of the various agricultural examining boards and it was decided to support any recommendation to establish a central organisation with reponsibility for the overall standards of agricultural examinations. This was the substance of the evidence given by the Journal Committee's Chairman, Wilfred Shirley, to the Pilkington Committee on 8 April 1965; Christopher York had earlier pointed out that the Society should not be afraid to surrender some of its authority as the RASE had never objected to work which it had initiated being taken over by others when it could be shown that it would thereby be carried out more effectively.[97]

The Society also convened a meeting with other agricultural examining bodies including the Royal Horticultural Society, National Poultry Diploma Board, City and Guilds of London Institute, National Certificate in Agriculture Examinations Board, Royal Institution of Chartered Surveyors, Chartered Land Agents' Society and representatives of the National Agricultural and National Dairy Examinations Boards. However, there was no strong feeling at the meeting that there was a need for a co-ordinating body.[98]

The original recommendation of the Pilkington Committee had been to establish a Council for Agricultural Examinations, under which would be constituted award-giving boards with responsibility for examination standards in the various branches of agriculture. That would have left the detailed adminstration of the examinations in the hands of bodies similar to the existing agricultural examination boards and was a generally acceptable arrangement. Nevertheless, the Department of Education and Science came out in favour of a joint committee consisting of representatives from organisations in the industry, the teaching profession and Government, and the Society was invited by the DES to undertake its administration. This was not felt to be a very satisfactory proposal as the RASE and its officers would, effectively, be operating as servants of Government and be required to carry out policy over which they would have little control. The view of the Society's Education Officer, Frank Russell, was that it was not in the best interests of the RASE to undertake the adminstration of the joint committee. There was general agreement that the Royal shall not undertake a task where it did not have full control over its own operations and its conclusion was therefore that the Society should decline the DES invitation.[99] Thus the Society administered the NDA and NDD examinations until they were phased out, but did not have a role in the administration of the OND and HND examinations which took their place. This may have been inevitable, and at the time the Society's resources were needed for the development of the NAC, but the lack of involvement by the RASE in formal education has been a cause for regret ever since.

Much more interest was shown by the Society at this time to a proposal from a prominent Council member, Mr J Everard Hosking, that it should institute a senior, professional award in agriculture. Hosking envisaged the establishment by the Society of a professional body, with members drawn from the best practitioners of agricultural thought and experience. Fellowships or their equivalent would be awarded as a result of the Society's own examinations which would establish an agricultural qualification of the highest standard. A working party was set up to consider the feasibility of this proposal and recommended that the Society, in collaboration with the other Royal Agricultural Societies, should institute a distinctive senior award in agriculture with an Associateship (ARAgS) leading to a Fellowship (FRAgS) of the Royal Agricultural Societies. The aim of this proposal was to create a high calibre qualification for outstanding agriculturists who, although already having a recognised qualification, might wish to have a professional seal set on their achievement.[100]

Applicants would propose a project in a particular field of agriculture and present a treatise, project essay, or dissertation at least one year after the project was approved. If successful, this could lead to the conferment of Associateship. Fellowship would be awarded not less than 10 years after the first stage and would be reserved for those over 35 years of age who were making a distinctive mark in the profession of agriculture. The conferment of awards was to be vested in a Council or Committee of Fellows made up, initially, of eminent people in the agricultural field who would be afforded Fellowships. The long term objective was the establishment of a professional body which, it was thought, would be of great benefit to the agricultural industry.

A foundation Council of Fellows was appointed in October 1969, consisting of persons nominated by the three participating national agricultural societies (RASE, Royal Highland, and Royal Welsh) and the scheme was launched on 1 April 1970 with E C R Tasker, the Society's Education Officer who succeeded Frank Russell, acting as Secretary. Early experience indicated that those candidates presenting themselves for the Associateship were drawn mostly from the teaching, administrative, or research sectors of agriculture, and that the scheme did not attract the progressive farmers for whom it had been especially intended. As H G Hudson (Chairman of the Council of Fellows) recognised, such people tend not to have the time or inclination to write specialised dissertations and for this reason the original terms of the Associateship were widened. They would now allow alternative modes of assessment including short submissions on innovative farm systems, or a more detailed report on the study of a new agricultural practice, backed up, where appropriate, by inspection and interview on farms for which the candidates were responsible.[101]

Despite these modifications, increasing concern was expressed within the Society's Education and General Purposes Committee about the operation of the scheme which, by the late 1970s, seemed to fall between being a recognition of services to agriculture and a postgraduate award. There was also confusion between the Associate and Fellowship scheme and the Society's own expanded Honorary Fellowship, which is conferred upon eminent persons in the area of farming and agriculture (current holders of this distinction are listed in an Appendix). After considerable deliberations, and investigation into the operation of the FRAgS by John Green (then Chairman of the Education and General Purposes Committee), it was finally decided that the RASE would withdraw from the scheme. It continues on a subscription basis administered by the other national agricultural societies and with the English Fellows still participating.[102]

Soon after the establishment of the Society at Stoneleigh concern was expressed by Basil Neame, Chairman of the Agricultural Apprenticeship Council and of the newly-formed Agricultural Industry Training Board, that the Society's activities, as set out in the Fact Finding Committee report, did not appear to place much emphasis on education within the NAC context.[103] The response of Christopher York and others was to stress that agricultural education *per se* was rather outside the report's remit; nevertheless, since the late 1960s the NAC has had an important role to play in various aspects of agricultural education. The British Agricultural Training Board (formerly the Agricultural, Horticultural and Forestry Industry Training Board) Training Centre at Stoneleigh has, since 1968, run extended instructional courses for people who wish to pass on skills to others while the Education and Careers Centre – developed out of an initiative by Miss Elizabeth Hess (Principal of the former Studley College in Warwickshire) in 1964 – established a permanent pavilion in 1970, shared with the Warwickshire College of Agriculture.[104] This provides advice and information on all aspects of agricultural education, courses and careers, particularly for visitors to the Royal Show. John Skew, formerly Principal Careers Officer in Warwickshire, did much to develop the contribution of the Centre, continuing with the Society in a part-time capacity following his retirement from professional life. He was elected an Honorary Member in 1983 in recognition of his contribution.

More recently the Society has been involved in rural training projects, having been awarded in 1984 a two-year consultancy contract by the Manpower Services Commission to assist in securing a better take-up in rural areas of the funds and opportunities available under the Youth Training Scheme. In 1986 the Society formally launched its Rural Employment and Training Unit. With a small staff of four this Unit seeks to obtain a high national profile for the specific employment and training problems of rural areas, at the same time co-operating with Government agencies, local authorities and private initiatives on specific schemes that will generate employment in such areas. As in so much of the Society's work it acts as a catalyst, organising seminars and conferences as well as co-operating with all the other agencies in the field. Meanwhile, in order to ensure that the approach is not simply theoretical but based on a full understanding of practical realities, the Society has for many years been responsible for a specific training project at the NAC. This changes its programme from time to time in accordance with Manpower Services Commission's funding arrangements, but the Rural Crafts Youth Training Scheme, as it is currently known, has a high reputation and has achieved a better than 70% employment record for the young people who were typically unemployable when they first joined the scheme.

The Society has taken a close interest in agricultural education at all levels; as Christopher Dadd observed in 1977, agricultural education had been the subject of nine reports since the war but the position still remained uncertain and unsatisfactory.[105] The Hudson Committee in 1975 concluded that there was a need for an educationally independent national validating and examining body for agriculture, a view supported by the RASE but resisted by the DES. More recently, validation of the BTEC examinations was considered to be beyond the Society's resources although the RASE has representation on that body. Over the years the RASE has made a number of representations about the closure of agricultural colleges and the contraction in the number of University departments of agriculture.

Much of the Society's work is concerned with continuing education and this encompasses the provision of services to, and joint initiatives with, agricultural colleges. The Farmscan competition evolved over a three-year period in collaboration with Barclays Bank, ADAS and the University of Exeter into a 'Farmscan Goes To College' programme which ran for three years promoting the use of computerised farm management games as an aid to the teaching of farm management as a subject.[106] This was followed by an important initiative which grew out of a meeting between HMI Mr Peter Brown and the Society's Agricultural Director. This led to the establishment of a highly successful self-help group – the National Computer Users Group in Agricultural Education which has pursued the objective of assisting colleges, through exchange of information, newsletters and regular workshops, with the integration of computers into agricultural education and teaching practices. The Computer Users Group, for which the Society provides the Secretariat, has matured into an important network attracting additional funding to sponsor research and development in computer applications in curriculum development. This initiative exemplifies the way in which the Society, whilst relinquishing its involvement in formal education, retains and expresses a deep and continuing interest in the provision of agricultural education and its role as a facilitator in developing new initiatives. More recently still, with the support of Lloyds Bank and a working party group drawn from college teachers and principals, the Society has established with the joint sponsors a Students' Day at the NAC. Launched in 1987, the first such day attracted over 2,500 agricultural students from establishments across the UK.

The Society's *Journal* remains pre-eminent both as a scholarly *and* a practical agricultural periodical. Since 1970 an annual *Farmer's Guide to the National Agricultural Centre* has been added to the established *Farmer's Guide to Agricultural Research* containing periodic reviews of developments at the various Stoneleigh Units and overviews of the NAC activities; the Units also report through the medium of the *NAC News* as well as distributing their own *Newsletters*. D H Robinson retired from the post of the Society's Editor in 1974 to be succeeded by Neil McCann (1974–1984) and Eric Carter, the current holder of the position. Issues of the Society's *Journal* have, during the 1970s and 1980s, contained articles dealing with a wide variety of agricultural topics, ranging from the practical, scientific and technical to the historical in emphasis and with conservation, 'adding value', agricultural strategy, and future planning well to the forefront. The Society's Audio-Visual Unit has, during the 1980s, produced a considerable volume of instructional material at a variety of levels while the latest (sixteenth) edition of *Fream's*, published in 1983 under the editorship of Professor Colin Spedding, continues the successful tradition of one of the Society's most enduring instructional enterprises.

Although all of the Society's activities can be viewed as 'educational', the NAC has come to have a particular role in the *general* education of the public in farming and countryside activities. The need for this was a theme running through many of the reports of the late 1960s and early 1970s which reviewed the likely trend of future development of the NAC. The Stoneleigh Farm and Country Centre opened in 1974 under the guidance of Jef Aartse Tuyn, then Special Projects Officer. The aim was to attract the 'unconverted' – people who knew little about agriculture or the Country Code – and the intensive livestock units were integrated into a Stoneleigh farm 'trail' which included various

Rosemary Bartlett, Jef Tuyn, Ron Treves and Emily Binions.

attractions such as the Bee Centre, Rare Breeds, and a children's farmyard. A series of Sunday Open Days attracted, during their first season of operation, some 60,000 visitors who were, it was thought, not normally likely to visit an interpretation centre. The Society's Farm Interpretation activities underwent a major review in 1982 following the closure of the Food and Farm Facts Unit at the Arthur Rank Centre (which had been initiated by a group of Hampshire Farmers in 1977 to provide independent information on farming issues) and the importance that the RASE attaches to this sphere of its activity is reflected in the recent creation of a Countryside Communications Unit headed by Jef Tuyn.[107]

In recent years intensive livestock production has come to have a poor image among consumers (who nevertheless, demand cheap food) and as early as 1966 the Stoneleigh operations attracted the attention of campaigners against 'factory farming'. Apart from demonstrating production techniques the Livestock Units have, over the years, received many thousands of the general public on open days and there are special viewing facilities built into these units for such visitors. The Units have been concerned with the development of systems sympathetic to animal welfare and the reception of the non-farming public and school children has an important educative function in showing that modern livestock systems are run by 'caring people who look after healthy, contented

The Conservation Pavilion at the Royal Show.

stock'. One of the current 'stars' at Stoneleigh is cow 878 in the Dairy Unit with a particular penchant for the 'Mars Bars' offered by school children who are often from inner city areas and seeing farm animals for the first time.[108] 'Farm Interpretation' is, however, a continuing process and increasingly it requires specialist facilities and skills. The role of the permanent livestock demonstration units is essentially technical and professional; this keeps them fully occupied and they have found it increasingly difficult to absorb significant numbers of urban visitors. Thus the NAC's role in this field is always under review.

Although the Society has encouraged organised visits of school children to the Royal Show over the years, this event essentially caters for the already-informed non-farming visitor; the Town and Country Festival is the more important focus for maintaining a rural-urban link. One very successful educative enterprise was the 'Adopt a Jersey Calf Scheme' whereby dairy farms were linked to schools and the care of a calf was a focal point for a farming project; the calves were paraded by children for judging at the Town and Country Festival. Apart from this August event and other open days at Stoneleigh, Stowford Farm has also been used to stage a 'Family, Farm and Craft Show' in conjunction with a number of other bodies including the Dartmoor National Parks Authority, Country Landowners' Association, Devon Trust for Nature Conservation, the Nature Conservancy Council and The Forestry Commission.

The Society's Farm Interpretation Unit, together with the Home Food Unit founded in 1980, was formerly located in the Arthur Rank Centre which is now the base for the Town and Country Festival. Since its establishment in 1972 the Arthur Rank Centre, initially under the direction of Canon Peter Buckler and from 1983 to 1987 Canon A J Russell, has come to have an important role in the socio-economic aspects of the countryside and rural community.[109] Not only has it been concerned with creating awareness of farming and rural affairs by providing information on them, but it has had an increased involvement in matters of rural welfare. An early example was its sponsorship in 1975 of a survey into the tied cottage system. This was carried out by Miss Moira Constable of the *Shelter* organisation and the report, *An Alternative to the Abolition of the Tied Cottage System,* found that while few farm workers wanted to see the abolition of the tied cottage, over half of the 300 interviewed felt some insecurity. As a result of this finding, a system of licensing was advocated which would guarantee re-housing if a farm employee lost his job. The report was produced in time to have a significant effect on the content of the Labour Government's Tied Cottage legislation. In spite of much concern at the time, the legislation did contribute successfully to the resolution of a real problem. This was an interesting example of the value of the Arthur Rank Centre's ability to act independently where the Society itself, for political reasons, would have had some difficulty.

It was shortly after this that the NAC Housing Association and the National Agricultural Centre Rural Trust were founded to aid retired workers by establishing rural housing associations. While progress on this project was very slow during the late 1970s because of interminable bureaucratic delays, a number of very beneficial schemes have since been completed. Recently, a major study *Rural Homes for Rural People* has focused attention on the way in which many rural communities are being broken up as the young are priced out of the rural housing market by influxes of outsiders associated with the remorseless march of 'counter-urbanisation'. Although the countryside contains acute social problems associated with low incomes, housing, service provision and transport, these are often overlooked as urban areas receive greater attention.[110] This has prompted the Arthur Rank Centre to encourage the Archbishop of Canterbury to establish a commission for rural areas to produce a countryside equivalent of *Faith in the City.* The Arthur Rank Centre has produced a number of studies on these and related issues over the years including *The Changing Village* (a Hampshire study) and *The Changing Farm* which is a study of the ethics of food production from a Christian viewpoint. A recent concern has been with the high incidence of stress and suicide in the farming community, itself indicative of the problems facing the agricultural industry in the late 1980s. For two decades, through the 1970s and 1980s, when the Society's financial resources were fully stretched, its involvement in this wide range of rural social issues would hardly have been possible without the

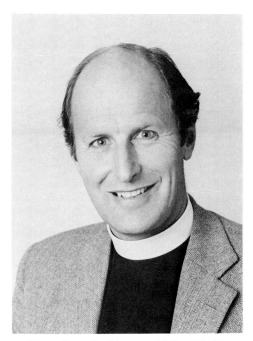

Peter Buckler, Director ARC 1973–83.   Tony Russell, Director ARC 1983–87.

continued financial support of the Arthur Rank Foundation and the personal inspiration and drive of its Chairman, Mr Robin Cowen, who was made an Honorary Vice-President of the Society in 1985.

The importance attached to the communication of farming matters to the urban majority is a reflection of the increased attention that has been focused upon agricultural matters in recent years when farming has increasingly come to be viewed unfavourably by the general public. Indeed, 'Agriculture in Contention' was the theme of Sir Michael Franklin's *Outlook* address in 1984. To concern about the environmental aspects of modern agricultural practice has been added impatience about the cost of support policies and what are seen as the absurdities of the CAP. As a result, agriculture has been subject to an increasing stream of critical commentaries, (of various degrees of authority) which receive a good deal of public attention.[111]

Although there is no specific 'conservation unit' at Stoneleigh (the view being taken that a 'holistic' conservation policy towards *all* of its farming operations is more appropriate) the RASE has taken a number of initiatives in the conservation field. The extension of the Society's landholding in the late 1970s provided new opportunities in this area and when land was acquired to the west of the showground adjacent to the Kenilworth by-pass a survey of its wildlife was instigated by George Jackson with the request, 'tell us what wildlife we have and how to look after it'. The acquisition of the John Eastwood Farm led to a major assessment of the integration of sound conservation policies with economic farm practice and extensive wildlife surveys and habitat appraisals have also been

289

carried out at the Society's William Scott Abbot Trust Sacrewell Farm.[112]

Following a review of policy towards farming and conservation in 1978 the Society's Technical Development Committee approved a proposal brought to them by Eric Carter, then Deputy Director-General of ADAS, and George Jackson, that the Society should seek to establish a Conservation Advice Centre at the Royal Show. Situated on the edge of the Arable Area, a demonstration site was developed jointly with ADAS, the Countryside Commission, the Nature Conservancy Council and the Farming and Wildlife Advisory Group. The Advice Centre, which provided an important means of contact for farmers visiting the Show, proved highly successful – so much so that the Ministry of Agriculture, the Countryside Commission and the Nature Conservancy Council joined with the Society to sponsor a permanent pavilion on the site which was opened at the 1987 Royal Show.

As agricultural issues became increasingly complex towards the late 1970s so the RASE was called upon to give opinions on a range of important matters relating to the environment, the occupancy of land, and farming practice and research. That it should do so was seen by some within the Society as being very much in conformity with the RASE's role as a 'Learned Society' which had perhaps become eclipsed since the establishment of Stoneleigh with its stress on technical development and demonstrations. This 'Learned Role' was the subject of a discussion by the Honorary Fellows in 1979; a note by John Green stressed that the Society had to 'understand and influence the circumstances in which the nation's agriculture is being practised'.[113] His review of the development of the Society since the Second World War noted the strong influence of the Society during the period preceding the 1947 Agriculture Act (reviewed in an earlier part of this *History*) and recognised that the 1950s was a period of relative inactivity on the part of the Society while the agricultural industry was cushioned by the 'feather bed' – a phrase immortalised by Stanley Evans in 1950.[114] Later, the move to Stoneleigh preoccupied the Society until new demands were put upon it in the late 1970s.

In 1977 an invitation was extended to the RASE by the Royal Commission on Environmental Pollution to submit evidence. A working party under the Chairmanship of John Green collected information and a report was prepared by Rodney Barker of the NAC ADAS Unit. The RASE's Report was divided into four parts – effects of pollution on agriculture, pollution risks from agriculture, planning considerations, and long-term developments, and included observations on the run-off and leaching of inorganic fertilizers, the disposal of manure and slurry, the use of pesticides, and straw disposal. The general conclusion was that the 'farmer's task was to use all the knowledge and resource that is available to his generation to maintain optimum physiological performance in a given situation with the minimum of adventitious aid' and that 'a farm should be in a geographical position to recycle its own wastes in such a way as to use as little energy and as few stimulants and antidotes as possible'. This was the way, it was thought, to reduce pollution problems.[115]

Also in 1977 the Society was invited to give evidence to the Northfield Committee which had been established 'to examine recent trends in agricultural land acquisition and occupancy as they affect the structure of the agricultural industry'. Its 26-paragraph submission reviewed the historical and present positions, farm structure, human motivations in landholding and occupancy, agricultural employment, taxation and landownership, and the transfer of agricultural freeholds. It concluded with the observation that 'the agricultural freehold is a public duty as well as a private right and that what differentiates it from other forms of capital is the fact that it has permanent value'.[116]

The need for the RASE to respond to such issues gave rise to consideration within the Society as to what was the proper framework for its contributions to be made efficiently, promptly, and with the requisite degree of authority. There was also the feeling among some senior members of the Society that since the move to Stoneleigh most attention had been given to technical events and activities and the Royal Show at the expense of leadership in the wider sphere of agriculture. Following an address by Oscar Colburn to the Farmers' Club in 1980 on the lack of strategic thinking within the agricultural industry, a paper by Henry Fell urged that the Society's Council should play a more positive part in developing agricultural policies. This stressed that the independent position of the Society was very important, and that there was a vacuum to be filled within agriculture as other bodies such as the National Farmers' Union and Country Landowners' Association had sectional interests and the MAFF was concerned with political issues; the RASE's Council, with its elected and nominated membership, contained an important non-aligned cross-section of the agricultural interest.[117]

In response to these ideas, the Chief Executive stressed that it would be very expensive to extend the Society's influence and play a larger part on the national agricultural platform and that in the short term, a London secretariat or regional structure to enhance its political influence was beyond its means. Rather, the Society should channel its resources into areas which were self-supporting and concentrate on the NAC in the specific areas of education and training, communication of technical information, and product evaluation. There were also doubts within the Society as to how far the Society should become involved in 'political' issues; although the paper submitted to the Northfield Committee was neutral in its argument and was prepared as an 'impartial and unbiased view of what was in the best interest of the national estate', there was no overall agreement that the occupancy of land was something on which the Society should properly take a view. This consideration mirrored very closely the nineteenth century deliberations on what were the 'forbidden topics' within the Society's proceedings, while Christopher York reasserted that 'agricultural politics' were properly within the RASE's domain – what it was not allowed to do was to involve itself with 'party politics'.[118]

The Society's 'thinking role' was extended during the early 1980s by means of the establishment of an Agricultural Policy Sub-Committee reporting to the Education and General Purposes Committee to deal with issues separate from the general business of the RASE. For a period, an Agricultural Policy Review Group had the remit of considering the longer-term issues facing the United Kingdom agricultural and food industry to ensure that the Society was able to make representations – privately or publicly – on such issues, with advice and comment, when called upon to do so. Items considered suitable for consideration by the Group included straw burning, rural infrastructure, and the position of young entrants into farming, and recent reports have reviewed the Society's role in the rural environment and in 'Third World' problems. Currently, the Society is called upon to give advice, or opinion, upon some twenty issues each year and such is the depth of expertise among the Society's Officers and its Council that a speedy and authoritative response is readily forthcoming.

THE SESQUICENTENARY OF THE RASE

The one hundred and fiftieth anniversary of the foundation of the English Agricultural Society was celebrated on 9 May 1988 when the RASE held a dinner in the Whitbread Porter Tun Room, the site of the old Chiswell Street Brewery. The dinner was hosted by the Society's President, the Earl of Selborne, and the chief guests were HRH the Princess Royal (President 1986–7) and Captain Mark Phillips, and HRH the Princess Alice, Duchess of Gloucester. Over 500 people were present including the Society's Vice Presidents, Trustees, Council members, representatives of the Society's sponsors, and leaders of every sector of the agricultural industry. All members who had joined the Society prior to 1938 were invited and of 123 in this category 25 were able to attend. The longest serving members of the RASE at the time of the sesquicentenary were the Lord Daresbury and Mr William Manning who were both elected on 7 December 1912.[119]

The anniversary dinner featured the best of English food – and wine – including beef from Shorthorn cattle whose pedigrees trace back to animals used at the first RASE dinner. These were supplied with the assistance of the Shorthorn Society, the oldest established breed society. It is interesting to note that the Shorthorn, the pride of Victorian breeders, is again coming into fashion as a high quality, dual purpose animal after a period of decline.

In his speech Lord Selborne remarked that the RASE's 150th anniversary fell at a particularly dramatic time in the Society's life, because negotiations for the purchase of the freehold of the main National Agricultural Centre site were well

Guests assemble for the one hundred and fiftieth anniversary dinner, 9 May 1988.

advanced and, in September it was announced that the Society had acquired the freehold of some 628 acres of land from the Stoneleigh Estate. The purchase was made possible by a generous interest-free loan from the Rank Foundation and to that Foundation, together with the Eastwood Foundation, and the Rare Breeds Survival Foundation of America, the RASE, as Lord Selborne acknowledged, owes a great debt of gratitude for continued generosity over a number of years. The Society is also interested in the acquisition of the Abbey and the balance of 715 acres of adjacent land, following the decision of the Leigh family to vacate Stoneleigh. Ambitious and imaginative plans have been formulated to bring the Science Museum's proposed new National Museum of Food and Farming to Stoneleigh, and to use the whole estate – the Abbey, its land, and the NAC – for continued service to the agricultural industry and the rural community. It remains to be seen whether these plans can be brought to fruition.

The year 1989 will mark both the 150th anniversary of the Society's first show and the centenary of the formation of the Ministry of Agriculture, Fisheries and Food (originally the Board of Agriculture).[120] The coincidence of these anniversaries has led to the designation of 1989 as British Food and Farming Year directed by a Council under the Chairmanship of HRH the Duke of Edinburgh. A programme of country-wide events and exhibitions is planned including a

Festival of Food and Farming to be held in Hyde Park during May 1989.

This celebration comes at a problematic time for the agricultural industry for, despite its success in achieving massive increases in productivity since 1950, agriculture has come to have an increasingly unfavourable 'image' such that the British farmer feels under 'siege', at a time of declining incomes, from environmental pressure groups.[121] It is to be hoped that the national celebration will act as a corrective to some of the misinformation that is propagated by the industry's critics. As Sir Frank Engledow and Leonard Amey pointed out at the start of the present decade, food 'surpluses' in the western world should not lead us to forget the need to provide for emergencies: indeed, in the summer of 1988 drought in the United States of America gave rise to considerable concern.[122]

Towards the end of the second part of this history it was suggested that the Society's founders would have been disappointed with the status of agriculture by the end of the nineteenth century despite the pioneering technical and scientific endeavours that were a feature of the early years of the RASE. As we have seen, as soon as cheap food became available on a significant scale on the world market, the agricultural interest was promptly abandoned by Government only to be rediscovered at times of war. Thus it could be observed in 1941 that:

> If the years from 1916 to 1923 are disregarded the course of events during the following decade appear as a projection of tendencies which had prevailed for almost 50 years prior to 1914.[123]

After the Second World War, the 1947 Agriculture Act ensured that there was no repeat of the earlier 'great betrayal' and, as has been emphasised in Part III, the RASE played a leading role in the formulation of this monumental Act. During the post-war period there was an outstanding technical revolution in farming and, just as in the mid-nineteenth century, the RASE was seen as:

> the focus of a great system, collecting from remote sources scattered rays of practical experience, and again diffusing them with increased intensity and effect through every region of the agricultural world; or the powerful heart which maintained in vigour the circulation of the lifeblood through the several organs of the agricultural body.[124]

This historic role as a *communicator* and *catalyst* of change, a dual theme which runs throughout this book, has been continued at Stoneleigh over the past quarter century.

The fruits of the most recent 'harvests of change' have not altogether been sweet for the practising farmer. It has been remarked that the 'sword of [agricultural] technology is double-edged' in that increased output has been thrown onto an inelastic market so that farmers have become locked into what

The Earl of Selborne, RASE President 1977–8

has been termed a 'treadmill' of technological change.[125] As Mrs Wheatley-Hubbard (formerly Chairman of the Technical Development Committee and Deputy President 1986–7) observed in 1979, 'I sometimes feel that with all the advances that have been made we are just having to run faster all the time in order to stand still!'[126]

Stoneleigh has existed in order to provide information on the best practice for the farmer and, in Sir Francis Pemberton's words, to enable the agriculturist 'to learn what is new and to go home to earn a better living'.[127] That living has to be earned not only in the context of the physical capabilities of a particular farm unit, but also in the political and economic environment within which the producer operates. Thus over the past 25 years the emphasis has shifted away from productivity to efficiency and cost reduction towards alternative enterprises and 'added value' with an increased regard for the environmental costs of progress. The time has long passed when there could be agreement with J C Morton's nineteenth-century assessment that:

> Agricultural progress, if of any interest or value whatever, simply means more food produced per acre . . .[128]

At the 1988 Royal Show – attended by 227,413 visitors (the second highest total at Stoneleigh) despite rather wet conditions – alternative enterprises were well represented under the umbrella of the Society's recently-founded Country-side Communications Unit. If the economic viability of many alternative enterprises is open to question, then research and development of industrial and energy crops is surely a better use of resources than 'set-aside' schemes.

For the future, it seems likely that with the decline of public funding of agricultural research and support services, the RASE will have an enhanced role in this area. The Society's President for 1977–8 (who is also Chairman of the Agricultural and Food Research Council) believes that the RASE can make an important future contribution in the marketing of research both at home and abroad. The competitive pressures on British agriculture will undoubtedly increase with full economic integration in the EEC. Support from the agricultural industry as a whole for the Food from Britain Organisation, responsible for the promotion of British food, has been far from sufficient and it may well be that the RASE will have a role here in ensuring that its efforts are adequately maintained and that a broad-based marketing strategy is put together to promote the collective interests of farming.[129]

We can only speculate what the Society's founders would have made of the current position of agriculture. It is to be hoped that they would find much to admire even if, inevitably, there would be much that was disturbing and puzzling to them. Their perusal of recent issues of the *Journal*, for example, would have revealed items both on 'Agriculture and the Nuclear Bomb' and 'War Game' enterprises as part of farm diversification, an apparent paradox which they might have found difficult to resolve![130]

This concluding section does not presume to make any judgement on what has been achieved at Stoneleigh during the past quarter century – that awaits the Society's next historian. However, the concept of the National Agricultural Centre has come to be greatly admired overseas and on average two delegations a year come to the Centre to find out how it was established and how it operates, and to see whether something similar could be developed in their own countries. Although the NAC is clearly a product of the British agricultural scene, and although society, culture and circumstances elsewhere are necessarily different, the concept is relevant to other countries and detailed studies are in progress in Portugal and Venezuela, for example, with a view to establishing centres on the NAC model. While the United States of America is too large a country for any single centre to be set up, the Agricentre International was established in Memphis, Tennessee in 1987 and has many attributes in common with Stoneleigh.[131]

One of the particular features of the Society's history has been the sense of continuity provided by the endeavours of its members and consultants over considerable periods of time. The remarkable 120 year connection of the Voelcker family with the Society has already been noted, but other long-serving consultants with more than 30 years of service include Cecil Warburton

Lt-Col Sir Walter Burrell, Bt, RASE President 1964 seen with the Ansdell portrait of his ancestor Sir Charles Burrell, Bt.

(Consulting Zoologist 1893–1944), F S Courtney, Charles Carruthers, Sir Rowland Biffen and S J Wright. The Society continues to recognise the worth of service in times of change through its long-service awards for farm and estate employees which were first instituted in 1924. The death in 1985 of Sir Walter Burrell (who played a major part in setting up Stoneleigh and the NAC) broke a long-standing family link with the Society for his ancestor Sir Charles Burrell was one of the founder members of the Society and was present at the Bristol meeting of 1842 which is featured on the front cover of this book.

In 1855 it was noted that the RASE had 'been established, not by Parliamentary grant, but by the voluntary contributions of many thousands of the most distinguished friends of agriculture in this century'.[132] It will be clear from the preceding pages how much the Society continues to owe to its more recent 'distinguished friends' and in 1988 the need for the non-partial, voluntary, Royal Agricultural Society of England has arguably never been greater at any time during the past 150 years. It faces massive challenges in the immediate future in continuing its record of service to the agricultural industry and to the nation as a whole. How those challenges were met will provide future generations with fascinating reading in the Society's *bicentennial* history.

NOTES AND REFERENCES

Abbreviations: *AHR: Agricultural History Review*
EHR: Economic History Review
JRASE: Journal of the Royal Agricultural Society of England.

PART I: THE FOUNDATION OF THE SOCIETY

1. Spencer's observation was at the Smithfield Club dinner held 11 December 1837, which was the occasion when he formally proposed the formation of the English Agricultural Society. His speech was reported in *Farmer's Magazine*, VIII, 1838, pp 47–8 and elsewhere in the agricultural and national press.

INTRODUCTION

2. J A Scott Watson, *The History of the Royal Agricultural Society of England 1839–1939*, 1939, p 14.

ANTECEDENT INSTITUTIONS

3. Alexander Ramsey, *History of the Highland and Agricultural Society of Scotland*, 1879.
4. John Dudgeon, 'Account of the Improvements which have taken place in the Agriculture of Scotland since the formation of the Highland Society', *JRASE*, I, 1840, pp 59–112.
5. The agricultural interests of the Royal Society are reviewed by R V Lennard, 'English Agriculture under Charles II: The Evidence of the Royal Society's "Enquiries"', *EHR*, IV, 1932, pp 27–45. On the Society of Arts (which took its 'Royal' prefix in 1908) see D Luckhurst and K W Hudson, *The Royal Society of Arts 1754–1954*, 1954. Robert Trow-Smith's *A History of the Smithfield Club*, 1979, supersedes earlier histories of this organisation; on the other early institutions with an agricultural connection or concern see H R Fletcher, *A History of the Royal Horticultural Society 1804–1968*, 1968; Monica C Grobel, 'The Society for the Diffusion of Useful Knowledge 1826–1846', unpub MA thesis, University of London, 1933; O J R Howarth, *The British Association 1831–1931: a Retrospect*, 1931. For the 'Old' Board of Agriculture see E Clarke, 'The Board of Agriculture 1793–1822', *JRASE*, ser iii, IX, 1898, pp 1–41; Rosalind Mitchison, 'The "old" Board of Agriculture 1793–1822', *English Historical Review*, LXXIV, 1959, pp 41–69; Nicholas Goddard, 'The Board of Agriculture and its Reports', in G E Mingay, ed, *The Agrarian History of England and Wales VI 1750–1850*, in press, 1988.
6. Clarke, 'Board of Agriculture', p 2.
7. Lennard, 'English Agriculture under Charles II', p 23.
8. O G C Allan, *William Shipley, Founder of the Society of Arts*, 1968. The early agricultural interests of the Society of Arts are dealt with by Sir Henry Trueman Wood, *A History of the Society of Arts*, 1913, pp 114–42 and Luckhurst and Hudson, pp 57–85.
9. See John G Gazley, 'Arthur Young and the Society of Arts', *Journal of Economic History*, I, 1941, pp 129–52; Hudson and Luckhurst, p 83; John G Gazley, *The Life of Arthur Young*, 1973, p 130. See *Annals of Agriculture*, I, 1786, pp 113–9 for a report of plough trials.
10. J French Burke, *British Husbandry*, 1834, p 23.
11. On Sinclair see Rosalind Mitchison, *Agricultural Sir John. The Life of Sir John Sinclair, 1754–1835*. For catalogues of the *General Views* see Clarke, 'Board of Agriculture', p 16; W F Perkins, *British and Irish Writers on Agriculture*, 2nd edn, 1939, pp 176–8; O R Macgregor, 'Introduction' to Lord Ernle, *English Farming Past and Present*, 6th edn, 1961, pp xcix–c. Young justified the work of the Board in Arthur Young, *On the Advantages which have Resulted from the Establishment of the Board of Agriculture*, 1809; for his involvement with

the Board see M Betham-Edwards, *The Autobiography of Arthur Young*, 1898, pp 219–61 and Gazley, *Life of Arthur Young*, pp 306–59. On Webb Hall's political interests see D Spring and T L Crosby, 'George Webb Hall and the Agricultural Association', *Journal of British Studies*, 1, 1962, pp 115–31.

THE CONTEXT OF THE SOCIETY'S FORMATION

12. On late eighteenth century local agricultural societies see Kenneth Hudson, *Patriotism with Profit: British Agricultural Societies in the Eighteenth and Nineteenth Centuries*, 1972; H S A Fox, 'Local Farmers' Associations and the Circulation of Agricultural Information in Nineteenth Century England' in H S A Fox and R A Butlin, eds, *Change in the Countryside: Essays on Rural England 1500–1900*, Institute of British Geographers Special Research Publication No. 10, 1979, pp 42–63; Nicholas Goddard, 'Societies and Shows' in G E Mingay, ed, *Agrarian History VI*, in press, 1988. The best known of these early local and regional societies, which were often modelled on the Society of Arts, is the Bath and West on which see Kenneth Hudson, *The Bath and West: a Bicentenary History*, 1976. 'Sheep-shearings' had part of the function of modern agricultural shows where leading agriculturists met on the estates of prominent landowners to exchange views; see E Clarke, 'Agriculture and the House of Russell', *JRASE*, ser iii, I, 1980, pp 129–36 and Susanna Wade Martins, *A Great Estate at Work*, 1980, pp 48-9. Early farming literature is surveyed in G E Fussell, *The Old English Farming Books from Fitzherbert to Tull, 1523 to 1730*, 1950 and *More Old English Farming Books: from Tull to the Board of Agriculture 1731–1793*. G E Mingay's *Arthur Young and his Times*, 1976, gives a selection of extracts from this prolific author's works. For early farming newspapers and magazines see Nicholas Goddard, 'The Development and Influence of Agricultural Newspapers and Periodicals 1780–1880', *AHR*, 31, pt ii, 1983, pp 116–131 and 'Books, Periodicals and Newspapers' in G E Mingay, ed, *Agrarian History VI*, in press, 1988. Stuart Macdonald, 'The Role of the Individual in Agricultural Change: The Example of George Culley of Fenton, Northumberland, in Fox and Butlin, *Change in the Countryside*, pp 5–21, considers the influence of individuals on the process of agricultural change.

13. G E Fussell, 'A Scottish Forerunner of Humphrey Davy. Archibald Cochrane, Earl of Dundonald, 1749–1831', *Scottish Farmer*, 57, 1949, p 625. For a discussion of Davy's and Grisenthwaite's work see E J Russell, *A History of Agricultural Science in Great Britain*, 1965, pp 67–80 and G E Fussell, *Crop Nutrition; Science and Practice before Liebig*, 1971, pp 159, 184-5 and 194-6. See also G E Fussell, 'Agricultural Science and Experiment in the Eighteenth Century: An Attempt at a Definition', *AHR*, 24, 1976, pp 44–7.

14. On post-1815 agricultural developments see Travis L Crosby, *English Farmers and the Politics of Protection*, 1977 and A R Wilkes, 'Adjustments in Arable Farming after the Napoleonic Wars', *AHR*, 28, 1980, pp 90–103. For early nineteenth century agricultural science see E J Russell, *op cit*; Boussingault is the subject of a full-length study: N McCosh, *Boussingault*, 1984.

15. 'Testimonial to William Shaw Esq.', *Farmer's Magazine*, ser ii, VII, 1843, p 54.

16. John Grey, 'A View of the Past and Present State of Agriculture in Northumberland', *JRASE*, II, 1841, p 155.

17. Many agriculturists attributed the low prices of the 1820s and 1830s to the deflationary effects of Peel's Currency Act of 1819 which returned the country to the gold standard (see Crosby, *op cit*, pp 57–8). Other 'political' issues were the maintenance of protection and abolition of the malt tax.

18. *Farmer's Magazine*, VIII, 1838, p 163.

19. *Agricultural Gazette*, 3 January 1846.

20. *Ibid*, 7 February, 25 July 1846, 30 July 1849; *Mark Lane Express*, 4 January 1836.

21. 'High-farming' refers to the relatively intensive farming methods adopted between about 1850 and 1875 and is particularly associated with the use of off-farm inputs such as fertilizers and manufactured feeding-stuffs. The term gained increased currency after the publication of J B Caird's pamphlet, *High Farming under Liberal Covenants, the Best Substitute for Protection*, 1849. See also P J Perry, 'High Farming in Victorian Britain: Prospect and Retrospect', *Agricultural History*, 55, 1981, pp 156–166, and 'High Farming in Victorian Britain: The Financial Foundations', *ibid*, 52, 1978, pp 364–79. For a general survey see J D Chambers and G E Mingay, *The Agricultural Revolution 1750–1880*, 1966, and C S Orwin and E Whetham, *History of British Agriculture 1846–1914*, 1964.

22. 'The Corn Laws', *Farmer's Magazine*, ser ii, VII, 1843, pp 177–82; *Mark Lane Express* 19, 26 February 1844.

23. *Agricultural Gazette*, 7 February 1846.

24. G Kitson Clark, 'The Repeal of the Corn Laws and the Politics of the Forties', *EHR*, ser ii, IV, 1951, p 9.

25. *Mark Lane Express* 1 December 1843, 15 January 1844; Earl Fitzwilliam, *First, Second and Third Addresses to the Landowners of England on the Corn Laws*, 1839. See also David Spring, 'Earl Fitzwilliam and the Corn Laws', *American Historical Review*, LIX, 1954, pp 287–304.

26. *Mark Lane Express* 3 June, 22 July, 7 October 1844.

27. John Morton and Joshua Trimmer, *An Attempt to Estimate the Effects of Protecting Duties on the Profits of Agriculture*, 1844. For a memoir of John Morton, see *Agricultural Gazette*, 4 October 1873. On J C Morton see E Clarke, 'John Chalmers Morton', *JRASE*, ser ii, XXIV, 1888, pp 691–6.

28. For memoirs of Holland, Davis, and Acland which stress their early free-trade leanings see *Agricultural Gazette* 10 December 1870, 4 February 1871, 8 June 1872. On the Anti-Corn Law League, George L Mosse, 'The Anti-League and the Corn Law Crisis of 1846', *Historical Journal*, III, 1960, pp 162–83; Crosby, *op cit*, pp 131–5.

29. *Mark Lane Express*, and *Farmers' Journal*, 15 January 1843.

30. *Mark Lane Express*, 27 May 1844.

31. Identified by R W Linker, 'Philip Pusey Esq., Country Gentleman 1809–55', unpub PhD thesis, Johns Hopkins University, 1962, p 446.

32. Reported in *Farmer's Magazine*, II, 1835, pp 59-63 and also cited by D C Moore, 'The Corn Laws and High Farming', *EHR*, ser ii, XVIII, 1965, p 549 and *The Politics of Deference*, 1976, p 342.

33. E Clarke, 'The Foundation of the Royal Agricultural Society', *JRASE*, ser iii, I, 1890, pp 2-3; Scott Watson, p 15; E A Wasson, 'The Third Earl Spencer and Agriculture', *AHR*, 26, pt i, 1978, pp 95; C David Edgar, 'Honest Jack Althorp – Founder of the Royal', *JRASE*, 141, 1980, pp 10–22; 'Royal Agricultural Society', *Farmer's Magazine*, III, 1835, pp 443–9; *Farmer's Magazine*, ser ii, II, 1840, pp 73–4; Shaw's role is reviewed by the present author, 'William Shaw "of The Strand" and the formation of the Royal Agricultural Society of England', *JRASE*, 143, 1982, pp 98–104.

34. *Agriculturist*, 2 January 1836.

35. *Farmer's Magazine*, IV, 1836, pp 2–3, 82–9, 115–6.

36. *Mark Lane Express*, 22 January 1838; 'On Agricultural Chemistry', *Farmer's Magazine*, V, 1836, pp 27–33, 77–81, 156–60, 235–6, 248–56, 250–1; VII, 1837, pp 551–2.

37. On Spencer's involvement with the Yorkshire Agricultural Society, see Vance Hall, *A History of the Yorkshire Agricultural Society 1837–1987*, 1987, pp 51–6; his meeting with Gibbs is recalled in B H T Gibbs, *The Smithfield Club. A Short History of its Origin and Progress*, 1857, p 14.

38. 'Smithfield Club Dinner', *Farmer's Magazine*, VIII, 1838, pp 47–8.

39. 'National Agricultural Institution', *ibid*, pp 1-3.

40. West Sussex Record Office, Goodwood MSS, 1597, Spencer to Richmond 10 January and 14 February 1838.

41. Henry Handley, MP, *A Letter to Earl Spencer on the Formation of a National Agricultural Institution*, 1838. See also *Farmer's Magazine*, VIII, 1838, pp 191–98. For a memoir of Handley see *ibid*, ser ii, XI, 1845, pp 1–4.

42. Goodwood MSS, 1458, Shaw to Richmond 21 February 1838; *Mark Lane Express* 1, 15 January 1838 and *Farmer's Magazine*, VIII, 1838, pp 162–5.

43. *Farmer's Magazine*, VIII, 1838, pp 164–5.

44. *Mark Lane Express* 19 March, 9 April 1838.

45. *Ibid*, 30 April 1838.

46. *Farmer's Magazine*, VIII, 1838, pp 440–48. The meeting was widely reported. On the Central, see *Bell's Weekly Messenger*, 14 May 1838.

THE EARLY DEVELOPMENT OF THE SOCIETY

47. Goodwood MSS, Spencer to Richmond 14, 22 February, 27 March 1838; Shaw also founded the London Farmer's Club on which see Kevin Fitzgerald, *Ahead of Their Time: A Short History of the London Farmer's Club*, 1967.

48. Proceedings of Council, 20 October 1948, Appendix B (Memorandum prepared by Sir John Russell for Research Committee).

49. Lynette J Peel, 'Practice with Science: the First Twenty Years', *JRASE*, 137, 1976, p 10.

50. Minutes of Committee of Management 13, 20 March 1839; Lynette J Peel, *op cit*, p 1.

51. On local farmers' clubs see H S A Fox, *op cit*, and Nicholas Goddard, 'Agricultural Societies' in G E Mingay, ed, *The Victorian Countryside*, I, 1981, pp 245–259.

PART II: THE VICTORIAN SOCIETY

'STORM CENTRES OF INNOVATION': EARLY ROYAL SHOWS

1. *Agricultural Gazette*, 26 December 1881.

2. Minutes of Committee of Management, 26 June 1838; *Cambridge Independent Press*, 20, 27 July 1839; Minutes of Committee of Management, 11 March 1840; Monthly Council, 3 November 1841; District Committee, 24 November 1841.

3. *Agricultural Gazette*, 1 May 1847; Monthly Council 25 March 1846; General Meeting 22 May 1861; Monthly Council 4 December 1867; General Meeting 1868; Monthly Council 6 July 1870, 1 November, 6 December 1876, 7 February 1877.

4. 'The Royal Agricultural Society's Meeting in 1872', *Farmer's Magazine*, ser iii, XXXIX, 1871, p 165; H H Dixon, 'The Royal Agricultural Society', *Gentleman's Magazine*, new ser, III, 1869, p 303.

5. *Farmer's Magazine*, ser iii, 1852, p 76; J A Scott Watson and M E Hobbs, *Great Farmers*, 1937, p 207.

6. *Agricultural Gazette*, 1 May 1847, 22 July 1854, 28 July 1855, 14 July 1860.

7. 'Report of the Miscellaneous Department at Warwick', *JRASE*, XX, 1859, p 323.

8. Dixon, 'The Royal Agricultural Society', pp 301-2; Monthly Council 3 May 1876.

9. Dixon, *loc cit*.

10. Agricultural Gazette, 19 October 1857, *Mark Lane Express*, 18 July 1859; *Agricultural Gazette* 9 January 1858 (letter from E W Moore).

11. Alfred Crosskill, 'Agricultural Shows and their Influence on Agricultural Progress', *Farmer's Magazine*, ser iii, XXIX, 1866, p 375; *Farmer's Magazine*, ser iii, XLVIII, 1875, p 407; Monthly Council 2 February, 5 April, 3 May 1876.

12. *Farmer's Magazine*, ser iii, LVI, 1879, p 357; Rodney Weaver, personal communication to J A Tuyn.

13. Joseph Darby, 'Reminiscences of Royal Shows', *Mark Lane Express Carlisle Supplement*, 7 July 1902, p 22.

14. The character of early Royal Shows is well conveyed by reports in the *Illustrated London News* especially 20, 27 July 1850, 16 July 1853, 11 August 1855, 1 August 1857.

15. *Farmer's Magazine*, ser iii, XL, 1871, p 147.

16. For a memoir of Thomas Gibbs see *ibid*, ser ii, XIX, 1849 p 220. For Brandreth Gibbs, *Agricultural Gazette*, 31 December 1853, 14 December 1872; *JRASE*, ser ii, XXI, 1885, pp 611–620.

17. H S Thompson, 'Agricultural Progress and the Royal Agricultural Society', *JRASE*, XXV, 1864, pp 1–52. Ransome's comments were in reply to C W Hoskyns's paper, 'The Progress of English Agriculture over the last Fifteen Years', *Journal of the Society of Arts*, IV, 1855, pp 271–86. See also J A Ransome, *Implements of Agriculture*, 1843.

18. Dan Pigeon, 'The Development of Agricultural Machinery', *JRASE*, ser iii, I, 1890, pp 257–75. See also Susan Blake, 'An Historical Geography of the British Agricultural Engineering Industry 1780–1914, 1974. (Unpublished thesis at Museum of English Rural Life, University of Reading.)

19. 'Oxford' and 'Cambridge' Implement Reports in *JRASE*, I, 1840, pp lxiv–lxx and II, 1841, pp xiii–xvii; Liverpool and Bristol Implement Reports in *ibid*, III, 1842, pp cii–cxviii and 341.

20. Josiah Parkes, 'Report on Drain-Tiles and Drainage', *JRASE*, IV, 1843, p 376 and 'Report on the Exhibition of Implements at the Southampton Meeting in 1844', *ibid*, V, 1845, pp 390–1, 'Shrewsbury', VI, 1846, pp 318–9, 'Newcastle-Upon-Tyne', VII, 1847, p 692, 'Northampton', VIII, 1848, pp 354-5; Earl Cathcart, 'Remarks on the Implement Department at Bury', *JRASE*, ser ii, III, 1867, p 589.

21. 'Southampton Report', p 272-3; 'Northampton Report', p 346; 'Newcastle Report', pp 693–6.

22. G E Fussell, *The Farmer's Tools*, p 113.

23. 'Liverpool Report', p cvii; Josiah Parkes, 'On a trial of Messrs Ransome's Portable Steam Thrashing Engine . . .', *ibid*, pp cxvi–cxvii; 'Bristol Report', p 351, 'Southampton Report', p 385, 'Northampton Report', pp 330–2, 334, 340–1; Col Challoner, 'Report on the Exhibition and Trial of Implements at the Exeter Meeting, 1850', *JRASE*, XI, 1850, pp 466–7.

24. William Fisher Hobbs, 'Report on the Exhibition and Trial of Implements at the Carlisle Meeting, 1855', *JRASE*, XVI, 1855, p 506.

25. Sir A K Macdonald, 'Report on the Exhibition of Implements at the Chester Meeting, 1858', *JRASE*, XIX, 1858, pp 313–4, 316.

26. Anon, 'Report on the Worcester Show-yard', *JRASE*, XXIV, 1863, pp 493–6; John Coleman, 'Report on the Trials of Implements at Oxford', *JRASE*, ser ii, VI, 1870, pp 441–61.

27. 'Chester Report', pp 328, 334; 'Bury Report', p 592-3.

28. 'Bury Report', p 593.

29. 'Cardiff Report', pp 434–5, 443, 446.

30. *Agricultural Gazette*, 21 April, 14 July 1855; 'Carlisle Report', p 525; 'Chelmsford Report', p 579; 'Salisbury Report', pp 424–5, 'Chester Report', pp 320–8. The steam trials are discussed by Clark C Spence, *God Speed the Plow*, 1960, and Harold Bonnett, *Saga of the Steam Plough*, 1965, especially pp 47–9. See also John Haining and Colin Tyler, *Ploughing by Steam*, 1970.

31. 'Reports of the Committees appointed to Investigate the Present State of Steam Cultivation', *JRASE*, ser ii, III, 1867, p 367; G E Fussell, *The Farmer's Tools*, pp 89–90; C S Orwin and E H Whetham, *A History of British Agriculture 1846–1914*, 1971, p 105.

32. John Algernon Clarke, 'Report on the Trials of Steam-Cultivating Machinery at Wolver-hampton, *JRASE*, ser ii, VII, 1871, pp 442–80; 'The Pause in the Development of Steam Cultivation', *Farmer's Magazine*, ser iii, LIII, 1878, pp 213–4; *Agricultural Gazette*, 24 March 1879.

33. Philip Pusey, 'On Mr. McCormick's Reaping-machine', *JRASE*, XII, 1851, p 160.

34. 'Lewes Report', pp 302–4; *Agricultural Gazette*, 22, 29 September, 1855; Samuel Sidney, 'On the Effect of Prizes on Manufacturers', *Journal of the Society of Arts*, X, 1861–2, p 376. Early reaping machines and the Society's trials are discussed in *The Farmer's Tools*, pp 115–37.

35. *The Farmer's Tools*, pp 134–5.

36. John Hemsley, 'Report on the Trials of Implements at Taunton', *JRASE*, ser ii, XI, 1875, pp 631–9; Jabez Turner, 'Report on the Exhibition of Implements at Birmingham', *ibid*, ser ii, XII, 1876, pp 596–8; John Coleman, 'Report on the Trials of Sheaf-binders and Miscellaneous Implements at the Bristol Meeting', *ibid*, ser ii, XV, 1879, pp 73–105.

37. 'Lewes Report', pp 304–5; E L Jones, 'The Agricultural Labour Market in England 1793–1872', *EHR*, ser ii, XVII, 1964–5, pp 322–38; E J T Collins, 'Harvest Technology and Labour Supply in Britain 1790–1870', *ibid*, XXII, 1970, pp 453–73; P A David, 'The Landscape and the Machine: Technical Interrelatedness, Land Tenure and the Mechanisa-tion of the Corn Harvest in Victorian Britain', in D N McCloskey, ed, *Essays on a Mature Economy: Britain after 1840*, 1971, pp 145–205. For a general discussion on mechanisation in the nineteenth century see E J T Collins, 'The Rationality of "Surplus" Agricultural Labour: Mechanisation in English Agriculture in the Nineteenth Century', *AHR*, 35, pt i, 1987, pp 36–46.

38. 'Lewes Report', pp 305–10.

39. *Implement Manufacturer's Review*, 6 December 1877.

40. Richard Milward, 'Report on the Exhibition of Livestock at the Gloucester Meeting of the Society', *JRASE*, XIV, 1853, p 457, noted by R J Colyer, 'Some Welsh Breeds of Cattle in the Nineteenth Century', *AHR*, 22, pt i, 1974, p 2; Henry Corbet, 'Report on the Exhibition of Livestock at Cardiff', *JRASE*, ser ii, VII, 1872, pp 374–5.

41. Cadwallader John Bates, *Thomas Bates and the Kirklevington Shorthorns*, 1897, p 266.

42. T C Hincks, *Hints for Increasing the Practical Usefulness of Agricultural Shows*, pp 14–17; 'On the Overfed State of Animals Exhibited at the Show of the Royal Agricultural Society', *Farmer's Magazine*, ser ii, XVIII, 1848, p 273.

43. *Farmer's Magazine*, ser iii, II, 1852, p 540.

44. *Agricultural Gazette*, 16 July 1853; *Farmer's Magazine*, ser iii, IV, 1853, pp 140–1, 174, 176–7.

45. 'Exhibitions of Breeding Cattle and the Royal Agricultural Society of England', *Farmer's Magazine*, ser iii, V, 1854, pp 104–6 and VI, 1854, pp 104–9, 164–5; J A Scott Watson and M E Hobbs, *Great Farmers*, 1937, p 365.

46. William Simpson, 'Report on the Exhibition of Livestock at the Carlisle Meeting of the Society', *JRASE*, XVI, 1856, p 504; Samuel Jonas, 'Chester Report', *ibid*, XVIII, 1858, p 365, John Dent Dent, 'Worcester' and 'Plymouth' Reports, *ibid*, XXIV, 1863, p 472 and ser ii, I, 1865, p 360; *Morton's Almanac for Farmers and Growers*, 1871, p 59.

47. Cadwallader John Bates, pp vii–viii, 308–11.

48. 'The Public Judge', *Farmer's Magazine*, ser iii, XXIV, 1863, p 257.

49. 'The Royal Agricultural Society – Mr E A Fawcett's Suggestions', *Farmer's Magazine*, ser iii, XLVII, 1875, p 78.

50. Monthly Council 8 December 1875 and 2 February 1876.

51. Discussions at General Meeting 10 December 1874 and in *Bell's Weekly Messenger*, 21 December 1874; *Mark Lane Express*, 14, 28 December 1874; *North British Agriculturist*, 16

December 1874; *Agricultural Economist*, 1 March 1875; *Agricultural Gazette*, 20 March, 3, 10, April 1876.

52. *The Farmer*, 20 October, 3 November 1873; *Agricultural Economist*, 1 December 1875, *North British Agriculturist*, 15 July 1874; Charles S Plumbe, *Judging Farm Animals*, 1919, pp 2–16; J E Nichols, *Livestock Improvement*, 1944, pp 25–6. For a memoir of Kinnaid see 'The Late Lord Kinnaid as an Agriculturist', *Farmer's Magazine*, ser iii, LIII, 1878, p 145.

53. *JRASE*, ser iii, XV, 1879, p 631; Thomas F Plowman, 'Agricultural Societies and their Uses', *Journal of the Bath and West and Southern Counties Association*, 31, 1885–6, pp 172–3.

54. *Agricultural Gazette*, 26 July 1845.

55. 'Liverpool Report', 1877, p 531.

56. For histories of prominent early implement firms see R A Whitehead, *Garretts of Leiston*, 1963 and D R Grace and D C Phillips, *Ransomes of Ipswich*, 1975. On the influence of the shows and trials Blake, thesis, p 49.

57. *Agricultural Gazette*, 11 July 1877; Wray Vamplew, 'The Progress of Agricultural Mechanics; the Cost of Best Practice in the mid-Nineteenth Century', *Tools and Tillage*, III, 1979, pp 204–14.

58. J C Morton, 'Agricultural Progress: its Helps and Hindrances', *Journal of the Society of Arts*, XII, 1863, pp 55–69; *Agricultural Gazette*, 20 February 1864; J Wrightson, 'Agricultural Machinery', in G Phillips Bevan, ed, *British Manufacturing Industries*, IX, 1876, p 150; W W Good, *Where are we Now? A Politico – Agricultural Letter to the Chairman of the Central Chamber of Agriculture, Clare Sewell Read Esq* MP, 1869, p 24.

59. Sidney, 'On the Effect of Prizes ...', p 376; Crosskill, 'Agricultural Shows and their Influence ...', p 376; *Agricultural Gazette*, 16 January 1864.

60. Thompson, 'Lewes Report', pp 312–4.

61. J C Morton, 'Some Lessons of Recent Agricultural Experience', *Journal of the Bath and West Society*, VIII, 1861, pp 220–39.

62. Quoted in Morton, 'Agricultural Progress', p 64.

63. *Agricultural Gazette*, 20 February 1864.

64. 'Agricultural Shows and their Influence', *loc cit*.

65. *Agricultural Gazette*, 15 August 1846.

66. E A Fawcett, 'Shorthorns: their General Utility for all Purposes', in J Wight, ed, *The Treasury and the Homestead*, I, 1877, p 81.

67. Robert Smith, 'Report on the Exhibition of Livestock at Chester', *Journal*, XIX, 1859, p 365; John Dent Dent, 'Report to Council on the Cattle Exhibited at Newcastle', *JRASE*, XXV, 1864, p 426 and 'Report on the Exhibition of Livestock at the Plymouth Meeting', *ibid*, ser ii, I, 1865, p366. See also Robert Trow-Smith, *English Livestock Husbandry*, 1700–1900, 1959, p 241; W Wells, 'Report on the Exhibition of Livestock at Manchester', *JRASE*, V, 1869, pp 51–78.

68. 'Worcester Report', p 473; D Reynolds Davies, 'Report on the exhibition of livestock at Oxford', *JRASE*, ser ii, VI, 1870, pp 556, 560; Richard Milward, 'Report on the Exhibition of Livestock at Hull', *ibid*, IX, 1873, p519; J Walton, 'The Development of Oxfordshire Agriculture 1750–1850', unpub D Phil thesis, University of Oxford, 1976, p 372.

69. See Edith Whetham, 'The Trade in Pedigree Livestock 1850–1900', *AHR*, 27, pt i, 1979, pp 47–50; 'Oxford Report', p 525. Master Butterfly's rather inauspicious Australian career is recalled by 'The Druid' in *Saddle and Sirloin*, 1869, pp 340–1.

70. See Martin Andrews, 'The Firm of Hare and Co Commercial Wood-Engravers', unpub BA dissertation, University of Reading, 1976.

71. Joseph Darby, 'Reminiscences of Royal Shows', *Mark Lane Express Carlisle Supplement*, 30 July 1902.

BREAKING THE CLOSED CIRCUIT: THE JOURNAL AND AGRICULTURAL SCIENCE

72. F M L Thompson, 'The Second Agricultural Revolution 1815–1880', *EHR*, ser ii, XXI, 1968, pp 62–77.

73. English Agricultural Society, Minutes of Committee of Management, 6 June 1838, pp 16–17.

74. F A Mackenzie, letter, *Farmer's Magazine*, new series, III, 1839, p 86.

75. H H Dixon, 'The Royal Agricultural Society', *Gentleman's Magazine*, new series, III, 1869, p 304.

76. J C Morton, 'The late Mr. H M Jenkins, FGS: A Memoir', *JRASE*, ser ii, XXIII, 1887, p 193.

77. R W Linker, 'Philip Pusey Esq., Country Gentleman 1809–55', unpublished PhD thesis, Johns Hopkins University, 1962, p 449. For other studies of Pusey see Ernest Clarke, 'Philip Pusey', RASE, ser iii, XI, 1900, pp 1–17 and Paolo E Coletta, 'Philip Pusey, English Country Squire', *Agricultural History*, 18, 1944, pp 83–91.

78. Sir James Caird, 'Agriculture', in T H Ward, ed, *The Reign of Queen Victoria*, II, 1887, p 130.

79. E B Pusey, letter, *Agricultural Gazette Literary Supplement*, 21 April, 1879.

80. Lawrence to Pusey, 'On Diminishing the Quantity of Roots in Fattening Cattle', 10 August 1854, p 8, Berkshire Record Office, D/EBpF8/2; *Agricultural Gazette*, 15 March 1862.

81. J S Henslow, 'Report on the Diseases of Wheat', *JRASE*, II, 1841, p 1.

82. *Agricultural Gazette*, 3 August 1861.

83. 'The Public Judge', *Farmer's Magazine*, ser iii, XXIV, 1863, p 257.

84. *Farmer's Magazine*, ser iii, XXXV, 1869, p 51.

85. *Ibid*, ser iii, XXXIII, 1868, p 39.

86. *Ibid*, ser iii, XXXV, 1869, p 54.

87. C P Le Cornu, 'The Potato in Jersey', *JRASE*, ser ii, VI, 1870, pp 127–44.

88. H H Dixon, 'The Royal Agricultural Society', p 304; 'The Prize System Again', *Farmer's Magazine*, ser iii, XLIII, 1873, p 483.

89. For a further analysis of *Journal* topics and contributors see N P W Goddard, 'The Royal Agricultural Society of England and Agricultural Progress 1838–1880', unpub PhD thesis, University of Kent at Canterbury, 1981, pp 154–170.

90. Professor Schübler, 'On the Physical Properties of Soils', *JRASE*, I, 1840 p 177 also quoted by Peel, 'Practice with Science', p 10.

91. Charles Daubeny, 'Lecture on the Application of Science to Agriculture', *JRASE*, III, 1842, pp 139–40, 143–4 and 'On the Public Institutions for the Advancement of Agricultural Science . . .', *ibid*, pp 383–4. Daubeny was Sibthorpian Professor of Rural Economy in the University of Oxford.

92. John Grey, 'A view of the past and present State of Agriculture in Northumberland', *ibid*, II, 1841, p 155.

93. Russell, *op cit*, pp 98–9.

94. *Organic Chemistry . . .*, 3rd edn, p 211.

95. J Thomas Way and G H Ogston, 'Report on the Analysis of the Ashes of Plants', *JRASE*, VII, 1846, pp 593–68; 'Second Report', *ibid*, VIII, 1847, pp 134–208; 'Third Report', *ibid*, IX, 1848, pp 136–74; 'Fourth Report', *ibid*, XI, 1850, p 497–541.

96. Justus Von Liebig, *Organic Chemistry in its Application to Agriculture and Physiology*, ed Lyon Playfair, 1st edn, 1840, p 85.

97. *Ibid*, 3rd edn, 1843, p 54. See also J B Lawes and J H Gilbert, 'On some points connected with Agricultural Chemistry', *JRASE*, XVI, 1856, p 417; Richard P Aulie, 'The Mineral Theory', *Agricultural History*, XLVIII, 1974, p 372; Margaret Rossiter, *The Emergence of Agricultural Science: Justus Von Liebig and the Americans 1840–1880*, 1975, p 42.

98. Michael O Stephens and Gordon W Roderick, 'The Muspratts of Liverpool', *Annals of Science*, 29, 1972, p 295.

99. Justus Von Liebig, *An Address to the Agriculturalists of Great Britain Explaining the Principles and Use of his Artificial Manures*, 1845, p 19.

100. See *Journal of the Farmer's Club*, December 1875, p 62. Other trials quickly established the Muspratt/Liebig products of little use – see, for example *Gardeners' and Farmers' Journal*, 11 March 1848.

101. Justus Von Liebig, 'On some points in Agricultural Chemistry', *JRASE*, XVII, 1856, p 315; Rossiter, *op cit* p 44; H S Thompson, 'On the Absorptive Power of Soils', *ibid*, XI, 1850, pp 63–74; J T Way, 'On the Power of Soils to Absorb Manure', *ibid*, p 313. Thompson's work is discussed by Vance Hall, *A History of the Yorkshire Agricultural Society*, 1987. The work of Way and others in this important research area is reviewed in S D Forrester and C H Giles, 'From Manure Heaps to Monolayers: the Earliest Development of Solute-Solid Absorption Studies', *Chemistry and Industry*, 13 November 1971, pp 1314–1321.

102. John Bennett Lawes, 'On Agricultural Chemistry', *JRASE*, VIII, 1847, pp 226–60.

103. J F W Johnston, 'The Present State of Agriculture in its Relations to Chemistry and Geology', *JRASE*, IX, 1849, pp 221–44.

104. Philip Pusey, 'On the progress of Agricultural Knowledge during the last Eight years', *JRASE*, XI, 1850, pp 383, 392. Hall, *op cit*, suggests that Pusey's view was very much influenced by H S Thompson. For Liebig's attack on Pusey see *Familiar Letters on Chemistry*, 3rd edn, 1851, pp 479–83.

105. J B Lawes and J H Gilbert, 'On Agricultural Chemistry – especially in Relation to the Mineral Theory of Baron Liebig', *JRASE*, XII, 1851 pp 38 and 40 (note by Pusey) also quoted by Russell, p 118.

106. J B Lawes and J H Gilbert, 'On Some Points connected with Agricultural Chemistry', *JRASE*, XVI, 1856, pp 497–8.

107. Philip Pusey, 'On the Source and Supply of Cubic Saltpetres, Salitre, or Nitrate of Soda, and its Uses in Small Quantities as a Restorative to Corn Crops', *JRASE*, XIII, 1852, p 358.

108. J F W Johnston, 'Present State of Agriculture . . .', p 217.

109. *Idem*, 'On Guano', *JRASE*, II, 1841, pp 305–10.

110. J T Way, 'Composition and Money Value of Guano', *JRASE*, X, 1849, p196. See also W M Mathew, 'Peru and the British Guano Market 1840–1870, *EHR*, ser ii, XXIII, 1970, p 121.

111. Russell, *op cit*, pp 93–5.

112. Duke of Richmond, 'On the Solution of Bones in Sulphuric Acid for the purposes of Manure', *JRASE*, IV, 1843, pp 408–9; John Hannam *et al*, 'On the use of bones as a Manure with Sulphuric Acid', *ibid*, V, 1845, pp 443–68 and 594–6', *idem*, 'An Experimental Inquiry into the Theory of the Action and Practical Application of Bones as a Manure for the Turnip Crop', *ibid*, VI, 1845, pp 71–2.

113. Nicholas Goddard, 'Nineteenth-Century Recycling: the Victorians and the Agricultural Utilisation of Sewage', *History Today*, 31, June 1981, pp 32–6.

114. William Hope, 'The Use and Abuse of Town Sewage', *Journal of the Society of Arts*, XVIII, 1869, p 302.

115. See, for example, Voelcker's conclusion in his 'Influence of Chemical Discoveries on the Progress of English Agriculture', *JRASE*, ser ii, XIV, 1878, pp 30–4.

116. Augustus Voelcker, Charles Gay Roberts, J C Morton, Robert Wolff and Edward Owen Greening, *Agricultural Economy*, 1874, pp 31–2.

117. *Ibid*, pp 40–4.

118. Josiah Parkes, 'On Draining', *JRASE*, VII, 1846, pp 249–72.

119. See David Spring, *The English Landed Estate in the Nineteenth Century: its Administration*, 1963, pp 143–5.

120. William Bullock Webster, 'On the Failure of Deep Draining on certain Strong Clay Subsoils, with a Few Remarks on the Injurious Effect of Sinking the Water too Far below the Roots of Plants in very Porous, Alluvial and Peaty Soils, *JRASE*, IX, 1848, pp 237–8.

121. Pusey, 'Note', to William Bullock Webster, 'On the Mischief arising from Draining Certain Clay Soils too Deeply, *ibid*, XI, 1850, pp 311–2.

122. H H Nicholson, *The Principles of Field Drainage*, 2nd edn, 1953, pp 80–2; A D Trafford, 'Field Draining', *JRASE*, 131, 1970, p 141.

123. *Agricultural Economist*, 1 March 1878; *Journal of the Farmer's Club*, May 1882, pp 75–6, quoted in J Bailey Denton, *Agricultural Drainage: A Retrospect of Forty Years Experience*, 1883. For assessments of the impact of Victorian underdrainage see H C Darby, 'The Draining of the English Claylands', *Geographische Zeitschrift*, 211, 1964, pp 190–201; R W Sturgess, 'The Agricultural Revolution on the English Clays', *AHR*, XIV, 1966, pp 104–21; E J T Collins and E L Jones, 'Sectoral Advance in English Agriculture, 1850–1880', *AHR*, XV, 1967, pp 65–81; A D M Phillips, 'Underdraining and the English Claylands 1850–80: A Review', *AHR*, XVII, 1969, pp 44–55.

124. 'The Royal Agricultural Society – Proceedings in Council', *Farmer's Magazine*, ser iii, XIII, 1858, p 495.

125. Farmer's Club Dinner Report, *Mark Lane Express*, 14 December 1874. For a memoir of Voelcker see *Farmer's Magazine*, ser iii, XXXIV, 1869, p 3.

126. See 'Fraud in Sale of Guano', *Farmer's Magazine*, ser ii, XV, 1847, pp 559–60. The question was extensively discussed in the Society's Council between 1847 and 1852.

127. Monthly Councils 2 March and 6 July 1870 (Reports of Chemical Committee).

128. See Bradburn v Royal Agricultural Society of England, *JRASE*, ser ii, VII, 1871, pp 465–9 and *Farmer's Magazine*, ser iii, XL, 1871, pp 15–16.

129. Special Council 21 August 1872; Kidd v Royal Agricultural Society of England', *JRASE*, ser ii, VIII, 1872, pp 481–682.

130. *Agricultural Economist*, 1 September 1876.

131. See 'SWC', 'Mr William Carruthers', and 'The Botanist's Work 1871–1909', *JRASE*, 70, 1909, pp 3–5, 5–12.

132. See 'The Royal Agricultural Society and the Improvement of Cereals', *Farmer's Magazine*, LIV, 1880, pp 44–5.

133. 'The English Agricultural Society and the Veterinary Art', *Farmer's Magazine*, new series, I, 1839, p 24; 'The English Agricultural Society', and 'The Royal Veterinary College', *ibid*, new series, I, 1858, p 451; 'The Veterinary College and the English Agricultural Society', *ibid*, new series, II, 1839, pp 38–9; Minutes of Committee of Management 5 September 1838 and 10 July 1839; *Animal Health: A Centenary 1865–1965*, HMSO, 1966, pp 135–6; 'Epidemic among Cattle', *JRASE*, I, 1840, pp cxcii–cxcvi. For an overview see J R Fisher, 'Animal Health and the Royal Agricultural Society in its Early Years', *JRASE*, 143, 1982, pp 105–110.

134. Sir Frederick Smith, *A History of Veterinary Literature*, III, 1930, p 127.

135. *Ibid*, p 89. For Simonds's autobiography see *Veterinarian*, LXVII, 1894, pp 315–24, 401–12, 487–500, 573–85, 651–62, 736–49, 811–23, 889–99.

136. James Beart Simonds, 'Report on Steppe Murrain or Rinderpest', *JRASE*, XVIII, 1857, p 270.

137. See Ruth D'Arcy Thompson, 'The Gamgees – Medical and Veterinary', *Veterinary History*, III, 1974, pp 3–7; Richard Perren, *The Meat Trade in Britain 1840–1914*, 1978, pp 50–68; *The Times* 10 and 13 November 1863 cited in *Animal Health*, 1966, pp 13–14.

138. Smith, IV, pp 100–102; *Animal Health*, pp 16–17; Simonds, Autobiography, p 742.

139. Monthly Councils 1 November and 6 December 1865; 'Deputation to the Lords of the Privy Council', *Farmer's Magazine*, ser iii, XXIX, 1866, pp 68–9 and 'The Cattle Plague', (Report

of St. James's Meeting 14 December 1865), *ibid*, pp 73–4; Monthly Council 7 February 1866 and 'Deputation to Lord Russell', *ibid*, pp 240–2. See also Thomas Mackay, ed, *The Reminiscences of Albert Pell*, 1908, pp 198–202 and T Duckham, 'The Progress of Legislation against Contagious Diseases of Livestock', *JRASE*, ser iii, IV, 1893, p 270.

140. *Animal Health*, pp 134, 136; Monthly Council 3 July, 11 December 1872; May 1874. On the economic aspects of cattle diseases see J R Fisher, 'The Economic Effects of Cattle Disease in Britain and its Containment', *Agricultural History*, 54, 1980, pp 278–93. On a recent assessment of control policy see A P Power and S A Harris, 'A Cost-Benefit Evaluation of Alternative Control Policies for Foot-and-Mouth Disease in Great Britain', *Journal of Agricultural Economics*, 24, 1973, pp 573–600.

SOME ISSUES AND CONTROVERSIES

141. H S Thompson, 'Address of the President to the General Meeting', *JRASE*, ser iii, III, 1867, p 428. See also 'Forbidden Topics at the Royal Agricultural Society', *Farmer's Magazine*, ser iii, XXXI, 1867, pp 79–80.

142. Chandos Wren Hoskyns, 'On Agricultural Statistics', *JRASE*, XVI, 1856, pp 554–606; *Farmer's Magazine*, IX, 1856, p 270.

143. 'The Charter of the Royal Agricultural Society *versus* Agricultural Statistics', *Farmer's Magazine*, IX, p 271.

144. 'The Charter of the Royal Agricultural Society' and report of half-yearly meeting, *Farmer's Magazine*, ser iii, XXIX, 1866, pp 420, 453–4.

145. *Agricultural Gazette*, 15 December 1866.

146. *Farmer's Magazine*, ser iii, XXIX, 1866, p 304.

147. Clay's letters are reproduced in A H H Matthews, *Fifty Years of Agricultural Politics*, 1915, pp 392–4.

148. 'The Present Position of the Royal Agricultural Society', *Farmer's Magazine*, ser iii, XXXIII, 1868, p 471; discussion at General Meeting 1871 reported in *ibid*, ser iii, XXXIX, 1871, p 463; 'The Royal Charter', *ibid*, pp 530–1; discussion at General Meeting 1873, *ibid*, ser iii, XLV, 1874, p 478; 'The Opening of the Winter Session in London', *Farmer's Magazine*, ser iii, XLVII, 1875, pp 1–2.

149. 'Horse Shows and the Prize System', *Farmer's Magazine*, ser iii, XXXVIII, 1871, p 274.

150. *Mark Lane Express*, 24 July 1843. See also reports of the Derby Meeting in *Farmer's Magazine*, ser ii, VIII, 1843, pp 103–4 and 119–20.

151. 'A Manufacturer', *The Manufacture of Agricultural Machinery Considered as a Branch of National Industry*, 1857, pp 19–22; William Day, *Mechanical Science and the Prize System in Relation to Agriculture*, 1857.

152. 'The Prize System – as now opposed by the Implement Makers', *Farmer's Magazine*, ser iii, XII, 1857, pp 116–7; 'RSB', (probably Robert Scott Burn) 'Agricultural Machinery and the Prize System', *ibid*, ser iii, XVI, 1859, p 296.

153. Ransomes and Sim, *Reasons for not Exhibiting at the RASE Meetings in Canterbury 1860 and Leeds 1861*, 1861.

154. Samuel Sidney, 'On the Effect of Prizes on Manufacturers', *Journal of the Society of Arts*, X, 1861–2, pp 376–88; J C Morton, 'Agricultural Progress: Its Helps and Hindrances', *ibid*, XII, 1863, pp 64–5', 'The Prize System, as put at the Society of Arts', *Farmer's Magazine*, ser iii, XXVI, 1864, pp 9–11.

155. 'Agricultural Progress', *loc cit*; Richard Garrett, letter, *Agricultural Gazette*, 16 January 1864.

156. *Agricultural Gazette*, 31 December 1853 and 15 December 1855.

157. Reports of the General Meetings of July and December 1857 reported in *Farmer's Magazine*, ser iii, XII, 1857, pp 162–3 and XIII, 1858, pp 70–1. Samuel Sidney (nom-de-

plume of Samuel Solomons, 1813–1883) attended agricultural shows for the *Illustrated London News* and was for a time Assistant Secretary to the Crystal Palace. In 1860 he was appointed Secretary to the Islington Agricultural Hall Company where, from 1864 until his death he organised the annual horse shows, notorious for their 'leaping' exhibitions. His best known work is *The Book of the Horse*, 1873.

158. For memoirs of Hoskyns see *Agricultural Gazette*, 7 January and 9 April 1877 and J S Arkwright's introduction to *Talpa: or the Chronicles of a Clay Farm*, 1903 edn; Acland did much to revive the Bath & West Society on which see Kenneth Hudson, *The Four Great Men of the Bath & West*, 1973, pp 11–16 and *idem*, *The Bath & West: a Bicentary History*, 1977, pp 88–116. Thompson's association with the Yorkshire Society is detailed by Vance Hall, *The Yorkshire Agricultural Society 1837–1987*, 1987.

159. H D Acland, *Letters and Memoirs*, 1902, cited by Hudson, 'Four Great Men', p 16; Earl Cathcart, 'Sir Henry Stephen Meysey Thompson, Bart: A Biographical Sketch', *JRASE*, ser ii, X, 1874, p 519; *Farmer's Magazine*, ser iii, XIII, 1858, p 71.

160. Minutes of Journal Committee 3 February, 3 March 1858; Monthly Councils 3 February, 3 March, 25 1858, 3 November, 7 December 1859. See 'Royal Agricultural Society - Proceedings in Council', *Farmer's Magazine*, ser iii, XIII, 1858 and 'An Investigator', letter, *Agricultural Gazette*, 16 June 1860 and Morton's obituary, *ibid*, 14 May 1888.

161. Editorship Committee, 9 March 1860; *Farmer's Magazine*, ser iii, XVII, 1860, p 484 and XVIII, 1860, pp 482–3; *Agricultural Gazette* 26 May and 9 June 1860.

162. *Farmer's Magazine*, ser iii, XVIII, 1860, p 480.

163. Special Council Meetings 27 May and 22 June 1859; 'The Administrative of the Royal Agricultural Society', *Farmer's Magazine*, ser iii, XVI, 1859, pp 15–16. See also *ibid*, XIX, 1861, pp 429–30. Brandeth Gibbs acted as Secretary *pro tem* during part of 1859.

164. Sidney at General Meeting 15 July 1859 reported in *Farmer's Magazine*, ser iii, XVI, 1859, pp 145–6.

165. Sidney at Half-Yearly Meeting 23 May 1860 reported in *ibid*, XVIII, 1860, pp 479–80. See also comment in *Agricultural Gazette*, 23 July 1859 and 12, 19, 26 May and 21 July 1860.

166. 'A Wednesday Afternoon at the Society's Rooms', *Farmer's Magazine*, ser iii, XIX, 1861, p 495.

167. *Agricultural Gazette* 12 January, 2 February 1861 and 'Old English Farmer', letter, 19 January 1861.

168. Monthly Councils 3 June and 1 July 1868.

169. J Bailey Denton, letter, *Agricultural Gazette*, 15 August 1869; *ibid*, 17 October 1868.

170. J C Morton, 'The Late Mr. H M Jenkins, FGS: A Memoir', *JRASE*, ser ii, XXIII, 1887, p 174.

171. *Agricultural Gazette*, 7, 14, 21 November, 12 December 1868.

172. Thompson's defence was at the December General Meeting, 1868; for Corbet's comments see *Mark Lane Express*, 7 September and 9 November 1868.

173. See comments in *Agricultural Gazette*, 15 October 1870, and *Farmer's Magazine*, ser iii, XXXVII, 1870, p 54 and XLIII, 1873, p 56.

THE LATER NINETEENTH CENTURY

174. J Wrightson, 'The Agricultural Lessons of "The Eighties"', *JRASE*, ser iii, I, 1890, p 275.

175. For surveys of this period see C S Orwin and E H Whetham, *British Agriculture 1846–1914*, 971, especially pp 240–83; P J Perry, *British Farming in the Great Depression 1870–1914*, 1974; *idem*, *British Agriculture 1875–1914*, 1973; Jonathan Brown, *Agriculture in England 1870–1947*, 1987.

176. C De Laune Faunce De Laune, 'Tobacco as a Farm Crop for England', *JRASE*, ser ii, XXIII, 1887, pp 213–52.

177. Primrose McConnell, 'Experiences of a Scotsman on the Essex Clays', *JRASE*, ser iii, II, 1891, pp 311–25.
178. Robert Trow-Smith, *Society and the Land*, 1953, pp 117–56.
179. 'The Tone and Tendency of the Autumn Meetings', *Farmer's Magazine*, ser iii, XX, 1861, p 436.
180. 'Country Newspapers', *Temple Bar*, X, 1864, p 131.
181. W E Bear, 'The Public Interest in Agricultural Reform', *The Nineteenth Century*, V, 1879, pp 1079–80.
182. C De Laune Faunce De Laune, 'On Laying Down Land in Permanent Grass', *JRASE*, ser ii, XVIII, 1882, pp 229–64.
183. William Carruthers, 'The Botanist's Work 1871–1909', *JRASE*, 70, 1909, pp 5–12.
184. Edward Kinch, 'Basic Cinder as Manure', *ibid*, ser iii, I, 1890, pp 129–38.
185. H M Jenkins, 'Report on the Practice of Ensilage, at Home and Abroad', *ibid*, ser ii, XX, 1884, pp 126–64; Augustus Voelcker. 'On the Chemistry of Ensilage', *ibid*, pp 482–504.
186. H M Jenkins, 'Dairying in Denmark', *ibid*, XIX, 1883, pp 155–84; 'Agricultural Lessons', p 279.
187. Monthly Councils 3 November 1875, 5 April, 3 May 1876.
188. *Ibid*, 1 November, 6 December 1876.
189. *Ibid*, and 6 February, 3 April 1878. See also 'The Woburn Experiments', *Farmer's Magazine*, ser iii, LVI, 1879, pp 378–80.
190. J A Voelcker and E J Russell, *Fifty Years of Field Experiments at Woburn Experimental Farm*, 1936; A E Johnson, 'Woburn Experimental Farm: a Hundred Years of Agricultural Research', *JRASE*, 138, 1978, pp 18–26. The experiments and investigations were regularly reported in the *Journal*.
191. *Agricultural Gazette*, 23 February, 29 June 1861.
192. *Mark Lane Express* 11, 25 January 1847; Reports of half-yearly meeting 1866', Agricultural and Middle-Class Education', 'The Present Position of the Royal Agricultural Society', *Farmer's Magazine*, ser iii, XXIX, pp 454, 467; XXXIII, 1868, p 471. See also C Lawrence, 'The Royal Agricultural College at Cirencester', *JRASE*, ser ii, I, 1865, pp 4–5.
193. Monthly Council 2 March 1864; *JRASE*, XXV, 1864, pp 542–3.
194. *Ibid*, pp 543–8; Monthly Councils 2 November 1864, 1 February, 6 December 1865.
195. T D Acland, *Agricultural Education; What It Is and How to Improve It, Considered in Two Letters to Sir Edward Kerrison, Bart, M P, 1865; Agricultural Gazette*, 25 February, 10 December 1865. Acland's views were also stated in T D Acland, *The Education of the Farmer Viewed in Connection with that of the Middle-classes in General: Its Objects, Principles and Cost*, 1857.
196. *Agricultural Gazette*, 15 December 1866.
197. Monthly Council 2 April 1867, Special Council 2 May 1867.
198. 'The Body and its Members', *Farmers Magazine*, ser iii, XLV, 1874, p 552; H M Jenkins, 'The Royal Agricultural Society', *JRASE*, ser ii, XIV, 1878, p890; Herbert J Little, 'Report on Agricultural Education: a Summary', *JRASE*, ser ii, XXI, 1885, pp 126–64 and 518–46; John Dent Dent, 'Notes on Agricultural Education at Home and Abroad', *JRASE*, ser iii, I, 1890, p 38.
199. Henry Edmunds, 'Eighty Years of Fream's Elements of Agriculture', *JRASE*, 134, 1984, pp 66–77. See also Gwyn E Jones, 'William Fream: Agriculturist and Educator', *JRASE*, 144, 1983, pp 30–44.
200. J H Gilbert, 'The Late Dr Voelcker', *JRASE*, XXI, 1885, p 327.
201. A P Thomas, 'Report of Experiments on the Development of Liver-Fluke (Fasicola Hepatica)', *JRASE*, ser ii, XVII, 1881, pp 1–29; James Beart Simonds', The Rot in Sheep: its Nature, Causes, and Treatment', *Ibid*, XXIII, 1862, pp 64–159.
202. Nigel Harvey, 'Can we Eliminate Liver Fluke?', *Country Life*, 2 March 1972.

203. Ralph Whitlock, *The Great Cattle Plague: An Account of the Foot and Mouth Epidemic of 1967–8*, 1968.

204. Russell, *op cit*, pp 106, 156–7, 163.

205. The first of Curtis's *Journal* papers appeared as 'Observations on the Natural History and Economy of the Turnip Saw-Fly, and its Black Caterpillar, called the Black Palmer, Black Conker, Black Jack, Black Slug, and Nigger, or Negro', *JRASE*, II, 1841, pp 364–89 and his series of articles continued until vol. XVIII, 1857.

206. George Ordish, *John Curtis and the Pioneering of Pest Control*, 1974, pp 86–7. See also *idem*, *The Constant Pest*, 1976.

207. F S Courtney, 'The Trials of Oil Engineer at Cambridge', *JRASE*, ser iii, V, 1894, p 697.

208. J C Morton, 'The Late Sir B T Brandreth Gibbs', JRASE, ser ii, XXI, 1885, p 612.

209. J C Morton, 'Jenkins', p 168.

210. *Agricultural Gazette*, 9 May 1888.

211. Ernest Clarke, 'John Chalmers Morton', *JRASE*, ser ii, XXIV, 1888, pp 691–6.

212. *Mark Lane Express*, 27 May 1844.

213. Chandos Wren Hoskyns, 'The Progress of English Agriculture During the last Fifteen Years', *Journal of the Society of Arts*, IV, 1856, p 274.

214. Susan Fairlie, 'The Corn Laws and British Wheat Production', *EHR*, ser ii, XXII, 1969, pp 102–3.

215. For a summary, see E L Jones, *Seasons and Prices*, 1964, pp 169–73, also James Caird, 'On the Agricultural Statistics of the United Kingdom', *Statistical Journal*, 1868, p 131.

216. J Z Titow, *Winchester Yields*, 1972, gives extensive information on medieval grain yields.

217. Observation by Robert Baker of Writtle in *Farmer's Magazine*, ser iii, VII, 1855, p 445. I am grateful to Mrs Pam Soanes for bringing this to my attention.

218. Richard Perren, *The Meat Trade in Britain 1840–1914*, 1978, p 3.

219. *Agricultural Economist*, 1 February 1878; James Caird, 'Fifty Years' Progress of British Agriculture', *JRASE*, ser iii, I, 1890, pp 26–7.

220. Perren, p 3. For statistics of the balance of value between home produced and imported food-stuffs between 1848 and 1885 see N L Tranter, *Population and Industrialisation*, 1973, p 151.

221. 'The Farmer's Newspaper', *Farmer's Magazine*, ser iii, VI, 1854, p 486.

222. G Leach, *Energy and Agriculture*, 1976, p 15.

223. In a discussion at the London Farmer's Club quoted by J R Fisher, *Clare Sewell Read 1826–1903: a Farmer's Spokesman of the Late Nineteenth Century*, University of Hull, 1975, p 19.

224. E L Jones, 'The Changing Basis of English Agricultural Prosperity 1853–73', *AHR*, X, 1962, pp 102–119; Fairlie, 'Corn Laws', p 99.

225. *Mark Lane Express*, 31 March 1903.

226. *Agricultural Gazette*, 9, 30 July 1877. These reminiscences were prompted by the occasion of the Liverpool Royal Show when the *Gazette* featured a number of reviews of the changes that had taken place in agriculture since the Society's first visit in 1841.

227. G T Brown, *Life on the Farm*, 1886, pp 111–2.

228. P K O'Brien, 'Agriculture and the Industrial Revolution', *EHR*, ser ii, XXX, 1977, p 171.

229. *The Times*, 18 September 1882 also quoted by Linker, thesis, p 499.

230. At the Society's General Meeting.

231. The revival of interest in agricultural science is noted by Fisher, thesis, p 92.

232. A W Stanton, 'Decadence of Agricultural Shows', in *Agricultural Annual and Mark Lane Express Almanac*, 1902, p 82.

233. *Cadwallader John Bates, Thomas Bates and the Kirklevington Shorthorns*, 1897, p v.

Part III: From Park Royal to Stoneleigh 1903–1963

1. Unpublished Report of RASE Fact-Finding Committee, 1961, paragraph 9, p 6.

The Failure of Park Royal

2. Rt Hon. Walter Long MP at Half-Yearly General Meeting 7 December 1899, *JRASE*, ser iii, X, 1899, p cxcv.
3. Monthly Council 26 July 1899, *ibid*, p lxxx–lxxxi.
4. The Special Show Committee first met on 30 October 1899 and presented a preliminary report to the Monthly Council 7 February 1900; the full report was considered by a Special Council on 7 March 1900. See *JRASE*, ser iii, XI, 1900, pp xxxii–xxxiv and xxxv–xlviii.
5. The Report was published in *ibid*, pp 65–86.
6. Clare Sewell Read at the half-yearly General Meeting 9 December 1897 reported in *ibid*, VIII, 1897, pp ccvii.
7. Special Council 7 March 1900, *ibid*, Xl, 1900, p xlviii.
8. See especially Monthly Councils 3 April 1901 and 5 November 1902, *ibid*, 62, 1901, pp xlix–lii and 63, 1902, p lxxxv.
9. See Monthly Councils 1 May, 5 June. General meeting 27 June, Monthly Council 31 July, 6 November, 1901; 5 November, 10 December 1902; General Meeting 11 December 1902, reported in *JRASE*, 62, 1901 pp xlix–lii, lxv–lxvi, lxxiii–lxxiv, lxxxiv; 63, 1902, pp lxxxv, xciv–xcv. Sutton's resignation was received at Monthly Council, 1 June 1904, and reported in *ibid*, 65, 1904, p xlviii.
10. 25 June 1904 and reported at Monthly Council 27 June, *ibid*, 65, p lii.
11. See Monthly Councils 6 October, 2 November, 7 December, 1904, 11 January 1905; General Meeting 21 June, and Annual General Meeting 1 August 1905 reported in *ibid*, 65, 1904 pp lvii–lxvii, lxvii–lxvii, lxxii–lxxvii, and 66, 1905, xxxiii–xxxviii, lvi–lix, lx–lxv. For Wilson's obituary see G G Rea, 'Sir Jacob Wilson, KCVO', *ibid*, pp 1–18.
12. *History of RASE 1839–1939*, 1939, pp 70–71.
13. Report of Council to General Meeting 22 May 1888, paragraphs 5, 6 and 8, December 1887, *JRASE*, 24, 1888, pp xi and xlii.
14. Monthly Councils 1 February, 12 April 1893 reported in *ibid*, ser iii, LV, 1893, pp xxviii–xxix and li–lii; the terms of the debenture issue are stated on p lxxix.
15. J P Goodwin, 'Mr Charles Adeane, CB', *ibid*, 104, 1943, p 5.
16. Special Council 7 March 1900, *ibid*, ser iii, XL, 1900, p xlvi. See also Sutton's letter in *Agricultural Gazette*, 22 July 1901.
17. Reported in *Agricultural Gazette*, 30 April 1900.
18. A W Stanton, 'Decadence of Agricultural Shows', in *Agricultural Annual and Mark Lane Express Almanac*, 1902, p 82.
19. Frederick King at the General Meeting 13 December 1894, *JRASE*, ser iii, V, 1894, p clxxxix.
20. 'Notes on the Royal Show' by 'A Member'. *Agricultural Gazette*, 1 July 1889.
21. General Meeting, 22 June 1904, *JRASE*, 65, 1904, p l.
22. Observation on the Windsor Show in *Agricultural Gazette*, 24 June 1889. On the industrial structure of London see P Hall, *The Industries of London since 1861*, 1962 and G Stedman-Jones, *Outcast London*, 1971, for its social implications.
23. Observation by Lord Middleton in Monthly Council 6 October 1904 reported in *JRASE*, 65, 1904, p lix.
24. The review of the society's affairs was established at the Monthly Council 27 July 1904. Conferences between the Society's Implement Committee and Stock Prizes Committee were held with the implement and stock exhibitors respectively on 5 October and recommendations considered at the Monthly Council 6 October. The decision to petition for the Supplementary Charter was taken at the Monthly Councils of 2 November and 7 December

and placed before the General Meeting of 8 December 1904; see *JRASE*, 65, 1904, pp lxxi, lxxxi, lxxxii–xciii.

25. Monthly Council 1 August, 1 November 1905; *ibid*, 66, 1905, lx–lxix, lxxi–lxxvii.

26. For the Society's reorganisation see Monthly Councils of 10 January, 7 February, 4 April, 1 August, 7 November; *ibid*, xxv–xxvii, xxvii–xxix, xxxii, xxxviii–xl, xl–xliv.

27. Monthly Council 1 February 1928.

28. J A Voelcker, 'Sir Ernest Clarke', *JRASE*, 84, 1923, pp 1–10.

29. Goodwin, *op cit*, p 5.

30. H Rider Haggard, *A Farmer's Year: being his Commonplace Book for 1898*, 1899, p 316 (footnote).

31. Scott Watson, *History*, p 169.

32. See 'Some Minor Farm Crops', I, *JRASE*, 74, 1913, pp 127–172, II, *ibid*, 75, 1914, 75–87, III, 76, 1915, pp 110–138.

33. Thomas McRow, 'The Doncaster Show 1912', *ibid*, 73, 1912, pp 175–7.

34. Gordon Mingay, *British Friesians: An Epic of Progress*, 1982, p 36.

35. W Worby Beaumont and R J Bayntun Hippisley, 'Trials of Agricultural Motors', *JRASE*, 71, 1910, p 190.

36. Anon, 'Sir Walter Gilbey Bart', *ibid*, 75, 1914, pp 136–47. On Gilbey's support for the continuance of a permanent showyard see his letter in *Mark Lane Express*, 6 November 1905.

FROM THE FIRST WORLD WAR TO THE CENTENARY SHOW 1914–1939

37. Edith H Whetham, *The Agrarian History of England and Wales, VIII, 1914–39*, 1978, pp 70–108 provides an account of farming policy during the First World War.

38. On farming profits and the labour question see particularly Peter E Dewey, 'British Farming profits and Government Policy during the First World War', *EHR*, ser ii, XXXVII 1984, pp 373–90; *idem*, Agricultural Labour supply in England and Wales during the First World War, *ibid*, 28, 1975, pp 100–12; *idem*, 'Food Production and Policy in the United Kingdom 1914–1918', *Trans Royal Historical Society*, 30, 1980, pp 71–89. On general food policy see L Margaret Barnett, *British Food Policy during the First World War*, 1985. The impact of the war on the countryside is reviewed by Caroline Dakars, *The Countryside at War 1914–1918*, 1987.

39. Monthly Council 9 December 1914.

40. *Ibid*, 6 December 1916.

41. *Ibid*.

42. *Ibid*.

43. *Ibid*, 24 January, 21 February 1917.

44. The War Emergency Committee met regularly during 1917 and 1918 and reported to the Monthly Council Meetings.

45. J P Goodwin, 'The work of the Agricultural Relief of Allies Committee', *JRASE*, 84, 1923, pp 371–380. The RASE library (Belgrave Square) holds a commemorative illustrated album containing the signatures of the Belgian farmers who received assistance. On the Society's earlier relief work see Sadie B Ward, 'The French Peasants' Seed Fund: a 19th Century Example of Disaster Relief', *JRASE*, 138, 1977, pp 60–70.

46. E H Whetham, 'The Agriculture Act, 1920 and its Repeal: the "Great Betrayal"', *AHR*, 22, pt i, 1974, pp 36–49.

47. *Idem, Agrarian History VIII*, pp 142–153.

48. J D F Green, 'Agricultural Broadcasting: A Memoir and a Point of View', *JRASE*, 142, 1981, p 18.

49. T Rooth, 'Trade Agreements and the Evolution of British Agricultural Policy in the 1930's, *AHR*, 1985, 33, pt ii, pp 173–90; 'The Turn of the Tide', *Farmer and Stockbreeder*, 31

December 1934. On policies for agricultural revival and rural reconstruction during the interwar period see Lord Addison, *A Policy for British Agriculture* 1939; Viscount Astor and Keith A H Murray, *Land and Life: the Economic National Policy for Agriculture*, 1932 and *idem, The Planning of Agriculture*, 1933; Viscount Astor and B S Rowntree, *The Agricultural Dilemma*, 1935 and *idem, British Agriculture*, 1938; M Fordham, *Rebuilding of Rural Britain*, 1925; Sir A D Hall, *Reconstruction and the Land* 1941; C S Orwin, *The Future of Farming*, 1931; Sir R G Stapledon, *The Land Now and Tomorrow*, 1935; J A Scott Watson, *Rural Britain Today and Tomorrow (Being a modern Cobbett's Tour)*, 1934; Sir William Dampier, *Politics and the Land*, 1928.

50. *Farmer and Stockbreeder*, 31 December 1928.
51. *Monthly Council* 3 February 1932; Whetham, *Agrarian History VIII*, p 243. On the development of interwar agricultural policy see A F Cooper, 'The Transformation of British Agricultural Policy 1912–1936', unpub. D Phil thesis, University of Oxford, 1980.
52. Monthly Councils 28 June, 3 November, 8 December 1920.
53. Scott Watson, p 128; Russell pp 174–5.
54. *Farmer and Stockbreeder* 4 July 1921.
55. For an account of the foundation of the Norfolk research station see *JRASE*, 71, 1910, pp 366–70.
56. B M Jenkin, review of Frederick Irvine Anderson, *Electricity for the Farm*, *JRASE*, 76, 1915, p 191.
57. Reported in *Farmer and Stockbreeder* 12 May 1924.
58. Monthly Council 2 November 1927; R Borlase Matthews, *Electro-Farming* or *The Application of Electricity to Agriculture*, 1928, p 5; *Farmer and Stockbreeder*, 9 May 1927.
59. Nigel Harvey, *The Farming Kingdom*, 1954, pp 109,163.
60. G H Garrad, 'The work of the Motor Tractor', *JRASE*, 79, 1918, pp 1–23; 'Report of the Judges on the Trials of Agricultural Motors', *ibid*, 81, 1920, pp 1–62; S J Wright, 'World Tractor Trials, 1930', *ibid*, 91, 1930, pp 202–236; *Farmer and Stockbreeder*, 15 September 1930.
61. Reported in *Farmer and Stockbreeder*, 19 January 1931.
62. E J T Collins, 'The Agricultural Tractor in Britain 1900–1940' in H Winkel and K Herrmann, eds, *The Development of Agricultural Technology in the 19th and 20th Centuries*, 1984, pp 27–8.
63. *Ibid*, pp 34–5.
64. On the Macdonald family see J A Scott Watson and M E Hobbs, *Great Farmers*, 1937, pp 248–9 and A McN., 'Mr Charles James Black Macdonald', *JRASE*, 91, 1930, pp 175–77.
65. G Foster Clarke, 'The Hop Control', *JRASE*, 86, 1926, pp 1–30 (pt i) and *ibid*, 87, 1927, pp 86–124; A W Street, 'The Agricultural Marketing Act, 1933', *ibid*, 94, 1933, pp 1–21; C S Orwin, 'The Agricultural Policy in Action', *ibid*, 95, 1934, pp 1–17.
66. W S Mansfield, 'The Farms of Messrs Chivers & Sons Limited', Histon Cambridgeshire', *ibid*, pp 142–151; Henry G Robinson, 'Messrs S E and J F Alley's Mechanical Farming', *ibid*, 93, 1932, pp 157–164; L G Troup, 'The Leckford Estate Limited', *ibid*, 98, 1937, pp 127–141. A number of other articles appeared in this series during the 1930s.
67. *Farmer and Stockbreeder*, 10 July 1922.
68. *Ibid*, 9 July 1923.
69. Monthly Council 21 February 1927. The Society administered the Quarantine Stations for six years, handing it over to the Ministry on 31 March 1934. See 'The London Quarantine Station', *JRASE*, 95, 1934, pp 406–411.
70. 'Twenty-Five years of Royal Shows', *Farmer and Stockbreeder*, 7 July 1930. See also the note by Lord Cornwallis, 'Lord Daresbury, CVO: 1905–1930', *JRASE*, 91, 1930, pp 1–2.
71. *Farmer and Stockbreeder*, 14 July 1930.
72. *Ibid*, 8 September 1940, 13 July 1931, 11 July, 15 August 1932 for critical comment on the shows.

73. Walter Elliot, 'The New Outlook in Agriculture', *Farmer and Stockbreeder*, 29 April 1935 (Supplement).

74. L C Tripper 'Members' Suggestions' at Annual General Meeting 6 December 1933.

75. Monthly Council 6 April 1932. Sir Douglas's proposal was to reduce the pig classes to four.

76. A full account of the Society's Centenary Show is given in Scott Watson's *History*, pp 184–199.

77. *Farmer and Stockbreeder*, 18 July 1939.

THE SOCIETY IN WARTIME

78. Monthly Councils 1 November, 6 December 1939.

79. Annual General Meeting 6 December 1939; *Farmer and Stockbreeder*, 12 December 1939.

80. Proceedings of Council, 29 October 1942.

81. 'The Inactivity of the RASE', *Farmer and Stockbreeder*, 7 September 1943.

82. Minutes of Executive Committee, 28 October 1943.

83. The Agricultural Improvement Councils, under the auspices of the Ministry of Agriculture and the Department of Agriculture for Scotland, had the function of formulating agricultural research and advising the Agricultural Research Council (founded in 1931) on the agricultural problems requiring investigation. On the latter body see G W Cooke, ed., *Agricultural Research 1931–1981*, 1981.

84. Minutes of Executive Committee and Council, 29 October 1942; Executive Committee Minutes, 18 February 1943.

85. Keith A H Murray, *Agriculture*, 1955, pp 307–8 (*History of the Second World War*, ed Sir Keith Hancock).

86. Whetham, *Agrarian History VIII*, pp 328–9.

87. See Murray, *op cit*, for the official history of the wartime food production campaign. Dorman-Smith was a former NFU President and his statement was reported in *Farmer and Stockbreeder*, 24 October 1939. When ejected from Churchill's Cabinet in 1940 he was recalled as the 'Only Minister of Agriculture within living memory (with the possible exception of Lord Ernle) in whom farmers, workers, and landowners had implicit trust and confidence' ('Blythe' in *Farmer and Stockbreeder*, 21 May 1940). Possession was taken of 374,965 acres of land between 1940 and 1947 on the grounds of bad husbandry and this involved the termination of 2,793 tenancies. For membership of the County War Agricultural Committees (1939–1945) and details of land possession see Anthony Hurd, *A Farmer at Westminster*, 1951, Appendix I, pp 109–123 and III, p 128. The observation on the statistic of yield in relation to grass conversion to tillage was made in the War Cabinet – see Minutes of War Cabinet 291 (40) 8 p 86.

88. *Farmer and Stockbreeder*, 24 October 1939.

89. *Ibid*, 12 December 1939.

90. Minutes of Executive Committee, 22 May, 27 June 1941. The initial members of the committee were Lord Mildmay of Flete, Sir Arthur Hazlerigg, Sir Merrik Burrell, Sir Roland Burke, Sir Archibald Weigall, The Earl of Radnor, Lord Cranworth, Sir George Courthope and Mr A H B Talbot-Ponsonby.

91. Minutes of Executive Committee, 23 April, 29 October 1942.

92. Reported in *Farmer and Stockbreeder*, 16 February 1943.

93. Minutes of Executive Committee, 28 October 1943.

94. The following organisations were represented: National Farmers' Union (four representatives), Highland and Agricultural Society of Scotland, Group of Peers, Council of Agriculture, Central Landowners' Association, National Union of Agricultural Workers, Transport and General Workers' Union, Land Union, Chartered Surveyors Institution, Land Agents' Society (all with two representatives). The drafting committee consisted of Sir George Courthope, T Hodgson (T & GWU), J K Knowles (NFU), J Turner (later Lord

Netherthorpe) (NFU), Maj R Proby (CLA), Lord Brocket (Land Union), T S Brown (NUAW). For a report of the meeting see J P Goodwin, 'Agreement on Essentials of Policy', *Farmer and Stockbreeder*, 18 April 1944.

95. Minutes of Council, 31 May 1944; Viscount Astor and B Seebohm Rowntree, *Mixed Farming and Muddled Thinking. An Analysis of Current Agricultural Policy*, 1945, p 25.

96. Reported in *Farmer and Stockbreeder*, 3 August 1943. Christopher York and others also issued a critical pamphlet, *The Husbandman Waiteth* by 'Three Members of Parliament'.

97. Minutes of War Cabinet, 55(43) 1 pp 220–1.

98. For surveys of post-war agricultural policy see I Bowler, *Government and Agriculture, A Spatial Perspective*, 1979; B A Holderness, *British Agriculture since 1945*, 1985, especially Chapters I and II, pp 1–27; J K Bowers 'British Agricultural Policy since the Second World War', *AHR*, 33, pt i, 1985, pp 66–76.

99. J D F Green, 'A Tale of Three Brothers', *JRASE*, 149, 1987, pp 206–210.

100. Laurence Easterbrook was agricultural correspondent of the *News Chronicle* and during the second world war was part of the Ministry of Agriculture's Information Department. See *RASE Review*, 1, No 4, September 1965, p 25.

101. Finance Committee, 14 March and 31 May 1944; Report of Executive Committee, 31 May 1944; Minutes of Council, 31 May 1944; 'No "Royal" in 1945', *RASE Quarterly Review*, January 1945 pp 1–2.

102. Minutes of Council, 24 October 1945; 'No Show in 1946', *RASE Quarterly Review*, October 1945, p 1.

103. Minutes of Council, 19 June 1946.

104. *Ibid.*, 11 September, 4 December 1946 and Annual General Meeting 4 December 1946; Publicity Sub-Committee 5 February 1947; Minutes of Council (Showyard Works Committee), 5 March 1947.

105. Recollection of Sir Francis Pemberton, personal communication to author.

106. 'Progress at Lincoln', *RASE Quarterly Review*, No 1, 1947, p 3; Minutes of Council, 30 July 1947; 'Blythe', *Farmer and Stockbreeder*, 8 July 1947; 'After Lincoln', *RASE Quarterly Review*, October 1947 p 2.

107. For a review of the origins of the NAAS see N McCann, 'The Background to the National Agricultural Advisory Service', *JRASE*, 137, 1976, pp 51–9; on the prewar development of advisory services see C J Holmes, 'Science and the Farmer: the Development of the Agricultural Advisory Service in England and Wales 1900–1939', *AHR*, 36, pt i, 1988, pp 77–86.

108. Proceedings of Council, 4 December 1946, report of Forestry and Biological Committee.

109. Proceedings of Council, 28 July and 20 October 1948, Research Committee Appendix B (memorandum prepared by Sir John Russell).

110. The full list of County Surveys was *Kent* (G H Garrad) 1954, *Sussex* (R H B Jesse) 1960, *Northumberland* (C Cecil Pawson) 1961, *Cheshire* (W B Mercer) 1963, *Hertfordshire* (R W Gardner) 1968, *Yorkshire* (W Harwood Long) 1969 and *Suffolk* (P J O Trist) 1971.

111. D A Bond, 'Recent History and Varieties of Field Beans in the UK', *JRASE*, 146, 1985, pp 144–159.

THE CHARACTER OF POST WAR SHOWS 1947–1962

112. 'What Oxford taught us', *RASE Quarterly Review*, August 1950, p 4.

113. 'The Royal Show of the Festival Year', *ibid*, October 1951, pp 1–5.

114. 'The Newton Abbot Show', *ibid*, September 1952, pp 1–4.

115. 'The Royal Show at Blackpool', in 'Royal Show Blackpool Supplement', *JRASE*, 114, 1953, p 7.

116. Hugh Barty-King, *Light Up the World, The Story of Dale Electric 1935–1985*, 1985, p 52.

117. Robert Trow-Smith, 'Speaking as an Onlooker', *NAC News*, May-June 1972.

118. 'The Newton Abbot Show', *RASE Quarterly Review*, September 1952, pp 1–4.

119. *Farmer and Stockbreeder*, 16 July 1957.

120. *Ibid*, 8 and 15 July 1958.

121. Author's conversation with Canon Peter Buckler, 3 February 1986. For a profile of Peter Buckler see *Farmers Weekly*, 24 December 1982.

122. *Farmer and Stockbreeder*, 12 July 1960.

123. *Ibid*, 11 July 1961.

124. *RASE Review*, November 1962, pp 7–8.

THE ROUTE TO A PERMANENT SITE

125. D H Robinson, *The New Farming*, 1938 p 15 and third edition, 1951, p 17

126. As was noted in *Farmer and Stockbreeder*, 6 March 1945 'the present generation is unaware of the intensity of the RASE determination never to return to the metropolis after the financial losses which followed three shows at Park Royal 1903–5'. See letter from Cosmo Douglas urging a London site and reply from R M Dodington suggesting a base in the 'centre of England' in *Farmer and Stockbreeder*, 30 January and 13 February 1945.

127. Christopher York wrote to Alec Hobson on 25 July 1950 and the letter was noted at the Selection and General Purposes Committee, 1 August 1950. Alec Hobson produced a report entitled *Secretary's Report on Considerations involved in a Permanent and/or Several Permanent Sites Compared with the Migratory System*, 21 April 1951.

128. F Neville Gascoigne, 'To Move or not to Move', *Farmer and Stockbreeder*, 8 December 1954.

129. Selection and General Purposes Committee, 1 April 1953.

130. Proceedings of Council, 2 December 1953.

131. *Ibid*, 2 March 1955, item 17.

132. Proceedings of Council, 12 December 1956 (Selection and General Purposes Committee Report).

133. *Ibid* and 6 March, 1 May, 4 July, 16 October 1957.

134. Stoneleigh was approved as the Society's permanent base – for the trial period – at the Council meeting of 19 October 1960. See also 'A Permanent Base for the Royal', *The Review*, November 1960, p 6.

'A GREAT NEW CONCEPT'

135. 'Reviewing the Recommendations of the Fact Finding Committee, which presented its Report to Council in 1961', *RASE Review*, Vol 2, No 1, December 1965.

136. Proceedings of AGM, 6 December 1961 and John Hobson, personal communication to author.

137. Gwyn E Jones, 'The Diffusion of Agricultural Innovations', *Journal of Agricultural Economics*, XV, 1963, pp 387–409.

PART IV: THE SOCIETY AT STONELEIGH: THE FIRST TWENTY-FIVE YEARS

ESTABLISHMENT AT STONELEIGH

1. In conversation with Denis Russell, reported in *NAC News* March-April 1977 p 26

2. 'Reception at Stoneleigh', *The Review*, June 1962, p 5

3. Author's conversation with Sir Francis Pemberton 11 May 1986 and subsequent personal communications

4. H M Tickler, now of Little Cheveney Farm, Marden, Kent

5. Conversation between Francis Pemberton and Robert Trow-Smith reported in *Farmer and Stockbreeder*, 2 July 1963

6. Author's conversation and correspondence with Christopher Dadd (29 January 1988) and Sir Francis Pemberton

7. *Farmer and Stockbreeder*, 23 April, 25 May 1963

8. *Ibid*, 9 July 1963

9. 'Royal Show Stoneleigh Abbey: The Demonstration Area', *The Review*, June 1963

10. Peter Buckler, 'Reflections on the Demonstration Area', *ibid*, November 1963

11. See *Farmer and Stockbreeder*, 14 July 1964

12. *Farmer and Stockbreeder Comment*, 9 July 1963

13. 'Blythe' was the author of the comment column in *Farmer and Stock-breeder*. See also John Cherrington, 'The Royal Begins to Grow Up', *Farmer and Stockbreeder*, 21 July 1964. The 'Bowler-hat Brigade' refers to the symbol of office of the show stewards: as an example of Cherrington's criticism see 'Away with this Bowler Hat Brigade!', *Farmer and Stockbreeder*, 9 August 1960

14. Proceedings of Council, 6 May 1964 (Report of Finance and General Purposes Committee, 25 March 1964)

15. *Ibid*, 10 December 1964 (Report of Finance and General Purposes Committee, 28 October 1964)

16. Reported in *Farmer and Stockbreeder*, 3 October 1967

17. John Hearth, 'Agricultural Exports: Time for Leadership', *NAC News*, November-December 1976, p 1

THE DEVELOPMENT OF THE NATIONAL AGRICULTURAL CENTRE

18. *RASE Review*, 1, no 2, March 1965 p 3

19. 'Message from The Hon Show Director', *RASE Review* 1, no 3, June 1965, p 3; Peter Bell, 'Growing Pains at Stoneleigh', *Farmer and Stockbreeder*, 21 November 1967; Proceedings of Council, 6 March 1968 (Report of Finance and General Purposes Committee, 17 January 1968)

20. Proceedings of Council, 29 September 1971 (Report of Executive Board, 15 June and 20 July 1971). The 'very good friends' remained anonymous at the time

21. *Farmer's Weekly* 12 May 1972 and P Wormell, *Anatomy of Agriculture*, 1978, p 523; for a profile of John Hearth see *Farmer's Weekly*, 9 July 1982

22. Proceedings of Council, 6 March 1974 (Council and Committee Structure Working Party – Report)

23. The committee structure that resulted from the Player Commitee deliberations owed much to suggestions made by Mr J D F Green (who had been invited to join the committee by Capt Player) although he recalls being in favour of equal county representation and against recognition of the new metropolitan counties. John Green was for ten years Chairman of the Education and General Purposes (now Rural Affairs) committee, an extension of the old Journal Committee, with responsibility for the Society's external relations.

24. Reported in *National Agricultural Centre News*, no 5, February 1970

25. RASE annual accounts and personal communication from J D M Hearth

26. Author's conversations with Canon Peter Buckler and Christopher Dadd. See also Peter Buckler, 'The Arthur Rank Centre', *JRASE*, 140, 1979, pp 157–161

27. Proceedings of Council, 3 July 1969 (item 10, Unity in Design of Centre)

28. A R Laing, 'The Planning and Development of the National Agricultural Centre', *JRASE*, 137, 1976, pp 120–124; J D M Hearth, 'Study the Style', *NAC News* May-June 1976, p 3

29. 'New Electro-Agricultural Centre at Stoneleigh', *RASE Review*, vol 2, no 6, December 1966

30. Rev John Dockery, 'Beekeeping', *ibid*, vol 2, no 1, December 1965. See also Eva Crane, 'Bees in the Pollination of Seed Crops', *JRASE*, 133, 1972, pp 119–34

31. Dorian Williams, 'National Riding Centre', *RASE Review*, vol 2, no 5, September 1966, p

15; Ann Martin, 'The National Equestrian Centre', *JRASE*, 136, 1975, pp 107–112; Devinna Cannon, 'My Kingdom for a Horse!', *ibid*, 144, 1983, pp 192–6

32. In conversation with author 3 February 1988

33. Joe Henson, 'The Rare Breeds Survival Trust', *JRASE*, 145, 1984, pp 93–100

34. Reported in *Ark*, XIII, no 11, 15 November 1986, p 373

35. J D M Hearth, 'New Lease means more Land for NAC', *NAC News* May-June 1978, p 2, and personal communication to author

36. 'New Land Extends Scope of NAC', *NAC News*, September 1980. See also report in *Farmers Weekly*, 20 June 1980. For a profile of Sir John Eastwood see C David Edgar, 'Sir John Eastwood – Challenger at the Frontier of Agriculture', *JRASE*, 142, 1981, pp 96–108

37. 'William Scott Abbot Trust', *RASE Review*, vol 1, no 1, 1964, p 14

38. For a memoir see G H Jackson, 'Louise Ryan and Stowford – An Appreciation', *JRASE*, 147, 1986, pp 159–60. The history of Stowford was recorded by Mrs Ryan in *An Obscure Place* (privately published, 1973)

39. 'By his Work Shall We Know Him', *NAC News*, January 1988, p 2; *Farmers Weekly* 8 July 1977

40. Chief Executive's reports to Council

41. In this section I have drawn upon various unpublished reports which relate to the demonstration units. I have also had a number of conversations with the Society's Agricultural Director, George Jackson, and I am grateful for his guidance in certain technical areas. Developments and projects at the various units are regularly reported in *NAC News*

42. D H Robinson, 'Events Leading to the Formation of the National Agricultural Centre at Stoneleigh', *JRASE*, 129, 1968, p 18

43. In conversation with the author 29 September 1987

44. Peter Bell, 'Growing Pains at Stoneleigh', *Farmer and Stockbreeder*, 21 November 1967

45. W Emrys Jones, 'The National Agricultural Centre – The Next 10 Years', (Appendix 'A' to Proceedings of Council, 30 September 1969)

46. Proceedings of Council, 12 May 1971 (Report of Works Committee, 23 March 1971)

47. *National Agricultural Centre News*, September 1971. See also R G Haines, 'The Agricultural Development and Advisory Service at the NAC', *JRASE*, 133, 1972, pp 153–5

48. Proceedings of Council, 9 December 1971, item 10

49. Christopher Dadd, 'NAC – a Centre for Information', *JRASE*, 134, 1973, p 149

50. Apart from reports in *NAC News* and unpublished material, for the development of the Pig Unit see Keith Thornton, 'The Pig Demonstration Area 1963–71', *JRASE*, 132, 1971, pp 147–157; G R Brent, 'A Review of Developments at the NAC Pig Demonstration Centre', *ibid*, 137, 1976, pp 113–119; P J Peet, 'Developments at the NAC Pig Demonstration Unit', *ibid*, 142, 1981, pp 152–162 and 'Recent Developments at the NAC Pig Unit', *ibid*, 147, 1986, pp 210–219

51. David F R Wortley, 'The Dairy Demonstration Unit', *ibid*, 134, 1973, pp 160–165; D F Devine, 'The National Agricultural Centre Dairy Unit', *ibid*, 137, 1976, pp 107–112 and 'The National Agricultural Centre Dairy Unit', *ibid*, 140, 1979, pp 170–174; Alastair M R Holden, 'The NAC Dairy Unit', *ibid*, 145, 1984, pp 160–165

52. G S Fraser, 'The Calf Rearing Unit', *ibid*, 132, 1971, pp 158–161; P D Alsford, 'The Calf and Beef Demonstration Units', *ibid*, 134, 1973, pp 166–171; D J Read, J B Kilkenny, D M Allen, 'Maize Silage Beef System', *ibid*, 142, 1982, pp 142–151

53. J R Dalton, 'The Sheep Unit', *ibid*, 133, 1972, pp 144–148; Alastair Dymond, 'The National Agricultural Centre Sheep Unit', *ibid*, 136, 1975, pp 113–121 and 140, 1979, pp 170–174

54. J Keys, 'The NAC Poultry Unit', *ibid*, 146, 1985, pp 174–183

55. N A Barron, 'A Review of the Early Development of the NAC Cereal Unit', *ibid*, 139, 1978, pp 158–163; M R Saull, 'The NAC Arable Unit', *ibid*, 146, 1985, pp 184–187. See also P S

Wellington, 'The Royal Show, the NIAB and the National Agricultural Centre', *ibid*, 139, 1978, pp 147–151

56. D M Barling, 'Winter Barley Development Work on the Cotswolds', *ibid*, 141, 1980, pp 165–164, *NAC News* May 1979

57. 'The Farm-electric Centre', *JRASE*, 133, 1972, pp 139–43; David Long, 'The Farm Buildings Centre', *ibid*. 134, 1973, pp 152–154; J D Young, B Brockway, P Wakeford, 'Joint Activities at the National Agricultural Centre – ADAS, FBIC and FEC', *ibid*, 138, 1977, pp 147–156; B N Brockway, 'The Farm Buildings Information Centre', *ibid*, 148, 1987, pp 194–198; J Hardcastle, 'The AFRC at the NAC', *ibid*, 147, 1986, pp 220–225

58. G H Jackson, personal communication to author

59. *Farmers Weekly* report, 28 April 1972

60. See *ibid*, 14 September 1973

61. Comment in *ibid*, 16 August 1974

62. *Ibid*, 4 April 1975

63. *Ibid*, 1 and 15 April 1977

64. *Ibid*, 22 July 1977

65. 'Goats and Much More', *RASE/NAC News* September 1987, pp 19–20

ROYAL SHOWS AT STONELEIGH: FROM SUMMER PAGEANT TO INTERNATIONAL AGRICULTURAL EXPOSITION

66. The theme of this section was suggested to me by Mr J D F Green

67. *Farmer and Stockbreeder*, 13 July 1965

68. *Ibid*, 12 July 1966

69. *Ibid*, 11 July 1967; tribute from Lord Digby, Proceedings of Council, 6 July 1967, item 8

70. *Ibid*, 9 July 1968, 8 July 1969; 'Blythe' in *ibid*, 14 July 1970

71. See Elizabeth Phillipo, 'Speaking as an Onlooker', *National Agricultural Centre News*, November 1971 and Robert Trow-Smith, *ibid*, May-June 1972

72. Quoted in *Farmer and Stockbreeder*, 7 April 1972

73. *Annual Report of Council* 1985; author's conversation with C R Ferens 9 October 1987

74. Chief Executive's memorandum on conference on 'The NAC – the next Five Years' held 1 November 1973 at Stoneleigh

75. *Farmers Weekly*, 8 and 15 July 1977

76. *Ibid*, 8 July 1977

77. *Ibid*, 4 and 11 July 1980

78. Information taken from unpublished audience profile reports prepared for the Society by Farm Research Ltd and Produce Studies Ltd

79. For a summary see T J Colwyn David, 'Livestock at the Royal Show: the Crathorne Report', *JRASE*, 132, 1971, pp 65–78 and *Farmer and Stockbreeder* 20 October 1970

80. Reports in *Farmers Weekly*, 9 July 1971, 7 July 1972, 6 July 1973

81. See *ibid*, 10 July 1981

82. Claude Culpin, 'Royal Agricultural Society Machinery Awards', *JRASE*, 144, 1983, pp 176–182

83. 'Demonstrations at the Royal Show 1972', *JRASE*, 133, 1972, p 162 and *Farmers Weekly*, 7 July 1972

84. Sir Shridath's address was published in *JRASE*, 144, 1983, pp 10–12; *NAC News*, June 1984, p 2

85. Author's conversation with Harry Fox 22 October 1987

86. Proceedings of Council, 3 March 1971 (Report of Technical Development Committee 19 January 1971)

87. 'Farming spells F-o-o-d and Fight for Markets', *Farmers Weekly*, 6 July 1973

88. 'The Editor's Diary', *Ibid*, 4 July 1975
89. 'A Taste of Britain in Royal High Street', *NAC News*, July–August 1977
90. *Farmer and Stockbreeder*, 8 July 1969
91. Mary Cherry, 'The Royal Show 1972', *JRASE*, 133, 1972, p 159
92. 'Demonstrations at the Royal Show 1973', *JRASE*, 134, 1973, pp 177–181; *Farmers Weekly*, 8 July 1973
93. *NAC News*, March 1978
94. Unpublished survey of overseas visitors to Royal Show, 1983, by Exhibition Surveys (Melton Mowbray)
95. Peter Adams, 'Agriculture's £6 million shop-window', *Farmers Weekly*, 27 June 1980
96. At Annual General Meeting, 29 May 1975

EDUCATION, THE RURAL COMMUNITY AND ENVIRONMENT, AND THE SOCIETY'S 'LEARNED ROLE'

97. Proceedings of Council, 5 May 1965 (Journal and Education Committee Report, 10 March 1965)
98. *Ibid*, 9 December 1965 (Journal and Education Committee Report, 20 October 1965)
99. *Ibid*, 3 May and 7 December 1967
100. *Ibid*, 5 December 1968 (Appendix 'A' to Report of Journal and Education Committee, 9 October 1968)
101. H G Hudson, 'The Fellowship and Associateship of the Royal Agricultural Societies', *JRASE*, 140, 1979, pp 71–77
102. Proceedings of Council, 10 March 1982 and 9 March 1983
103. *Ibid*, 4 May, 8 December 1966 (Report of Journal and Education Committee, 9 March and 12 October 1966)
104. R Swann, 'Two Decades of Organised Farm Training', *JRASE*, 147, 1986, pp 19–25; K N Neilson, 'The ATB Management Centre', *JRASE*, 148, 1987
105. Christopher Dadd, 'Agricultural Education: Where Now?, *NAC News*, March-April 1977; Eric Tasker, 'The Society's Role in Agricultural Education', *JRASE*, 135, 1974, pp 7–16
106. N A Barron, 'Farmscan: New Horizons in Farm Management Education', *JRASE*, 138, 1977, pp 137–146. I have also drawn upon information provided by George Jackson in this section
107. J Aartse Tuyn, 'Stoneleigh Farm and Country Centre – An exercise in Farm Interpretation', *JRASE*, 136, 1975, pp 122–126 and 'Review of the Farm Interpretation Unit', *ibid*, 145, 1983, pp 166–73
108. Geoff Hughes, 'Secret Weapon Aims for Mars', *NAC News*, November 1987, p 11
109. For a review see Anthony Russell, 'The Arthur Rank Centre and the Changing Social Context of British Farming', *JRASE*, 144, 1983, pp 183–91
110. There is an extensive literature on these aspects of 'rural deprivation'. See, for example, Philip Lowe et al, *Deprivation and Welfare in Rural Areas*, 1986; R W Gilg, *An Introduction to Rural Geography*, 1985; Howard Newby, *Green and Pleasant Land*, 1979
111. Examples include Richard Body, *Agriculture: The Triumph and the Shame 1982* and *Farming in the Clouds*, 1984; J K Bowers and P Cheshire, *Agriculture, the Countryside, and Land Use*, 1983; Marion Shoard, *The Theft of the Countryside*, 1980 and *This Land is Our Land*, 1987
112. See E S Carter and J Hall, 'Farming, Conservation and Wildlife', *JRASE*, 141, 1981, pp 55–67; Peter Manning, 'Monitoring Wildlife: a Survey at Crewe Farm Stoneleigh 1980', *ibid*, 143, 1982, pp 147–63; P H Manning, 'Sacrewell Farm – a Study of Wildlife', *ibid*, 146, 1985, pp 47–81
113. See *JRASE*, 140, 1979, pp 10–11
114. Stanley Evans was Parliamentary Secretary to the Ministry of Food and his charge was made

at a Manchester press conference on 14 April 1950. The theme provided the title for a book by A G Street, *Feather-Bedding*, 1954

115. See *JRASE*, 139, 1978, pp 16–23
116. *Ibid*, pp 10–15
117. Proceedings of Council, 9 September, 10 December 1981
118. *Ibid*, 10 March 1982, 9 March 1983, 10 December 1980

THE SOCIETY'S SEQUICENTENARY

119. A short account of the anniversary dinner appeared in *NAC/RASE News* June 1988. Membership information supplied by Neil Ramsey, Assistant Secretary, personal communication to author 14 June 1988.
120. For an early history see Sir Francis Floud, *The Ministry of Agriculture and Fisheries*, 1927.
121. See, for example, comments by John Collier (Chairman of West Riding Branch of the NFU) at opening of the Great Yorkshire Show, reported in *The Times* 13 July 1988.
122. Sir F Engledow and Leonard Amey, *Britain's Future in Farming* 1980, Chapter 14, pp 136–141.
123. D A E Harkness, *War and British Agriculture*, 1941, p 48.
124. Seventh Annual Meeting of Bakewell Farmer's Club reported in *Farmer's Magazine*, ser iii, VIII, 1855, p 392.
125. E J T Collins, 'Agricultural Revolution in a Modern Industrial Economy: Britain 1950–1980', 1983, pp 28–30. The 'treadmill' view comes from Willard A Cochrane, *The Development of American Agriculture*, 1979, and cited by Collins.
126. *NAC News* June 1979.
127. Sir Francis Pemberton, personal communication to author, 29 February 1988.
128. J C Morton, 'Agricultural Progress: its helps and hindrances', *Journal of the Society of Arts*, XII, 1863, p 54.
129. Lord Selborne, personal communication to author, 21 June 1988.
130. T H R Davies, 'Agriculture and the Nuclear Bomb', *JRASE*, 142, 1981, pp 68–78; S Crocker, 'Diversification: Pitfalls or Profits?', *ibid*, 147, 1986, p 29.
131. J D M Hearth, personal communication to author, 21 May 1988.
132. See notice in *JRASE*, 146, 1985, p 208.
133. Sixteenth Annual Meeting of the Debenham Farmer's Club reported in *Farmers Magazine*, ser iii, VIII, p 541.

Appendices

The Society wishes to record its gratitude to the following organisations and companies whose commitment to agricultural progress is or has been reflected in their contributions to the development of the NAC Demonstration Units.

Arable Unit Sponsors

1977　　　The Cereal demonstration Unit is established under the management of the RASE in conjunction with the following sponsors:
ICE AGRICULTURAL DIVISION
ICI PLANT PROTECTION DIVISION
BARCLAYS BANK
The following sponsors joined between 1977 and 1984:
MASSEY-FERGUSON (UK) LTD
RHM AGRICULTURE LTD
MAFF-ADAS
THOMAS PHILLIP PRICE TRUST

1984　　　The Unit broadened to become the NAC Arable Unit with the current sponsors:
RASE (Managing)
ICE FERTILISERS (was ICI AGRICULTURE DIVISION)
ICE AGROCHEMICALS (was ICI PLANT PROTECTION DIVISION)
MASSEY-FERGUSON (UK) LTD
BRITISH SUGAR plc
CIBA-GEIGY AGROCHEMICALS
MAFF-ADAS
WILLIAM SCOTT ABBOTT TRUST
FARMERS WEEKLY

Beef and Calf Unit Sponsors

1966　　　Cattle centre established by the RASE and BOCM Silcock, with BOCM as Managing Sponsors.
1967　　　Calf unit set up by the above.
1975　　　MEAT AND LIVESTOCK COMMISSION became Managing Sponsors.
BOCM SILCOCK remain as sponsors of the unit.
FISONS LTD (Fertiliser Division) became sponsors.
1981/2　　FISONS retire and ELANCO PRODUCTS LTD become sponsors.

Present Sponsors

MEAT AND LIVESTOCK COMMISSION (managing)
RASE
BOCM SILCOCK LTD
ELANCO PRODUCTS LTD

323

Dairy Unit Sponsors

1970	Established by:
	RANK HOVIS McDOUGALL LTD (RHM)
	GASCOIGNE
	GUSH AND DENT AGRI LTD
	SIMPLEX OF CAMBRIDGE LTD
	RASE
1973/4	SIMPLEX retire.
1976	CIBA-GEIGY (UK) AGROCHEMICAL DIVISION become sponsors
1978	GASCOIGNE and GUSH AND DENT retire.
	FULWOOD AND BLAND and BARCLAYS BANK become sponsors
1982	BARCLAYS BANK retire as sponsors.
1983	RHM retire.
	DALGETY AGRICULTURE become Managing Sponsors.
1984	UKF FERTILISERS become sponsors.
1988	ROYAL ASSOCIATION OF BRITISH DAIRY FARMERS (RABDF) become sponsors.

Present Sponsors

DALGETY AGRICULTURE (Managing)
FULLWOOD AND BLAND LTD
RASE
CIBA-GEIGY (UK) AGROCHEMICAL DIVISION
UKF FERTILISERS
RABDF

Pig Unit Sponsors

1963	Established by RASE and R SILCOCK AND SONS LTD (later BOCM SILCOCK LTD) with R Silcock and Sons Ltd acting as Managing Sponsor.
1968	MEAT AND LIVESTOCK COMMISSION become sponsors.
1988	NATIONAL PIG DEVELOPMENT COMPANY (NPDC) and the FARM ELECTRIC CENTRE become sponsors.

Present Sponsors

BOCM SILCOCK LTD (Managing)
RASE
MEAT AND LIVESTOCK COMMISSION
NATIONAL PIG DEVELOPMENT COMPANY
FARM ELECTRIC CENTRE

Sheep Unit Sponsors

1968	Unit established and included the rare breeds gene bank
	RASE (Managing)
	MESSRS BARKERS AND LEE SMITH (later Paul and Whites Foods Ltd and then Pauls Agriculture)
	MESSRS BOOTS
	MESSRS COOPER, MCDOUGAL AND ROBERTSON
1970	MESSRS BOOTS retire as sponsors.
1973	ICI LTD (Agricultural Division) become sponsors.
1984	MEAT AND LIVESTOCK DIVISION become sponsors.
1986	ICI LTD (Agricultural Division) now ICI FERTILISERS retire as sponsors.
	TRIDENT FEEDS and WHAT'S NEW IN FARMING become sponsors.

1987   PAULS AGRICULTURE retire as sponsors.

1988   BP NUTRITION (UK) LTD become sponsors.

Present Sponsors
> RASE (Managing)
> BP NUTRITION (UK) LTD
> COOPERS ANIMAL HEALTH LTD
> MEAT AND LIVESTOCK COMMISSION
> TRIDENT FEEDS
> WHAT'S NEW IN FARMING

Poultry Unit Sponsors

1965   Unit established by RASE and SPILLERS LTD with SPILLERS LTD acting as the Managing Sponsor.

1968/74   SPILLERS LTD retire and J E HEMMINGS AND SONS LTD become Managing Sponsor.

1983   THE EGG AUTHORITY and MAFF-ADAS become sponsors.

1988   J E HEMMINGS AND SONS LTD retire and the RASE become Managing Sponsor.

Present Sponsors
> RASE (Managing)
> MAFF-ADAS

Audio Visual Unit

1978   Unit established by RASE (Managing Sponsor) with LLOYDS BANK as co-sponsor.

1982   NFU MUTUAL became sponsors.

Present Sponsors
> RASE (Managing)
> LLOYDS BANK
> NFU MUTUAL

Conference Centre

1987   NAC Conference Unit created to administer both the UK and overseas conferences.

Present Sponsors
> RASE (Managing)
> Agricultural Mortgage Corporation (AMC)
> ADAS

Food and Farm Facts Unit

1977   Unit established with the aim of fostering communications between Town and Country. The Unit was funded through the Arthur Rank Centre by generous contribution from a number of farming organisations and trusts and by member subscriptions.

1983   The Food and Farm Facts Unit was disbanded but much of its work continued under the auspices of the Farm Interpretation Unit which was sponsored by the RASE.

Countryside Communications Unit

1987   The RASE Farm Interpretation Unit broadened its horizons and became the Countryside Communications Unit sponsored by the RASE and the Louise Ryan Endowment Fund.

Rural Employment and Training Unit

1986   Unit established by RASE and sponsored by The Rank Foundation.

PRESIDENTS OF THE ROYAL AGRICULTURAL SOCIETY OF ENGLAND
President 1988–9: Her Majesty The Queen
(Deputy President: The Earl of Selborne KBE, DL)

1839	3rd Earl Spencer
1840	5th Duke of Richmond
1841	Philip Pusey
1842	Henry Handley MP
1843	4th Earl of Hardwicke
1844	3rd Earl Spencer
1845	5th Duke of Richmond
1846	1st Viscount Portman
1847	6th Earl of Egmont
1848	2nd Earl of Yarborough
1849	3rd Earl of Chichester
1850	4th Marquis of Downshire
1851	5th Duke of Richmond
1852	2nd Earl of Ducie
1853	2nd Lord Ashburton
1854	Philip Pusey
1855	William Miles MP
1856	1st Viscount Portman
1857	Viscount Ossington
1858	6th Lord Berners
1859	7th Duke of Marlborough
1860	5th Lord Walsingham
1861	3rd Earl of Powis
1862	{ HRH The Prince Consort / 1st Viscount Portman }
1863	Viscount Eversley
1864	2nd Lord Feversham
1865	Sir E C Kerrison Bart MP
1866	1st Lord Tredeger
1867	H S Thompson MP
1868	6th Duke of Richmond
1869	HRH The Prince of Wales KG
1870	7th Duke of Devonshire
1871	6th Lord Vernon
1872	Sir W W Wynn Bart MP
1873	3rd Earl Cathcart
1874	Edward Holland
1875	1st Viscount Bridport
1876	2nd Lord Chesham

1877	Lord Skelmersdale
1878	Col Kingscote CB MP
1879	HRH The Prince of Wales KG
1880	9th Duke of Bedford
1881	William Wells
1882	John Dent Dent
1883	6th Duke of Richmond and Gordon
1884	Sir Brandeth Gibbs
1885	Sir Massey Lopes Bart MP
1886	HRH The Prince of Wales KG
1887	2nd Lord Egerton of Tatton
1888	Sir M W Ridley Bart MP
1889	Her Majesty Queen Victoria
1890	Lord Moreton
1891	2nd Earl of Ravensworth
1892	1st Earl of Feversham
1893	1st Duke of Westminster LG
1894	8th Duke of Devonshire KG
1895	Sir J H Thorold Bart
1896	Sir Walter Gilbey Bart
1897	HRH The Duke of York KG
1898	5th Earl Spencer KG
1899	9th Earl of Coventry
1900	HRH The Prince of Wales KG
1901	3rd Earl Cawdor
1902	HRH Prince Christian KG
1903	HRH The Prince of Wales KG
1904	16th Earl of Derby KG
1905	9th Lord Middleton
1906	F S W Cornwallis
1907	4th Earl of Yarborough
1908	9th Duke of Devonshire KG
1909	7th Earl of Jersey GCB
1910	Sir Gilbert Greenall Bart
1911	HM King George V
1912	9th Lord Middleton
1913	2nd Earl of Northbrook
1914	Earl Powis
1915	Duke of Portland KG
1916	7th Duke of Richmond and Gordon
1917	Charles Adeane CB
1918	Hon Cecil T Parker
1919	Sir J B Bowen-Jones Bart
1920	HRH The Prince of Wales KG
1921	R M Graves
1922	HRH The Duke of York KG
1923	Lt Col E W Stanyforth
1924	Ernest Mathews CVO
1925	Sir Gilbert Greenall Bart CVO
1926	Lord Desborough GCVO

1927	1st Viscount Tredegar CBE
1928	3rd Lord Harlech CB
1929	Earl of Harwood KG
1930	HRH The Duke of Gloucester KG
1931	Sir Arther Hazelrigg Bart
1932	Lord Mildmay of Flete
1933	9th Duke of Devonshire KG
1934	Earl of Stradbroke KCMG
1935	HRH The Duke of Kent
1936	Sir Merrick R Burrell Bart CBE
1937	U Roland Burke
1938	Earl of Plymouth
1939	HM King George VI
1940	John Evens
1941	Lord Mildmay of Flete PC
1942	Lord Mildmay of Flete PC
1943	Lord Mildmay of Flete PC
1944	Rt Hon Col Sir George Courthope Bart MC MP
1945	Rt Hon Col Sir George Courthope Bart MC MP
1946	Viscount Bledisloe PC GCMG KBE
1947	Lt Col Sir Archibald Weigall Bart KCMG
1948	The Rt Hon The Earl of Halifax KB OM
1949	HRH The Princess Elizabeth Duchess of Edinburgh
1950	HRH The Princess Royal
1951	Lt Col H J Cator MC
1952	Earl Fortescue KG
1953	The Earl of Derby MC
1954	HM The Queen
1955	The Duke of Portland KG
1956	The Duke of Northumberland
1957	HRH The Duke of Edinburgh KG KT
1958	The Duke of Beaufort KG GCVC
1959	The Lord Digby DSO MC TD VMH
1960	HM Queen Elizabeth The Queen Mother
1961	Col Sir Robert E S Gooch Bart DSO
1962	The Duke of Northumberland KG
1963	HRH The Duke of Edinburgh KG KT OM GBE PC
1964	Lt Col Sir Walter Burrell Bart CBE TD DL
1965	Lord Netherthorpe LLD BSc
1966	HRH The Princess Margaret Countess of Snowdon
1967	The Most Hon The Marquess of Abergavenny OBE
1968	HRH Princess Alexandra
1969	Viscount Cobham KG GCMG PC JP TD
1970	The Lord Rank LLD
1971	HRH The Duchess of Gloucester
1972	HM The Queen
1973	The Rt Hon Sir Christopher Soames GCMG GVCO CBE MA
1974	HM Queen Elizabeth the Queen Mother
1974/5	Francis W W Pemberton CBE MA

1975/6	HRH The Duchess of Kent
1976/7	Sir Henry Plumb
1977/8	HRH The Prince of Wales KG KT GCB
1978/9	Christopher York DL
1979/80	HRH The Prince Philip Duke of Edinburgh KG KT OM GBE PC
1980/1	Lord Porchester KG KT OM GBE PL
1981/2	HRH The Duke of Gloucester GCVO
1982/3	Sir Nigel Strutt TD TL
1983/4	Lord Sieff of Brimpton OBE MA
1984/5	HRH The Duke of Kent GLMG GCVO
1985/6	HRH The Princess Alexandra GCVO
1986/7	HRH The Princess Royal GCVO
1987/8	The Earl of Selborne KBE DL

Year when
first elected

TRUSTEES

1957	HRH The Prince Philip, Duke of Edinburgh, KG, KT, OM, GBE, PC
1959	Her Majesty Queen Elizabeth the Queen Mother
1972	HRH Princess Alice, Duchess of Gloucester
1982	HRH The Duke of Gloucester, GCVO
1968	Abergavenny, The Marquess of, KG, OBE
1966	Green, J D F
1951	Pemberton, Sir Francis, CBE, DL
1970	Lord Plumb of Coleshill, DL, FRAgS
1974	Smith-Ryland, C M T
1960	Wheatley-Hubbard, Mrs E R, OBE
1948	York, Christopher, DL

VICE-PRESIDENTS

1971	Butler, Sir Richard, MA(Agric Cantab)
1973	Ferens, C R, MA, FRICS
1970	Forwood, Sir Dudley, Bt
1957	Harris, J H, JP, DL
1970	Matson, R T
1971	Reeves, D W
1949	Ryman, W J
1950	Smith, P L
1958	Stoddart, A D
1984	Strutt, Sir Nigel, TD, DL
1958	Woodward, G. Philip

HONORARY VICE-PRESIDENTS

1949	Benson, W A, TD, DL
1985	Cowen, R F H
1980	Eastwood, Sir John
1987	Nickerson, Sir Joseph
1985	Rosenberg, M M
1986	Lord Sieff of Brimpton, OBE, MA
1971	Thompson, Sir Edward, MBE, TD, DL

MEMBERS OF COUNCIL
Chairman of Council: C M T Smith-Ryland

1983	Appleton, E A
1959	Barclay, Captain C G E
1983	Barton, Mrs A M, OBE
1986	Beckett, A M, MBE
1974	Benyon, W R, MP
1982	Bernays, R E J
1985	Bowden, R H
1983	Bruce, Dr R, BSc(Agric), PhD, FCIB, FRAgS
1985	Buchanan, Mrs E F C, MA Oxon
1980	Burrough, C J
1980	Bush, J B, JP, MA
1970	Clinton, The Lord
1983	Colbatch Clark, C
1981	Copas, T A
1972	Creak, Miss E
1984	Cumber, W, BSc
1982	Cunningham, Professor J M M, CBE
1979	Dalton, D C
1976	Dampney, T D, TD, JP
1976	Eady, Mrs R
1978	Farrant, M J
1974	Freemantle, Commander The Hon J, RN Ret'd, KStJ, JP
1979	Furness, J W, ARICS
1970	Godber, The Hon R T
1985	Greaves, G A
1984	Harris, J McR, ARICS
1988	Heywood, T J
1981	Hill, A G
1970	Hobson, W H D
	Hosking, W J S

1975	Houghton Brown, P J
1974	Hughes, J C
1979	Hull, J
1982	Hutchinson-Smith, Group Capt D W, AFC, DL
1972	Iliffe, R P R
1972	Lee, M P
1985	Legh, The Hon D P C, FRICS
1966	McCreadie, A T
1970	Meyrick, Sir David, Bt, FRICS
1981	Miles, R J
1983	Moorhouse, P
1986	Morris, P W, MA, NDA, DipTAd, CIAgrE
1977	Naish, C D
1975	Naish, J A
1960	Neame, C D, FRAgS
1984	Needler, H M
1985	Oliver-Bellasis, H R
1986	Overton, M, MRCVS
1988	Parkes, Mrs J
1980	Pease, Capt N C
1981	Pemberton, A F, MA
1976	Pile, R E L, MA
1971	Posnett, R J
1969	Price, J E, JP
1982	Raynham, Viscount
1982	Robertson, D I
1978	Robson, G
1976	Sapsed, P D
1975	Scott, D L U
1975	Simper, N E E
1986	Skelton, R
1974	Smart, S W
1985	Southwell, G
1983	Speakman, E J C, JP
1974	Stearn, E F R, OBE, MA, MSc, FRAgS
1980	Stovold, P J F
1984	Stubbs, D H
1978	Trevelyan, J C R, JP
1986	Tutton, A R, OBE, TD, JP
1984	Warde-Aldam, Major W, JP, DL
1987	Weaver, L
1975	Wilson-Wright, J M
1971	Wyatt, J P
1979	York, Col E C

NOMINATED COUNCIL MEMBERS

1977	Baker, Dr H K, BSc, DipAg
1984	Bell, Professor R L, CB, BSc, PhD, CEng, FIM, FInstP, FIAgrE
1988	Bennett, A J, BSc, DTA, MSc
1976 } 1982	Carter, E S, CBE, BSc, FIBiol
1976	Cooper, Sir Richard P, Bt
1981	Cotton, M J, JP, FRICS
1978 } 1987	Fell, H R, FRAgS
1988	Goldsmith, W K, FCA, CBIM, FRSA
1986	Gourlay, S A
1987	Hadnett, R
1987	Harris, A G
1980	Hughes, H V, BSc(Hons)
1985	Laing, N A G
1985	Lambert, H U A
1985	MacNichol, I D R, FRICS
1984	May, Professor B A, BSc, NDAgrE, CEng, MIMechE, FIAgrE
1980	Miles, Professor C W N, CBE, MA, FRICS
1982	Muddiman, C T
1987	Newman, D C
1988	Norman, R F, CEng, MSc
1988	North, J J, BSc, MS, DipAgric, FIBiol
1980	Payne, C G
1985	Pearce, D G, FBIM
1983	Russell, The Rt Rev'd Anthony, DPhil, The Bishop of Dorchester
1973	Shaxson, M
1966	Steele-Bodger, Professor A, CBE, BSc, MA, FRCVS
1985	Thompson, D R B
1988	Vowles, J, CIAgrE
1988	Webster, P

OFFICERS OF THE SOCIETY

Honorary Treasurer	Richard T Matson
Honorary Director of Royal Show	The Hon R T Godber
Editor of Journal	Eric S Carter, CBE, BSc, FIBiol
Consulting Architect	S Dunham, Charter Building Design Group
Honorary Consulting Engineer	W E Klinner, CEng, FIAgrE, Mem ASAE
Honorary Consulting Veterinary Surgeon	Prof A O Betts, BSc, MA, PhD, MRCVS, Principal, Royal Veterinary College
Solicitors	Halsey, Lightly & Hemsley
	Wright, Hassall & Co
Bankers	National Westminster Bank Ltd
Auditors	Price Waterhouse

Appendices

Showground Services Manager	D A Cooper
Site Engineer	M Thompson
Clerk of Works	B W Sammons

SECRETARIES/PRINCIPAL OFFICIALS OF THE RASE

SECRETARIES
English Agricultural Society:

1838–1839	William Shaw

Royal Agricultural Society of England:

1839–1859	James Hudson
1859–1868	H Hall Dare
1868–1887	H M Jenkins
1887–1905	Sir Ernest Clarke
1906–1920	Thomas McRow
1921–1946	T B Turner, MVO
1946–1961	Alec Hobson, CBE, MVO
1962	R R Meyric Hughes: Paul M Osborne (Acting)
1963–1969	C V Dadd, OBE, MA, DipAgric(Cantab), FRAGS

JOINT DIRECTORS

1969–1972	C V Dadd (and Agricultural Director 1972–1977)
	W D Draffan, MBE

CHIEF EXECUTIVE

1972–1989	J D M Hearth, CBE, MA, CBIM
1989–	Robin Hicks

HONORARY DISTINCTIONS

HONORARY FELLOWSHIP OF THE SOCIETY

SIR DEREK BARBER, MRAC, HonDSc(Bradford)
PROFESSOR P M BIGGS, CBE, DSc, DVM(HC), FRCVS, FRCPath, FIBiol, FRS
J BINGHAM, FRS
SIR KENNETH BLAXTER, FRS
PROFESSOR D K BRITTON, CBE
E S CARTER, CBE, BSc, FIBiol
OSCAR COLBURN, CBE, JP, FRAGS
DR G W COOKE, CBE, PhD, FRS
PROFESSOR M McG COOPER, CBE, BAgrSc, BLitt, FRSE
DR B A CROSS, CBE, MA, PhD, ScD, MRCVS, FIBiol, FRS
J D FRYER, CBE, MA, FIBiol
H J HAMBLIN, OBE, BA, MIAgrE
SIR WILLIAM MACGREGOR HENDERSON, FRS
PROFESSOR J P HUDSON, CBE, GM, PhD, VMH, FIBiol
J E MOFFITT, CBE, FRAGS
DR R A NEVE, OBE
SIR CHARLES PEREIRA, BSc, PhD, DSc, FRS
DR E J C POLGE, BSc(Agric), PhD, FRS
W H G REES, CB, BSc, MRCVS, OVSM
SIR RALPH RILEY, DSc, FRS
PROFESSOR C R W SPEDDING, CBE, MSc, PhD, DSc, FIBiol

Sir Nigel Strutt, td, dl, frags
Professor B G F Weitz, obe, DSc, MRCVS, FIBiol
Dr P S Wellington, cbe, DSc, PhD, ARCS, FLS, FIBiol, frags

Honorary Membership of the Society

Overseas
Dr N E Bourlaug, PhD
Dr R F Chandler
Dr L T Evans, ao, MAgrSc, DPhil, DSc
Sir Vincent Fairfax, cmg
H Heemskerk
C D Hill
Dr David Hopper
W Ives, cbe

United Kingdom
Canon P Buckler, obe, BSc, NDA, frags
C Culpin, obe, MA, DipAgric(Cantab), FIAgrE
C V Dadd, obe, MA, DipAgric(Cantab), frags
Nigel Harvey, MA, ARICS
Lord Plumb, dl, frags
Dr D H Robinson, PhD, BSc, NDA
The Rt Revd Anthony Russell, DPhil
A J Skew, erd, frags

Honorary Directors of the Royal Show

The first Honorary Director was appointed in 1843. Before that, Mr Humphrey Gibbs was Director of the Show.

1843–1874	Sir Brandreth Gibbs
1875–1892	Sir Jacob Wilson
1893–1898	The Hon Cecil Parker
1899–1904	Percy Crutchley
1905	Sir Jacob Wilson
1906–1930	Lord Daresbury
1931–1950	Sir Roland Burke, kcvo
1951–1952	Michael Mason
1953–1955	Lt-Col Guy Blewitt, dso, mc
1956–1962	W A Benson
1963–1967	Francis W W Pemberton, cbe, MA, frags
1968–1972	A A C MacArthur, frags
1973–1977	Sir Dudley Forwood, bt
1978–1982	J H Harris, jp
1982–1987	C R Ferens, MA, frics
1987–	The Hon R T Godber

Honours and Awards
Gold Medal for Distinguished Services to Agriculture

AWARDS
1933 Sir Thomas Hudson Middleton, KCIE, KBE, CB, FRS
1934 Sir Arnold Theiler, KCMG
1935 Lord Ernle, MVO, PC
1936 Sir William Cecil Dampier, ScD, FRS
1938 Sir Merrik R Burrell, BT, CBE
1939 Sir George Stapledon, CBE, DSc, FRS
1942 Sir George Courthope, MC
1947 Viscount Bledisloe, GCMG, KBE, PC
1950 Sir Roland Burke, KCVO
1954 Sir John Russell, OBE, DSc, FRS
1955 Sir James A Scott Watson, CBE, MC, LLD
1956 Sir Ian Clunies Ross, CMG, DVSC, HonLLD(Melbourne)
1969 Baron Netherthorpe of Anston
1971 Col Sir Robert E S Gooch, BT, DSO
1974 Frank Sykes, CVO, CBE, DL, FRAGS
1979 Sir Edmund Bacon, BT, KG, KBE, TD
1983 Lord Plumb, DL, FRAGS

Technology Award

1985 Volac Limited (Quantock Veal Limited)
Milk Marketing Board, Breeding and Production Division
1986 F B C Ltd
1987 Traileyre Systems Ltd
1988 Pig Improvement Company
Robert Young & Co. Ltd

Medal for Surveyors in the Land Agency and Agricultural Division of the RICS

AWARDS
1957 Ronald Allen
1958 John T Duberley
1959 Anthony Hector, NDA
1960 Ian R Tuckey
1961 John R M Ridgwell
1962 Jeremy A W Leech
1963 Ronald Cecil Brobson
1964 Andrew George Buchanan, BA
1965 A C H Bond
1966 P E H Greenhow
1967 R W Jonas
1968 M P MacLay
1969 L H J Tollemache
1970 Peter Thomas Day
1971 N D Moore
1972 Graham Candy, BSc
1973 T B Vesey

1974   H M A Nicholson
1975   A Winnington
1976   C G H Turney
1977   C R Walley
1978   W J Abbott
1979   Miss L T Burtenshaw
1980   G E T Heelis
1981   R D Thomas
1982   T Dansie
1983   J F Bengough
1984   J A Fife
1985   R C R Feilden
1986   P V Lindon, BA
1987   T Warde-Aldam, BA
1988   J P Kennedy, BSc

Bledisloe Veterinary Award

AWARDS
1961   Sir John Ritchie, CB, BSc, FRCVS, DVSM, FRSE
1964   G N Gould, JP, FRCVS
1973   G B S Heath, BSc, MRCVS
1975   Dr J B Brooksby, CBE, DSc, MRCVS, FRSE
1976   J T Stamp, CBE, DSc, FRCVS, FRSE
1977   P M Biggs, DSc, MRCVS, MRCPath, FRS
1978   L E A Rowson, OBE, MA, FRCVS, FRS
1979   Dr W Plowright, CMG, DVSC, FRCVS
1980   A C L Brown, MRCVS
1981   Dr J M Payne, BSc, PhD, FIBiol, MRCVS
1982   Dr B A Cross, BSc, MA, PhD, ScD, MRCVS, FIBiol, FRS
1983   Professor J D L King, PhD, MVSC, BSc, FRCVS, FIBiol
1984   Dr W B Martin, DVSM, MRCVS, PhD, FRSE
1985   M R Muirhead, BVMS, FRCVS, DPM
1986   D W B Sainsbury, MA, PhD, BSc, MRCVS, FRSH
1987   P R Ellis, BSc(VetSci), MPH, MRCVS
1988   W H G Rees, CB, BSc, MRCVS, DVSM

Gold Medal for Landowners

AWARDS
1958   The Earl of Iveagh, KG, CB, CMG
1959   Captain G L Bennett Evans, OBE
1962   J R Blackett-Ord
1964   Lt-Col Sir Richard Verdin, OBE, TD, DL, JP
1967   Major Sir Richard Proby, BT, MC, DL
1969   Earl de la Warr, PC, GBE
1972   Sir Michael Culme-Seymour, BT, DL
1974   Lord de Ramsey, KVO, TD
1975   Lord Bradford, TD, JP
1976   The Duke of Northumberland, KG, FRS
1978   Miss E A Johnstone, JP, FRAGS
1979   The Earl of Lonsdale

1980 THE DUKE OF DEVONSHIRE
1981 THE EARL OF SELBORNE
1983 G M T FOLJAMBE
1984 MAJOR J R MORE-MOLYNEUX, OBE, DL
1985 J G QUICKE, CBE
1986 W R BENYON, MP
1987 PETER KIRTON DENNIS

RESEARCH MEDAL FOR RESEARCH WORK OF BENEFIT TO AGRICULTURE

AWARDS
1955 SIR FREDERICK BAWDEN, MA, FRS
1956 G D H BELL, CBE, PhD, BSc, FRS
1957 ARTHUR WALTON, PhD, BSc(Agric)
1958 W A SEXTON, BSc, PhD, FRIC
      W G TEMPLEMAN, MSc, PhD, DIC
1959 ALAN ROBERTSON, BA, DSc
1960 PROFESSOR R L WAIN, PhD, DSc, FRIC, FRS
1961 RAYMOND HULL, PhD, DIC
1962 A T PHILLIPSON, MA, MRCVS, PhD, DVSC(Hons), FRSE
1963 R L MITCHELL, Phd, BSc, FRIC, FRSE
1964 K L BLAXTER, BSc(Agric), PhD, DSc, NDA(Hons), FRS
1965 BASIL KASSANIS, PhD, DSc
1966 CHARLES CLIVE BALCH, PhD, DSc
1967 GEORGE WILLIAM COOKE, PhD, FRIC, FRS
1968 W F RAYMOND, CBE, MA, FRSC
1969 J C HAWKINS, BSc, NDA, FIAgrE
1970 J M HIRST, DSc, PhD, FRS
1971 JAMES M B ROY, MA, DipAgric(Cantab), PhD
1972 J M PAYNE, PhD, BSc(VetSci), MRCVS
1973 J K A BLEASDALE, BSc, PhD
1974 F H DODD, BSc, PhD
      F K NEAVE, BSA
1975 J H BINGHAM, BSc(Hons)
1976 R B HEAP, BSc, PhD, MA, FIBiol
1977 L R TAYLOR, DSc, FIBiol
1978 J EADIE, BSc(HonsAgric)
1979 D J GREENWOOD, BSc, PhD, DSc, FRIC
      P PORTER, BSc, PhD, DSc
1980 R J WILKINS, BSc, PhD, FIBiol
      D A DOLING, BSc, BAgr, PhD, MIBiol
1981 B H HOWARD, BSc, PhD
1982 J J ROBINSON, BSc, PhD
1983 J MATTHEWS, BSc, CEng, FInstP, FIAgrE
1984 C T WHITTEMORE, NDA, BSc, PhD
1985 S M WILLADSEN, DVetMed, LicMedVet
1986 R T PLUMB, BSc, PhD, CBiol, MIBiol
      G S G SPENCER, BSc, PhD
1987 P I PAYNE, BSc(Hons), PhD
1988 A I DONALDSON, MA, MVB, PhD, ScD, MRCVS
      PROFESSOR J D LEAVER, BSc, PhD, MIBiol, FRAGS

BURKE PERPETUAL CHALLENGE TROPHY

AWARDS

1971 MASSEY FERGUSON (UK) LTD (Ferguson System)
1972 RANSOME, SIMS & JEFFRIES (Reversible plough)
1973 STANHAY LTD (Precision seed drill)
1974 HOWARD ROTAVATOR CO LTD (Rotary cultivation)
1975 F W McCONNEL LTD (Power arm machinery)
1976 BOMFORD AND EVERSHED LTD (Cultivating and hedge cutting equipment)
1977 R J FULWOOD & BLAND LTD (Dairy and feeding equipment)
1978 JOHN WILDER (ENGINEERING) LTD (Forage harvesting and grain drying equipment)
1979 F A STANDEN & SONS (ENGINEERING) LTD (Sugar beet harvesters)
1980 ICI PLANT PROTECTION DIVISION (Direct drilling equipment)
1981 SANDERSON (FORKLIFTS) LTD (Agricultural materials handling vehicles)
1982 DOWDESWELL ENGINEERING CO LTD (Plough manufacture)
1983 P J PARMITER & SONS LTD (Cultivation and materials handling equipment)
1984 RDS FARM ELECTRONICS LTD (Electronics on farm machinery)
1985 KIDD FARM MACHINERY (Forage and feed machinery)
1986 A C BAMLETT LTD (Seed drilling and fertilizer application equipment)
1987 LAND ROVER LTD (Design, development and supply of 4-wheel drive vehicles)
1988 FORD NEW HOLLAND LTD (Development, manufacture and marketing of tractors world wide)

SELECT BIBLIOGRAPHY

(Place of publication is London unless otherwise stated)

ACLAND, H D. *Letters and Memoirs*, 1902

ACLAND, T D. *The Education of the Farmer Viewed in Connection with that of the Middle-Classes in General: Its Objectives, Principles and Costs*, 1857

ACLAND, T D. *Agricultural Education: What it is and How to Improve it, Considered in Two Letters to Sir Edward Kerrison, Bart, MP*, 1865

ADDISON, Lord. *A Policy for British Agriculture*, 1939

ALLAN, D G C. *William Shipley Founder of the Society of Arts*, 1968

ANON, *Animal Health: A Centenary 1865–1965*, HMSO, 1966

ASTOR, Viscount and MURRAY, Keith A H. *Land and Life: the Economic National Policy for Agriculture*, 1932

ASTOR, Viscount and MURRAY, Keith A H. *The Planning of Agriculture*, 1933

ASTOR, Viscount and ROWNTREE, B Seebohm. *Mixed Farming and Muddled Thinking: An Analysis of Current Agricultural Policy*, 1945

AULIE, Richard P. 'The Mineral Theory', *Agricultural History*, XLVIII, 1974, pp 369–382

BARLING, D M. 'Winter Barley Development Work on the Cotswolds', *JRASE*, 141, 1980, pp 156–164

BARNETT, L Margaret. *British Food Policy during the First World War*, 1985

BATES, Cadwallader John. *Thomas Bates and the Kirklevington Shorthorns*, 1897

BEAR, W E. 'The Public Interest in Agricultural Reform', *The Nineteenth Century*, V, 1879, pp 1079–1090

BEVAN, G Phillips. *British Manufacturing Industries*, 1876

BETHAM-EDWARDS, M. *The Autobiography of Arthur Young*, 1898

BODY, Richard. *Agriculture: the Triumph and the Shame*, 1982

BODY, Richard. *Farming in the Clouds*, 1984

BONNETT, Harold. *Saga of the Steam Plough*, 1965

BOWERS, J K. 'British Agricultural Policy since the Second World War', *AHR*, 33, pt i, 1985, pp 66–76

BOWERS, J K & CHESHIRE, P. *Agriculture, the Countryside and Land Use*, 1983

BOWLER, I. *Government and Agriculture: a Spatial Perspective*, 1979

BROWN, Jonathan. *Agriculture in England 1870–1947*, Manchester, 1987

BROWN, G T. *Life on the Farm*, 1886

BURKE, J French. *British Husbandry*, 1834

CAIRD, James B. *High Farming under Liberal Covenants: the Best Substitute for Protection*, 1847

CAIRD, James B. 'On the Agricultural Statistics of the United Kingdom', *Statistical Journal*, XXXI, 1868, pp 127–145

CAIRD, Sir James. 'Agriculture', in Ward, T H, ed, *The Reign of Queen Victoria*, II, 1887, pp 129–152

CARTER, E S and HALL, J. 'Farming, Conservation and Wildlife', *JRASE*, 141, 1981, pp 55–62

CATHCART, Earl. 'Sir Henry Stephen Meysey Thompson, Bart: A Biographical Sketch', *JRASE*, ser ii, X, 1874, pp 519–41

CHAMBERS, J D and MINGAY, G E. *The Agricultural Revolution 1750–1880*, 1966

CLARKE, Ernest. 'John Chalmers Morton'. *JRASE*, ser ii, XXIV, 1888, pp 691–6

CLARKE, Ernest. 'The Foundation of the Royal Agricultural Society', *JRASE*, ser iii, I, 1890, pp 1–19

CLARKE, Ernest. 'Agriculture and the House of Russell', *JRASE*, ser iii, I, 1890, pp 129–36

CLARKE, Ernest. 'The Board of Agriculture 1793–1822', *JRASE*. ser iii, IX, 1898, pp 1–41

CLARKE, Ernest. 'Philip Pusey', *JRASE*, ser iii, XI, 1900, pp 1–17

CLARK, G Kitson. 'The Repeal of the Corn Laws and the Politics of the Forties', *EHR*, ser ii, IV, 1951, pp 1–13

COLETTA, Paolo. 'Philip Pusey, English Country Squire', *Agricultural History* 18, 1944, pp 83–91

COLLINS, E J T. 'Harvest Technology and Labour Supply in Britain 1790–1870', *EHR*, XXII, 1970, pp 453–73

COLLINS E J T. 'Agricultural Revolution in a Modern Industrial Economy: Britain 1950–1980', in *Agricultural Revolution* [papers presented to the Economic History Society conference at Canterbury 1983], Leeds, 1983, pp 19–35

COLLINS, E J T. 'The Rationality of "Surplus" Agricultural Labour: Mechanisation in English Agriculture in the Nineteenth Century', *AHR*, 35, pt i, 1987, pp 36–46

COLLINS, E J T. 'The Agricultural Tractor in Britain 1900–1940', in Harald Winkel and Klaus Herrmann, eds, *The Development of Agricultural Technology in the 19th and 20th Centuries*, Ostfildern, 1984, pp 23–47

COLLINS, E J T and Jones, E L. 'Sectoral Advance in English Agriculture, 1850–1880', *AHR*, xv, 1967, pp 65–81

COLYER, R. 'Some Welsh Breeds of Cattle in the Nineteenth Century', *AHR*, 22, pt i, 1974

CROSBY, T L. *English Farmers and the Politics of Protection*, Hassocks, 1977

CROSBY, T L and SPRING, D. 'George Webb Hall and the Agricultural Association'. *Journal of British Studies*, 1, 1962, pp 115–31

CULPIN, Claude. 'The Royal Agricultural Society of England Machinery Awards', *JRASE*, 144, 1983, pp 176–82

CURTIS, J. 'Observations on the Natural History and Economy of the Turnip Saw-Fly, and its Black Caterpillar, called the Black Palmer, Black Conker, Black Jack, Black Slug and Nigger, or Negro', *JRASE*, II, 1841, pp 364–89

DADD, Christopher. 'NAC – a Centre for Information', *JRASE*, 134, 1973, pp 149–151

DAKARS, Caroline. *The Countryside at War*, 1987

DAMPIER, Sir William. *Politics and the Land*, 1928

DARBY, H C. 'The Draining of the English Claylands', *Geographische Zeitschrift*, LII, 1964, pp 190–201

DAUBENEY, Charles. 'Lecture on the Application of Science to Agriculture', *JRASE*, III, 1842, pp 136–159

DAUBENEY, Charles. 'On the Public Institutions for the Advancement of Science', *JRASE*, III, 1842, pp 364–386

DAVID, P A. 'The Landscape and the Machine: Technical Interrelatedness, Land Tenure and the Mechanisation of the Corn Harvest in Victorian Britain', in McCloskey, D N, ed, *Essays on a Mature Economy: Britain after 1840*, 1971, pp 145–205

DAY, William. *Mechanical Science and the Prize System in Relation to Agriculture*, 1857

DE LAUNE, C De Laune Faunce. 'On Laying Down Land in Permanent Grass', *JRASE*, ser ii, XVIII, 1882, pp 229–64

DE LAUNE, C De Laune Faunce. 'Tobacco as a Farm Crop for England', *JRASE*, ser ii, XXIII, 1887, pp 213–52

DENT, J Dent. 'Notes on Agricultural Education at Home and Abroad', *JRASE*, ser iii, I, 1890, pp 37–47

DENTON, J Bailey. *Agricultural Drainage: A Retrospect of Forty Years' Experience*, 1883

DEWEY, Peter E. 'Agricultural Labour Supply in England and Wales during the First World War', *EHR*, ser ii, 28, 1975, pp 100–112

DEWEY, Peter E. 'Food Production and Policy during the First World War', *Trans Royal Historical Society*, 30, 1980, pp 71–89

DEWEY, Peter E. 'British Farming Profits and Government Policy during the First World War', *EHR*, ser ii, XXXVII, 1984, pp 373–90

DIXON, H H ('The Druid'). 'The Royal Agricultural Society', *Gentleman's Magazine*, new series, III, 1869, pp 264–304

DIXON, H H ('The Druid'). *Saddle and Sirloin*, 1869

DUDGEON, John. 'Account of the Improvements which have taken place in the Agriculture of Scotland since the Formation of the Highland Society', *JRASE*, I, 1840, pp 59–112

EDGAR, C David. 'Honest Jack Althorp – Founder of the Royal', *JRASE*, 141, 1980, pp 10–22

EDGAR, C David. 'Sir John Eastwood: Challenger at the Frontiers of Agriculture', *JRASE*, 142, 1981, pp 96–108

EDMUNDS, Henry. 'Eighty Years of Fream's Elements of Agriculture', *JRASE*, 134, 1973, pp 66–77

ENGLEDOW, F and AMERY, L. *Britain's Future in Farming*, Berkhamsted, 1980

ERNLE, Lord. *English Farming Past and Present*, 6th edn, 1961

FAIRLIE. 'The Corn Laws and British Wheat Production', *EHR*, ser ii, XXII, 1969, pp 88–119

FAWCETT, E A. 'Shorthorns: their General Utility for all Purposes', in J Wight, ed, *The Treasury and the Homestead*, I, Dublin 1877

FISHER, J R. *Clare Sewell Read 1826–1903: a Farmer's Spokesman of the Late Nineteenth Century*, University of Hull, 1975

FISHER, J R. 'The Economic Effects of Cattle Disease in Britain and its Containment', *Agricultural History*, 54, 1980, pp 278–93

FISHER, J R. 'Animal Health and the Royal Agricultural Society in its Early Years', *JRASE*, 143, 1982, pp 105–110

FITZGERALD, Kevin. *Ahead of their Time: a Short History of the London Farmer's Club*, 1967

FITZWILLIAM, Earl. *First, Second and Third Addresses to the Landowners of England on the Corn Laws*, 1839

FLETCHER, H R. *A History of the Royal Horticultural Society 1804–1968*, 1968

FORRESTER, S D and GILES, C H. 'From Manure Heaps to Monolayers: the Earliest Development of Solute-Solid Absorption Studies', *Chemistry and Industry*, 13 November 1971, pp 1314–1321

FOX, H S A. 'Local Farmers' Associations and the Circulation of Agricultural Information in Nineteenth Century England', in Fox, H S A and Butlin, R A, *Change in the Countryside, Essays on Rural England 1500–1900*, Institute of British Geographers, Special Publication No 10, 1979, pp 42–63

FUSSELL, G E. 'A Scottish Forerunner of Humphrey Davy, Archibald Cochrane, Earl of Dundonald, 1749–1831', *Scottish Farmer*, 57, 1949, p 625

FUSSELL, G E. *The Old English Farming Books from Fitzherbert to Tull, 1523 to 1730*, 1950

FUSSELL, G E. *More Old English Farming Books: from Tull to the Board of Agriculture 1731–1793*

FUSSELL, G E. *The Farmer's Tools*, 1953

FUSSELL, G E. *Crop Nutrition: Science and Practice before Liebig*, 1971

FUSSELL, G E. 'Agricultural Science and Experiment in the Eighteenth Century: An Attempt at a Definition', *AHR*, 24, 1976, pp 44–7

GARRAD, G H. 'The work of the Motor Tractor', *JRASE*, 79, 1918, pp 1–23

GAZLEY, John G. 'Arthur Young and the Society of Arts', *Journal of Economic History*, I, 1941, pp 129–52

GAZLEY, John G. *The Life of Arthur Young*, Philadelphia 1973

GIBBS, B T B. *The Smithfield Club: A Short History of its Origin and Progress*, 1857

GILG, R W. *An Introduction to Rural Geography*, 1985

GODDARD, Nicholas. 'Nineteenth-Century Recycling: the Victorians and the Agricultural Utilisation of Sewage', *History Today*, 31, June 1981, pp 32–6

GODDARD, Nicholas. 'Agricultural Societies', in Mingay, G E, ed, *The Victorian Countryside*, I, 1981, pp 245–59

GODDARD, Nicholas. 'William Shaw "of the Strand" and the formation of the Royal Agricultural Society of England', *JRASE*, 143, 1982, pp 98–104

GODDARD, Nicholas. 'The Development and Influence of Agricultural Newspapers and Periodicals 1780–1880', *AHR*, 31, pt ii, 1983, pp 116–131

GODDARD, Nicholas. 'Books, Newspapers and Periodicals', 'Societies and Shows' and 'The Board of Agriculture and its Reports' in Mingay, G E, ed, *An Agrarian History of England and Wales 1750–1850*, in press, Cambridge 1988

GOOD, W W. *Where are we Now? A Politico-Agricultural Letter to the Chairman of the Central Chamber of Agriculture, Clare Sewell Read Esq, MP*, 1869

GRACE, D R and PHILLIPS, D C. *Ransomes of Ipswich*, Reading 1975

GREEN, J D F. 'Agricultural Broadcasting: A Memoir and a Point of View', *JRASE*, 142, 1981, pp 17–23

GREEN, J D F. 'A Tale of Three Brothers', *JRASE*, 149, 1987, pp 206–10

GREY, John. 'A View of the Past and Present State of Agriculture in Northumberland', *JRASE*, II, 1841, pp 151–92

HAGGARD, H Rider. *A Farmer's Year: Being his Commonplace Book for 1898*, 1899

HAINING, John and TYLER, Colin. *Ploughing by Steam*, 1970

HALL, P G. *The Industries of London Since 1861*, 1962

HALL, Vance. *A History of the Yorkshire Agricultural Society 1837–1987*, 1987

HANDLEY, Henry. *A Letter to Earl Spencer on the Formation of a National Agricultural Institution*, 1838

HANNAM, John. 'On the Use of Bones as a Manure with Sulphuric Acid', *JRASE*, V, 1845, pp 443–68 and 594–6

HANNAM, John. 'An Experimental Inquiry into the Theory of the Action and Practical Application of Bones as a Manure for the Turnip Crop, *JRASE*, VI, 1845, pp 71–2

HARKNESS, D A E. *War and British Agriculture*, 1941

HARVEY, Nigel. *The Farming Kingdom*, 1954

HENSLOW, J S. 'Report on the Diseases of Wheat', *JRASE*, II, 1841, pp 1–25

HENSON, Joe. 'The Rare Breeds Survival Trust', *JRASE*, 145, 1984, pp 93–100

HINCKS, T C. *Hints for Increasing the Practical Usefulness of Agricultural Shows*, 1845

HOLDERNESS, B A. *British Agriculture since 1945*, Manchester 1985

HOLMES, Colin J. 'Science and the Farmer: the Development of the Agricultural Advisory Service in England and Wales 1900–1939', *AHR*, 36, pt i, 1988, pp 77–86

HOPE, William. 'The Use and Abuse of Town Sewage', *Journal of the Society of Arts*, XVIII, 1870, pp 298–304

HOSKYNS, Chandos W. *Talpa; or the Chronicles of a Clay Farm: An Agricultural Fragment*, 1852

HOSKYNS, Chandos W. 'The Progress of English Agriculture during the Last Fifteen Years', *Journal of the Society of Arts*, IV, 1855, pp 271–86

HOSKYNS, Chandos W. 'On Agricultural Statistics', *JRASE*, XVI, 1856, pp 554–606

HUDSON, Kenneth. *Patriotism with Profit: British Agricultural Societies in the Eighteenth and Nineteenth Centuries*, 1972

HUDSON, Kenneth. *The Four Great Men of the Bath and West*, 1973

HUDSON, Kenneth. *The Bath and West: a Bicentenary History*, Bradford-on-Avon, 1976

HURD, Anthony. *A Farmer at Westminster*, 1951

JENKINS, H M. 'The Royal Agricultural Society of England', *JRASE*, ser ii, XIV, 1878, pp 855–93

JENKINS, H M. 'Report on the Practice of Ensilage, at Home and Abroad', *JRASE*, ser ii, XX, 1884, pp 126–64

JENKINS, H M. 'Dairying in Denmark', *JRASE*, ser ii, XIX, 1883, pp 155–84

JOHNSON, A E. 'Woburn Experimental Farm: a Hundred Years of Agricultural Research', *JRASE*, 138, 1978, pp 18–26

JOHNSTON, J F W. 'On Guano', *JRASE*, II, 1841, pp 301–21

JOHNSTON, J F W. 'The Present State of Agriculture in its Relations to Chemistry and Geology', *JRASE*, IX, 1848, pp 200–36

JONES, E L. 'The Changing Basis of English Agricultural Prosperity 1853–73', *AHR*, X, 1962, pp 102–119

JONES, E L. *Seasons and Prices*, 1964

JONES, E L. 'The Agricultural Labour Market in England 1793–1872', *EHR*, ser ii, XVII, 1964–5, pp 322–38

JONES, Gwyn E. 'The Diffusion of Agricultural Innovations', *Journal of

Agricultural Economics, XV, 1963, pp 387–409

JONES, Gwyn E. 'William Fream: Agriculturist and Educator', *JRASE*, 144, 1983, pp 30–44

KINCH, Edward. 'Basic Cinder as a Manure', *JRASE*, ser iii, I, 1890, pp 124–38

LAWES, J B and GILBERT, J H. 'On Agricultural Chemistry – especially in Relation to the Mineral Theory of Baron Liebig', *JRASE*, XII, 1851, pp 1–40

LAWES, J B and GILBERT, J H. 'On some Points connected with Agricultural Chemistry', *JRASE*, XVI, 1856, pp 411–502

LAWRENCE, C. 'The Royal Agricultural College of Cirencester', *JRASE*, ser ii, I, 1865

LEACH, Gerald. *Energy and Agriculture*, Guildford, 1976

LE CORNU, C P. 'The Potato in Jersey', *JRASE*, ser ii, VI, 1870, pp 127–44

LENNARD, R V. 'English Agriculture under Charles II: the Evidence of the Royal Society's "Enquiries", *EHR*, IV, 1932, pp 27–45

LIEBIG, Justus von, *Organic Chemistry in its Application to Agriculture and Physiology* (ed Lyon Playfair), 1st edn, 1840; 2nd edn 1842; 3rd edn 1843

LIEBIG, Justus von. *An Address to the Agriculturists of Great Britain Explaining the Principles and Use of his Artificial Manures*, 1845

LIEBIG, Justus von. 'On some Points in Agricultural Chemistry', *JRASE*, XVII, 1856, pp 289–326

LITTLE, H J. 'Report on Agricultural Education: a Summary', *JRASE*, ser ii, XXI, 1885, pp 126–64 and 518–46

LOWE, Philip et al. *Countryside Conflicts: the Politics of Farming, Forestry and Conservation* 1985

LOWE, Philip and others. *Deprivation and Welfare in Rural Areas*, Norwich, 1986

LUCKHURST, D and HUDSON, K W. *The Royal Society of Arts 1754–1954*, 1954

MACDONALD, Stuart. 'The Role of the Individual in Agricultural Change: the Example of George Culley of Fenton, Northumberland', in H S A Fox and R A Butlin eds, *Change in the Countryside: Essays on Rural England 1500–1900*, Institute of British Geographers Special Publication No. 10, pp 1–22

MACKAY, Thomas. ed. *The Reminiscences of Albert Pell*, 1908

MANNING, Peter. 'Monitoring Wildlife, a Survey at Crewe Farm Stoneleigh 1980', *JRASE*, 143, 1982, pp 147–63

MANUFACTURER, A, *The Manufacture of Agricultural Machinery considered as a Branch of National Industry*, 1857

MATTHEW, W M. 'Peru and the British Guano Market 1840–1870', *EHR*, ser ii, XXIII, 1970 pp 112–28

MATTHEWS, A H H. *Fifty Years of Agricultural Politics*, 1915

MATTHEWS, R Borlase. *Electro-Farming*, 1928

McCLOSKEY, D N. ed. *Essays on a Mature Economy: Britain after 1840*, 1971

McCONNELL, Primrose. 'Experiences of a Scotsman on the Essex Clays', *JRASE*, ser iii, II, 1891, pp 311–25

McCOSH, N. *Boussingault*, Dordrech, 1984

MIDDLETON, Sir Thomas. *Food Production in War*, Oxford, 1923

MINGAY, G E. *Arthur Young and his Times*, 1976

MINGAY, G E. *British Friesians: An Epic of Progress*, Rickmansworth, 1982

MITCHISON, Rosalind. *Agricultural Sir John. The Life of Sir John Sinclair 1754–1835*, 1962

MITCHISON, Rosalind. 'The "old" Board of Agriculture 1793–1822', *English Historical Review*, LXXIV, 1959, pp 41–69

MOORE, D C. *The Politics of Deference*, Hassocks, 1976

MOORE, D C. 'The Corn Laws and High Farming', *EHR*, Ser ii, XVIII, 1965, pp 544–61

MORTON, John Chalmers, *The Handbook of Farm Labour*, 1868

MORTON, John Chalmers, 'The Late Mr H M Jenkins, FGS, A Memoir, *JRASE* Ser ii, XXIII, 1887, pp 168–91

MORTON, John Chalmers. 'Agricultural Education', JRASE, ser ii, I, 1865, pp 436–64

MORTON, John Chalmers. 'Agricultural Progress: its Helps and Hindrances, *Journal of the Society of Arts*, XII, 1863–4, pp 55–69

MORTON, John Chalmers. 'Some Recent Lessons of Agricultural Experience', *Journal of the Bath, and West Society*, IX, 1861, pp 213–66

MOSSE, George L. 'The Anti-League and the Corn Law Crisis of 1846', *Historical Journal*, III, 1960, pp 162–83

O'BRIEN, PK. 'Agriculture and the Industrial Revolution', *EHR*, ser iii, XXX, 1977, pp 166–81

PERKINS, W F. *British and Irish Writers on Agriculture,* 2nd edn, Southampton, 1939

PERREN, Richard. *The Meat Trade in England 1840–1914*, 1978

PERRY, P J. *British Agriculture 1875–1914*, 1973

PERRY, P J. *British Farming in the Great Depression 1870–1914*, Newton Abbot, 1974

PERRY, P J. High Farming in Victorian Britain: The Financial Foundations. *Agricultural History*, 52, 1978 pp 364–79

PERRY, P J. 'High Farming in Victorian Britain: Prospect and Retrospect'. *Agricultural History*, 52, 1981 pp 156–61

PHILLIPS, A D M. 'Underdraining and the English Claylands 1850–80: A Review', *AHR*, XVII, 1969, pp 44–55

PHILLIPS, David and WILLIAMS, Allan. *Rural Britain: a Social Geography*, 1984

PLOWMAN, Thomas F. 'Agricultural Societies and their Uses', *Journal of the Bath and West and Southern Counties Association*, ser iii, 17, 1885–6, pp 168–88

PLUMBE, Charles S. *Judging Farm Animals*, New York, 1919

POWER, A P and HARRIS, S A. 'A Cost-Benefit Evaluation of Alternative Control Policies for Foot-and-Mouth Disease in Great Britain', *Journal of Agricultural Economics*, 24, 1973, pp 573–601

PUSEY, Philip. 'On the Progress of Agricultural Knowledge during the last Eight Years', *JRASE*, XI, 1850, pp 381–442

PUSEY, Philip. 'On the Source and Supply of Cubic Saltpetres, Salitre, or Nitrate of Soda, and its Uses in Small Quantities as a Restorative to Corn Crops', *JRASE*, XIII, 1852, pp 374–91

RAMSEY, Alexander. *History of the Highland and Agricultural Society of Scotland*, Edinburgh, 1879

RICHMOND, Duke of. 'On the Solution of Bones in Sulphuric Acid for the Purposes of Manure', *JRASE*, IV, 1843, pp 408–9

ROBINSON, D H. *The New Farming, 1939*; 2nd edn, 1951

ROBINSON, D H. 'Events Leading to the Formation of the National Agricultural Centre at Stoneleigh', *JRASE*, 129, 1968, pp 1–18

ROOTH, T. 'Trade Agreements and the Evolution of British Agricultural Policy in the 1930s', *AHR*, 1985, 33, pt ii, pp 173–190

ROSSITER, Margaret. *The Emergence of Agricultural Science: Justus von Liebig and the Americans 1840–1880*, 1975

RUSSELL, E J. *A History of Agricultural Science in Great Britain*, 1965

SCHÜBLER, Professor. 'On the Physical Properties of Soils', *JRASE*, I, 1840, pp 177–218

SHOARD, Marion. *The Theft of the Countryside*, 1980

SHOARD, Marion. *This Land is Our Land*, 1987

SIDNEY, Samuel. 'On the Effect of Prizes of Manufacturers', *Journal of the Society of Arts*, X, 1861–2, pp 374–82

SIDNEY, Samuel. *The Book of the Horse*, 1873

SIMONDS, James Beart. 'Report on Steppe Murrain or Rinderpest', *JRASE*, XVIII, 1857, pp 197–270

SIMONDS, James Beart. 'The Rot in Sheep: its Nature, Causes, and Treatment', *JRASE*, XXIII, 1862, pp 64–159

SIMONDS, James Beart. 'Autobiography', *Veterinarian*, LXVII, 1894, pp 315–24, 401–12, 487–500, 573–85, 651–62, 736–49, 811–23, 889–99

SMITH, Sir Frederick. *A History of Veterinary Literature*, III, 1930

SPENCE, Clark C. *God Speed the Plow*, Urbana, Ill., 1960

SPRING, David. 'Earl Fitzwilliam and the Corn Laws', *American Historical Review*, LIX, 1954, pp 287–304

SPRING, David. *The English Landed Estate in the Nineteenth Century: its*

Administration, 1963

STAPLEDON, R G. *The Land Now and Tomorrow*, 1935

STEDMAN-JONES. G. *Outcast London*, 1971

STEPHENS, Michael O and RODERICK, Gordon W. 'The Musprats of Liverpool', *Annals of Science*, 29, 1972, pp 287–311

STREET, A G. *Feather Bedding*, 1954

STURGESS, R W. 'The Agricultural Revolution on the English Clays', *AHR*, XIV, 1966, pp 104–21

THOMPSON, F M. 'The Second Agricultural Revolution 1815–1880', *EHR*, ser ii, XXI, 1968, pp 62–77

THOMPSON, H S. 'On the Absorptive Power of Soils', *JRASE*, XI, 1850, pp 63–74

THOMPSON, Ruth D'Arcy. 'The Gamgees – Medical and Veterinary', *Veterinary History*, III, 1974, pp 3–7

TITOW, J Z. *Winchester Yields*, Cambridge, 1972

THOMAS, A P. 'Report of Experiments on the Development of Liver-Fluke (Fasicola Hepatica)', *JRASE*, ser ii, XVII, 1881, pp 1–29

TRAFFORD, A D. 'Field Draining', *JRASE*, 131, 1970, pp 129–52

TRANTER, N L. *Population and Industrialisation*, 1973

TROW-SMITH, Robert. *Society and the Land*, 1953

TROW-SMITH, Robert. *English Livestock Husbandry 1700–1900*, 1959

TROW-SMITH, Robert. *A History of the Smithfield Club*, 1979

VAMPLEW, Wray. 'The Progress of Agricultural Mechanics: the Cost of Best Practice in the Mid-nineteenth Century', *Tools and Tillage*, III, 1979, pp 204–14

VOELCKER, Augustus. 'Influence of Chemical Discoveries on the Progress of English Agriculture', *JRASE*, ser ii, XIV, 1878, pp 805–54

VOELCKER, J A. 'On the Chemistry of Ensilage', *JRASE*, ser ii, XX, 1884, pp 482-504

VOELCKER, J A. 'Sir Ernest Clarke', *JRASE*, 84, 1923, pp 1–10

VOELCKER, J A and RUSSELL E J. *Fifty Years of Field Experiments at Woburn Experimental Farm*, 1936

VOELCKER, Augustus, *et al. Agricultural Economy*, 1874

WADE-MARTINS, Susanna. *A Great Estate at Work*, 1980

WARD, Sadie B. 'The French Peasants' Seed Fund: a 19th century example of Disaster Relief', *JRASE*, 138, 1977, pp 60–70

WASSON, E R. 'The Third Earl Spencer and Agriculture', *AHR*, 26, pt i, 1978, pp 89–99

WATSON, J A Scott. *Rural Britain Today and Tomorrow (being a Modern Cobbett's Tour)*, 1934

WATSON, J A Scott. *The History of the Royal Agricultural Society of England*, 1939

WATSON, J A Scott and HOBBS, M E. *Great Farmers*, 1937

WAY, J T. 'Composition and Money Value of Guano', *JRASE*, X, 1849, pp 196–230

WAY, J T. 'On the Power of Soils to Absorb Manure', *JRASE*, XI, 1850, pp 313–79

WEBSTER, William Bullock. 'On the Failure of Deep Draining on Certain Strong Clay Subsoils, with a Few Remarks on the Injurious Effects of Sinking the Water too far Below the Roots of Plants in very Porous Alluvial and Peaty Soils', *JRASE*, IX, 1849, pp 237–8

WILKES, A R. 'Adjustments in Arable Farming after the Napoleonic Wars', *AHR*, 28, 1980, pp 90–103

WOOD, Henry Trueman. *A History of the Society of Arts*, 1913

WORMELL, P. *Anatomy of Agriculture*, 1978

WHETHAM, Edith H. 'The Agricultural Act 1920 and its Repeal: the "Great Betrayal"', *AHR*, 22, pt i, 1974, pp 36–49

WHETHAM, Edith H. *The Agrarian History of England and Wales, VIII, 1914–39*, Cambridge 1978

WHETHAM, Edith H. 'The Trade in Pedigree Livestock 1850–1900', *AHR*, 27, pt i, 1979, pp 47–50

WHITEHEAD, R A. *Garretts of Leiston*, 1963

WIGHT, J. ed. *The Treasury and the Homestead*, I, 1877

WRIGHTSON, J. 'Agricultural Machinery', in Bevan, G Phillips, ed, *British Manufacturing Industries*, IX, 1876

WRIGHTSON, J. 'The Agricultural Lessons of "The Eighties"', *JRASE*, ser iii, I, 1890, pp 275–88

YOUNG, Arthur. *On the Advantages which have resulted from the Establishment of the Board of Agriculture*, 1809

Index

Note: page numbers in italic refer to illustration captions.

Abergavenny, Marquess of 212, 224
Abu Dhabi 279
Acland, Sir Thomes Dyke 16, 111, 123–4, 131
Acton Council 147
Adams, Peter 280
ADAS (Agricultural Development and Advisory Service) 234, 246, 254, 259, 273, 274, 284, 290
Adeane, Charles R W 148, *149*, 152, 156–8, 171
Adulteration of Seeds Act (1869) 99
'Advances in Cereal Technology (Royal Show Symposium, 1983) 261
Advisory Committee on Agricultural Education (Pilkington Committee) 281–2
Agricentre International 296
Agricultural and Food Research Council 234, 254
Agricultural Apprenticeship Council 283
Agricultural Central Co-operative Association 213, 218
Agricultural class of horses (shires) 64
Agricultural Cooperative Association 92, 98
Agricultural Development Act (1939) 166
Agricultural Development and Advisory Service *see* ADAS
Agricultural Economist 98, 135
Agricultural Economy (Agricultural Cooperative Association) 92
Agricultural Education Association 213, 218
Agricultural Engineers' Association 40, 186, 196, 213, 216, 217, 266
Agricultural Gazette 13, *15*, 15, 71, 74, 80, 97, 110, 111, 122, 132
Agricultural Gazette Literary Supplement 80
Agricultural Hall Company 147
Agricultural Holdings Act (1875) 121
Agricultural, Horticultural and Forest Industry Training Board 234, 283
Agricultural Improvement Council (AIC) 165, 176–7
Agricultural Industry Training Board 283
Agricultural Land Service 213
Agricultural Machinery & Tractor Dealers' Association 213, 218
Agricultural Research Council 167, 213, 218
Agricultural Research Institute, Oxford 149
Agricultural Show Exhibitors' Association 213, 216, 217
'Agricultural Societies and their Uses' (Plowman address) 70
Agricultural Society of France 153

Agricultural Training Board 234
Agriculture Act (1920) 153
Agriculture Act (1937) 166
Agriculture Act (1947) 171, 290, 294
Agriculture House (NFU HQ) 213
'Agriculture in Contention' (Franklin *Outlook* address) 289
Ainsworth-Davis, J R 150
Aintree racecourse 49
Akester, W D 219
Alice, HRH The Princess, Duchess of Gloucester *230*, 292
Alice in Wonderland 127
Alley, S F and J E 160
Alternative Livestock Enterprises *276*
Alternative to the Abolition of the Tied Cottage System, An (Shelter report) 288
Althorp, Viscount *see* Spencer, 3rd Earl
America(s) 61–2, 70, 76, 154
Amey, Leonard 294
Amos, C E 52, 130
Andrews of Reading 55–6
Anglesey cattle 64
Anglican Church 229
'Animal Health' (Royal Show Symposium, 1985) 261, *261*
Animal Health Trust 213, 218
Anti-Corn Law League 15, 16
ARAgS (Associateship of Royal Agricultural Societies) 282, 283
Ardingly School 124
Ark (Newsletter of Rare Breeds Survival Trust) 235
Arthur Rank Foundation 288–9
    see also Arthur Rank, Centre; Rank Village *both under* Stoneleigh; *see also* Rank (J Arthur) Group Charity
Askham Bryan College, Yorkshire 253
Association of Agriculture 231, 218
Association of British Manufacturers of Agricultural Chemicals 213, 217
Association of Independent Crop Consultants 234
Audience Profile Report (1983) 267
Australia 70, 76, 109, 154
Aveling and Parks agricultural 61
Ayre and Kidd of Hull 97

BAEC *see* British Agricultural Exports Council
Bailey Denton, J 114
Baker, Robert 16, 134
Banks, Sir Joseph 4
Barclaycard Leisure Festival 'Recro' (1980) 226
Barclays Bank 239, 284
Barker, Rodney 290
Barley '79 254
Barrett agricultural implements 46, 55
Barron, N A 252
Bartlett, Rosemary 223

Bates, Thomas 64, 68, 70
Battersea Show 39, 69, 146
Baxter agricultural implements 46
Bawtry 252
Bear, W E 118
Beart of Godmanchester 48, 49
Beche, H de la 27
Bedford, Francis, Duke of Bedford 119, 121, 146, 157
Bedford School 124
Bedford Show 36, 69
Bedford Square (former RASE premises) 147, 172
Beef Recording Association (UK) 213, 217, 233
Belgium 103, 153
Belgrave Square (present RASE premises) 172, 212, 277
Bell, Rev Patrick 59
Bell's reaper 60
Bell's Weekly Messenger 22, 107
Benion, J E 205
Benson, W A 'Billy' 184, 189, 205, 206
Bentall agricultural implements 71, 73
Berzelius 10
Bestalls agricultural implements 46
BHS *see* British Horse Society
Biddell agricultural implements 46, 51, *54*, 73
Biffen, Professor R H (later Sir Rowland Biffen) 148, 175, 297
Billy J Kramer and the Dakotas 209
'Bioscience in Crop Improvement' (Royal Show Symposium, 1986) 261
Bird, Douglas J 193
Birley, Sir Oswald 182
Birmingham Show/trials 28, 36, 61, 69, 109, 128, 138, 139, 150
Blackpool Show 184, 193
Bledisloe, Lord 157, 160–1, 172, 174–5, 178, 180, 182, 191, 193
Bledisloe Veterinary Award 181
Blewitt, Lt Col Guy 184
Blonde d'Aquitaines 270
Blythe 210
Board of Agriculture 1, 3, 4, 6, 8, *10*, 10, *11*, 19, 21, 44, 84, 107, 125, 147
    see also RASE
BOCM Ltd 189
BOCM Silcock 248
Book of the Farm series (Morton) 125
Booths (stock breeders) 30, 68, 70
Border Leicester sheep 189
Bourne, John 197, 199
Boussingault, Jean Baptiste 10
Bowly agricultural implements 68
Boyton meeting (1985) 265
BP LANDWORK 252
'Breeding for Beef – A Discussion' (RASE conference, 1964) 259

Breed Promotion and Sale Centres 270
Brent, Gerry 248
Bristol Show 31, 49, 149, 185–7, 195
British Agricultural Exports Council
  (BAEC) 212, 217, 275
British Agricultural Training Board 283
British Association for the Advancement
  of Science 3, 6, 88
British Beekeepers' Association 213, 218,
  233
British Council 262
British Egg Marketing Board 213
British Electrical Development
  Association 213
British Equestrian Federation 234
British Food and Farming Year, 1989 293
British Friesian 150
British Friesian Society 171
British Holstein 150
British Holstein Cattle Society 150
British Horse Society (BHS) 214, 217,
  233
British Husbandry 79
British Limousin Cattle Society 234
British Museum 99
British Show Jumping Association
  (BSJA) 214, 217, 233
British Simmental Cattle Society 234
British Sugar Corporation 252
British Texel Sheep Society 234
British Veterinary Association 214, 216,
  217
British Wool Marketing Board 214
Brougham, Henry 4
Brown, G T 137
Brown, Peter 285
Brown, Thomas 160
Brown Institution 126
BSJA *see* British Show Jumping
  Association
BTEC examinations 284
Buckingham, Duke of 17
Buckland, Rev Dr 131
Buckler, Canon Peter 187, 189, 208–9,
  225, 229, 231, 242, *271*, 288, *289*
Bunsen, Baron 131
Burgess and Key agricultural implements
  60
Burke, U Roland (later Sir Roland
  Burke) 162, 163, 171, 172, 173, 182,
  191–3, 280
Burke Perpetual Challenge Trophy 182,
  273
Burnell, Waite, Huggins & Co 61
Burrell, Lt Col Walter (later Sir Walter
  Burrell) 194, 196–7, 199, 205, 215, 219,
  220, 246, *271*, *297*
Burrell, Sir Merrik 163–5, 167, 175, 182
Bury St Edmunds Show 36, 56, 57
Bushe agricultural implements 46
Bygrave agricultural motor trial 150

Cadwallader, Mr 207
Cafe Royal 224
Caird, Sir James 80, 135
Caley, E S 16, 24
Callaghan, A D 223
Calor Ltd 272
Cambridge of Market Lavington 53, 72

Cambridgeshire Agricultural Society 182
Cambridgeshire Association 24
Cambridge Show 27, 36, 43, 48, *72*, 128,
  182, 187–90, 195, 197, 199, 242, 263
Cambridge University *72*, 112, 123, 128,
  176
  School of Agriculture 157, 178, 205,
    253
Canada 76, 279
Canadian Herefords 270
Canadian Holstein Friesians 270
Candolle, de 11
Cantelupe Farm, Haslingfield 223, 257
Canterbury, Archbishop of (Robert
  Runcie) 288
Canterbury Show 36, 43, 44, 57, 64, 109
CAP (Common Agricultural Policy) 171,
  279, 289
Cardiff Show 56, 57, 64, 152, 201
Carlisle report (1855) 55, 68
Carlisle Show 36, 38, 39, 43, 44, 58, 74
Carr, J B C 216, 219
Carroll, Lewis 127
Carr-Taylor, David 265
Carruthers, Charles [William] 99–100,
  119, *120*, 126, 148, 297
Carter, Eric 285, 290
Carter, W Ray B 219, *220*, 245, 247
Cashmore, W H 272–3
Castle Martin cattle 64
Cathcart, Earl 50, 100, 111
Cator, Col Harry 191, 193–5
Cattle Diseases Prevention Act (1866)
CEGB (Central Electricity Generating
  Board) 210
Cement and Concrete Association 210,
  214, 217
Central Agricultural Society 12, 13,
  17–19, 22, 24
Central Chamber of Agriculture 107
Central Electricity Generating Board *see*
  CEGB
Central Landowners' Association *see* CLA
Central Paris Society 1, 17, 19, 26
Chadwick, Edwin 114
Chamberlain, Neville 166
Chamber of Agriculture Journal 114
Chambers of Agriculture 99
Chandos, Marquis of 17, 18
Changing Farm, The 288
Changing Village, The 288
Channel Island cattle 63, 64
Charity Commissioners 157
Charles, John *see* Spencer, 3rd Earl
Charolais cattle 270
Chartered Auctioneers and Estate Agents
  Institute 217
Chartered Land Agents' Society 180, 218,
  281
Chelmsford Show 50, 58–9, 74, *76*, 76
Cherrington, John 210
Chesford Grange Hotel, Kenilworth 259
Chesham, Lord 114
Chester Show 36, 55, 57, 59, 64, 68, 75,
  159
Cheviot sheep 64
Childers, J W 79
Chivers' fruit farms, Histon 160
Christianity 229, 288

'Chrys' cartoon *198*
Cirencester Agricultural College *see* Royal
  Agricultural College, Cirencester
City and Guilds of London Institute 281
CLA (Central Landowners' Association),
  later Country Landowners' Association
  169, 199
Clark, Kitson 14
Clark, Peter *271*
Clarke, J A 59, 85, 114
Clarke, Ernest (later Sir Ernest Clarke)
  131, *132*, 143, 144, 146–8
Clay, Charles 107
Clayton, Shuttleworth & Co 49, 50, *56*,
  56
Clinton, Lord 268
Clive, Brig A F L 215
Clun Forest sheep 189
Clydesdale pigs 64
Cockle Park experimental station 158, 189
Colbred sheep 189
Colburn, Oscar 189, 291
Coleman, Professor 100
College of Preceptors 123
Collison, Lord 215
Colonial Service 221
Colt, Messrs 229
Common Agricultural Policy *see* CAP
Communications (Board of Agriculture) 8
'Communications in Agriculture' (Royal
  Show Symposium, 1987) 261
Commonwealth 175
Compound Animal Feeding Stuffs
  Manufacturers' National Association
  214, 218
Constable, Moira 288
Cooper, Sir Richard 148
Corbet, Henry 36, *37*, 40, 43, 64, 66, 107,
  115, 118
Cornes agricultural implements 46
Corn Laws 12–16, 18, 21, 104
Corn Production Act (1917) 151, 153
Cornwallis, F S W (later Lord
  Cornwallis) 147, 195
Cotswolds 15, 253, 262
Cotswold sheep 64, 76
Council of Agricultural for England *see*
  under RASE
Council of Fellows (of the Royal
  Agricultural Societies) 282–3
Council of Industrial Design 218
Country Code 285
Country Landowners' Association 214,
  215, 217, 287, 291
Countryside Commission 290
County Councils' Association 202
County Surveys 177
Courthope, Sir George (later Lord
  Courthope) 169, 171
Courtney, F S 160, 297
Cowen, Robin 289
Crathorne Report (1970) 268, 270, 272
Creagh-Scott, Lt Col J 167
Crosskill, Alfred 40, 51, 74
Crosskill agricultural implements 46, 48,
  51, *54*, 60, 71
Crowther, Dr E M 178
Crutchley, Percy 140, 142, 171
Crystal Palace *see* Great Exhibition

Culpin, Claude 273–4
Cumber, John 220, 221, 237, *237*
Cunard Shipping Company 221
Curtis, John 127–8, *129*
Czechoslovakia 166

Dadd, Christopher 205–7, 215, 219, *220*, 221, 223, 225, 229, 234, 240, 241, 243, 245, 247, 252, 263, *271*, 282, 284
Daily Express 209
Dairy Burke Trophy *180*, 272
Dairy Shorthorn Association 150
Dairy Shorthorn 150, 163, 270
Dale Electric Company 184
Dalgety-Spillers 272
Dampier-Whetham, W C (later Sir William Dampier) 158
Dampney, T D 216
Darby, Joseph 42, 77, 136
Dare, Henry Hall 114
Daresbury, Lord *see* Greenall, Sir Gilbert
Darlington Show 156
Dartmoor National Parks Authority 287
Daubeny, Charles 85, *86*
Davies, A J 245–6
Davis, Hewitt 16
Davy, Sir Humphrey 8, 10
Denison, Evelyn (later Lord Ossington) 58
Denmark 120, 124
Dent, John Dent 68, 69, 75, 99, 114, 125
Department of Education and Science (DES) 282
Derby, Earl of 146
Derby, the (racing) 40
Derby Show 49, 108, 148, 149
Deutsche Landwirtschafts-Gesellschaft 130
Development Commission 157
Devon Breed Society 242
Devon cattle 63, 76
Devon County School 124
Devonshire, Duke of 162
Devon Trust for Nature Conservation 287
Dick, Professor 102
Dictionary of the Farm 6
Digby, Lord 'Eddie' 215, 219
Dillamore, Ernest *271*, 280
Directory of Country Foods 255
Disraeli, Benjamin 118
Dixon, H H ('The Druid') 33, 38–40, 79, 84, 85
Doncaster Show 149, 161
Dorman-Smith, Sir Reginald 166
Dorset County School 124
Dorset Horned sheep 189, 243, 250
Downing College, Cambridge *72*, 112
Downton Agricultural College *145*
Draffan, W D 219
Dray agricultural implements 60
Ducie, Earl 15–16, 66, 68, 69
Dugdale, J Marshall 140
Dundonald, Earl 10
Dunnington-Jefferson, Sir John 191, 193–6
Dymond, Alastair 236, 255

Easterbrook, L F 172
Eastwood, Sir John 239, *240*

Edinburgh, Duke of 175, 185–6, *240*, 293
Edinburgh College 102
Edinburgh University 125
Edinburgh Veterinary College 102
Education and Careers Centre 283–4
'Education and Training for International Agricultural Development' (Royal Show Symposium, 1984) 261
Education Act (1872) 117
Edwards, Dr Joseph 216
EEC (European Economic Community) 165, 279
Egg Marketing Board 218
Electricity Council 217, 233
Electricity for the Farm 158
Electro-Agricultural Centre (later Farm-Electric Centre) 233
Elements of Agriculture: A Text-Book (Fream) (aka *Fream's*) 125, *126*
  Ainsworth-Davis's revision (1911) 150, 164
  Robinson's revision (1949) 176, 179
  Spedding's revision (1983) 125, 285
Elizabeth II, Queen 179, *180*, 279
Elliot, Walter 162
Ellman, John 4, 113
Empire Dairy Council 155–6
Engledow, Sir Frank 178, 294
English Agricultural Society *see* RASE
English Farming Past and Present 136
Ernle, 136
Etheridge agricultural implements 49
European Economic Community *see* EEC
'Eurotechnik' display 274
Evans, R H 171
Evans, Stanley 290
Eve, Jim 239
Everall, John 215
Evershed, H 85
Eversley, Lord (C Shaw Lefevre) 18, 24, 79
Exall agricultural implements 46, 55
Exeter, Marquis of 22
Exeter Show 43, 44, 53
Exeter University 284
Eyth, Max von 130

Fairlie, 136
Faith in the City 288
Farm Buildings Association 214, 217, 233
Farm Buildings (Information) Centre 214, 217, 223, 233, 234, 254
Farm Electric Centre (formerly Electro-Agricultural Centre) 234, 254
Farmer and Stockbreeder 154, 163, 164, 167, 186, 207, 262
Farmer's Advocate (Ontario) 145
Farmers' Central Agricultural Society 24
Farmers' Club 96, 157, 214, 218, 291
Farmer's Guide to Agricultural Research, The 160, 179, 285
Farmer's Guide to the National Agricultural Centre 285
Farmer's Journal 16
Farmer's Magazine 18, 21, 36, 70, 78, 117, 124
Farmers' Publishing Group (*Farmers' Weekly*) 234

Farmer's Series (of Society for the Diffusion of Useful Knowledge) 4
Farmers' Weekly 254, 273, 277
Farmer's Year, A (Haggard) 148
Farm Holiday Bureau 234
Farmhouse Holiday Bureau 255
Farming and Wildlife Advisory Group 290
Farm Management Association 217, 233
Farmscan competition 284
Fatstock Marketing Corporation 214, 218
Fattening (of pigs) 243
Faunce-De Laune, C De Laune 119
Fawcett, E A 69, 75
Fell, Henry 291
Fellowes, Carol 171, 183, 203
Ferens, Richard 264
Fertilizer Manufacturers' Association 214, 216, 217
Feversham, Lord 40
Field 85
'Fifty Years' Progress of British Agriculture' (Caird) 135
Finn/Dorset Horn rams 250
First World War (Great War) 151, 158, 159, 164, 166
Fisken agricultural implements 58
Fisons Ltd 224, 245
Fitzwilliam, Earl 14
Flies Injurious to Stock (Ormerod) 128
Follow 'N' Flock 250
Food from Britain Organisation 278, 296
Ford, Daphne *271*
Fordson Model 'N' 159
Foreign Office 26
Foresters 181
Forestry Commission 169, 214, 218, 268, 287
Forwood, Sir Dudley 234–5, 264
Fowler of Leeds 59, 130
Fox, Harry 276
Fox, Howard V 219, 223
FRAgS (Fellowship of Royal Agricultural Societies) 282, 283
France 124, 127, 153, 278–80
Franco-Prussian War (1870–1) 153
Frankish, W 140
Franklin, Sir Michael 289
Frank Parkinson Agricultural Trust 225, 231
Fream, William 125, 144, *145*, 148, 160
Fream's see Elements of Agriculture: A Text-Book
Freemasons' Tavern (locale of foundation of RASE) 22, 24, 25, 132
French Burke, J 79
French Peasants' Seed Fund 153
Frere, P. H. 84, 111–12, 114–15
Freund, William 196, 199, 206
Friesian cattle 270
Friesland sheep 189
Fussell, G E 51

Game Laws 108
Gamgee, John 102–3, 105
Gardner agricultural implements 46
Garrett, Richard 73
Garrett agricultural implements 46, 48, 60, 71

Gascoigne, F Neville 192
General Views (Board of Agriculture) 8
'Georgical Committee' (of Royal Society) 3
Geological Society of London 115
George VI, King 163, 171
Germany 103, 122, 124, 130, 279
Gibbs, Humphrey 44
Gibbs, B H B (later Sir Brandreth) 19, 35, 41, 44, 130
Gilbert, J H 85, 122, 127
Gilbey, Sir Walter 140, 142, 143–4, *150*, 151, 171
Gilchrist-Thomas process 120
Glasnevin (Dublin) 124
Gloucester Chamber of Agriculture 159
Gloucester Show 43, 64, 66, 150
Goat Society 258
Godfrey, E H 148
Gooch, Sir Robert 206, 215
Gooch agricultural implements 71
Good, W W 73
Graham, Sir James 27, 131
Graham Cherry Organisation 199
Grand National Archery Society 234
Grant agricultural implements 46
'Great Betrayal' 153, 167
Great Depression 154
Greater Felcourt Farm, East Grinstead 159
Great Exhibition (Crystal Palace) 39, 47, 59, 61
Great War *see* First World War
Great Yorkshire Show 186, 191
Green, John D F 154, *168*, 231, 283, 290
Greenall, Sir Gilbert (later Lord Daresbury) 148, 161–2, 280, 292
Greening, E O 98
Greenwell, Sir Peter 215, 235
Grey, Sir Charles 103
Grey of Dilston 12, 87
Grisenthwaite, William 10
Groundsell agricultural implements 48
Group of Peers 169
Guernsey cattle 64
Guide to Methods of Insect Life (Ormerod) 128
Guide to On-Farm Trialling 254
Guild of Agricultural Journalists 214

Haddon, R W (later Sir Richard Haddon) 164–5, 172
Haggard, H Rider 148
Hailstone, Bernard *240*
Haines, Guy 246
Hall, George Webb 6, *11*
Hampshire College of Agriculture 253
Hampshire sheep 64
Handbook of Farm Labour (Morton) 57
Handel Festival 40
Handley, Henry 1, 12, 18, 21, *23*, 24, 79, 91, 113
Hardcastle, J 254
Hare and Co 77
Harewood House 143, 144, 146, 147
Harper Adams College 178
Harris, Joe 264
Harrogate showground 186, 191, 256
Hartlib, Samuel 3

Harvey, Nigel *166*
Hazelrigg, Sir Arthur (later Lord Hazelrigg) 163, 168, 191, 197
Healey, Fred 205
Health & Safety Executive 234, 274
Hearth, John D M 221, 223, 225, 239, 266
Hellriegal and Wilfrath 127
Hemmings, J E & Son Ltd 251
Henslow, Professor J S 82, *83*
Henson, Joe 235
Herd Book 64, 69
Hereford Breed Society 242
Hereford cattle 63, 64, 76–7
Hereford Herd Book Society 270
Hess, Elizabeth 283
Higgs, Clyde 199
Highland and Agricultural Society of Scotland 1, 2–3, 6, 17–19, 22, 24, 69, 78, 102, 105, 169
Hills, E H 121
Hills Bequest 157, 178
Hincks, T C 66
HND examinations 282
Hobbs, William Fisher 33, *34*, 55
Hobson, Alec 171–3, 179, 186–7, 191–3, 199, *201*, 201–2, 205, 215
Hobson, Harry 171
Hobson, John 202
Holland, Edward 16, 105–6, *106*, 122–3
Home Farm, Stoneleigh 197, 205
Hornsby of Grantham 46, 55, 61
Hosking, J Everard *271*, 282
Hoskyns, Chandos Wren 13, 14, 17, 44, 90, 105, 111, *112*, 114, 123, 133
House of Commons 170
Howard, E Maxwell 219
Howard of Bedford 46, 59, 71, 74
Hudson, H G 283
Hudson, James 25, 79, 113–14
Hudson, R S (later Lord Hudson) 165, 193
Hudson Committee 283–4
Hughes, Cledwyn (later Lord Cledwyn) 224
Hughes, H V 253
Hull Show 76
Humphrey Gibbs & Co 44
Hunt, Gilbert 216
Hunt agricultural implements 71
Hurd, Anthony (later Lord Hurd) 165, 172, 173, 191
Hussey reaper 59–60, 62
Huxley, Thomas 115

ICI Crop (or Plant) Protection Ltd 238, 276
Illustrated London News 110
Implement Manufacturer's Review 63
Imports Board 169
Inclosure Commissioners 94
Incorporated Society of Auctioneers and Landed Property Agents 214, 218
Industrial Training Board 281
Institute of Agricultural Engineering, Oxford 159, 273
Institute of Agricultural Secretaries 234
Institute of Corn and Agricultural Merchants 217
Inter-county Dairy Herd Trophy 181

International Dairy (Kilburn Show, 1879) 120
International Exhibitions 39, 278–80
Intervention Board 279
'In Town Tonight' (radio programme) 162
Ipswich Show 162
Islington Agricultural Hall Company *110*
Iveagh, Earl of 180

Jackson, George H 223, 246, 262, 289, 290
James, Cynthia 280
Jenkins, H M 28, 79, 80, 104, 114, *116*, 119, 120, 124, 131, 143, 147
Jersey cattle 64
John Eastwood Farm 268, 289
Johnson, J F W 89, 90
Johnston, Cuthbert 11, 13, 21, 25
Jonas, Samuel 68
Jones, Peter 273
Jones, Rupert 115
Jones, W Emrys (later Sir Emrys Jones) 245
Jopling, Michael 236
Journal of RASE see under RASE

Kenya 234
Kenya Co-operative Creameries Ltd 219
Kerrison, Sir Edward 123
Keyser, John 279
Kidlington Aerodrome 185
Kilburn Show 28, 36, 38, 40–3, *41*, *42*, 116, 120, 139, 142, 146
Kilburn stock report 70
King's College, Newcastle 189
Kingscote, Sir Nigel 140, 148
Kingscote agricultural implements 68
Kinnaid, Lord 70
Kinross Show 70
Klinner, W E 274
Knepp Castle 164
Königliche Landwirtschaftliche Gesellschaft von England und ihr Werf, Die 130

Labour Party/Government 171, 288
Laing, A R 232
Land Agents' Society 214
Laval cream-separator 120
Lawes, J B 85, 88–9, 91, 92, 121, 122, 127
Lawes Agricultural Trust 157
Lawrence, Charles 80
Leamington trials 109
Le Couteur, Col (of Jersey) 21
Leckford fishing 160
Leeds Show 36, 109
Leicester sheep 63
Leigh, Lord 197, 239, 242, 293
Letter (Handley, 1838) 91
Lever Foods Ltd 243
Lewes Show 36, 43, 60, 63, 66
Liebig, Justus von 6, 87–9
Limousin cattle 270
Lincoln Red Breed Society 242
Lincoln sheep 64
Lincoln Show 36, 60, 68, 149, 164, 171–4, 181, 191, 193, 197
Liverpool Show 31, 36, 37–8, 39, 48, 53, 61, 128, 149
Liverpool University 250

Livestock Export Council of Great
  Britain 214
Livestock Export Information Centre 272
Lloyd's Bank 285
Lockinge Estate, Ardington 159
London Farmer's Club 70, 107, 113, 114
London University 123, 126
Longhorn cattle 64
Luckin, P S 225
Luxmore Committee on Agriculture
  Education 179

'Mac' cartoon of 1965 Royal Show
  officials *271*
MacArthur, A A C 'Archie' 219, 220, 277
McCann, Neil 285
McCormick agricultural implements 47,
  59–61, *62*, 62
Macdonald, C J B 160
Mackenzie, S J J 148–9
McRow, Thomas 147, 160, 171
MAFF (Ministry of Agriculture,
  Fisheries and Food) 196, 198, 214, 216,
  217, 219, 224, 246, 279, 290, 291
  see also Ministry of Agriculture
Maidstone Show 138, 139
Maine Anjou cattle 270
Manchester Show/trials 39, 43, 61, 75,
  128, 150, 152
Manning, William 292
Manpower Services Commission 284
'Mansion House Fund' 42
Manual of British Husbandry 6
Maplin Sands reclamation 91
*Mark Lane Express and Agricultural
  Journal* 1, *5*, 13, 16, 21, 22, 36, *37*, 97,
  108, 118, 138
Marks and Spencer 227–8
Marriner, Harold *271*
Mason, Michael *182–3*
Massey-Ferguson Group 224
Mastal, H D 140
'Master Butterfly' (prize Shorthorn) *76*
Matthews, R Borlase 159, 171
Meat and Livestock Commission (MLC)
  233–4, 242, 257, 272
Meuse-Rhine-Issel cattle 270
Meyric Hughes, R R 202, 205
Meysey-Thompson, Sir Harry *see*
  Thompson, H S
Middle East Agribusiness 275
Middleton, Lord 142
Mildmay of Flete, Lord 163
Miles, Sir William 16
Milk Marketing Board (MMB) 175, 188,
  214, 218, 234, 245
Milward, Richard 64
Mineral Theory 89
Ministry of Agriculture 151, 152, 165–6,
  169–73, 181–3, 186, 187, 293–4
  see also MAFF
Ministry of Food 153, 169, 182
Ministry of Munitions 152
Ministry of Works 173
MLC *see* Meat and Livestock Commission
MMB *see* Milk Marketing Board
Model, Craft and Country Show 226
Montgomery Martin, Robert 18
Montgomeryshire cattle 64

Morning Post 80
Morrison, W S 170
Morton, John 15–16, 51, 57, 72–3
Morton, John Chalmers 14, *15*, 15–16,
  31, 36, 37, 43, 68, 71–4, 77, 82, 85, 97,
  105, 107, 109–15, 122–5, 130–2, 136, 295
Muckle, T B 273
Murchison, Sir Roderick 115
Museum of English Rural Life 182
Muspratt of Liverpool 88, 89

NAAS (National Agricultural Advisory
  Service) 27, 175, 177, 182, 205, 214,
  245
NAC *see* National Agricultural Centre; *see
  also* Stoneleigh
NACAB *see* Advisory Board *under*
  National Agriculture Centre
NAC News (formerly *Quarterly Review*)
  172, 242, 285
Napoleonic Wars 10
National Advisoy Council on Education
  for Industry and Commerce 281
National Agricultural Advisory Service *see*
  NAAS
National Agricultural Examination Board
  281
National Agricultural Centre (NAC) 189,
  186, 189, *204*, 205–81 *passim*
  Advisory Board (NACAB) *213*, 215–19,
    245–6
  Housing Association 288
  Rural Trust 288
  see also Stoneleigh
National Association of Agricultural
  Contractors 214, 217
National Association of Corn and
  Agricultural Merchants 214, 217
National Beekeeping Centre 233, 234
National Cattle Breeders' Association
  214, 217
National Celebration of British Food and
  Farming (1989) 265–6
National Cereals Demonstration 253
National Certificate in Agriculture
  Examinations Board 281
National College of Agricultural
  Engineering, Silsoe 273
National Computer Users' Group in
  Agricultural Education 285
National Diary Examination Board 281
National Diploma in Agriculture *see* NDA
National Diploma in Dairying *see* NDD
National Equestrian Centre 233, 237
National Farmers' Union of England and
  Wales *see* NFU
National Federation of Young Farmers'
  Clubs 214, 217, 234
National Institute of Agricultural Botany
  see NIAB
National Institute of Agricultural
  Engineering (NIAE) 209, 214, 218, 274
National Master Farriers', Blacksmiths'
  and Agricultural Engineers'
  Association 234
National Museum of Food and Farming
  293
National Pet Show 227

National Pig Breeders' Association 171,
  214, 217
National Poultry Diploma Board 281
National Proficiency Tests Council 234
National Sheep Breeders' Association
  182, 214, 217, 272
National Union of Agricultural Workers
  see NUAW
National Westminster Bank 272
Nature Conservancy Council 287, 290
NDA (National Diploma in Agriculture)
  125, 179, 282
NDD (National Diploma in Dairying)
  125, 179, 282
Neame, Basil 283
Netherthorpe, Lord 205, 213, 214, 216,
  219, *222*, 223, 224, 263, *271*
Newbury agricultural implements 73
Newcastle Show 36, 37–8, 44, 63, 75, 143,
  149, 184–5, 189, 194, 195, 207–8, 242
Newcastle University 243
New Farming, The (Robinson) 190–1
'New Outlook, The' (in farming) 162–3
Newport Show 159
Newton, Sir Douglas (later Lord
  Eltisley) 159, 162, 163
Newton Abbot Show 182–4, 186
New Zealand 279
NFU (National Farmers' Union of
  England and Wales) 155, 167, 169, 174,
  182, 196, 198–9, 212–17, 234, 255, 291
NIAB (National Institute of Agricultural
  Botany) 175, 178, 209, 214, 217, 238,
  252, 276
NIAE *see* National Institute of
  Agricultural Engineering
Nickerson, Sir Joseph 221
Norfolk Agricultural Station 158, 176,
  178
Norfolk Horn sheep 235
Norfolk Red Poll cattle 64
Northampton Show 51
Northfield Committee on agricultural
  land acquisition 291
North Midland Railway Company 111
Norwegian Show, Oslo 187
Norwich Show 50, 185–6, 193–5
Nottingham Show 128, 151–2, 184, 195,
  197
NUAW (National Union of Agricultural
  Workers) 199, 214, 215, 217

O'Brien, P K 137
OND examinations 282
Order of Citeaux 207
*Organic Chemistry in its Application to
  Agriculture and Physiology* (Liebig) 6,
  87–8
Ormerod, Miss Eleanor 127–8
Orwin, C S 149, 160
Osborn, Paul 202–3, 205, 219
Oslo Show 187
Ossington, Lord *see* Denison, Evelyn
Outlook 289
Oxford Downs sheep 64, 76
Oxford Show 31, 36, 43, *46*, 48, 50, 56–7,
  63, 64, *65*, 76, 131, 163, 182, 185, 187,
  195, 197
Oxford University 123

Pardoe, Mrs Peggy 225
Paris Agricultural Show 278
Paris Central Society *see* Central Paris Society
Parker, Cecil T 130, 140
Parkes, Josiah 49, 52, 93, 94, 96
Park Royal (abortive RASE showground) 139, 142, *143*, 144–9, 151, 158, 191, 195, 197
Park Royal Estates Company 147
Park Royal Limited 141
Parliament 24, 107, 111, 170
Peel, Sir Robert 22, 24
Peet, Bernard 248
Pell, Albert 103
Pemberton, Francis W W (later Sir Francis Pemberton) 182, 187, 189, 199, *204*, 205–8, *206*, 210, 215, 216, 218–21, 239, 246, 252, 263, *271*, 280–1, 295
Penny Cyclopaedia (of Society for the Diffusion of Useful Knowledge) 6, 79
Perrin, John 187
Perrott, J 223
Peruvian guano 90, *90*, 97
Peterborough Show 160
Petheridge, F R 176
Phillips(s) agricultural implements 46
Philosophical Transactions of the Royal Society 3
Pigeon, Dan 47
Pig Farming 257
Pig Industry Development Authority (PIDA) 189, 214, 217, 242
Pilkington Committee *see* Advisory Committee on Agricultural Education
Player, Capt Steve 220, 221
Playfair, Lyon (later Lord Playfair) 88, 94, 96
Plowman, Thomas 70
Plumes Tavern 142
Plymouth Show 44, 61, 68, 75, 139
Portman, Lord 66, *67*
'Potato Disease and its Prevention, The' (essay competition) 100
Potato Marketing Board (PMB) 214, 218, 252, 257
Pot-Culture Station, Woburn 122
Poultry Stock Association 214, 217
Pregnant Sow 243
Principles of Agriculture (Thaer) 11
Prior, James (later Lord Prior) 246
Privy Council 103, 104
Prize Essays and Transactions (Highland Society) 78
Produce Packers' Association 214, 218
'Profitable Framing in a Competitive World' (RASE Conference, 1963) 259
Public Money Drainage Act (1846) 93
Punch 118
Pusey, Edward Bouverie 80
Pusey, Philip 28, 39, 47, 49, 59, 61, 66, 79–80, *81*, 82, 85, 89–90, 92, 94, 109, 111, 113, 115, 121, 122, 131, 137
Pym, Sir Francis 12

Quarterly Journal of Agriculture 78
Quarterly Review 80
Queen's Park Rangers Football Club 141

RABDF *see* Royal Association of British Dairy Farmers
Ramphal, Sir Shridath 274
Randell, Charles 103, 114, 121
Rank, Lord 221, 224, 229, 231
Rank (J Arthur) Group Charity 231
Rank Foundation 293
Ransome, J Allen 44, 46, 108
Ransome and Sim of Ipswich 21, 46, 48, 52–3, *54*, *58*, 71, 74, 109
Rare Breeds Survival Trust 234–6, *235*, 251
RASE (Royal Agricultural Society; formerly English Agricultural Society) *passim*
  Accountancy Department 223
  Advisory Committee on Propaganda and Publicity 172, 174, 205
  Agricultural Department 223
  Agricultural Policy Review Group 292
  Agricultural Policy Sub-Committee 292
  Agricultural Relief of the Allies Committee 153
  Arable Policy Working Group 252
  Associateship (ARAgS) 282, 283
  Audio Visual Unit 254, 285
  Botanical and Zoological (Forestry and Orchards) Committee 176
  Cattle Plague Committee 103–4
  Central Executive Committee 216
  Charter 28, 104–7, 109–10, 132, 152, 155, 156, 172, 180, 211, 215, 241, 262
  Chemical Committee 96–7, 99, 121, 158
  Chemical Laboratory 143
  Committee of Management 25, 26, 31, 100
  Conference on post-war agricultural policy 169–70
  Council 38, 40, 58, 59, 66, 69, 81, 84, 85, 93, 96–7, 102–5, 111, 113–14, 124–5, 141, 142, 144–8, 155–9, 162–5, 168, 169, 171, 183, 186, 191–9, 201–2, 206, 211, 215–16, 218–19, 221–4, *222*, 224–5, 291, 292
  Country Meeting Committee 31, *32*, 33–5, 39
  Demonstrations Committee 243, 245
  Development Fund (Appeal) 224–5, 246
  Drafting Committee 169
  Eastwood Foundation 293
  Editorship Committee 114
  Education and General Purposes Committee *168*, 283, 292
  Education Committee 123, 154
  Electro-Farming Conference 159
  Executive Committee 163–4, 167, 168, 171, 172, 206, 219–23, 291
  Fellowship (FRAgS) 282, 283
  Finance and General Purposes Committee 211, 215–16, 219, 220
  Finance Committee 113, 148, 157, 178, 180, 192–3, 222
    Special Committee (to review finances) 156–7
  Forestry and Biological Committee 176
  General Purposes Committee 220, 222
  Geological Committee 27
  Gold Medal 180, 182, 273
  Honorary Fellowship 283, 290
  Initial Gifts Committee 224
  Journal (JRASE) 9, 11, 27–9, 59, 77–94, *81*, *83*, 98–9, 102, 104–5, 110–12, 114–15, 117, 119–20, 122, 125, 127, *129*, 130, 131, 144, 146, 148–9, 158–60, 164, 178–9, 222, 233, 274, 285
    Committee 79, *81*, 81–2, *84*, 99, 105, *112*, 114–15, 120, 281
  'Learned Role' 290
  Livestock and Sponsorship Executive 223
  Marketing Department 221, 223
  NAC News (formerly *Quarterly Review*) 172, 242, 285
  Objectives 25–6
  Planning and Works Committee 232
  Policy Committee 172, 192–5
  Poultry Review Group 252
  Public Relations Department 221, 233
  Quarterly Review 172, 191, 199, 209, 233
    see also *NAC News* under RASE
  Report of Council 227
  Report of pollution and agriculture 290-1
  Research Committee 158–60, 177–8, 182
  Reserve Fund 158
  Royal Show Committee 220
  Secretarial Department 223
  Selection and General Purposes Committee 152, 156, 163, 183–4, 194, 198, 199, 201
  Selection Panel 220, 222
  Shows 31–77, *32*, *39*, *41*, *42*, *45–8*, *50–3*, 108, 128, 138, 139–42, 146–52, 160–3, 172–5, 181–98, *198*, 262–81, *264*, *269*, *271*, *273*, *275*, *276*, *278*, *287*
    Centenary 163, 164, 174
    Fact-Finding Committee/Report 199–200, 203, 214–15, 241, 262, 283
    Fiftieth Anniversary 118, 132
    National Centre *see* National Agricultural Centre; *see* also Stoneleigh
    Policy Committee 196
    Sesquicentenary (1989) 265–6, 292
    Special Committee 140–1
    Working Party 195
  Silver Medals 268, 272–4
  Supplementary Charter 146
    revised (1979) 239
  Technical Development Committee 220, 222, 252, 265, 290
  Veterinary Committee 100, 102
  War Emergency Committee 152–3
  Working Party on staff structure 220
  Working Party on Council and Committee structure 221–2, 224
  Works Committee 220, 246
Rayns, Frank 158, 176
Rare Breeds Survival Foundation of America 293
Read, C S 88, 136
Reading Show 159, 160
Reading University 182

Farming Club 192
Rearing and Weaning (of pigs) 243
Red and White Canadian Fresians 270
Reed, Charles 205
Reed, Howard 114
Remarks on the Present State of Agriculture (Lefevre) 18
Rew, Sir Henry 157
Rham, Rev W L 6, *9*, 79, 85
Richardson, C H 223
Richmond, Duke of 16, 19, *20*, 21, 22, 24, 25, 28, 79, 131
Richmond agricultural implements 46
Ricketts and Burrell 59
Ritchie, Sir John 181
Roberts, James Denby *271*
Robinson, Dr D H 176, 178–9, 190, 243, 285
Robinson, W C *271*, 280–1
'Role of Women in Agricultural Extension' (Royal Show Symposium, May 1987) 262
Rosenberg, Michael 235, *235*, 236, 272
Rothamsted research centre 85, 88–9, 91–2, 121, 157–8, 176, 178
Rowett Institute 189
Royal Agricultural College, Cirencester 26, 122–4, 125, 253–4
Royal Agricultural Society of England *see* RASE
Royal Agricultural Society of the Commonwealth 175
Royal Agricultural Society of Ireland 102
Royal Ascot week 145
Royal Association of British Dairy Farmers (RABDF) 214, 217, 256, 272
Royal Buckinghamshire Agricultural Association 17, 117
Royal Commission on Agriculture 120, 124
Royal Commission on Environmental Pollution 290
Royal Forestry Society of England, Scotland, Wales and N Ireland 214, 218, 268
Royal Highland and Agricultural Society 125, 185, 283
Royal Horticultural Society 3, 4, 281
Royal Institution of Chartered Surveyors 214, 218, 281
Royal Norfolk Costessey Showground 185
Royal Shows *see under* RASE
Royal Smithfield Club *2*, 3, 4, 6, 17, 19, 40, 44, 68, 214, 217
Royal Society 3
Royal Veterinary College 26, 100–2, 126
Royal Welsh Agricultural Society 283
Rumania 153
Rural Craftsmen 181
Rural Crafts Youth Training Scheme 284
Rural Employment and Training Unit 284
Rural Homes for Rural People 288
Rural Industries Bureau 214, 218
Russell, Canon Anthony J 229, 231, 288, *289*
Russell, Frank 179, 282, 283
Russell, Sir John 176–7
Russia 102

'Rusticus' 22
Ryan, Mrs Louise 241

Sacrewell Farm, Thornhaugh 240–1, 290
    Arable Fair 252, 256
Salisbury Show 43, 59, 61, 64, 109
Samuelson agricultural implements 61
Sanday, G H 140
Savills 239
Scampton Aerodrome 159
Schaik, Simon Van 274
Schloesing and Muntz 127
Schubler, 10
Science Museum 293
Scotch Horned cattle 63
Scotch Polled cattle 63
Scottish Midland Counties Show, Kinross 70
Scott Report (on post-war rural conditions) 168
Scott Abbot, Mary 240
Scott Abbot, William 240
Scott Watson, Professor Sir James A 1, 27, 142, 144, 149, 160, 177, 178
Scragg agricultural implements 49, 50
Second World War 137, 153, 163–70, 290
Seed Trade Association Bureau of the United Kingdom 214, 217
Selborne, Earl of 292–3, *295*
Select Committee on Agricultural Distress (1836) 12, 18
Sewell, Professor William 100–1
Shaw, William 1, *5*, 11–14, 16–19, 21, 25, 31, *32*, 36, *37*, 78, 109, 121, 122, 132, 137
Shaw Lefevre, C *see* Eversley, Lord
Sheep '88 258
Shell Chemicals 235
Shelter organisation 288
Shipley, William 3
Shirley, Wilfred 281
Shorthorn cattle 63, 64, 69, 70, 75, 76–7, 118
Shorthorn Cattle Society 234
Short-wool sheep 64
Shrewsbury Show 49, 63, 71, 280
Shropshire sheep 64, 76
Sidney, Samuel 43, 70, 84, *110*, 110–13
Silcock, R and Sons 187, 242–3
Silcock, Richard 189
Simental cattle 270
Simonds, James Beart *101*, 101–3, 124, 127
Sinclair, Sir John 2, 6, 8
Sir John Eastwood Foundation 239
Skew, John 284
Slater, Dr W K 177
Small Pig Keepers' Council 171, 179
Smith, Robert 75
Smith, Sidney 114
Smith, Sir Frederick 102
Smithfield Club *see* Royal Smithfield Club
Smithfield Show 68, 197
Smith of Deanston (James Smith) 12, 19, 46, 93, 94, *95*
Smith of Woolston 59
Smith-Ryland, Charles M T *222*, 223
Smythe of Peasenhall 71, 73

Soames, Sir Christopher 279
Society for the Diffusion of Useful Knowledge 3, 4, 6, 19, 22, 78
Society of Arts 3, 4, 8, 27, 44
    Agricultural Committee 4
Somerville, Lord 4
Somerville, Professor W 157–8
Southampton Show 49, 51, 53, 63, 162
South Devon cattle 270
South Down sheep 63, 64
South Kensington Institute for Agriculture 128
Sow and Litter 243
Sparrey, C A M 223
Spedding, Professor Colin R W 125, 285
Spence, Joseph 89
Spencer, 3rd Earl (John Charles; Viscount Althorp) 1, *2*, 4, 6, 12, 14, 16, 17, 19, 21, 22, *23*, 25, 28, 78, 113, 131, 137
Spiers, A G 18
Spillers 243
Spooner, William 102
Sprengel, 10
Stanhope, Earl 16
Stannard, Derek 233, *271*
Stanton, A W 138
Stanyforth, E W 140, 156
Stapledon, Sir George G 158, 164, 176
Steele-Bodger, A 216, 219
Stock Exchange 131
Stoneleigh (National Agriculture Centre (NAC)) 186, *204*, 205–81 *passim*, 293, 296
    Abbey 238, 242
    ADAS Unit 254, 259, 290
    'Adopt a Jersey Calf Scheme' 287
    Arable Marquee 275
    Arable Research Centres 254
    Arable Unit/Area 253, 275, 290
    Arthur Rank Centre 228–9, *228*, 231, 286, 288
    Autumn Rare Breeds Show and Sale 235
    Basic Slag Stand 229
    Beef-crosses *249*
    Beef Demonstration Unit 243, 249–50
    Beef '82 and '86 258
    Bee Centre/Pavilion 233, 286
    'Best of Country Living Feature' 268
    British Agricultural Training Board Training Centre 283
    Bull Centre 245
    Bull Performance Testing Unit 242, 250
    Central Concourse 231, *232*
    Cereals '88 258
    Cereal Unit 252–4
    Church Pavilion 229
    Clock Tower 237
    Conference Hall 231, 237, 247, 259
    Conservation Advice Centre 290
    Conservation Pavilion *287*
    Council, Stewards and Governors' Pavilion 231, 237
    Countryside Communications Unit 286, 296
    Country Sport area 268
    Dairy Unit 243, 248–9, 286

Deed of Variation 239
Deer Unit 255, *255*
Demonstration Area 209–10, *244*, 263, 268, *275*
Education and Careers Centre Pavilion 283
European Poultry Fair 257
Farm and Country Centre 285
Farm Buildings Centre 207–9, 242
Farmers' Club Building 237
Farmer Wheat System plots 275–6
Farm Interpretation activities 286–8
Farm Woodland Area 268
Field Vegetable Centre 275
Flower Show 212, 238, 268
Food and Farm Facts Unit 286
Food Hall exhibition 277–8, *278*
'From Seed to Harvest' 257
Grand Ring 226, 236–7
Grandstand 212, 237
Grecian Lodge Drive 239
Hall of Residence 231
Home Food Unit 288
International Dairy Show (later International Dairy Farming Event) 256
International Pavilion 237, 280
International Symposia 261–2; *261*
John Cumber Park 237
John Eastwood Farm 239
Landscape Industries '88 258
Livestock Demonstration Units 277, 286
Manor Fields Farm 239
Members' Pavilion 212, 231, 237
Model, Craft and Country Show 226
'Muck' events 256–7
National Grassland Demonstration 210, 256
  Committee 214, 217
National Pet Show 227
National Pig Fair 257
National Sheep Fair 256
National Small Farming Event and Goat '87 257–8, *258*
New Crop Opportunities Demonstration plots 275
Newsletters 250, 285
'Outlook' conference 261
Pig Unit/Demonstration Centre 242–3, 247–8
Poultry Demonstration Unit 243, 251–2
Rank Village *229*, 231, 237, 272
Rare Breeds Pavilion 235, 286
Royal Pavilion 207, *230*, 231, 237
Royal Shows 261–81, *264*, *269*, *271*, *273*, *275*, *276*, *278*, *287*
'Science into Practice' exhibition 268
Sheep Demonstration Unit 243, 250–1, *251*, 256, 268
Showground Plan *236*
Soil Centre 275
Soils Marquee 275
Students' Day 285
Sunday Open Days 286
Tate and Lyle food exhibition 277
Town and Country Centre 237, 242, 268

Town and Country Festival 225, *226*, *227*, 265, 287, 288
Tree Collection 268
UKF Grassland Demonstration 258
Woodland and Plantations Competition 268
Stowford Farm, Ivybridge 241, 287
'Family, Farm and Craft Show' 287
Stratton, Richard 69
Studley College, Warwickshire 283
Suffolk (County Survey) 177
Suffolk pigs 64
Suffolk Red Poll cattle 64
Suffolk sheep 235
Sussex Breed Society 242
Sussex cattle 63, 64, 270
Sutton, Martin 141, 142, 144–5
Sutton seeds 151
Sykes, Frank 199, 205, 211, 219, *271*, *279*, 279–80

Talbot-Ponsonby, Arthur 180
Talbot-Ponsonby prize for agriculture 180
Tasker, E C R 283
'Taste of Britain' promotion 277
Taunton Show 36, 44, 61
Taylor, P R 221, 264
Technical Centre for Agricultural and Rural Co-operation 262
Textbook of Agricultural Entomology, A (Ormerod) 128
Thaer, 10, 11
Thatcher, John V 216, 218, 219, 245
Third World problems 292
Thomas, A P 127
Thompson, H S (later Sir Harry Meysey-Thompson) 15, 44, 60, 61, 73, 89, 92, 104–5, 111, 114–15, 122, 124
Thompson, Professor F L 78, 84
Thornton, Hobson and Co 171
Thornton, Keith 243, 248
Three Counties Showground, Malvern 258
  Sheep '88 256, 258
Tied Cottage legislation 288
Timber Growers' Organisation 214, 218
Times, The 16, 102, 118, 137, 160, 172
Torr, William 31, 68, 114
'Towards an Agro-Industrial Future' (Royal Show Symposium, 1988) 262
Town and Country Festival 225, *226*, *227*, 265, 287, 288
Towneley, Col 66, 76
Towneleys (stock breeders) 30
Transactions of Highland and Agricultural Society 3, 6
Transactions of New South Wales Agricultural Society 114
Trent College 124
Treves, Ron 223
Trimmer, Joshua 16
Tring Agricultural Discussion Society 159
Trist, P J O 177
Tropical Agricultural Machinery Centre 274
Trow-Smith, Robert 186, 188–9, 207, 264, *264*

Trumpington Farming Company 205, 253
Trumpington Show (Cambridge) 187–9
Tupper, Captain Henry 215
Turner, T B 160, 171
Turners (stock breeders) 30
Tuxford of Boston 55
Tuyn, Jef Aartse 245, 285, 286
Twyford showground site 139, 141

Uley cultivator 51, 73
United States 61–2, 70, 76, 154, 278
University Grants Committee 177
Usher of Edinburgh 58
Uthwatt Committee 168

Verney, Sir Harry 132, *136*
Veterinarian 79
Victory Churn Contest 165
Voelcker, Augustus 27, 92, 96–7, *98*, 122–4, 126, 130
Voelcker, J Augustus 119–22, *120*, 147–8, 157
Voelcker, Eric *99*, 176, 296
Volvo UK 235
Wages Board 153
Wakefield Farmers' Club 106
Walton, Mrs M *271*
War Agricultural Executive Committees ('War Ags') 151, 167, 190
Warburton, Cecil 128, 175, 296
War Cabinet (WW2) 167
Warwickshire College of Agriculture 234, 246, 283
Warwickshire Young Farmers 234
Warwick Show 36, 38, 40, 108
Way, J T 88–9, 90–1, 96
Webb, Jonas 31
Webb, Owen 206
Webster, Daniel 131
Webster, William Bullock 93–4
Wedlake agricultural implements 46, 71
Weigall, Sir Archibald 155, 164, 172–4, 183
Wellcome Foundation 272
Wellington, Dr P 252
Wellington, Duke of 22
Wells, John 97
Wells Organisation 224
Welsh breeds of cattle 63–4
Welsh Plant Breeding Station, Aberystwyth 158
Werrington Park meeting (1986) 265
West County Down sheep 64
West Cumberland Agricultural Society 74
Westfield Vineyard meeting (1987) 265
Westminster, Duke of 130, 143–4
Wheat Act (1932) 156, 163
Wheat '77 253, 257
Wheat '84 (Cambridge) *253*
Wheatley, Col 165, 171
Wheatley-Hubbard, Mrs E R 235, 265, 295
Whipsnade Zoo 234
Whitehead agricultural implements 50
Whitgift School 124
Wilkes, John 4
Willesden Council 147
Williams, Dorian 233

Williams, G T 212
Williams, O G 245
Williams, Robert 265
Williams, Tom (later Lord Williams)
172–3
William Scott Abbot Trust 240, 256, 290
Wilson, C H M 216
Wilson, Sir Jacob 44, 130, 140–2
Wiltshire and Hampshire Agricultural
College 122
Windsor Show 39, 63, 146, 172, 184
Centenary 163, 164, 174
Fiftieth Anniversary 118, 132, 163
Woburn experimental farm 26, 119,
121–2, 126, 146, 148, 156–7

Woburn Sheep Shearing 4
Wolfson Foundation 231
Wolverhampton Show 43, 59, 64, 160
Women's Institutes 181
Wood, Walter A 61
Wood agricultural implements 48, 61
Woolley, Sir Harold 215
Wool Marketing Board 218
Worcester Show 56, 57, 68
Wright, S J 159, 205, 272, 297
Wright Rain Ltd 273
Wrightson, Professor J 71, 73, 116, 120,
122, 125
Wroxall Abbey 197
Wynn, Sir Watkin W 114

York, Christopher 170, 191, 193–9, 211,
220, 224–6, 281, 283, 291
Yorkshire Agricultural Society 19, 111,
186, 191
York Show 66, 181, 185, 191, 193
Youatt, William 4, 6, *7*, 25, 26, 79, 101–2,
113
Young, Arthur 4, 6, *10, 11*
Young Farmers' Clubs 175, 177, 181
Youth Training Scheme 284

Zoological Society 234
Zuckerman, Sir Solly (later Lord
Zuckerman) 234